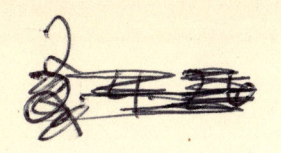

The Role of Inventories in Business Cycles

MOSES ABRAMOVITZ

Occasional Paper 26

NATIONAL BUREAU OF ECONOMIC RESEARCH

The Role of Inventories in Business Cycles

MOSES ABRAMOVITZ

Occasional Paper 26: May 1948

NATIONAL BUREAU OF ECONOMIC RESEARCH, INC.

1819 Broadway, New York 23, N. Y.

Price: fifty cents

Copyright, 1948, by National Bureau of Economic Research, Inc.
1819 Broadway, New York 23, N. Y. All Rights Reserved
Manufactured in the U.S.A. by John N. Jacobson & Son, Inc.

PREFACE

THIS PAPER REPORTS BRIEFLY some results of a larger study of cyclical fluctuations in commodity stocks undertaken as part of the National Bureau's general investigation into business cycles. It was read, substantially in its present form, before the Econometric Society in Chicago, December 30, 1947. Several passages have been expanded and a few notes added, but no significant alteration or enlargement has been attempted.

The community's stockpile of goods, which embody some quantity of labor and other resources but have not yet reached the hands of their final consumers or users, is what we commonly call the stocks or inventories of business. The goods are of the most diverse origins, physical qualities, and ultimate destinations. They are held at many stages of production by concerns performing very different functions. Wheat, hides, and bituminous coal, for example, differ significantly in the rapidity with which their supply can be adjusted to changes in demand. The risk of holding women's dresses is much greater than the risk of holding cloth, which in turn is greater than that of holding raw cotton. The speculative dealer holds stocks for a purpose different from that of the manufacturer who fabricates the material or the wholesaler who distributes the fabricated product. These differences, and many others, produce radical dissimilarities in the movements of inventories, and make the problem of detecting uniformities and framing useful generalizations extraordinarily complex. And the problem is rendered still more difficult by a scarcity of reliable statistical records.

These circumstances have conditioned the scope and character of the National Bureau's inventory research. In view of the great differences in the behavior of stocks of different types and in the factors governing their behavior, it seemed best to focus attention initially upon some important category of stocks. The category so far studied most intensively is the inventory held by manufacturers. Within this category, we have been driven to recognize several distinct types of stocks, whose relation to business cycles varies from case to case, but that together account for the behavior of the total. The decision to concentrate effort on manufacturers' stocks has been doubly rewarding. It has enabled us to study this major block of stocks with sufficient care to reveal its complex nature. At the same time, it has enabled us to understand better the forces controlling inventories held in other branches of business.

The principal purpose of the investigation is to determine what relations fluctuations in manufacturers' stocks bear to business cycles. The study deals with both cycles in inventories and cycles in the accumulation of inventories. The plan is to use what estimates there are of manufacturers' total inventories to establish certain broad characteristics of cyclical behavior. In the process, movements in manufacturers' stocks are compared with those in stocks held by other major divisions in the economy, and the general relation between total business inventories and business cycles indicated. To gain an understanding of the cyclical behavior of manufacturers' stocks revealed by over-all estimates, I have depended on a collection of series representing manufacturers' holdings of individual commodities of many types. These commodities were divided into significant classes, the characteristic behavior of each class established, and the causes of the behavior investigated. By combining these results with estimates of the importance of the several classes, a reasonable account of the behavior of manufacturers' stocks as a whole became possible.

The present paper sets forth some of the results of this investigation and attempts to indicate their significance for business-cycle theory. In such a brief essay, however, the argument is necessarily pared to its essentials and the supporting evidence confined to examples and illustrations. A revised draft of my full report, which makes good these deficiencies, is now about completed and will be ready for publication soon.

Both in preparing this paper and in the larger investigation, I have been greatly helped by my colleagues at the National Bureau. My special thanks go to Carolyn C. Landau and Judith Moss who are assisting me in the general study of inventory cycles. The argument was greatly clarified by Martha Anderson's editorial suggestions. The charts were drawn by H. Irving Forman.

M. A.

As indicated in the Preface, this essay is a condensed version of parts of a larger study. It attempts merely to outline my views on the matters dealt with, leaving the full argument and most of the supporting evidence to be presented later.

I should like to begin with a fairly commonplace idea: from the standpoint of business-cycle theory, investment is not an autonomous variable determined by factors independent of cycles. It is rather a controlling factor which is itself governed by forces inherent in business cycles. Many considerations support this view, but one of the most significant is that inventories are an important object of short-term investment. And whatever we may think about other objects of investment, inventories and inventory investment *are* closely related to current levels of consumption and production and to rates of change in them. Hence an adequate explanation of business cycles should include an explanation of how inventories behave.

To grasp how important a factor inventories are in the generation and development of business cycles, we need only examine Simon Kuznets' estimates of gross national product. These demonstrate that a very large share of the cyclical changes in gross national product has regularly taken the form of changes in the volume of inventory investment.[1] For example, during the five business cycles identified by the National Bureau between the two World Wars, the average increase in gross national product between the trough and peak years

---

[1] By 'inventory investment' or 'volume of inventory investment', I mean the net value of the *physical additions* to stocks in a given period, over and above any goods sold or otherwise used up. 'Inventory disinvestment', as I use the term, refers to the net value of the physical change in inventories when this change is negative. Both terms are equivalent to the first differences in inventories, that is, to the rate of change in inventories per unit of time (of course, after the effect of price changes upon the book value of stocks has been allowed for). A 'change in the volume of inventory investment' implies a comparison between inventory investment in one period and inventory investment in another, that is, a comparison between the rates of change in inventories in two periods.

A simple example will illustrate the meaning of these terms. Let the value of inventories, measured in constant prices, be $1,000 at the end of Year 1, $1,200 at the end of Year 2, $1,500 at the end of Year 3 and $1,300 at the end of Year 4. The inventory investment (or the volume of inventory investment) is $200 during Year 2 and $300 during Year 3. During Year 4 there is inventory *dis*investment of $200. The *change* in inventory investment is +$100 between Years 2 and 3 and −$500 between Years 3 and 4.

of business expansions was some $12 billion in 1929 prices. The average increase in inventory investment from trough to peak years was nearly $3 billion—about 23 percent of the average expansion in gross national product. The average share of such a variable process as the fabrication of producer durable equipment, on the contrary, was only 14 percent, that of construction only 6 percent, and that of the output of consumer durable goods, 13 percent. During contractions, the average share of inventory investment change in the average change in gross national product was even more impressive—47 percent. The other major elements of investment all cut smaller figures: producer durable equipment, 26 percent; construction, 11 percent; consumer durable goods, 19 percent.[2]

Since this paper is concerned mainly with manufacturers' inventories, it is pertinent to notice the part played by this category of stocks. According to Kuznets' figures, fluctuations of inventory investment by manufacturers accounted for about half the total cyclical change in aggregate inventory investment in both expansions and contractions. In other words, they were of about the same importance as changes in the volume of construction or in the output of durable producer or consumer goods taken separately.[3]

[2] These figures are based on gross national product estimates in *National Product since 1869* (National Bureau of Economic Research, 1946). Kuznets' inventory investment component is derived from inventory estimates based largely, although not exclusively, on end-of-year book value figures reported by corporations to the Bureau of Internal Revenue or on other estimates of book values at the ends of calendar years. To get estimates in constant prices, the book value figures were corrected for price changes, allowance being made for the age of inventories in each industry group and for end-of-year markdowns. For manufacturing industries, I made revised estimates to allow for the diverse elements of cost applying to purchased materials, goods in process, and finished goods, respectively. Inventory investment in any year is the difference between the value of inventory at the end of the given year and that at the end of the preceding year after both values have been corrected for price changes. The methods by which inventory estimates and corrections for price changes were made are explained fully in my forthcoming book.

[3] Similar calculations were made by Simon Kuznets in Commodity Flow and Capital Formation in the Recent Recovery and Decline, 1932-1938 (National Bureau of Economic Research, *Bulletin 74*, June 25, 1939). The importance these figures attribute to inventory fluctuations is probably limited to the relatively short business cycles identified in the National Bureau chronology. For example, the increase in inventory investment plays a much smaller role in the long upswing from 1921 to 1929 than in the three short expansions

From the viewpoint of proximate causation, these surprising results may confidently be laid to two facts. The first is simply that the technique and organization of production and distribution in this country cause the quantity of stocks carried to be large relative to the gross national product of a year. Between 1919 and 1938 the average value of commercial inventories was about 35 percent of gross national product per annum.[4] This means that if the physical quantity of stocks grew 6 percent in the course of a year from an assumed position of stability—which one might fairly take to be a moderate change—this would of itself involve an increase in gross product of approximately 2 percent. A 10 percent change in gross product, on the contrary, would be deemed large in any peacetime year. Thus, a moderate change in stocks can easily constitute a considerable fraction of a large annual change in gross national product.

The second fact is that during short business cycles of the so-called 'forty-month' variety, investment in stocks, measured in constant prices, tends to be at or near its cyclical maximum when output, that is, gross national product, reaches a peak. Similarly, disinvestment in stocks tends to be close to its cyclical maximum when output reaches a trough. These tenden-

and two short contractions into which the National Bureau divides this period. The same point has been noticed by Alvin H. Hansen in his *Fiscal Policy and Business Cycles* (Norton, 1941), Chapter II.

The differential importance of inventory investment in long and short cycles cannot be clearly established on the basis of our experience in the five business cycles between 1919 and 1938, for which annual estimates of gross national product and its components are now available. As indicated, however, illustrations suggesting such a difference can be found, and there are good *a priori* reasons for thinking that a difference would normally exist. Both the statistical indications and the theoretical considerations are set forth in detail in my forthcoming monograph.

The importance attributed to inventory investment by these figures is further limited by the fact that they do not (and, of course, cannot) distinguish between planned and unplanned investment. It is clear, however, that a change in output can be said to have been caused by a change in the volume of inventory investment only to the extent that the change in inventory investment was planned by the business enterprises holding the stocks. Otherwise, the change in inventory investment might simply reflect an unexpected change in demand while the change in output was due to other causes. For some further remarks on this subject, see Section III.

[4] 'Commercial inventories' here refer to all stocks held by American business, including those held on farms. It excludes stocks held by consumers, governments, and philanthropic institutions.

cies are clearly revealed by comparisons of inventory investment —not only in the aggregate but also by manufacturers and dealers—with the National Bureau chronology of business-cycle turns or with the cyclical peaks and troughs of, say, the Federal Reserve Board Index of Industrial Production. Consequently, the contribution of inventory investment to output is positive and close to a maximum for the cycle in peak years, and its contribution to output is negative and close to a minimum in trough years. Other things being equal, therefore, the timing of the turns of inventory investment cycles during business cycles operates to maximize the contribution of changes in the rate of inventory investment to changes in output between trough and peak years of business, and between peaks and troughs.

The timing of inventory investment cycles is crucial for an understanding of business cycles. On it depends not merely the magnitude of the influence wielded by stocks in accentuating expansions and contractions, but also the answer to the moot question whether inventories are regularly instrumental in bringing these movements to an end and in setting a reverse movement going. It is unfortunate, therefore, that the only comprehensive estimates of stocks for a considerable period are annual. For from the annual data, one cannot determine with any assurance whether the peaks and troughs of inventory investment have tended to come in the very same months as the cyclical turns of business or not. As far as they go, however, the annual estimates indicate that inventory investment tends neither to lead nor to lag behind output and business at large. And our experience is that when annual data behave like this, the average lead or lag, if any, that might be revealed by monthly data covering several cycles is small—rarely longer than three months.

This observation, crude as it is, is of great theoretical interest. For it is commonly believed that businessmen tend to keep stocks in approximately constant proportion to output or sales. This notion, often encountered in applications of the acceleration principle to inventory investment, implies that inventories—not inventory investment—will move synchronously with output and sales, and that inventory investment and *rates of change* in output and sales reach cyclical maxima and minima at about the same time. Indicators of output, in manufacturing in any event, show, however, that while the peak rate of change in output sometimes occurs near turns in business, it more often comes much earlier. This induces an expectation, on the theory here in question, that inventory investment will frequently turn considerably before business does; but this, as I have just said, is at variance with experience.

The same general difficulty emerges from an inspection of the *volume* of stocks (in contrast to their rate of change) over the course of business cycles. The peak and trough levels of inventories held by both business at large and manufacturers alone have regularly lagged behind the peaks and troughs of business, rather than moved in roughly synchronous fashion, as the more common theory implies. And though annual data are poor guides to timing, I think these data, supplemented by such broad monthly series as are available, justify the conclusion that the lag of the physical volume of stocks behind output is not less than six months. Thus the common theory about the relation between inventories and output is obviously in need of serious revision.

Although confusion in the literature is rampant, similar observations about the timing of inventories are not lacking. Lloyd Metzler's recent papers on inventory cycles, for example, provide illustrations of economic models based on the assumption that the cyclical turns of inventories occur later than those of business at large.[5] His models also leave room for the fact, though they do not require, that the peaks and troughs of inventory investment occur near the peaks and troughs of business, rather than considerably earlier. Both observations are, as I have stated, in general accord with the evidence. And I suggest that the two chief problems in this area of inventory research are: (1) to determine whether inventory

---

[5] The Nature and Stability of Inventory Cycles, *Review of Economic Statistics*, Aug. 1941, pp. 113-29; Business Cycles and the Modern Theory of Employment, *American Economic Review*, June 1946, pp. 278-91; and Factors Governing the Length of Inventory Cycles, *Review of Economic Statistics*, Feb. 1947, pp. 1-15.

investment, which I have described loosely as turning 'near' the peaks and troughs of business, may not actually lead by a short interval and thus constitute one of the forces that together turn the business tide; (2) to explain the lag in the volume of inventories behind output and the lag in inventory investment behind the rate of change in output. A valid explanation, when attained, will be of great value. It will help provide a basis for more satisfactory predictive models, and it will furnish insight into conundrums such as the division of inventory changes into 'intended' and 'unintended' elements, without which an adequate statement concerning the role of stocks in business cycles is impossible. This paper is offered as a contribution to the second of these problems.

It is my conviction that progress toward an understanding of the cyclical behavior of stocks has been blocked chiefly by the fact that inventories have generally been treated as a homogeneous mass within which differences in behavior are not significant and to all parts of which much the same explanation is appropriate. True, one sometimes finds gross and inadequate distinctions, such as between finished and unfinished goods, or categories with nonoperational definitions such as Keynes' "working capital" and "liquid capital". By contrast, I believe that a sound explanation of the behavior of stocks can be reached only when fairly numerous categories are distinguished, and I propose to support this view by analyzing the large block of stocks—about 40 percent of the total—that is held by manufacturers.

II

The various classes of stocks held by manufacturers differ from one another with respect both to the motives that control inventory policy and to the ability of manufacturers to implement their policies promptly and completely. As a result the cyclical behavior of these classes of stocks differs materially, and the behavior of manufacturers' stocks in the aggregate is to be understood as simply the composite of the disparate fluctuations of the various parts.

To demonstrate this, manufacturers' stocks must be divided into at least three major categories: (1) raw materials, (2) goods in process and (3) finished goods. I define these categories from the standpoint of the manufacturer who owns the goods, not from that of the stage of fabrication. Thus any materials or supplies purchased by a manufacturer and not yet employed in the process of fabrication in his plant constitute raw materials, however much they may have been fabricated at earlier stages. Goods in process consist of commodities the manufacturer has begun to manipulate, but that are not yet in the condition in which they are usually sold by him. Finished goods are commodities a manufacturer is ready to sell either to distributors or consumers or to other manufacturers for further fabrication. Within these major groups still other categories must be distinguished. My analysis will run in terms of the cyclical fluctuations in the *volume* of inventories rather than in terms of cycles of inventory investment.

Of the three major categories, goods in process—comprising about 20 percent of all manufacturers' stocks—are the category whose behavior can most confidently be determined *a priori*. This is fortunate, for data on goods in process are all but nonexistent. The relation of this group of stocks to output can be stated categorically if confined to manufacturers whose activities approximate a single-stage or continuous operation—probably about half the total. In their plants, technical factors fix the relation between output and goods in process. If a small lead of goods in process over output is allowed for, direct and proportional variation must be the rule.

Goods in process in industries that combine several discontinuous stages or operations are not bound to output by rigid technical necessity. There is reason to believe, however, that in these industries, too, goods in process and output move in generally similar cycles. First, the goods being processed at each individual stage of a multistage operation must vary with the activity of that stage according to the rule applying to continuous-process industries. Secondly, while goods 'between stages' may, if manufacturers so desire, be allowed to lag behind output or even to vary inversely, the consequent accumulation of partly processed goods is, in many situations, of no advantage or positively disadvantageous. In such situations, manufacturers avoid the accumulation of surplus stocks of semifabricated goods, and materials flow from stage to stage in much the same fashion as they do through single stages.

The conclusions valid for continuous-process industries are, therefore, applicable in qualified form to goods in process in the aggregate. It is probably safe to say that total stocks of goods in process rise and fall together with output, that their movements are roughly proportional to those of output, and that they tend to reach their cyclical peaks and troughs at about the same time as output.

Turning to raw materials, which normally constitute about 40 percent of manufacturers' stocks, I shall develop my views by considering four examples of commodities supplied to manufacturers under different conditions: raw silk, crude rubber, newsprint and raw sugar, each a basic staple. The statistics for these commodities consist entirely of data in physical units. By means of average cyclical patterns, Chart 1 illustrates the behavior of stocks of these commodities in the hands of manufacturers during cycles in the rate at which each commodity is processed. Such cycles are marked off by the cyclical peaks and troughs of automobile tire prodution in the case of rubber, of silk deliveries in the case of silk, of newsprint consumption in the case of newsprint and of sugar meltings in the case of sugar. The National Bureau method of calculating cyclical patterns is described in the Appendix Note. At this point it is enough to know that the patterns purport to represent the typical standings of these commodity stocks at various stages of cycles in the fabrication of these goods, and except for sugar, as I shall explain, they do so quite adequately. For purposes of comparison, the chart shows also the average cycle patterns of the various indicators of the rate of raw material processing mentioned above.

The patterns of the four inventory series are markedly dissimilar. Raw silk stocks move up and down with the rate of silk deliveries but stocks lag by a short interval. Newsprint stocks, on the contrary, fall when newsprint consumption rises,

CHART 1

Stocks of Raw Materials
Average Cyclical Patterns during Cycles in Manufacturing Activity

FIG. 1
Crude Rubber
3 Cycles, 1923-1938
—— Crude rubber stocks, U.S. and afloat for U.S.
---- Automobile tires, pneumatic casings, production

Average duration: 57.7 months

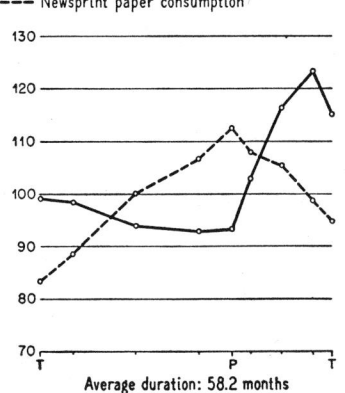

FIG. 2
Raw Silk
5 Cycles, 1920-1933
—— Raw silk stocks at mills
---- Raw silk deliveries to mills

Average duration: 30.8 months

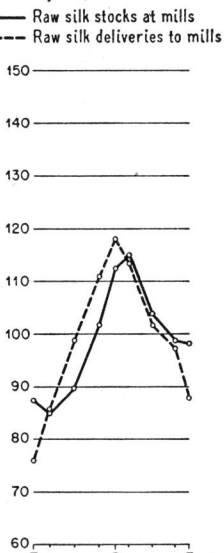

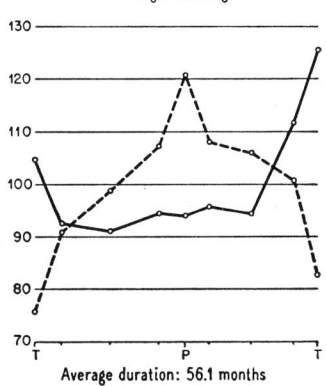

FIG. 3
Newsprint
4 Cycles, 1919-1938
—— Stocks at publishers and in transit to publishers
---- Newsprint paper consumption

Average duration: 58.2 months

FIG. 4
Raw Sugar
10 Cycles, 1893-1940
—— Raw sugar stocks
---- Sugar meltings

Average duration: 56.1 months

but there is some evidence of an upturn at the very end of expansion. Again, when consumption falls, stocks rise during most of the contraction, but begin to fall in the last stage. One can, if one wishes, think of this as a very long lag. The other two commodities display still other patterns. Rubber stocks typically vary inversely with rubber consumption, while the *average* pattern of raw sugar stocks moves inversely with activity at the beginning of expansion and at the end of contraction, but otherwise shows little response to fluctuations in sugar refining.

These differences may, at first sight, seem surprising, but I believe their explanation goes far to suggest a theory about the movements of manufacturers' stocks of raw materials as a whole. To begin with crude rubber held by United States manufacturers: the inverse behavior of these stocks is about as unlike the usual expectation concerning the behavior of inventories during business cycles as is possible. The reasons are simple. (1) The output of crude rubber on plantations is fairly stable in the short run. It is little affected by weather conditions, and it responds very sluggishly to changes in demand because the price must sink very far before it becomes worth while to suspend the tapping of mature trees and to disperse plantation labor forces. (2) Crude rubber deteriorates if kept long in the tropics. Hence only pipe line stocks are maintained in the Far East. (3) The few large automobile tire manufacturers in the United States are the world's chief consumers of rubber. They cannot, in any short period, radically alter the share of the total output they normally buy without causing enormous changes in price. Hence, something like a constant fraction of the total output flows to United States manufacturers steadily. (4) Cyclical fluctuations in the demand for crude rubber for automobile tires are relatively large. When demand increases, therefore, stocks in manufacturers' hands soon begin to fall. When demand declines, stocks rise.

Contrast this situation with that affecting mill stocks of raw silk. If a short lag is allowed for, these stocks have typically grown and declined together with manufacturing activity. Whence the difference between silk and rubber? As in the case of rubber, the output of raw silk is fairly steady and responds very sluggishly to changes in demand. Like rubber, silk is grown in the Far East and must make a long journey to the United States, the principal consuming area. Also, silk consumption fluctuates much more widely than the supply of raw silk. There is one crucial difference. In the case of rubber, manufacturers have been the chief holders of the crude material; their inventories, therefore, absorb the effect of disparities between the current rate of output of rubber and its current rate of utilization. In the case of silk, dealers' stocks in both this country and Japan serve as buffers between the producers of silk and the manufacturers who consume it. Manufacturers in this country can quickly obtain additional supplies by drawing on domestic warehouse stocks, and current supply, if not immediately required, tends to pile up in the hands of dealers. Thus manufacturers can quickly adjust their stocks as they desire. In such circumstances, their holdings tend to follow the rate of fabrication with a short lag. This rule is confirmed by the behavior of other commodities when manufacturers are able quickly to make large changes in the rate at which they receive supplies.

Newsprint and sugar stocks illustrate the effect of still other conditions of supply. Publishers' stocks of newsprint have a long lag or inverse pattern because newsprint is bought on long-term contracts, and the rate of delivery of paper to each publisher is usually set only once a year. The inverted average pattern of sugar stocks conceals their erratic fluctuations during individual cycles in meltings. These erratic movements reflect the similarly erratic movements of sugar crops, for which United States refineries are a major market.

These examples, supported by others of the same sort, suggest a general theory about cyclical fluctuations in stocks of raw materials which may be stated in the following terms: 1) If manufacturers had perfect control over their stocks of raw materials, they would increase and reduce their holdings with fluctuations in their output. Manufacturers would follow this course for several reasons. To begin with, stocks of raw materials have a pipe-line function. They include goods in transit to the manufacturer's plant when delivery is taken at the shipping point. And they include all goods arriving at a plant, being unpacked, sorted, checked, and passed through the establishment's distributing system to the processing shops. Moreover, a manufacturer needs a reserve of materials, the size depending upon his rate of activity, to ensure continuous operation against irregularities in the arrival of supplies and to meet promptly any likely near-future expansion of sales.

Whether manufacturers try to maintain a constant ratio of stocks to output is not clear. Conceivably, when their rate of activity is high, they can operate with fewer weeks' supply on hand because more categories of materials are then moving steadily into production. Fear of delays in the arrival of supplies and of price rises near the peak of business, however, work in the other direction and tend to induce manufacturers to keep a larger stock than usual for the volume of business. From the data now available we cannot determine whether the ratio of raw materials inventories to output typically remains constant. But I regard the generalization that stocks of raw materials typically move in the same direction as manufacturing activity to accord well with the facts when manufacturers are able quickly to alter the rate at which they receive supplies. This tendency is, I think, well illustrated by raw silk stocks.

2) Even under the best conditions—the case of silk is again a good illustration—the rate of raw material receipts cannot be adjusted instantaneously to the rate of consumption. Though supplies may be procured from dealers in this country or from other manufacturers in a position to fill orders from stock, days, perhaps weeks, are required to pack and ship the goods. The interval presumably depends chiefly on the backlog of orders, the means and availability of transport, and the distance. If the goods must be made to order—the normal situation for some types of goods—the interval between order and arrival is stretched several weeks, sometimes longer, depending on the length of the production period and the promptness with which a supplier can attend to a particular order.

Unless manufacturers anticipate cyclical turns in their rate of activity accurately and act promptly, therefore, a few days to a couple of months may elapse between, say, a downturn in their output and a consequent diminution in the rate at which they receive raw materials. Meanwhile stocks will continue to accumulate. This lag will be lengthened by whatever period intervenes between a curtailment of output and the time a manufacturer takes cognizance of it by reducing his rate of purchases. And the lag will be further lengthened unless the new rate of purchases is below the rate to which consumption may have fallen by the time the newly ordered goods begin to arrive. Thus a lag of several months is reasonable even when no special obstacles to an adjustment of supplies to requirements are present. In the case of raw silk, for example, where manufacturers draw their supplies from dealers in the same section of the country, the lag of stocks at cyclical turns in the rate of silk deliveries has been about two months. Presumably, it is somewhat longer in the stocks of other goods.

This expectation, that cycles in inventories conform positively with a lag to cycles in output, is valid, I think, for the bulk of raw materials stocks. An analysis of Census data shows that about two-thirds of all the raw materials used by United States manufacturers are the products of mines or of other manufacturers in this country. As far as this portion of their supplies goes, manufacturers are in a position to buy from stock or from suppliers who can rapidly adjust output to demand and who can ship goods in the main by rail or motor transport. To this class of goods we should add both raw materials that are the products of United States agriculture and imports, as long as manufacturers procure their supplies from domestic dealers who hold considerable stocks.

Even after making some allowance for goods bought on long-term contract, as in the case of newsprint, I think the proportion of raw materials whose supply can be rapidly—not immediately—adjusted to requirements does not fall far short of 75 percent. For this class of goods, as stated, I think we can expect stocks of raw materals to follow manufacturing activity with a short lag, say, of two to four months.

3) When manufacturers encounter special obstacles in adjusting their supplies to requirements the lag is longer. About

10 percent of the supplies used by United States manufacturers are imported. The part procured from domestic dealers rather than directly from abroad creates no special problem, provided the dealers carry ample stocks. For the remainder, however, a long interval must elapse between a manufacturer's decision to purchase and the arrival of the goods at his plant. We must expect stocks of such goods to lag by a much longer interval than do stocks of goods procured from domestic sources. The same will be true of goods bought on long-term contract, the quantity of which is unknown. The two groups together may account for some 10 percent of raw materials stocks and the effect of their behavior is to lengthen the lag that characterizes raw materials stocks as a whole.

4) A final class of goods in which adjustments are difficult are the products of agriculture, where supply, controlled largely by natural conditions, is virtually independent of short-run changes in demand. Over 20 percent of manufacturers' raw materials come from such sources. In many, perhaps most, cases wholesalers, not manufacturers, hold most of the stocks and absorb the haphazard effects of fluctuations in agricultural output. When manufacturers are the chief holders, however, their inventories of raw materials tend to fluctuate in random fashion during business cycles, injecting an element of irregularity into the behavior of the category as a whole.

We have now reviewed two major divisions of manufacturers' stocks: goods in process, about 20 percent of the total, which vary directly and in rough proportion with manufacturing activity; and raw materials, about 40 percent of the total, which, in the aggregate, probably lag behind activity by three or four months, or perhaps more. I turn now to the third major division—finished goods. These are the goods ready for shipment to purchasers whether for final use, for distribution, or for further fabrication. They ordinarily make up about 40 percent of all manufacturers' stocks.

Here again some distinctions are necessary. The primary division is between goods made to order and goods made to stock. Next, goods made to stock must be divided between goods whose output in the short run responds mainly to impulses from the side of demand and those whose output responds mainly to impulses from the side of supply. For purposes of statistical verification, one may identify these two classes (not wholly satisfactorily) with goods made from nonagricultural raw materials and those made from agricultural raw materials. Finally, goods made from nonagricultural raw materials should be divided into durable staples and perishables. Of these several groups, the behavior of all except perishables is illustrated in Chart 2. Here again the statistics consist of data recorded in physical units.

As far as goods made to order are concerned, it is easy to predict that finished stocks will rise and fall with production or shipments. Finished goods made to order are, in fact, simply the goods in the pipe line between production at one end and delivery at the other. When manufacturing activity is higher, there will be more goods in this pipe line; when it is lower, the pipe line will be less well filled.[6] The importance of the group cannot be fixed precisely, but some rough estimates suggest that it accounts for 15 to 20 percent of all finished goods or perhaps 6 to 8 percent of all manufacturers' stocks. An example of the behavior of goods in this group is provided in Chart 2, Figure 1, where inventories of steel sheets made to order are compared with inventories of such goods made to stock. The contrast is striking. The inventories of goods made to order rise and fall with shipments, as we expect; the inventories of goods made to stock vary inversely.

Figure 2 indicates that this inverse behavior of finished goods made to stock is characteristic of staples made from non-

[6] This is not to say that the movements of stocks of goods made to order will always tend to be strictly proportional to the movements of output and shipments. Mr. P. H. Brundage suggests that when demand is high, goods tend to be shipped more promptly in order to satisfy the needs of customers. When business falls off, orders may be canceled or goods may be billed when finished but actual delivery delayed at the purchaser's request. These considerations suggest that the ratio of stocks to output may be lower than usual near the end of expansion and rise immediately after the turn of business. They suggest also the possibility that the turn of stocks may actually lag behind output and shipments at peaks. On the same line of argument, one would expect stocks of goods made to order to be somewhat high for the volume of business towards the end of contraction and lower after the upturn.

CHART 2
Stocks of Finished Goods
Average Cyclical Patterns

Fig. 1
Steel Sheet Stocks During 4 Cycles in Shipments
1919 – 1932
——— Made to order
- - - - Made to stock

Average duration: 40.0 months

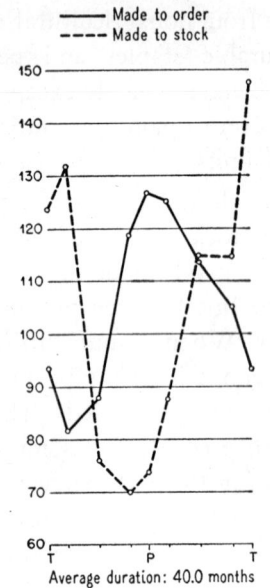

Fig. 2
Finished Staples Made from
Nonagricultural Raw Materials
17 Commodities
——— During business cycles
- - - - During cycles in manufacturing activity

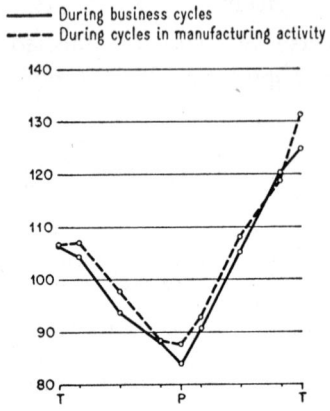

Fig. 3
Finished Staples Made from
Agricultural Raw Materials
9 Commodities
——— During business cycles
- - - - During cycles in production

16

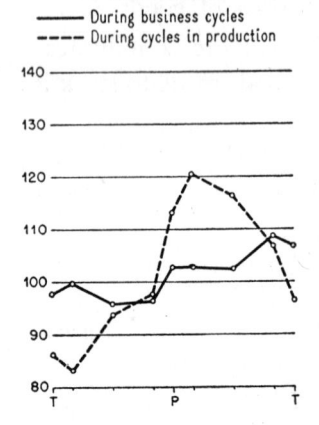

agricultural raw materials.[7] I have estimated that such staple finished goods produced from nonagricultural raw materials and normally made to stock account for about half of finished goods inventories and, consequently, for about one-fifth of all manufacturers' stocks. Records for this category are fairly plentiful, and whether we observe the fluctuations in such stocks during cycles in manufacturing activity in the industries holding the stocks or during cycles of business at large, their pattern is clearly inverse. Consequently, the fluctuations of this group of stocks, which continue to rise during contractions after goods in process and raw materials have begun to fall and continue to fall during expansions after the other two divisions have begun to rise, must contribute materially to the over-all lag observed in total manufacturers' inventories.

These behavior characteristics are clear, but their explanation is elusive. Production and shipments data for goods of this type reveal what one would expect: a close connection between rates of production and of shipments, reflecting the rapid adjustment manufacturing industries that do not depend upon agriculture for supplies can make to changes in demand. The cyclical turns in production, to be sure, tend to lag behind those in shipments by a short interval. This lag probably stems from two conditions. The first is uncertainty about the trend of demand near cyclical turns. When sales and shipments turn down, for example, it is hard to tell, for a time, whether the downturn represents the beginning of a period of contraction or simply a transient reversal of an uptrend to be followed within a few weeks by a renewed surge of orders. It is natural, therefore, to delay curtailing manufacturing operations for a short time. A second cause of the lag is the time consumed in fabrication. Even after a manufacturer reduces the input of materials into the process of fabrication, some weeks must pass, on the average, before the output of finished goods begins to fall. Failure to forecast turns in demand thus helps to account for the fact that stocks tend to rise at the

[7] The 17 commodities whose cyclical behavior is summarized in Figure 2 include merchant pig iron, lead, slab zinc, steel sheets, refined copper, newsprint, gasoline, paper (all grades), portland cement, oak flooring, southern pine lumber, lubricants, automobile tires, inner tubes, kitchen sinks, bath tubs and lavatories.

beginning of contraction and to fall at the beginning of expansion. But questions still remain. After demand has been falling and stocks have accumulated for some months, why is production not curtailed sufficiently to bring output below shipments? Why are stocks allowed to continue to accumulate? These same questions apply to expansions when stocks continue to decline for many months after demand has turned up.

I suggest the following answer with some diffidence. While manufacturers are willing to cut their purchases of raw materials drastically when surplus stocks begin to accumulate, since the burden of such cuts falls on their suppliers, they are reluctant to alter the operations of their own plants radically. For this there are two reasons. One is that in view of the perennial uncertainty surrounding the business future, manufacturers wish to minimize the costs involved in changing their rate of operations, of which the chief is probably the cost of dispersing large numbers of workers who may have to be reassembled in the not distant future. A second, less rational, reason is the dislike, often expressed by business men, of spreading overhead costs over a smaller output. In consequence, manufacturers seem content to adjust their rates of production tardily and incompletely to changes in shipments and to resign themselves to the resulting accumulation of stocks of finished goods. This hypothesis, in my view, reasonably accounts for the difference between the short lag of raw material stocks and the inverse behavior of durable, staple finished goods made from nonagricultural commodities.

Several limitations on this statement, however, are of great importance. First, it applies to durable staples alone. Manufacturers of goods that may lose value rapidly, either because of physical deterioration or change in style, can hardly afford to accumulate any considerable stock. Hence, though data are not available, we should not expect the minor inventory category of perishable goods made for the market to vary inversely with output. Accumulations of staples, however, are relatively safe. Producers of such goods can, therefore, tolerate a policy of tardy and inadequate adjustments of output to changes in demand.

A second point is that even in the case of staple goods, accumulation of stocks cannot go on indefinitely. Let a contraction last long enough, say more than two years, and a substantial number of such stocks begins to turn down. Let the contraction last three years and the number that begins to decline becomes a substantial majority. A classification of the behavior of these stocks by the duration of the contraction phase in manufacturing activity shows that the tendency for stocks to begin to decline before production has reached its trough mounts steadily with the length of the phase. In short, let the contraction be long enough, let stocks pile up high enough, and output will be cut drastically. The longer the contraction the stronger is this tendency. With appropriate changes of wording, the like is true of expansions.

Finally, these observations apply only to commodities whose output responds, in the short run, chiefly to impulses from the side of demand. The opposite case, commodities whose output in the short run responds chiefly to changes in the supply of raw materials, is illustrated by the composite patterns of Chart 2, Figure 3.[8] These stocks of fabricated commodities made from agricultural raw materials rise and fall with output in their industries although stocks lag behind output by a short interval, on the average. This behavior is unlike that of the nonagricultural staples, which vary inversely with output in their industries. During business cycles, the stocks of fabricated farm products behave irregularly—again in contrast to nonfarm products, which fluctuate inversely during business cycles.

The explanation is simple. Some—not all—farm products cannot be stored economically in crude form, either because they would deteriorate or because they are too bulky. For them, increased output of the crude material causes the output of the fabricated product to rise. Since the rise in production has been stimulated by an augmented supply of crude materials, not by an increase in demand, output soon outruns consumption. Hence stocks of finished goods rise with output

[8] The 9 commodities whose cyclical behavior is summarized in Figure 3 include linseed oil, inedible tallow, crude cottonseed oil, refined cottonseed oil, shortenings, evaporated milk and cold storage holdings of pork, lard and beef and veal.

after an interval long enough to allow output to overtake and exceed consumption. But since changes in the supply of agricultural raw materials, which in this case are the governors of the entire process, are usually not correlated with the state of business, stocks of finished goods made from such materials behave irregularly during business cycles.

III

By way of conclusion, I should like to develop very briefly a few implications of these observations and of the theory of inventory fluctuations to which they point.

As already stated, the total stocks of business men can be divided into numerous significant categories. The cyclical behavior of these categories reflects differences in the motives behind inventory policy and in the ability of business men—for reasons of technique, market organization, or contractual arrangements—to implement their policies. The validity of this view is, I think, demonstrated in the case of manufacturers' stocks. Here the observed lag of total inventories behind output is to be explained as the net resultant of the disparate behavior of at least seven classes of stocks: (1) goods in process, which vary together with output; (2) raw materials purchased from domestic manufacturers or dealers, which lag by, say, two or three months; (3) raw materials purchased from distant sources or on long-term contracts, which lag behind output by many months; (4) finished goods made to order which, like goods in process, are closely tied to output; (5) perishable finished goods sold from stock, which probably lag behind output by a few months; (6) staple finished goods made to stock, which vary inversely with output in short cycle phases and positively with a long lag in long phases; (7) agricultural raw materials and finished goods made from such materials, which, under certain conditions, inject an irregular element into the movements of manufacturers' stocks.

The need to distinguish numerous classes of stocks, moreover, is not confined to manufacturers' inventories. Aggregate inventories of wholesalers and retailers also appear to have lagged behind sales by about six months, and I am confident that close study will reveal that the lag of total distributors' stocks reflects great differences in the ability of merchants in different trades to keep the rate at which they receive goods in line with the rate at which they can dispose of them. It must be expected, therefore, that the ability of some merchants to adjust stocks to sales is so limited as to produce a long lag of stocks behind sales or even an inverse relation between sales and inventories.

From these general considerations, several important inferences may be drawn. The first is that no simple, general explanation of inventory fluctuations is valid. An adequate theory of inventory cycles must explain the disparate behavior of the several categories of stocks that move in significantly different ways.

A second inference is that if we are to put our knowledge of inventory cycles into fully quantitative form by the construction and empirical evaluation of a mathematical model, the results are likely to be more valid if the model takes into account subdivisions of aggregate stocks distinguished by industry and type. The point is, of course, obvious in a general way, but its importance may perhaps be heightened by considering some of the ways in which its neglect can cause difficulties. For example, raw materials, goods in process, and finished goods vary with output in distinctly different ways, but their importance is not the same in each industry. Shifts in the distribution of demand among industries, such as ordinarily accompany business cycles and occur also independently of cycles, must tend, therefore, to alter the relation between total inventories and output. In the same way, stocks of finished goods made to order and finished goods made to stock behave in radically different fashion. Changes in the distribution of demand or in marketing practices will also tend to modify the importance of these categories and thus to complicate the relation between aggregate stocks and output. Again, the behavior of staple finished goods made to stock depends upon the length of the cycle. Such stocks vary inversely with output during short expansions or contractions, but they tend to vary directly with output in the last stages of long movements. This in turn must tend to make the relation between aggregate stocks and output a variable. Under the circumstances it is likely to be more fruitful to try to take account of the shifting relation between stocks and output by studying each significant category of stocks in each important industry group separately and by combining the results in an appropriate way than by attempting to discover a single rule that expresses directly the changing relation between total stocks and total output.

Still a third general inference concerns our understanding of cycles in inventory investment as distinct from cycles in stocks themselves. As noted above, aggregate inventory investment tends to turn near the turns of output and to lag behind the peaks and troughs in the rate of change in output. An explanation of this behavior is, of course, more complicated than an explanation of the relation between cycles in the level of stocks and in the level of output. It is clear, however, that differences in the desire and ability of businessmen to keep stocks in line with output are necessary, if not sufficient, elements of a theory of inventory investment cycles. One may, for example, observe the same sort of contrasts in the cyclical behavior of investment in stocks of different types as were shown above to be characteristic of cycles in the volume of stocks. The peaks of investment in stocks of raw materials whose supply cannot be adjusted promptly to changes in demand occur much later in the cycle than the peaks of investment in stocks of materials whose supplies are easily adjusted. And the same is true of investment in stocks of finished staples, for in this case the desire of manufacturers to keep stocks in line with output is diluted by conflicting pressures.

It follows from these suggestions that the lag of inventory investment behind the rate of change in output is determined by a complex combination of conditions affecting different inventory categories. Hence a simple application of the acceleration principle to the movements of stocks is far from satisfactory. This apparent difficulty with a common element of cycle theory, however, facilitates, rather than complicates, an interpretation of the course of business cycles. For, as indicated above, there is good evidence that the rate of growth of output usually begins to decline long before business reaches a peak. If the volume of inventory investment were closely tied to the rate of change in output, as at least a simple formulation of the acceleration principle suggests, we should expect inventory investment also to decline early in expansion. But since inventory investment is a major element of capital expenditures, it must influence the timing of peaks in output and incomes. Hence if inventory investment actually did move synchronously with the rate of change of output, it would be difficult to account for the considerable interval that, in fact, usually intervenes between the peak in the rate of growth of output and the peak of the business cycle itself. At least part of the explanation for the existence of this interval lies in the absence of any close temporal connection between the rate of change in output and in total inventory investment. The continued growth of inventory investment after the rate of change in output begins to decline helps employment and output to continue their expansion. With some modifications, this hypothesis applies also to contractions.

The explanation of cycles in manufacturers' stocks can be used to throw light also on the connection between businessmen's plans and the observed movements of stocks. Of course, unambiguous causal significance can be attributed to inventory investment as an explanation of output changes only to the degree that the investment observed was planned or intended by the businessmen concerned. It is obvious also that we have no objective way of separating planned from unplanned changes in stocks. Implications with respect to intentions are, however, imbedded in the theory of cycles in manufacturers' stocks advanced above. One clear example is implied by the hypothesis that business men do not foresee turns in demand and consequently do not reduce orders for materials or curtail their output until after their own sales have begun to decline. The inference is that the rise in stocks of raw materials and finished goods immediately after a downturn of business is largely unplanned. The declines in stocks that follow upon the heels of upturns in business are, on this hypothesis, similarly fortuitous.

If this interpretation is correct, poor forecasting, which results in unintended inventory investment after business peaks, and disinvestment after troughs, makes these business reversals less sharp than they would otherwise be. It also seems likely, although it is by no means certain, that businessmen attempt later to wipe out the inventory surpluses or deficits thus created and that this intensifies the subsequent swings, whether of expansion or contraction.

One final implication of this analysis concerns the information required for the further development of inventory research. The character of the theory I have been discussing emphasizes the importance of augmenting the detail in which inventory information is reported. In the field of manufacturing, for example, the Department of Commerce now reports monthly the current book value of total inventories held by all manufacturers and by each of eleven industries. These series, which begin with December 1938, have added enormously to our current information about stocks. When their time-coverage becomes sufficiently long, they will prove to be of great benefit to business-cycle studies also. Our analysis suggests that an additional division distinguishing raw materials, goods in process, and finished goods is of first-rate importance. Almost equally vital is information enabling us to distinguish between inventories of finished goods made to order and to stock, and between durable, staple, and perishable finished goods. These supplements to our statistics, however, will not yield their full benefits until we are in a position to allow more adequately for the effect of price changes upon book values. Broadly speaking, we need additional information of two sorts: more knowledge about current practices in accounting for inventories and better information about changes in the unit costs of inventory commodities, particularly of goods in process and finished goods, than is now provided by standard price series. At best, however, the process of computing physical volume indexes by correcting book value figures for price changes will provide only rough approximations. The more widely we are able to extend our records of stocks in physical units, the more we shall be able to substitute accurate data for crude estimates.

Appendix Note

The National Bureau Method of Calculating Cyclical Patterns

The method by which the measures underlying Charts 1 and 2 were derived involves the following steps:

1) The seasonally corrected data of a given series are divided into cycle segments, which may be marked off according to any one of several plans. For example, if the purpose is to portray the cyclical behavior that is peculiar to a given series, the segments are marked off by the dates of the lower turning points, or troughs, of the series itself. (If a series typically behaves inversely during business cycles, the segments are marked off by its upper turning points.) In Chart 1, for instance, the cycle segments in the series representing the processing of raw materials (auto tire production, silk deliveries to mills, newsprint paper consumption, and sugar meltings) were marked off in this way. To show the behavior of a given series during the cycles in some related activity, the segments are marked off by the lower turning points in the related series. This is the procedure followed with the various stock series in Chart 1, with the two series in Figure 1 of Chart 2, and with the various series whose average patterns are represented by the broken lines in Figures 2 and 3 of Chart 2.

To show the behavior of a given series during cycles in general business the cycle segments are marked off by the trough dates of business at large as fixed by the National Bureau chronology of business cycles. This is the procedure followed with the various series whose average patterns are represented by the solid lines in Figures 2 and 3 of Chart 2. Whatever plan is used to mark off cycle segments, the succeeding steps are identical.

2) Within each cycle segment the average of the monthly values is computed, and the monthly values are converted into percentages of this average. The resulting figures are called 'cycle relatives'.

3) Each cycle segment is then divided into nine stages. Stage I covers the three months centered on the date of the initial trough, determined by the date of the trough of the given series if the segments are marked off according to the first plan described above, and by the date of the trough of the related series or of general business if the second or third plan is used. Stage V covers the three months centered on the peak, and stage IX the three months centered on the terminal trough. The peak and terminal trough are again dated according to the turns of the given series, the related series, or general business, as the case may be. Stages II to IV cover successive thirds of expansion, that is, the interval between the initial trough and peak. Stages VI to VIII cover successive thirds of contraction, that is, the interval between the peak and terminal trough.

4) The cycle relatives for the months included in each stage are averaged, yielding a nine-stage pattern for each cycle segment.

5) The average standings in each stage are averaged for the various cycle segments covered by a series to yield average cycle patterns. These are the graphs displayed in Charts 1 and 2.

6) For purposes of summary illustration, the averaging process was carried one step further in Chart 2, Figures 2 and 3, where the average patterns of several series for different commodities are combined into grand averages.

The National Bureau method of deriving business cycle measures is described in detail in *Measuring Business Cycles*, by A. F. Burns and W. C. Mitchell (National Bureau of Economic Research, 1946). The arithmetical computations are performed by a more direct and economical method than that sketched above, which, though accurate, is roundabout.

Officers
(1948)

C. Reinold Noyes, *Chairman*
Boris Shishkin, *President*
W. W. Riefler, *Vice-President*
George B. Roberts, *Treasurer*
W. J. Carson, *Executive Director*
Martha Anderson, *Editor*

Directors at Large

Chester I. Barnard, *Chairman, New Jersey Bell Telephone Company*
Arthur F. Burns, *Columbia University*
W. L. Crum, *University of California*
Oswald W. Knauth, *New York City*
Simon Kuznets, *University of Pennsylvania*
H. W. Laidler, *Executive Director, League for Industrial Democracy*
Shepard Morgan, *Vice-President, Chase National Bank*
C. Reinold Noyes, *New York City*
George B. Roberts, *Vice-President, National City Bank*
Beardsley Ruml, *Chairman, Board of Directors, R. H. Macy & Company*
Harry Scherman, *President, Book-of-the-Month Club*
George Soule, *New York City*
N. I. Stone, *Consulting Economist*
J. Raymond Walsh, *WMCA Broadcasting Co.*
Leo Wolman, *Columbia University*

Directors by University Appointment

E. Wight Bakke, *Yale*
C. C. Balderston, *Pennsylvania*
Corwin D. Edwards, *Northwestern*
G. A. Elliott, *Toronto*
H. M. Groves, *Wisconsin*
Gottfried Haberler, *Harvard*
Clarence Heer, *North Carolina*
R. L. Kozelka, *Minnesota*
Wesley C. Mitchell, *Columbia*
Paul M. O'Leary, *Cornell*
W. W. Riefler, *Institute for Advanced Study*
T. O. Yntema, *Chicago*

Directors Appointed by Other Organizations

Percival F. Brundage, *American Institute of Accountants*
Arthur H. Cole, *Economic History Association*
Frederick C. Mills, *American Statistical Association*
Boris Shishkin, *American Federation of Labor*
Warren C. Waite, *American Farm Economic Association*
Donald H. Wallace, *American Economic Association*

Research Staff

Arthur F. Burns, *Director of Research*

Moses Abramovitz
Harold Barger
Morris A. Copeland
Daniel Creamer
Solomon Fabricant
Milton Friedman
Millard Hastay
W. Braddock Hickman
F. F. Hill

Thor Hultgren
Simon Kuznets
Clarence D. Long
Ruth P. Mack
Frederick C. Mills
Wesley C. Mitchell
Geoffrey H. Moore
Raymond J. Saulnier
George J. Stigler

Leo Wolman

OCCASIONAL PAPERS IN PRINT

1 *Manufacturing Output, 1929-1937* (December 1940) $ .25
Solomon Fabricant
3 *Finished Commodities since 1879, Output and Its Composition* (August 1941), William H. Shaw $ .25
5 *Railway Freight Traffic in Prosperity and Depression* (February 1942), Thor Hultgren $ .25
6 *Uses of National Income in Peace and War* (March 1942) Simon Kuznets $ .25
10 *The Effect of War on Business Financing: Manufacturing and Trade, World War I* (November 1943) $ .50
R. A. Young and C. H. Schmidt
11 *The Effect of War on Currency and Deposits* (September 1943) Charles R. Whittlesey $ .35
12 *Prices in a War Economy: Some Aspects of the Present Price Structure of the United States* (October 1943) $ .50
Frederick C. Mills
13 *Railroad Travel and the State of Business* (December 1943) Thor Hultgren $ .35
14 *The Labor Force in Wartime America* (March 1944) $ .50
Clarence D. Long
15 *Railway Traffic Expansion and Use of Resources in World War II* (February 1944) $ .35
Thor Hultgren
16 *British and American Plans for International Currency Stabilization* (January 1944) $ .35
J. H. Riddle
17 *National Product, War and Prewar* (February 1944) $ .50
Simon Kuznets
18 *Production of Industrial Materials in World Wars I and II* (March 1944) $ .50
Geoffrey H. Moore
19 *Canada's Financial System in War* (April 1944) $ .50
B. H. Higgins
20 *Nazi War Finance and Banking* (April 1944) $ .50
Otto Nathan
22 *Bank Liquidity and the War* (May 1945) $ .50
Charles R. Whittlesey
23 *Labor Savings in American Industry, 1899-1939* (Nov. 1945) Solomon Fabricant $ .50
24 *Domestic Servants in the United States, 1900-1940* (April 1946) George J. Stigler $ .50
25 *Recent Developments in Dominion-Provincial Fiscal Relations in Canada* (March 1948), J. A. Maxwell $ .50
26 *The Role of Inventories in Business Cycles* (May 1948) $ .50
Moses Abramovitz

THE STRUCTURE

OF

POSTWAR PRICES

FREDERICK C. MILLS

OCCASIONAL PAPER 27

NATIONAL BUREAU OF ECONOMIC RESEARCH

THE STRUCTURE
OF
POSTWAR PRICES

FREDERICK C. MILLS

Occasional Paper 27: July 1948

NATIONAL BUREAU OF ECONOMIC RESEARCH
1819 Broadway, New York 23, N. Y.

I acknowledge with warm appreciation the research assistance of Maude R. Pech, the editorial services of Martha Anderson, and the contributions of H. Irving Forman in preparing the charts that accompany the text.

Price: Seventy-five cents

Copyright, 1948, by National Bureau of Economic Research, Inc.
1819 Broadway, New York 23, N. Y. All Rights Reserved

Manufactured in the United States of America by the
Academy Press, New York

CONTENTS

I	The Incidence of Inflation, 1939-1947	1
II	Major Changes in the Structure of Prices, 1939-1948	6
III	Changes in the Components of Selling Price, Manufactured Goods, 1939-1947	16
	Elements of the Cost Structure	16
	Prices of Raw Materials and Manufactured Goods	20
	Wages and Productivity	22
	Profits	24
IV	Some Historical Comparisons	27
	Major Changes in the Structure of Prices, 1924-27 to 1948	27
	Three Periods of Economic Expansion	33
	Prices during Two World Wars	39
	Patterns of Price Expansions and Contractions	43
V	Summary	46
	Comment by D. H. Wallace	51

TABLE
1	Changes in Physical Quantities Produced or Exchanged and in their Aggregate Values, 1939-1947	2
2	Prices and Wages, 1939-1948	6
3	Wholesale Prices, Commodity Classes of the Bureau of Labor Statistics, 1939-1948	9
4	Wholesale Prices, Commodity Classes of the National Bureau of Economic Research, 1939-1948	11
5	Retail Prices by Commodity and Service Classes, 1939-1948	14
6	Estimated Changes in Average Selling Price of Manufactured Goods and in its Major Components, 1939-1947	17
7	Prices of Raw and Manufactured Goods, 1939-1948	20
8	Prices of Raw and Manufactured Goods, 1924-27 to 1948	21
9	Changes in Average Hourly Earnings and in Output per Manhour in Selected Manufacturing and Mining Industries, 1939-1947	23
10	Corporate Profits and Selling Price per Unit of Product, Selected Manufacturing and Mining Industries, 1939-1947	25
11	Prices and Wages, 1924-27 to 1948	28
12	Prices and Wages, 1912-14 to 1948	30
13	Wholesale Prices, Commodity Classes of the Bureau of Labor Statistics, 1924-27 to 1948	31
14	Wholesale Prices, Commodity Classes of the National Bureau of Economic Research, 1924-27 to 1948	31

TABLE
15 Retail Prices by Commodity and Service Classes, 1924-27 to 1948   32
16 Changes in Quantities, Unit Prices, and in Aggregate Values during Three Periods of Economic Expansion   34
17 Prices during Two World Wars   40
18 Monthly Rates of Change in Wholesale Prices during Expansions in Peace and War, Specific Cycles   44
19 Monthly Rates of Change in Wholesale Prices during Contractions in Peace and War, Specific Cycles   45

APPENDIX TABLE
1 Wholesale Prices, Commodity Classifications of the National Bureau of Economic Research, Selected Dates, 1939-1948   52
2 Wholesale Prices, Commodity Classifications of the Bureau of Labor Statistics, Selected Dates, 1939-1948   54
3 Prices Received and Prices Paid by Farmers, Selected Dates, 1939-1948   55
4 Construction Costs, Selected Dates, 1939-1948   56
5 Average Hourly Earnings, Manufacturing Industries, Selected Dates, 1939-1948   57
6 Average Hourly Earnings, Nonmanufacturing Industries, Selected Dates, 1939-1948   58
7 Consumer Expenditures, Retail Prices, and Estimates of Volume of Consumer Purchases, Selected Periods, 1939-1947   59
8 Wholesale Prices, Commodity Classifications of the National Bureau of Economic Research, Monthly Indexes, 1943-1948   59

CHART
1 Changes in Selected Elements of the Economy, 1939-Fourth Quarter 1947   3
2 Relations among Elements of the Price Structure, Sept. 1938-Aug. 1939 to February 1948   7
3 The Changing Tempo of Inflation, 1939-1948   8
4 Monthly Changes in Wholesale Prices by Commodity Groups, 1939-1948   13
5 Estimated Changes in Average Selling Price of Manufactured Goods and in its Major Components, 1939-1947   18
6 Relations among Elements of the Price Structure, 1924-27 to February 1948   29
7 Changes in Quantities and in Aggregate Values during Three Periods of Economic Expansion   35
8 Prices during Two World Wars   41
9 Wholesale Prices during Expansions in Peace and War, Specific Cycles   45

I THE INCIDENCE OF INFLATION, 1939-1947

Since the outbreak of war in Europe in 1939 the economy of the United States has undergone a major inflation. Practically every sector of the economy and every economic process has been affected by declines in the worth of the monetary unit. Increases in the aggregate dollar values of goods produced and of services rendered substantially exceed increases in the physical volume of output and of services. This divergence is of the essence of inflation.

The degree of divergence between physical volume and value aggregates for selected elements of the economy, from 1939 to the fourth quarter of 1947, is indicated in Table 1 and Chart 1. The differences are measures of the role inflationary factors have played in swelling the monetary measures of output, trade, and employment.[1] The physical gains have been notable—27 percent in agriculture (1947 over 1939), 82 percent in manufacturing, 54 percent in the flow of goods to consumers,[2] 70 per cent in employment in manufacturing, 118 percent in volume of revenue freight carried by railroads. Here is a record of exceptional accomplishment during eight years. But in almost every field (revenue freight is the notable exception) the gains in aggregate value far outstripped the quantity advances. The monetary value of goods produced or of services rendered increased more than 200 percent in agriculture, manufacturing, and manufacturing employment; retail sales scored gains of much the same order; monetary values increased more than 100

[1] Inflation is here defined as the condition that exists when the aggregate value of all goods and services entering into exchange in a given economy advances more rapidly than the physical volume of the same goods and services. Inflation is thus an economy-wide condition. A divergence between value and volume aggregates for one class of goods is not inflationary if the price rises in this sector are offset by declines among other classes of goods or services. Thus no one of the volume and value comparisons in Table 1 is by itself an accurate index of the degree of inflation. Only a comparison comprehending economy-wide aggregates would provide a single, accurate index of inflation. But the fact that for every series in Table 1 the increase in aggregate value exceeded the increase in physical volume is clear evidence that the pressures toward higher values were truly inflationary.

[2] This estimate is derived by deflating consumer expenditures by the consumers' price index. Consideration of other retail price indexes yields a somewhat more conservative estimate — 40 to 50 percent; see App. Table 7.

TABLE 1

Changes in Physical Quantities Produced or Exchanged
and in Their Aggregate Values, 1939-1947

	% Change, 1939-IV 1947	
	Physical quantity	Aggregate value
Agricultural production	+27[a]	+272[a]
Mineral production	+46	+156
Manufacturing production	+82	+248
Construction activity	+34	+150
Revenue freight (ton miles)	+118	+136
Retail sales	+73	+226
Consumer expenditures	+54	+156
Employment in manufacturing[b]	+70	+248
Employment in mining[b]	+34	+171

[a] Change from 1939 to 1947. The movement for net farm income between these dates is +242.
[b] Employment is here measured in manhours. The corresponding change in number of production workers is +57 percent in manufacturing, +3 percent in mining.

percent in mineral production, construction, consumer expenditures, and employment in mining. The customary accounting and monetary measurements of economic activity and of productive accomplishment have been swelled by the factitious gains of inflation.

Such inflationary differences as these, which are manifest in unequal movements of prices, wages, and profits, affect producing and consuming groups unequally. From these inequalities stem the major economic difficulties that grow out of inflation (and, in the reverse situation, out of deflation). Trading relations among economic groups are altered. The worth of wheat in terms of coal, of raw cotton in terms of cotton cloth, of wool in terms of shoes, of labor in terms of beef—all these are modified; some traders gain in relative position, some lose. These changes affect individuals; they also modify the conditions under which broad economic groups cooperate in the productive process. The terms on which agricultural and industrial producers exchange goods, on which wage earners, share holders, and bondholders divide the receipts of corporate enterprise on which producers of capital equipment trade with producers of consumer goods may be profoundly altered under the unequal incidence of inflationary price advances.

Such shifts do not mean, merely, changes on quotation boards or alterations in books of account. The price records define, in fact fundamental relations between the aggregate physical rewards of given producing groups and their aggregate physical contribution to the economy. Thus if during a given period the average sellin

CHART 1

Changes in Selected Elements of the Economy
1939 – Fourth Quarter 1947

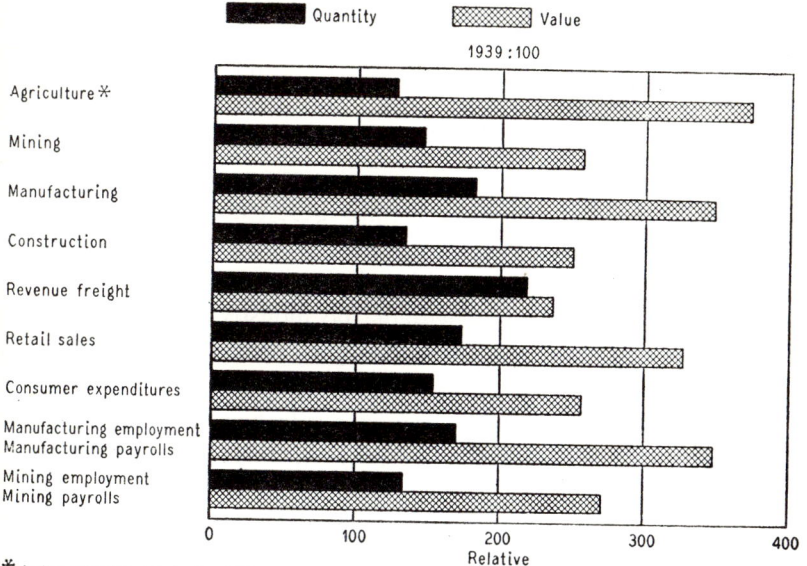

■ Quantity ▦ Value

1939 : 100

Agriculture *	
Mining	
Manufacturing	
Construction	
Revenue freight	
Retail sales	
Consumer expenditures	
Manufacturing employment	
Manufacturing payrolls	
Mining employment	
Mining payrolls	

Relative: 0, 100, 200, 300, 400

* Index numbers relate to 1947.

price of farm products rises 20 percent more than the average price of goods bought by farmers, there has been a gain of 20 percent in the aggregate real remuneration of farmers for their services in producing a constant aggregate quantity of farm products. For the same aggregate physical contribution farmers can withdraw from the common pot 20 percent more of the goods and services they purchase for their own use. If the average hourly earnings of wage earners increase 10 percent more than the cost of goods and services they buy, there has been an advance of 10 percent in the aggregate real rewards of wage earners for their services during a constant period of working time. If dividends per unit of manufactured product rise 15 percent more than the prices of goods bought by dividend recipients, there has been a gain of 15 percent in the aggregate real rewards of corporate shareholders for the services rendered by their capital in producing a constant quantity of manufactured goods. Relative prices, as counters, merely define changes in the relations between the aggregate real rewards and the aggregate physical contributions of given producing groups. When unit prices change considerably during fairly short periods, and at quite different rates for different economic elements, relations between the total 'inputs' and the total 'takeouts' of different groups will change substantially. The economic and social consequences may be far reaching.

We should note one other important consequence of wide and unequal movements of elements of the price system. The structure of costs in individual plants, in industries, and in the economy at large may be greatly altered, with corresponding changes in the operating characteristics of the productive units involved. We may think of elements of the cost structure as components of the selling price of the product. At a given time these components (e.g., material costs, labor costs, overhead costs, profits) stand in a definite relation to one another, and this relation is a major factor in the price policy of the entrepreneur or the industry concerned and in the broader policies that determine employment decisions, operating programs, and plans for expansion or contraction of output or plant. Wide price movements in the economy at large always modify these relations. This modification may be such as to encourage or discourage expansion of employment and output, to stimulate or retard mechanization, to promote or discourage search for new types or sources of materials, to advance or reduce selling prices. It may raise or lower the 'break-even' point in industrial operations and thus affect one of the central elements in the operating decisions of entrepreneurs.

In speaking of the various consequences of unequal price changes we have assumed a certain base period or a certain set of base relations with reference to which later relations are defined. In fact these relations are in process of continuous change in the economy at large. No one set of relations may be taken as 'normal', whether we are thinking of terms of exchange among producing groups, of the ratio of rewards to contributions for a given economic group or of the structure of costs in a given industry. Some change we shall find, no matter what base is chosen as a standard of reference. Yet periods may differ widely in degree and rapidity of price change. From September 1938 to August 1939 in the United States there were merely modest variations in the general price level and in relations among elements of the price system. From June 1946 to February 1948 there were major changes in the price level and violent shifts in the relations among prices.

In appraising shifts in price relations from a stated base period two factors are of primary importance. If the relations prevailing in a given base period have existed for some time, so that productive practices and business policies have been generally adapted to them, departures from these price relations will entail more extensive economic changes than would the same departures from transient relations to which there has been no general adaptation of business procedures and policies. In the second place, the degree and rapidity of change from an established set of price relations have an obvious bearing on the effects of these changes. Shifts in price relations that may be merely a healthy stimulus if effected at a leisurely tempo may bring major economic dislocations if the rate of change is rapid. In interpreting the price shifts that have accompanied the inflationary movements of recent years, therefore, we must take account of the conditions prevailing in the period used as a standard of reference and of the extent and rapidity of the alterations that have occurred since the base period.

It would be misleading to suggest that prices play the role of an independent variable in economic processes. In considerable degree price movements merely reflect changes in underlying factors of production, distribution, and consumption. In some degree, of course, price changes are active elements, to which physical processes require adjustment. This means, among other things, that in observing the movements of prices during any period we are dealing with one, only, of the aspects of economic change; we are tracing some, only, of the clues to an understanding of economic behavior and of the operations of a functioning economy.

With these considerations in mind we turn to an examination of the price structure existing at the beginning of 1948. Prevailing terms of exchange reflect the diverse pressures of wartime needs and shortages and of postwar adjustments, of changes in supply conditions, of extraordinary advances in the purchasing power of domestic consumers and of changes in their tastes and wants, of foreign purchasing and United States aid to foreign countries, of striking modifications in the relative bargaining power of different factors of production, of governmental controls and supports, all superimposed upon a set of relations that had developed during the interwar period of expansion, boom, sustained depression, and extensive governmental action in the economic sphere, and all operating on a price and cost system whose parts vary widely in their flexibility under the pressures of changing market conditions. Our present concern is with the nature and extent of the shifts resulting from these various pressures, and with some of their economic implications.

II Major Changes in the Structure of Prices, 1939-1948

The everyday experiences of individuals who must balance income against outgo have made most Americans familiar with the chief shifts in the economic terrain that have resulted from unequal movements of prices, wages, and other elements of the price system since 1939. The entries in Table 2, shown graphically in Chart 2, give precision to these general impressions. The base is the twelve-month period preceding the outbreak of war in Europe. Changes are

TABLE 2
Prices and Wages, 1939-1948

INDEX NUMBERS

	9/1938-8/1939	Mar. 1942	June 1946	Feb. 1948
Farm prices[d]	100	160	231	296
Per capita weekly earnings, mfg. labor[e]	100[a]	152	188	226
Food prices, retail[f]	100	124	153	215
Wholesale prices[f]	100	127	147	210
Hourly earnings, mfg. labor[f]	100[a]	129	172	205
Prices paid by farmers[d]	100	120	152	201
Retail prices, all[g]	100[a]	124	150	192
Construction costs[h]	100	115	147	190
Consumers' price index[f]	100	115	134	168
Industrial stock prices[i]	100	71	166	126
Rent[j]	100	104	104	111

AVERAGE MONTHLY RATES OF CHANGE[b]

	8/1939-3/1942	3/1942-6/1946	6/1946-2/1948[c]	6/1946-3/1947	3/1947-5/1947	5/1947-2/1948
Farm prices[d]	+2.2	+0.9	+1.4	+3.2	−1.4	+0.3
Per capita weekly earnings, mfg. labor[e]	+1.6	+0.5	+1.0	+1.2	+0.8	+0.8
Food prices, retail[f]	+0.9	+0.4	+2.0	+3.3	−0.5	+1.0
Wholesale prices[f]	+1.0	+0.3	+2.1	+3.6	−0.8	+1.0
Hourly earnings, mfg. labor[f]	+1.0	+0.7	+1.0	+1.0	+1.2	+0.8
Prices paid by farmers[d]	+0.7	+0.5	+1.6	+2.3	+0.4	+1.0
Retail prices, all[g]	+0.8	+0.4	+1.4	+2.2	−0.05	+0.7
Construction costs[h]	+0.5	+0.5	+1.5	+1.8	+1.0	+1.0
Consumers' price index[f]	+0.5	+0.3	+1.3	+1.9	−0.1	+0.8
Industrial stock prices[i]	−0.8	+2.6	−1.2	−2.1	−3.4	+0.02
Rent[j]	+0.1	−0.01	+0.3	+0.1	+0.1	+0.7

[a] January-August 1939:100.
[b] In deriving the average monthly change the percentage change between two dates is divided by the number of months in the given period.
[c] In showing rates of change, the period since June 1946 is subdivided since price rises come in two spurts interrupted by a short decline.
[d] Bureau of Agricultural Economics.
[e] Per capita earnings in manufacturing industries are here derived by dividing weekly payrolls by number of production workers employed, both series reported by the Bureau of Labor Statistics.
[f] Bureau of Labor Statistics.   [g] Department of Commerce.
[h] Composite, see App. Table 4.   [i] Standard and Poor's Corporation.
[j] The rent index is one element of the Bureau of Labor Statistics consumers' price index. It represents rental cost to wage earners and lower-salaried workers in large cities.

CHART 2
Relations among Elements of the Price Structure
Sept. 1938-Aug. 1939 to Feb. 1948

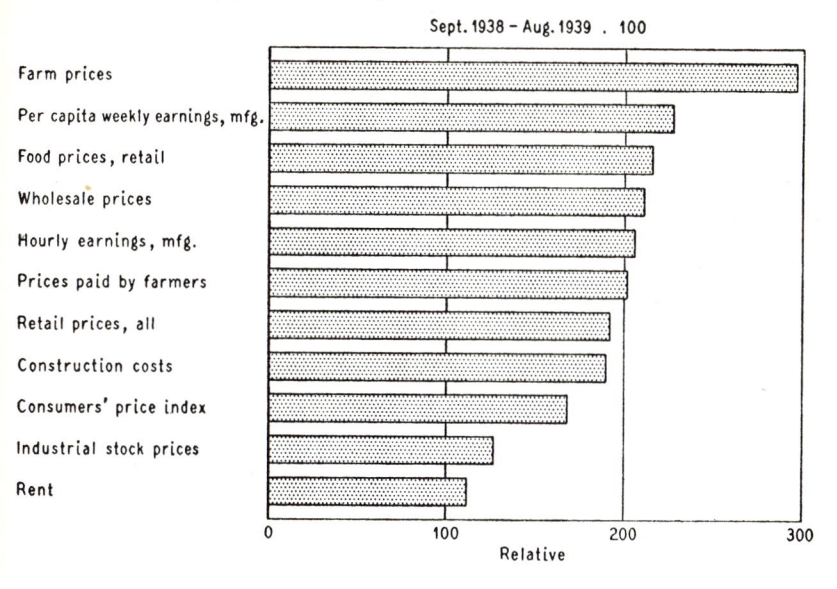

Sept. 1938 − Aug. 1939 . 100

Farm prices	
Per capita weekly earnings, mfg.	
Food prices, retail	
Wholesale prices	
Hourly earnings, mfg.	
Prices paid by farmers	
Retail prices, all	
Construction costs	
Consumers' price index	
Industrial stock prices	
Rent	

Relative

measured from this base to March 1942 (the month of the first broad fixing of prices under the General Maximum Price Regulation), June 1946 (the date of the termination of price control under wartime regulations),[3] and February 1948.

The extreme items in Table 2, for February 1948, are very far apart, ranging from farm prices, which rose almost 200 percent, to rents, which increased only 11 percent. The prices of equity shares in industrial corporations, which advanced only 26 percent, are near the bottom. The general cost of living for urban workers (the consumers' price index) rose 68 percent. (This index is held down, of course, by the stable rent element.) It is notable that measures for 7 of the 11 classes listed stand in a central group, for which price increases ranged from 90 to 126 percent. Here are wholesale prices, general retail prices and prices paid by farmers, construction costs, and wages, both hourly and per capita.[4] Apart from the extreme

[3] Temporary and partial controls had been restored by the end of July 1946; those for all except rents, rice, and sugar were removed in November 1946 by Presidential action.

[4] Per capita weekly earnings are, of course, a measure of income; they are not the price of a commodity or of a standard unit of effort. But taken together, average per capita weekly earnings, average hourly earnings, and unit labor costs (for which some estimates are given later) provide basic information about exchange relations and economic status.

CHART 3
The Changing Tempo of Inflation
1939 – 1948
Percentage Change per Month

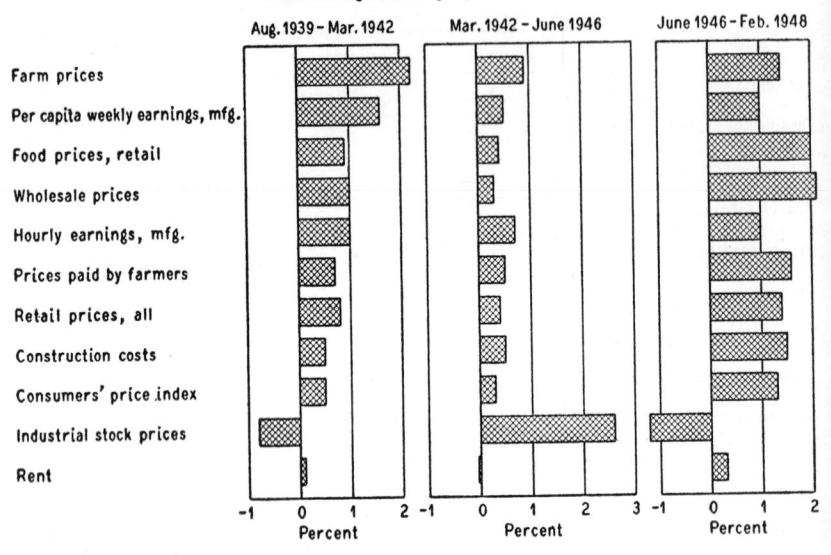

Aug. 1939 – Mar. 1942   Mar. 1942 – June 1946   June 1946 – Feb. 1948

- Farm prices
- Per capita weekly earnings, mfg.
- Food prices, retail
- Wholesale prices
- Hourly earnings, mfg.
- Prices paid by farmers
- Retail prices, all
- Construction costs
- Consumers' price index
- Industrial stock prices
- Rent

advances in farm prices and the modest increases in rents and stock prices, the general inflationary movement just about doubled the unit prices of commodities and services for the broad classes here represented.

The monthly rates of change recorded in Table 2 and Chart 3 show that the most rapid advances came in the periods preceding and following price control. The effectiveness of the controls, where imposed, is clear.[5] Stock prices (which were not controlled) gained materially in the interim period from March 1942 to June 1946; farm prices, which were subject to regulations less stringent than those applying to commodities in general, continued to rise at a rate close to 1 percent a month; hourly earnings in manufacturing increased 0.7 percent a month; other groups (except rents) advanced, but at relatively low rates.

A sharp and general upward spurt followed the termination of

[5] The price indexes and rates of change in Table 2 are for quoted prices. Later references in this paper (see text, note 10; and App. Table 7, note) call attention to some of the limitations of quoted prices arising from upgrading, deterioration of quality and service, and black market operations during the period of price control. The introduction of these sources of error, and their later removal, lessen the accuracy of available quotations, but the general record of price movements is probably not materially distorted by them.

wartime controls (again excepting rents, for which controls were retained, and stock prices). Wholesale prices in general, food prices at retail, and farm prices led in this resumed advance, which persisted at relatively high rates for nine months. After March 1947 there was a short period of retardation or decline. The price advance was renewed on a broad front in May 1947; most of the series here represented reached peaks, for the postwar movement to date, in January 1948. The monthly rates of advance in the several commodity price indexes were in this period well below those of 1946-47. The rate of increase in hourly earnings in manufacturing declined only slightly, however. The differential between price and wage advances characteristic of the 1946-47 rise was sharply reduced in 1947-48. Commodity prices fell off between January and February 1948; modest advances prevailed thereafter.

The degree of divergence of price and cost movements among these broad groups of goods and services is pronounced. But each entry in Table 2 is itself an average behind which lie wide internal differences. Tables 3 and 4 indicate the range of these differences for goods sold in wholesale markets—a broad category comprehending

TABLE 3

Wholesale Prices, Commodity Classes of the Bureau of Labor Statistics, 1939-1948

INDEX NUMBERS

	9/1938-8/1939	Mar. 1942	June 1946	Feb. 1948
Farm products	100	156	213	281
Foods	100	135	159	242
Textile products	100	145	164	222
Building materials	100	124	145	215
All commodities	*100*	*127*	*147*	*210*
Hides and leather products	100	126	132	209
Chemicals and allied products	100	128	127	178
Fuel and lighting materials	100	105	119	177
Housefurnishing goods	100	120	129	166
Metals and metal products	100	110	119	164
Miscellaneous	100	122	134	163

AVERAGE MONTHLY RATES OF CHANGE

	8/1939-3/1942	3/1942-6/1946	6/1946-2/1948	6/1946-3/1947	3/1947-5/1947	5/1947-2/1948
Farm products	+2.2	+0.7	+1.6	+3.4	−1.9	+0.6
Foods	+1.4	+0.3	+2.6	+5.4	−2.4	+0.9
Textile products	+1.4	+0.3	+1.8	+3.1	−0.2	+0.7
Building materials	+0.8	+0.3	+2.4	+4.1	−0.2	+1.0
All commodities	*+1.0*	*+0.3*	*+2.1*	*+3.6*	*−0.8*	*+1.0*
Hides and leather products	+0.8	+0.1	+2.9	+4.7	−1.1	+1.4
Chemicals and allied products	+1.0	−0.1	+2.0	+4.1	−2.0	+0.7
Fuel and lighting materials	+0.2	+0.3	+2.4	+1.6	+1.3	+2.9
Housefurnishing goods	+0.6	+0.1	+1.4	+1.5	+1.2	+1.1
Metals and metal products	+0.4	+0.2	+1.9	+2.7	+0.6	+1.1
Miscellaneous	+0.7	+0.2	+1.1	+1.9	+0.4	+0.4

all major commodity transactions between business buyers and sellers.

Table 3 sets forth the familiar groupings of the Bureau of Labor Statistics. The prices of farm products at wholesale—at the top of the list—reflect the high prices at the farm already noted. Foods, textiles, and building materials come next; near the bottom are housefurnishings and metals. The range from 163 for the lowest group to 281 at the top is very wide indeed for a period of only eight years.[6]

A different perspective on the incidence of inflationary forces during this period is provided by the classifications of commodities represented in Table 4. The groups overlap in diverse ways (e.g., metals enter into capital equipment, durable goods, manufactured goods, etc.; foods are also consumer goods, producer goods for human consumption, farm products, nondurable goods, etc.); in their totality they give a detailed and suggestive picture of the diversity of conditions in wholesale markets.[7]

The wide range between goods for use in capital equipment (which advanced only 59 percent) and foods at the producer goods stage (which advanced 196 percent) attests the variety of conditions in wholesale markets during these eight years. Where the classifications set up groups with directly opposed qualities differences of behavior are in general pronounced. Farm products rose more than nonfarm products; raw materials more than manufactured goods; nondurables more than durables; goods intended for human consumption more than goods intended for use in capital equipment. The difference is small between producer goods and consumer goods, but this is due to a sharp divergence between two classes of producer goods. Producer goods intended, after fabrication, for human consumption are at the top of the list; goods entering into capital equipment are at the bottom.

At the upper end of the spectrum provided by this exhibit are concentrated soft goods—foods, farm products, nondurables—and, notably, such goods at the producer stage. At the lower end are metals and other minerals, durable goods, capital equipment, nonfarm products—goods thought of as products of the heavy indus-

[6] In May 1920, at the peak of prices following the first World War, the range between extreme items for the same commodity groups was wider — from 194 for metals to 345 for textiles (indexes on the 1914 base).

[7] For descriptions of these classes of commodities see *Prices in Recession and Recovery* (National Bureau of Economic Research, 1936), App. II, pp. 470-90. Producer goods, the reader may note, include the materials of industry, raw or semiprocessed, and all forms of capital equipment. Consumer goods are those ready for final consumption.

TABLE 4
Wholesale Prices, Commodity Classes of the National Bureau of Economic Research, 1939-1948

	INDEX NUMBERS			
	9/1938-8/1939	Mar. 1942	June 1946	Feb. 1948
Producer goods for human consumption, foods	100	152	198	296
Producer goods for human consumption, all	100	150	186	270
Foods	100	140	174	255
Crops	100	148	190	253
Raw materials	100	140	180	253
American farm products	100	144	176	249
Animal products	100	139	159	245
Producer goods for human consumption, nonfoods	100	148	174	245
Nondurable goods	100	138	166	237
Human consumption goods	100	137	162	232
Consumer, processed foods	100	128	143	222
Producer goods, all	100	130	155	221
All commodities	*100*	*130*	*152*	*216*
Consumer goods	100	129	148	210
Building materials	100	118	142	202
Manufactured goods	100	123	135	195
Consumer, processed nonfoods	100	125	134	188
American nonfarm products	100	117	130	186
Durable goods	100	116	129	179
Nonmetallic minerals	100	108	120	170
Metals	100	112	121	165
Goods entering into capital equipment	100	111	120	159

	AVERAGE MONTHLY RATES OF CHANGE					
	8/1939-3/1942	3/1942-6/1946	6/1946-2/1948	6/1946-3/1947	3/1947-5/1947	5/1947-2/1948
Producer goods for human consumption, foods	+2.1	+0.6	+2.5	+5.4	−2.9	+0.8
Producer goods for human consumption, all	+1.8	+0.5	+2.2	+4.4	−1.5	+0.8
Foods	+1.5	+0.5	+2.3	+4.6	−2.4	+1.0
Crops	+1.6	+0.6	+1.7	+3.4	−0.6	+0.4
Raw materials	+1.4	+0.6	+2.0	+3.4	−1.0	+1.1
American farm products	+1.6	+0.4	+2.1	+4.1	−1.6	+0.8
Animal products	+1.5	+0.3	+2.7	+5.2	−2.8	+1.2
Producer goods for human consumption, nonfoods	+1.5	+0.3	+2.0	+3.4	+0.2	+0.8
Nondurable goods	+1.4	+0.4	+2.2	+4.0	−1.4	+0.9
Human consumption goods	+1.3	+0.4	+2.2	+3.9	−1.2	+0.9
Consumer, processed foods	+1.1	+0.2	+2.7	+5.5	−2.0	+0.9
Producer goods, all	+1.1	+0.4	+2.1	+3.5	−0.6	+1.1
All commodities	*+1.0*	*+0.3*	*+2.1*	*+3.5*	*−0.8*	*+1.1*
Consumer goods	+1.0	+0.3	+2.1	+3.5	−1.0	+1.1
Building materials	+0.6	+0.4	+2.1	+3.3	+0.7	+1.0
Manufactured goods	+0.8	+0.2	+2.2	+3.7	−0.6	+1.0
Consumer, processed nonfoods	+0.8	+0.1	+2.0	+3.0	+0.5	+1.1
American nonfarm products	+0.6	+0.2	+2.2	+2.9	+0.4	+1.5
Durable goods	+0.5	+0.2	+1.9	+2.8	+0.7	+1.1
Nonmetallic minerals	+0.3	+0.2	+2.1	+1.6	+1.2	+2.3
Metals	+0.4	+0.2	+1.8	+2.6	+0.3	+1.1
Goods entering into capital equipment	+0.4	+0.2	+1.6	+2.3	+0.5	+1.0

tries. The pattern is consistent; in many respects it represents a distinctive departure from that usually characteristic of cyclical expansions.[8] In the lagging of metals and durable goods generally and of the broad class of nonfarm products, in the marked leadership of foods and of farm products generally, in the relatively large advance in the prices of consumer goods, the present rise differs from the usual cyclical pattern. The consumption sector of the economy is usually the most stable; in the present rise foods have outstripped every other major category of goods. The price increases of 1939-48 impinge on the pockets and the budgets of final consumers more immediately and more heavily than do the price rises that accompany the usual cyclical expansion.[9]

The monthly rates of change in Table 4 and Chart 4 reflect the fairly rapid increase among soft goods in the period prior to price control, the general stability of wholesale prices during the four years of general control, and the sharp advances since June 1946. In general, the commodity groups that led in the earlier advances

[8] The following list, based upon materials in National Bureau files, presents different categories of commodities in the order of the degree of the rise in prices in wholesale markets during expansions. The standing is based upon averages for peacetime business cycles in the United States during the last 80 years, but later cycles, more fully represented in the available records, are much more heavily weighted than earlier ones in this averaging process. The averages for the different groups do not relate to precisely the same cycles. The groups at the top of the list are those showing the biggest price increases in cyclical expansions.

EXPANSIONS DURING PEACETIME CYCLES IN GENERAL BUSINESS

	Price	Quantity	Value
		(percentage increase)	
Metals	+19	+52	+70
Raw materials	+18	+21	+38
Producer goods for human consumption	+18	+20	+36
American nonfarm products	+17	+38	+54
Producer goods, all	+17	+29	+46
Durable goods	+16	+47	+62
Goods entering into capital equipment	+16	+46	+61
Animal products, domestic	+16	+7	+24
Nonmetallic minerals	+15	+33	+48
All commodities	*+15*	*+23*	*+38*
Human consumption goods	+15	+17	+32
Nondurable goods	+15	+12	+27
Foods	+14	+2	+16
American farm products	+13	+7	+22
Manufactured goods	+12	+24	+37
Consumer goods	+11	+12	+23
Crop products, domestic	+11	+8	+20

[9] We should note, however, that in several major peacetime expansions the record is close to that of wartime cycles. In the expansion phase of such major cycles advances in the prices of farm products have usually exceeded those in the prices of commodities in general at wholesale.

CHART 4
Monthly Changes in Wholesale Prices by Commodity Groups
1939 – 1948
Percentage Change per Month

	Aug. 1939–Mar. 1942	Mar. 1942–June 1946	June 1946–Feb. 1948
Producer foods for human consumption			
Producer goods for human consumption			
Foods			
Crops			
Raw materials			
American farm products			
Animal products			
Producer nonfoods for human consumption			
Nondurable goods			
Human consumption goods			
Consumer, processed foods			
Producer goods, all			
All commodities			
Consumer goods			
Building materials			
Manufactured goods			
Consumer, processed nonfoods			
American nonfarm products			
Durable goods			
Nonmetallic minerals			
Metals			
Goods entering into capital equipment			

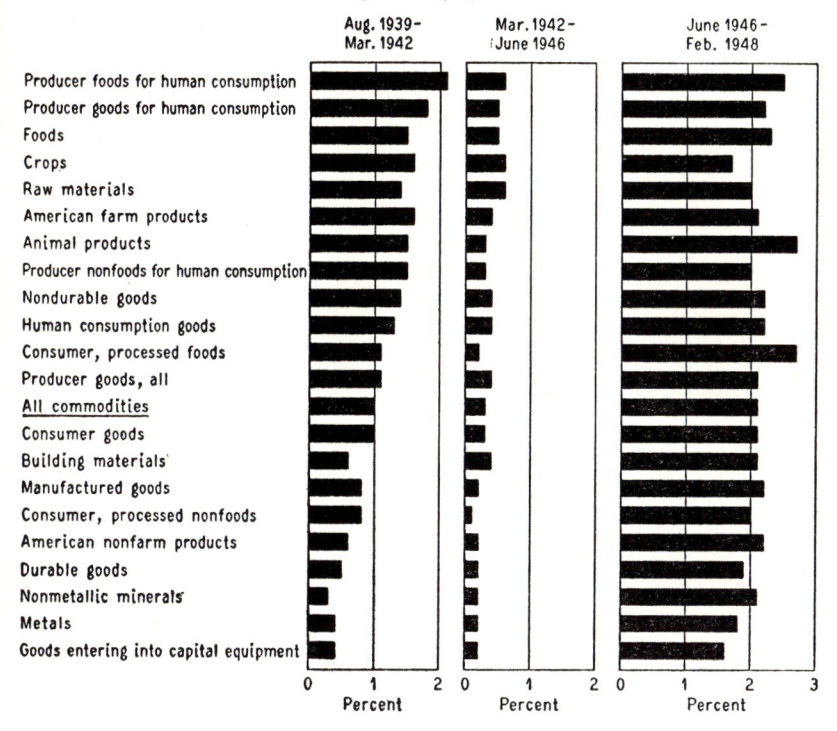

have been in the forefront of the rise since the ending of price control. In the more recent period processed foods advanced more rapidly than some of the earlier leaders. But the general array of commodity groups was much the same in February 1948 as in June 1946. Our economy remains one that is uptilted, with soft goods—foods, producer goods for human consumption, and farm products—at the high-priced end of the market spectrum.

The system of retail prices (Table 5) was marked by a range of price movements somewhat narrower than that recorded in wholesale markets, but the differences among group indexes are notable. Rents, at one end, rose only 11 percent; foods, at the other, more than 100 percent. The retail array reflects that of wholesale prices in that soft goods—foods and apparel—are above the heavier goods in the consumer budget.[10]

[10] To the degree that quoted prices understate actual prices (because of black market operations during the period of price control) the measurements in Table 5, and in

TABLE 5
Retail Prices by Commodity and Service Classes, 1939-1948

INDEX NUMBERS

	9/1938-8/1939	Mar. 1942	June 1946	Feb. 1948
Food[a]	100	124	153	215
Apparel[a]	100	123	156	194
Retail prices, all[b]	100	124	150	192
Housefurnishings[a]	100	120	154	190
Consumers' price index[a]	100	115	134	168
Anthracite coal[a]	100[d]	112	138	167
Bituminous coal[a]	100[d]	110	126	166
Miscellaneous[a]	100	109	127	145
Department store prices[c]	100	124	126	141
Fuel, electricity, and ice[a]	100	105	111	131
Rent[a]	100	104	104	111

AVERAGE MONTHLY RATES OF CHANGE

	8/1939-3/1942	3/1942-6/1946	6/1946-2/1948	6/1946-3/1947	3/1947-5/1947	5/1947-2/1948
Food[a]	+0.9	+0.4	+2.0	+3.3	−0.5	+1.0
Apparel[a]	+0.8	+0.5	+1.2	+1.9	+0.2	+0.6
Retail prices, all[b]	+0.8	+0.4	+1.4	+2.2	−0.05	+0.7
Housefurnishings[a]	+0.6	+0.6	+1.2	+1.9	−0.1	+0.7
Consumers' price index[a]	+0.5	+0.3	+1.3	+1.9	−0.1	+0.8
Anthracite coal[a]	+0.6[e]	+0.4	+1.1	+1.3	−2.0	+1.5
Bituminous coal[a]	+0.4[e]	+0.3	+1.6	+1.1	+0.4	+2.1
Miscellaneous[a]	+0.3	+0.3	+0.7	+0.9	+0.3	+0.6
Department store prices[c]	+0.8	+0.04	+0.6	+0.9	+0.1	+0.4
Fuel, electricity, and ice[a]	+0.2	+0.1	+0.9	+0.7	+0.05	+1.2
Rent[a]	+0.1	−0.01	+0.3	+0.2	+0.1	+0.7

[a] Bureau of Labor Statistics. [b] Department of Commerce. [c] Fairchild Publications.
[d] Average of four quarters, September 1938-June 1939. [e] September 1939-March 1942.

In this section we have examined certain major features of the structure of domestic prices as it has been left by the upheavals of the last eight years. In closing we note the following distinctive aspects of the period, and of present price relations.

1) The pressures on the price system reflected world-wide shortages of goods for which needs are urgent. Marked advances in the purchasing power of domestic consumers accentuated pressures arising from foreign needs. Rising costs of materials and labor contributed to the forces tending toward higher prices of manufactured goods.

2) The pressures on the prices of consumption goods were heaviest where the demands of final consumers, transmitted through retail and wholesale markets, focus on supplies in primary and secondary

Note 10 concluded:
preceding tables, are inaccurate. Thus prices actually paid for some food products in both wholesale and retail markets were higher in June 1946 than the quoted prices used in computing official indexes. For these goods the rise since then has been somewhat less than that indicated. Premium payments for automobiles in recent transactions raise these prices above current quotations.

markets. Competitive forces, acting in these markets without the restraints that often characterize price policies in markets where competition is less severe, interact to force prices up sharply on the basis of demand.

3) In the markets for durable goods, especially producer durables, demand has been strong but probably less insistent than for perishable goods; supplies, moreover, have been more readily increased. Deliberate price policy, formulated with reference to long-range considerations bearing on market position, labor relations, and public opinion, as well as to current costs, plays a significant role in determining the selling prices of durable goods. Related to this in the formulation of price policy is the fact that in the production of such goods relatively stable overhead charges are large elements of selling price. Rising volume may so lower overhead charges per unit of product that rising material and labor costs may be absorbed without reducing the strategically important profit margins per unit of product. In the next section we examine evidence on this matter.

4) A notable expansion of the money supply was a central factor in the generation of pressures on the price system. The influence of this expansion, which was partially restrained during the period of general price and wage controls, was strongly felt when controls were removed.

5) The general pattern of price advances between 1939 and 1948 differs significantly from that characteristic of cyclical expansions. Heavy, durable goods did not exercise their usual leadership; prices of goods in the consumption sector of the economy, usually fairly stable in business cycles, advanced most sharply. Consumers are closer to the strategic center of the present price rise, and the fortunes of consumers as buyers of goods are more immediately involved than in customary cyclical price advances.

6) The resumption of rapid advances in food prices in the early summer of 1947 reflected accentuation of foreign needs and developing shortages of domestic supplies of feed crops and important food products, coming at a time when the money purchasing power of domestic consumers was high and still increasing. Advances in wage rates in certain key industries and corresponding price advances gave further stimulus to the renewed upswing. Improvements in domestic and world food prospects in January 1948 altered the outlook and sharply reversed price movements for farm products and foods. The prices of heavy goods gained, relatively, in early 1948.

III CHANGES IN THE COMPONENTS OF SELLING PRICE, MANUFACTURED GOODS, 1939-1947

Elements of the Cost Structure

From the viewpoint of the man who buys materials, hires labor, and utilizes capital equipment in the production of goods the important price relations are those that enter into his cost structure—material costs, labor costs, overhead costs—and determine the profit margins that are of such central importance in an enterprise economy. Factors other than unit prices and hourly wages are here involved, of course. Productivity is a major determinant of labor costs; unit overhead costs are a function of volume of output. The price and cost factors that enter into the business man's calculations thus consist of direct payments for materials, supplies and labor, and overhead charges of diverse sorts, all modified by the effectiveness with which productive effort is utilized and by the volume of business done. The resulting components of selling price do not, in general, correspond to quoted market prices of commodities and services, but major movements in these components may be estimated. We pass to a review of certain of these elements.

The indexes in Table 6 and Chart 5 define estimated changes in selling prices and in various cost factors in manufacturing industries, all reduced to 'per unit of product' terms. The records for different manufacturing industries vary, of course, in cost and selling price changes. These estimates are designed to indicate average changes for all industries; their sources are noted in the table.

The eight years covered brought major shifts in the structure of manufacturing costs and notable changes in the conditions under which manufacturers operate. That the present postwar situation is one of flux, with major shifts still in process, is indicated by the magnitude of the changes between 1946 and 1947.

We consider first the movements of the two main categories of costs—direct costs, which include outlays for materials and labor, and the composite of overhead charges, taxes, and profits. In the years since 1939 advances in direct costs were substantially larger than those in the supplementary charges here called overhead costs, taxes, and profits. By 1946 direct costs had increased 51 percent, per unit of goods produced; supplementary charges advanced only 24 percent. Both components have jumped sharply in 1947; direct costs were 90 percent higher than in 1939, while overhead charges,

TABLE 6

Estimated Changes in Average Selling Price of Manufactured Goods and in Its Major Components, 1939-1947

	INDEX PER UNIT OF MANUFACTURED PRODUCT		
	1939	1946	1947
Selling price	100	144	178
Direct costs	100	151	190
Cost of materials	100	148	190
Labor costs	100	166	190
Overhead costs, taxes, and profits	100	124	145
Overhead (excl. income and excess profits taxes and profits)	100	104	103
Federal and state income and excess profits taxes	100	381	547
Profits, after taxes	100	134	200

The measure of change in the selling prices of manufactured goods is derived from the index of the National Bureau of Economic Research, adjusted to improve comparability with indexes of cost elements derived from monetary aggregates and production indexes. The index of material costs is based on a National Bureau index of the prices of producer goods at wholesale, with adjustment to take account of the time lag between the purchase of materials and the sale of the finished product. ('Materials' here include raw materials proper and semifinished goods bought for further processing.) The other indexes of the cost and profit components of selling price are estimates based on relevant records of the physical volume of production and the dollar value of sales of manufactured goods, payrolls and profits, and taxes paid by manufacturing industries. The measures of unit cost and profit changes thus derived are consistent with reported statistics of sales, aggregate output, payrolls, and profits, but each is subject to an appreciable error of estimate.

The following sources were used in making these estimates.

Production of manufactured goods: Board of Governors of the Federal Reserve System.

Sales of manufactured goods: Corporate sales from Department of Commerce adjusted to include estimated sales of noncorporate manufacturing enterprises.

Payrolls: Bureau of Labor Statistics.

Profits and income and excess profits taxes: Corporate data from Department of Commerce adjusted to include estimates for noncorporate manufacturing enterprises.

taxes, and profits were some 45 percent higher. The increases in direct costs exceeded those in the selling prices of manufactured goods; the chief lifting force on the prices of finished products was exerted by the expenses that fluctuate directly and immediately with the volume of business done—expenses that constitute some 75 percent of the value of product for manufacturing industries in the aggregate.

Between 1939 and 1946 labor costs per unit of product advanced more rapidly than material costs. The increases that followed the end of price control in 1946 carried materials up sharply, and in 1947 the two components of direct costs stood at the same level, with reference to the 1939 base. The advances in both elements of direct costs exceeded the average increase in unit selling prices.

The relation of changes in labor costs to changes in the unit selling prices of manufactured goods since 1939 is of exceptional interest. Historically, unit labor costs have lagged behind selling

CHART 5
Estimated Changes in Average Selling Price of Manufactured Goods and in its Major Components 1939 – 1947

Index per Unit of Manufactured Product

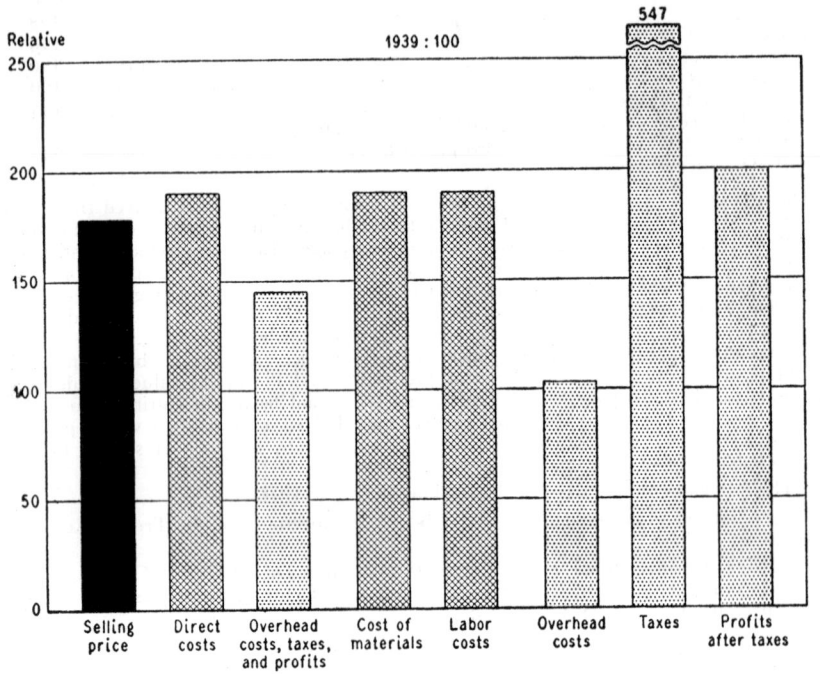

1939 : 100

- Selling price: ~178
- Direct costs: ~190
- Overhead costs, taxes, and profits: ~146
- Cost of materials: ~192
- Labor costs: ~192
- Overhead costs: ~105
- Taxes: 547
- Profits after taxes: ~202

prices during periods of major change in the price level.[11] In the present case the advance in labor costs has exceeded that in selling prices, for manufacturing industries as a whole. The explanation is to be found, partly, in labor shortages and in the strong bargaining position of labor during the period of the present survey. This accretion of power helped to offset any tendency toward lagging wage adjustments; indeed, in some industries it reversed the lag. A second factor is the character of the price rise. It was a rise that carried foods and other consumer goods up most sharply in price. The effects were felt immediately by wage earners, and there was consequent immediate pressure for relief through higher wage rates.

Material costs, as averaged for all manufacturing industries, kept general pace with selling prices until 1946. (Materials of manu-

[11] In six of seven comparisons (based on Census data) of advances in the average unit selling prices of manufactured goods and in average labor costs per unit of product, covering 1899-1939, the increase in selling prices exceeded that in estimated labor cost. However, the margin of difference was slight in the last half of this period.

facture include semiprocessed goods; the prices received for these goods by some manufacturers constitute costs for other manufacturers.) This average situation conceals a divergence already noted (in Tables 3 and 4). Materials that enter into perishable and semidurable goods for human consumption rose sharply between 1939 and 1946; the heavy materials that enter into capital equipment and durable consumer goods lagged well behind in the general advance. When controls were abrogated in 1946 the prices of both classes of materials increased (consumption goods more rapidly) and the general index of material costs per unit of manufactured product rose relatively more than selling prices. Indeed, in this latest stage of the price advance, material costs caught up with labor costs (which in 1946 were at higher levels, relatively to 1939).

The index that measures changes in the composite of services represented by 'overhead, taxes, and profits' defines the resultant of three quite divergent movements. Federal and state income and excess profits taxes, per unit of product, were in 1946 almost four times as high as in 1939; in 1947 they were more than five times as high. Unit profits after taxes rose some 34 percent to 1946, 100 percent to 1947. The sharp recent advance in profits was scored despite the relatively large increases in both elements of direct costs. The explanation lies in the behavior of overhead charges proper—charges for rent, interest, depreciation, salary payments, etc.—which are not directly related to the volume of business done, and which lag, typically, in their response to changes in the purchasing power of money. (This is notably true of depreciation when charged on the basis of original cost.) During the last eight years, while direct costs and taxes have been increasing sharply, the aggregate of overhead costs has made more modest advances; large volume has reenforced conditions making for relatively low unit overhead costs.[12] This fortunate conjuncture rendered business exceptionally profitable, although wages and the prices of materials were high and productivity gains in recent years were low in comparison with past records.[13]

In interpreting this profit record one somewhat fortuitous factor is to be noted. Rising prices have brought advances in inventory

[12] Overhead costs of this nature made up about 20 percent of the total value of manufactured products in 1939, in 1946 about 15 percent, and in 1947 some 12 percent.

[13] In 1939 profits (after payment of federal and state income and excess profits taxes) of manufacturing corporations aggregated $2,958 million, as compared with $4,403 million in 1929 and $1,418 million, the annual average for the decade 1929-38. Profits in

valuations that exceed the gains in the physical volume of inventories. Such gains from inventory valuation adjustments amounted to almost $3 billion for manufacturing corporations in 1946.[14] Gains in 1947 were lower, but still substantial. If we take account of *operating* profits alone, for manufacturing corporations (deducting from given profit figures estimates of inventory valuation gains) the index of profits per unit of product for 1946 (1939:100) becomes 92, indicating a drop of some 8 percent. For 1947 the index of operating profits per unit of product is 163, somewhat less than the index of selling prices of manufactured goods. In so far as inventory valuation gains are realized by manufacturers, and not canceled by subsequent price declines, the indexes of unit profits in Table 6 are appropriate measures. If profits from operations alone are in question, account must be taken of inventory valuation adjustments.

Prices of Raw Materials and Manufactured Goods

In the preceding section we have presented an index of estimated changes in material costs per unit of manufactured product. Direct

TABLE 7
Prices of Raw and Manufactured Goods, 1939-1948

	9/1938-8/1939	June 1946	Feb. 1948	% change June 1946-Feb. 1948
INDEXES OF THE NATIONAL BUREAU OF ECONOMIC RESEARCH			
Raw materials	100	180	253	+41
Producer goods, raw	100	176	256	+45
Manufactured goods	100	135	195	+44
American farm products			
Raw	100	212	284	+34
Processed	100	154	228	+48
American nonfarm products			
Raw	100	147	221	+50
Processed	100	121	168	+39
INDEXES OF THE BUREAU OF LABOR STATISTICS			
Raw materials	100	181	251	+39
Semimanufactured goods	100	141	208	+48
Manufactured goods	100	134	192	+43

Note 13 concluded:
1939 were 5.2 percent of sales as compared with 6.3 percent in 1929 and 2.9 percent, the average for 1929-38. When 1939 is used as a standard of reference for the aggregate of all manufacturing enterprises, these relations may be borne in mind. Profits for that year, in absolute amount and as a percentage of sales, fell below the 1929 peak levels, but were well above the average for the decade 1929-38. It does not follow that 1939 would necessarily be a representative year for any individual corporation.

[14] See National Income, *Survey of Current Business*, Supplement, July 1947, p. 34.

comparison of the prices of raw materials and processed goods yields additional evidence on this aspect of manufacturing operations. Shifts in raw-processed price relations are, of course, one of the factors making for changes in manufacturing margins and in unit costs of production.

Price advances since 1939 among the materials of industry have greatly exceeded those in manufactured goods (Table 7). The prices of farm products have risen more than those of nonfarm products, but the margin of difference between the movements of the prices of raw and processed goods between 1939 and February 1948 is about the same in the two groups.[15] For the major categories of goods here represented raw material costs rose more than the prices of processed goods. Between June 1946 and February 1948, however, the prices of processed farm products rose more rapidly than the prices of raw farm products. Recent changes in the prices of nonfarm products conformed to the pattern of earlier movements.

To escape from possible transitory conditions during the twelve months, September 1938-August 1939, we go back 20 years for a standard of reference in defining price changes affecting manufacturing margins. The indexes in Table 8 show somewhat smaller 1948

TABLE 8
Prices of Raw and Manufactured Goods, 1924-27 to 1948

	1924-27	June 1946	Feb. 1948
INDEXES OF THE NATIONAL BUREAU OF ECONOMIC RESEARCH			
Raw materials	100	127	179
Producer goods, raw	100	128	186
Manufactured goods	100	109	157
American farm products			
Raw	100	136	182
Processed	100	119	176
American nonfarm products			
Raw	100	118	179
Processed	100	101	140
INDEXES OF THE BUREAU OF LABOR STATISTICS			
Raw materials	100	126	175
Semimanufactured goods	100	104	152
Manufactured goods	100	110	158

[15] Relative price changes among raw and processed goods classified somewhat differently are shown by the following summary. The prices of raw materials rose most sharply since 1939, and diverged most widely from the prices of processed goods, for crop products. But for animal products and minerals gaps also have been created.

	Index numbers, Sep. 1938-Aug. 1939:100					% change,	
	June 1946		Feb. 1948		June 1946-Feb. 1948	
	Raw	Mfd.	Raw	Mfd.	Raw	Mfd.
Crops	250	158	316	219	+26	+39
Animal products	178	145	259	235	+46	+62
Minerals	129	117	187	158	+45	+35

differences between the prices of raw materials and of processed goods, on the earlier base, but the general relations are the same. The prices of manufactured goods rose less than the unit prices of primary products entering into them. The relative changes among the major classes of goods are different, however, on the two bases. On the earlier base the differential is much wider for nonfarm than for farm products. A considerable part of the recent rise in the prices of raw farm products represented recovery from a relatively depressed condition in 1938-39. But as of 1948 the prices of primary products were high, in relation to the prices of processed goods, for both farm and nonfarm products whether the base of comparison be 1938-39 or 1924-27.[16]

Wages and Productivity

The last eight years, as we have seen, brought advances in unit labor costs that closely paralleled advances in material costs and somewhat exceeded the rise in the unit selling price of manufactured goods. The two factors affecting labor costs are the price of labor per manhour and the number of manhours per unit of output. For certain manufacturing industries indexes relating to these factors are available (Table 9).

We have noted in an earlier section the approximate doubling of average hourly earnings in manufacturing between 1939 and 1947. The relative gains were slightly greater in industries producing nondurable goods than in the heavy industries. (Average hourly earnings in dollars are still somewhat lower in the former group, however.) In general, there is a heavy clustering of industries around the average figure for all manufacturing, but the range between the lowest figure (+65 percent for malt liquors) and the highest (+166 for cotton manufactures) is considerable.

The estimates of changes in output per manhour stand on a much lower level. They indicate modest over-all gains in manufacturing, averaging about 1 percent a year. The rate of gain is below those that prevailed in the 'thirties, in the 'twenties, and in the decade

[16] The price history of 1914-1939 is characterized by one striking reversal of the record for 1890-1914. In the earlier period the rise in prices of raw materials exceeded that of manufactured goods; during the twenty-five years 1914-39 raw materials were progressively cheapened, relatively to manufactured goods. Persistent agricultural difficulties, rising productivity in the extractive industries, and marked increases in wage rates in manufacturing industries were some of the factors in this reversal, a reversal that has its surprising features because of the great gains in manufacturing productivity. The recent sharp advance in the prices of primary products represents a shift back to earlier price relations, a relative cheapening of manufactured goods in terms of raw materials.

TABLE 9

Changes in Average Hourly Earnings and in Output per Manhour in Selected Manufacturing and Mining Industries, 1939-1947

	% Change, 1939-IV 1947	
	Average hourly earnings	Output per manhour
All manufacturing	+100	+7
Durable goods	+93	+5
Nondurable goods	+104	+9
Cotton manufactures	+166	−19
Canning and preserving	+134	
Wool manufactures	+125	+23
Lumber and timber basic products	+118	
Sawmills	+120	−30
Furniture and finished lumber products	+114	
Confectionery	+110	+14
Boots and shoes	+109	+2
Paper and pulp	+108	−12
Butter	+105	
Leather	+104	+22
Tobacco manufactures	+102	+37
Flour	+99	−13
Chemicals and allied products	+98	
Paints	+86	−15
Stone, clay, and glass products	+95	
Glass products	+86	−5
Cement	+77	+13
Rubber products	+92	
Nonferrous metals and their products	+92	
Iron and steel and their products	+90	
Slaughtering and meat packing	+89	+8
Printing, publishing, and allied industries	+79	
Newspapers and periodicals	+78	+10
Automobiles	+66	
Petroleum refining	+66	+2
Malt liquors	+65	−26
Canned milk		−42
Mining	+98	+9
Quarrying and nonmetallic mining	+114	
Bituminous coal	+106	+13
Metal mining	+94	
Iron ore	+85	−15
Anthracite coal	+91	−7
Crude petroleum	+76	+37

Sources: Hourly earnings data are from the Bureau of Labor Statistics. In interpreting the percentages of change from 1939 to 1947 the reader will note that some of the advances (e.g., for construction and petroleum refining) were from relatively high levels in 1939, some (e.g., for cotton textiles) from relatively low levels.

The estimates of productivity changes for all manufacturing and for the durable and nondurable categories are derived from production indexes of the Board of Governors of the Federal Reserve System and employment records of the Bureau of Labor Statistics. These over-all indexes must be regarded as approximative only. Indeed, since some of the production indexes for individual industries are derived by the Federal Reserve Board from estimated manhours data, the productivity index for all manufacturing in Table 9 rests, in part, on the productivity estimates of the Federal Reserve Board. For individual industries, productivity changes are derived from production index numbers of the Bureau of Labor Statistics and the Board of Governors of the Federal Reserve System and from manhours data of the Bureau of Labor Statistics. The productivity estimates depend, for their significance, on the accuracy and comparability of the two basic series for each industry. A considerable margin of error attaches to each of the derived industry figures, but the series of estimates as a whole indicate the general movement of manhour productivity and suggest the diversity of industrial experience during this period.

preceding the first World War.[17] A check to productivity gains is to be expected during the extensive industrial shifts that war and postwar readjustment entail. However, if we repeat the record of the years following the first World War we shall experience a substantial gain in productivity when readjustment to a peace basis is possible. War-bought gains in technical knowledge, in modes of organization, and in equipment provide the bases for such an advance; high labor costs spur management into utilizing improved productive procedures. Such an acceleration of productivity advances, of which, indeed, there are encouraging signs in the early summer of 1948, would greatly enhance our ability to operate under the present cost structure and to meet the problems of the years immediately ahead.

Hourly earnings and manhour output data that seem reasonably comparable, on an industry basis, have been placed side by side in Table 9. The relative values are indicative, of course, of the character of changes in labor costs per unit of product. When the average advance in earnings has exceeded the gain in productivity, unit labor costs have risen. The recorded changes in earnings and productivity point to a highly variegated labor cost structure among manufacturing industries today. In all cases unit labor costs have risen with the general price advance since 1939. The indicated advance in unit costs has been greatest in cotton goods, least in tobacco manufactures (among the manufacturing industries here represented). In general unit labor costs have kept pace with, or have slightly exceeded, the rise in selling prices.

Profits

In studying profits as a component of the selling price of goods we must also use indirect methods. We may derive indexes of changes in profits per unit of goods sold from records of aggregate profits and total output, or approximate changes in profits per unit of goods sold from aggregate sales and aggregate profits, when unit price figures are available for the 'deflation' of sales. The second method enables us to check the results obtained by the first method. The final indexes do not have the accuracy of direct price quotations but they are useful indicators of the general magnitudes involved. Changes between 1939 and 1947 are measured by the entries in Table 10.

[17] The rate of gain in output per manhour in manufacturing industries as a whole was about 3.1 percent a year between 1931 and 1939, 5.6 percent between 1921 and 1929, and 2.5 percent between 1899 and 1914.

TABLE 10

Corporate Profits and Selling Price per Unit of Product,
Selected Manufacturing and Mining Industries,[a] 1939-1947

| | \multicolumn{6}{c}{INDEX PER UNIT OF PRODUCT} |
| | Corporate Profits after Tax | | | Selling Price | | |
	1939	1946	1947	1939	1946	1947
Manufacturing industries	100	132	197	100	145	182
Durable goods						
Lumber and timber basic products	100	440		100	191	
Iron and steel and their products	100	224		100	115	
Furniture and finished lumber products	100	176		100	131	
Nonferrous metals and their products	100	132		100	128	
Nondurable goods						
Textile mill products	100	470		100	146	
Paper and allied products	100	326		100	145	
Leather and leather products	100	245		100	144	
Rubber products	100	196		100	123	
Food and kindred products	100	173		100	186	
Petroleum and coal products	100	172		100	131	
Chemicals and allied products	100	95		100	133	
Tobacco manufactures	100	69		100	120	
Mining	100	119	150	100	131	163
Bituminous coal	100[b]	1,224		100	136	
Crude petroleum	100	149		100	138	
Metal mining	100	62		100	122	

The indexes of profits per unit of product are derived from the data on corporate profits compiled by the Department of Commerce (*Survey of Current Business*, Supplement, July 1947) and the indexes of the physical volume of output, for corresponding industries, constructed by the Board of Governors of the Federal Reserve System. Because the industrial classifications underlying the Commerce and Federal Reserve groupings are not the same in all respects, the derived indexes of unit profits are to be regarded as approximative only. The resulting figures for 1946 and 1947, which are derived directly from data on profits and output, differ somewhat from the figures in Table 6, which were somewhat differently derived.

[a] In listing individual industries those with negative earnings in the base year, or in the later years named, are necessarily excluded, since relative numbers would not be meaningful. The indexes for the total of all manufacturing industries, which do take account of losses, are thus not averages of, nor are they necessarily consistent with, the indexes for the small number of individual industries listed.

[b] This base is affected by a strike which reduced earnings in 1939.

For the composite of manufacturing industries the average advance in profits per unit of goods turned out was over 30 percent between 1939 and 1946[18]—somewhat lower than the average increase in selling prices (about 45 percent). The range of variation

[18] A check on this general result is possible by utilizing records of changes in total sales of manufacturing corporations (Department of Commerce compilations) and in the average selling price of manufactured goods. From these, measures of relative change in output may be estimated for comparison with indexes of total profits of manufacturing corporations. The resulting measure of profits per unit of product indicates an advance of 41 percent from 1939 to 1946. Though somewhat greater than the more directly derived index, it confirms the indication of the latter concerning the general magnitude of the increase.

in the experience of individual industries is, however, very wide. For tobacco manufacturers unit profits appear to have declined 31 percent; for textile mill owners unit profits increased 370 percent.[19] Among the industrial groups listed in Table 10 profits per unit of product advanced less than selling price for foods, tobacco, chemicals; they increased conspicuously more for textile mills, lumber, paper and pulp, leather and leather products, and iron and steel.

For the last year we have somewhat less adequate records of corporate profits. Figures compiled by the Department of Commerce permit an estimate of profits per unit of product for all manufacturing corporations for 1947. The index, which stands at 197 (1939:100), points to a very sharp advance in unit profits in manufacturing between 1946 and 1947. This gain is somewhat greater than the indicated increases between 1946 and 1947 in the average unit labor cost and the average selling price of manufactured goods.

[19] In interpreting relative measures of profits we must recall that profits, as a residual share, are subject to very wide swings, and may, indeed, be negative at times. This point is particularly relevant to the selection of a base of comparison. In the accompanying tabulation the absolute magnitude of corporate profits in 1939, the present base, is compared with the amounts realized in 1929, and in the average for the three years 1936, 1937, and 1938. Absolute figures for 1946 and (where available) for 1947 are also given.

CORPORATE PROFITS AFTER FEDERAL AND STATE INCOME AND EXCESS PROFITS TAXES
(millions of dollars)

	1929	1936-38	1939	1946	1947
Manufacturing industries	4,403	2,323	2,958	6,338	10,365
Durable goods					
Lumber and timber basic products	79	32	36	182	
Iron and steel and their products	719	212	249	738	
Furniture and finished lumber products	33	18	39	94	
Nonferrous metals and their products	194	116	124	227	
Nondurable goods					
Textile mill products	123	61	131	844	
Paper and allied products	95	71	87	360	
Leather and leather products	39	17	32	91	
Rubber products	10	24	50	195	
Food and kindred products	428	316	430	1,026	
Petroleum and coal products	614	190	204	550	
Chemicals and allied products	376	291	416	837	
Tobacco manufactures	124	105	111	112	
Mining	416	289	272	407	578
Bituminous coal	9	−2	5	82	
Crude petroleum	110	135	93	190	
Metal mining	238	144	159	77	

Source: Department of Commerce, National Income Unit.

Corporate profits in 1939 were below their 1929 level, but above the average of the three years 1936-38. For all manufacturing industries, indeed, earnings in 1939 were higher than in any year between 1930 and 1938. Comparison of earnings in 1939 and in other years, for individual industries, will help the reader interpret the movements from the 1939 base shown in Table 10.

The evidence here reviewed points to some general conclusions concerning the present state of manufacturing industries:

1) Between 1939 and 1947 labor costs, material costs, and profits, per unit of manufactured product, rose by approximately the same relative amounts. (Profits from rising values of inventories are here added to operating profits.)

2) One important factor contributing to profits in 1947 was the relatively modest advance of overhead costs. Such costs declined substantially as a fractional part of the value of product. Large volume combined with the lagging advance of fixed charges made high profits possible in 1947.

3) A stepping up of depreciation charges on the basis of present cost levels will increase overhead charges and correspondingly reduce profit margins. Advances in overhead charges are to be expected when depreciation charges, rents, and other lagging items have been adjusted to present price levels.

4) The present cost and price structure of manufacturing industries is heavily dependent on large volume. A situation in which material costs, labor costs, and profits, per unit of goods produced, are all higher than selling prices (relatively to the 1939 base) seems anomalous. It would be so, of course, without the great increase (about 75 percent) in the number of units of goods produced and sold. The present industrial system, while highly productive, is more exposed to strain when sales and output decline than was the cost and price structure of the years immediately preceding the war. (In those years the level of output at which profitable operation was possible was, for many plants, lower than it now is.)

IV Some Historical Comparisons

Major Changes in the Structure of Prices, 1924-27 to 1948

The reference of measurements of price, wage, and cost changes to 1939 is desirable if we are concerned with shifts during the eight years after the outbreak of war in Europe. But such comparisons are affected by the relations among elements of the price system that prevailed in 1939. These relations, in part fortuitous, in part reflecting cyclical conditions of the base period, in part reflecting established cost structures and established terms of exchange, do not necessarily constitute a 'normal' state of affairs to which the price system may be expected to return. Any base period suffers from similar defects in that it reflects transitory relations as well as those of more enduring type. To get a different perspective on the relations prevailing in 1948 among major elements of the price system we refer them to a more distant base, as we did in the preceding section in discussing manufacturing margins. For present purposes we shall employ the same four years in the middle 1920's, a period mid-way in the general upward movement of that decade. The years 1924 to 1927 span one business cycle; temporary cyclical conditions will thus not affect base-period relations.

Table 11 and Chart 6 contain measures of movements in major elements of the price system between 1924-27 and 1948. The relatives for February 1948 on the 1924-27 base are, in general, lower than those in Table 2 on the 1938-39 base; for most elements of the system we are studying prices of 1938-39 were below those of 1924-27. The two exceptions are stock prices, which were some 10 percent higher in 1938-39 than in 1924-27, and the hourly earnings of manufacturing labor, which were about 20 percent higher.

TABLE 11

Prices and Wages, 1924-27 to 1948

	1924-27	9/1938-8/1939	Feb. 1948
Hourly earnings, mfg. labor	100	121[a]	249
Per capita weekly earnings, mfg. labor	100	89[a]	201
Farm prices	100	64	190
Construction costs	100	99	188
Wholesale prices	100	77	162
Food prices, retail	100	73	156
Prices paid by farmers	100	74	148
Industrial stock prices	100	111	140
Consumers' price index	100	80	134
Rent	100	69	77

For definitions and sources see notes to Table 2.
[a] January-August 1939.

The reference of 1948 price relations to a base twenty years earlier, rather than to 1938-39, changes the general ranking of elements somewhat. Food prices are lower on the earlier base, construction costs higher. The most notable shift relates to wages. The hourly earnings of manufacturing labor outrank all other elements in the gains made since 1924-27. For the rest, we find farm prices and the per capita weekly earnings of workers in manufacturing industries near the top in both listings (Tables 2 and 11); rents, industrial stock prices, and the consumers' price index are at the bottom. Wholesale prices occupy a middle place.

The general agreement of the two tables confirms the conclu-

CHART 6
Relations among Elements of the Price Structure 1924-27 to February 1948

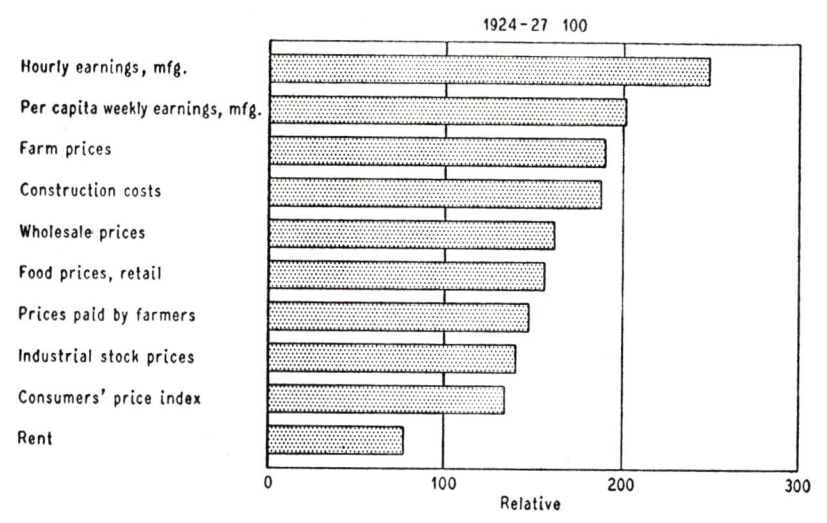

- Hourly earnings, mfg.
- Per capita weekly earnings, mfg.
- Farm prices
- Construction costs
- Wholesale prices
- Food prices, retail
- Prices paid by farmers
- Industrial stock prices
- Consumers' price index
- Rent

sions previously drawn about the nature of the 1948 price structure. During the twenty years, as during the eight years that span the war, the net shifts in price relations were such as to improve materially the exchange position of farmers and manufacturing labor, and to reduce the relative worth of rented properties, of equity shares, and of commodities and services entering into the consumers' price index (of which rent is an important element, it will be recalled).[20] The recent advances in farm prices offset net losses between 1924-27 and 1939; the recent advances in hourly earnings of manufacturing labor were superimposed upon earlier gains. (Substantial advances were made in industrial productivity between 1924-27 and 1948. The benefits of these accrued more immediately to manufacturing labor than to most other producing or consuming groups.) The gain in weekly earnings was lower because of a marked reduction, during the twenty years, in the length of the working week. The extraordinary divergence of construction costs and rents is one of the most significant features of this record. Industrial stock prices gained, relatively, between 1924-27 and 1938-39, and have lost, relatively, since 1939.

[20] As the reader will note, although the various indexes in Table 11 relate to exchange values, the units employed differ. Wage earnings are on an hourly and on an (over-all) per capita basis, physical goods on a commodity unit basis, industrial stock prices on an equity share basis. These are not, of course, precise and perfectly comparable indexes of relative well-being.

Reference to a still earlier base reveals the character of some long-period changes in economic relations. Indexes for February 1948 on the 1912-14 base are given in Table 12. Among all the goods and services represented in this table an hour of manufacturing labor has gained most, relatively, since 1912-14. The weekly earnings of manufacturing labor and construction costs stood next in order. The rise in farm prices exceeded the advance in the living costs of industrial wage earners and in wholesale prices. Measurements on a base more than thirty years removed in time are, of course, less accurate in a dynamic economy than are measurements on more recent bases, but they are useful indicators of the long period shifts that have marked our economic development since the outbreak of the first World War.

TABLE 12

Prices and Wages, 1912-14 to 1948

	1912-14	1924-27	9/1938-8/1939	Feb. 1948
Hourly earnings, mfg. labor	100	229	278[b]	568
Per capita weekly earnings, mfg. labor	100	226	201[b]	455
Construction costs	100	215	211	403
Industrial stock prices	100	204	227	287
Farm prices	100	146	94	277
Food prices, retail	100	164	119	256
Prices paid by farmers	100	165	122	245
Consumers' price index	100	177	141	238
Wholesale prices	100	144	111	233
Rent	100[a]	163	113	126

For definitions and sources see notes to Table 2.
[a] 1913-14.
[b] January-August 1939.

We turn to the system of wholesale prices. The commodity groups distinguished by the Bureau of Labor Statistics are shown, on the 1924-27 base, in Table 13. The indexes for February 1948 are lower, for all groups, than those on the 1938-39 base (Table 3), but the general ranking is not widely different. The forces that dominated the recent advance shaped also the net changes during the twenty years. Farm products, building materials, and foods advanced in relative worth; fuel and light, housefurnishings, chemicals, and metals lost, relatively to all commodities at wholesale. Textiles gained during the shorter period, lost somewhat during the longer period.

Other categories of goods at wholesale are ranked on the 1924-27 base in Table 14. Here, too, the array is of the same general character as that on the 1938-39 base. Farm products, raw materials, foods

TABLE 13

Wholesale Prices, Commodity Classes of the
Bureau of Labor Statistics, 1924-27 to 1948

	1924-27	9/1938-8/1939	Feb. 1948
Building materials	100	90	193
Hides and leather products	100	89	186
Farm products	100	64	181
Foods	100	73	178
All commodities	*100*	*77*	*162*
Metals and metal products	100	93	153
Textile products	100	65	144
Housefurnishing goods	100	85	140
Fuel and lighting materials	100	79	139
Chemicals and allied products	100	76	136
Miscellaneous	100	75	122

(notably foods at the producer goods stage) stand near the top on both bases. Minerals, manufactured goods, nonfarm products stand in the lower halves of the two arrays. Building materials stand relatively higher on the earlier basis than on the later; so also does the general class of producer goods. On both bases the advance in producer goods prices reflects very sharp rises in producer goods intended for human consumption. Relative prices for the heavy materials that enter into capital equipment are low on both bases.

The evidence we have here reviewed, utilizing bases respectively eight years and twenty years removed from the present situation,

TABLE 14

Wholesale Prices, Commodity Classes of the
National Bureau of Economic Research, 1924-27 to 1948

	1924-27	9/1938-8/1939	Feb. 1948
Producer goods for human consumption, foods	100	71	210
Animal products	100	75	184
Foods	100	72	182
American farm products	100	72	179
Raw materials	100	71	179
Building materials	100[a]	88	179
Producer goods for human consumption, all	100	66	177
Consumer, processed foods	100	77	170
Producer goods, all	100	77	170
Crops	100	65	165
Nondurable goods	100[a]	71	165
All commodities	*100*	*77*	*165*
Durable goods	100[a]	92	164
Human consumption goods	100	71	164
Consumer goods	100	77	161
Manufactured goods	100	81	157
Consumer, processed nonfoods	100	83	155
American nonfarm products	100	83	154
Metals	100	92	153
Producer goods for human consumption, nonfoods	100	62	152
Nonmetallic minerals	100	85	145
Goods entering into capital equipment	100[a]	88	140

[a] 1926.

points to a tilting of the price structure that has elevated soft goods —farm products, nondurables, food products in finished form and, still more, food products in unprocessed or semiprocessed form. Metals and other minerals, nonfarm products, goods entering into capital equipment (other than building materials) have lagged behind. The general conformity of the results obtained from measurements on the two bases indicates that these findings are not materially affected by transitory conditions in any one base period. Although the 1938-39 situation differed from that of 1924-27, the general rankings of the elements of the price system are much the same whether the base of reference be eight or twenty years distant. Movements from 1924-27 to 1938-39 were not always in the same direction as those from 1938-39 to 1948, but recent changes have been of a magnitude to dominate the record of changes within the system of wholesale prices and largely to determine the relative status of the producing groups here represented.

Records for retail prices are less comprehensive for the twenty-year comparison than for more recent years. Changes since 1924-27 in the chief categories of goods and services for which we have quotations are shown in Table 15. The general index of consumers' prices in February 1948 stands 34 percent above the base period average—an advance much smaller than the rise of 68 percent between 1938-39 and February 1948. The distribution of the groups is much the same, whether the base of reference be 1924-27 or 1938-39. The present structure of retail prices, as set forth in Tables 5 and 15, reflects rather fundamental shifts which have modified the relations of 1924-27 as well as those of 1938-39. Advances in cost to the consumer have been relatively less for living quarters, for fuel, for electricity than for other major items entering into his budget. Increases have been relatively large for food, for apparel,

TABLE 15

Retail Prices by Commodity and Service Classes, 1924-27 to 1948

	1924-27	9/1938-8/1939	Feb. 1948
Apparel	100	84	164
Housefurnishings	100	84	161
Food	100	73	156
Bituminous coal	100[a]	88	146
Miscellaneous	100	99	143
Consumers' price index	100	80	134
Anthracite coal	100[a]	79	132
Fuel, electricity, and ice	100	86	113
Rent	100	69	77

Source: Bureau of Labor Statistics.
[a] October 1922-September 1925.

for housefurnishings. In appraising these changes in unit costs account may be taken of changes in consumer incomes and of changes in the distribution of consumer expenditures among various classes of goods and services. Shifts in aggregate consumer expenditures are shown in Appendix Table 7.[21]

Three Periods of Economic Expansion

We may learn something about the particular features of the most recent inflationary rise by comparing volume and value changes of this period with those of two earlier periods (Table 16 and Chart 7). One covers 1914-20, when inflationary advances were clear to all observers; the other covers 1921-29, a period of notable economic expansion, but with price advances of restricted scope. For the purposes of this comparison we use annual data, and measure the movements of recent years against 1938 as base, rather than 1939. The year 1938, a cyclical low, is comparable with 1914 and 1921, the bases of relatives measuring changes during the two earlier periods. (The reader should note, however, that these dates do not relate to cyclical depressions of equal severity.)

Between 1914 and 1920 the aggregate output of physical goods in the United States increased some 17 percent. Manufacturing and mining scored advances of about one-third, in production; for agriculture the gain was about 7 percent. But the aggregate value of agricultural products more than doubled; that of manufactured goods trebled. In the markets for securities the volume of transactions expanded greatly but unit prices for stocks, in contrast to major commodity groups which more than doubled, were in 1920 only slightly above their 1914 level.[22] Farm realty prices increased 65 percent from 1915 to 1920.[23] These were substantial gains in a

[21] Detailed expenditure records are given in National Income, *Survey of Current Business,* Supplement, July 1947, pp. 41-4.

[22] Stock prices reached their high in July 1919; the average price was lower in 1920 than in 1919. For commodity prices, which were affected later by forces of recession, the reverse was true. In 1920 industrial stock prices (Standard and Poor's index) were 52 percent higher than in 1914, but utilities and rails were 25 percent lower. The use in this index of weights based on total shares outstanding gives industrials relatively less weight in this period than public utility and railroad stocks.

Quantity figures for securities (i.e., number of shares traded) are not of the same order as those for the other elements in Table 16, which relate to the current flow of goods or services. Nevertheless, the comparisons are useful for the light they throw on relative activity at different periods in different sectors of the national economy.

[23] From estimates of the Bureau of Agricultural Economics on average price per acre of farm real estate.

TABLE 16

Changes in Quantities, Unit Prices, and in
Aggregate Values during Three Periods of Economic Expansion[a]

	1914	1920	1921	1929	1938	1947
Total production[b]						
quantity	100	117	100	170	100	189
price	100	235	100	100	100	201
value	100	275	100	170	100	380
Agriculture[c]						
quantity	100	107	100	119	100	131
price	100	209	100	120	100	287
value	100	224	100	143	100	376
Mining[d]						
quantity	100	134	100	175	100	154
price	100	217	100	96	100	160
value	100	291	100	168	100	246
Manufacturing[e]						
quantity	100	130	100	188	100	223
price	100	241	100	92	100	179
value	100	313	100	173	100	399
Construction[f]						
quantity	100	65	100	174	100	145
price	100	265	100	103	100	176
value	100	171	100	179	100	256
Manufacturing employment and wages[g]						
total employment	100	118	100	131	100	192
average hourly earnings	100	263	100	111	100	198
payrolls	100	310	100	146	100	381
Securities[h]						
quantity	100	313	100	658	100	84
price	100	101	100	345	100	139
value, derived	100	316	100	2,270	100	117
value, actual					100	88

[a] The periods compared are not expansion phases of business cycles.

[b] Quantity and unit price measures are weighted averages of indexes of agriculture, mining, manufacturing, and construction. The weights, averages of 1927 and 1931 estimates of value added, are agriculture 22, mining 7, manufacturing 59, and construction 12. Value indexes are derived from quantity and unit price measures.

[c] Agricultural production is estimated by the Bureau of Agricultural Economics. Unit price is an average of farm prices. Value of agricultural production is derived from quantity and price measurements.

[d] Mineral production is estimated by Harold Barger and Sam Schurr for 1914-29; for 1938-47 the index of the Board of Governors of the Federal Reserve System is used. The index of wholesale prices of raw minerals is that of the National Bureau of Economic Research. Value indexes are derived from quantity and price measures.

[e] Manufacturing production 1914-29 is estimated by Solomon Fabricant; for 1938-47 the production index of the Board of Governors of the Federal Reserve System is used. The index of wholesale prices of manufactured goods is that of the National Bureau of Economic Research. Value indexes are derived from quantity and price measures.

[f] Bradstreet's value of contracts awarded is used for 1914-20; for 1921-47 the value of new construction activity is computed by the Department of Commerce. Unit price is a composite of construction cost indexes of Aberthaw Construction Company, American Appraisal Company, Associated General Contractors of America, and *Engineering News-Record*. Volume of construction is derived from value and unit price measures.

[g] Total employment, an index of manhours worked in manufacturing industries 1914-29, is computed by Solomon Fabricant; for 1938-47 indexes of number employed and hours worked are those of the Bureau of Labor Statistics. Payroll data for 1914-29 are from the Census of Manufactures; for 1938-47 the Bureau of Labor Statistics index is used. Average hourly earnings are derived from payroll and employment measures.

Notes to Table 16 are concluded on page 36.

CHART 7

Changes in Quantities and in Aggregate Values during Three Periods of Economic Expansion

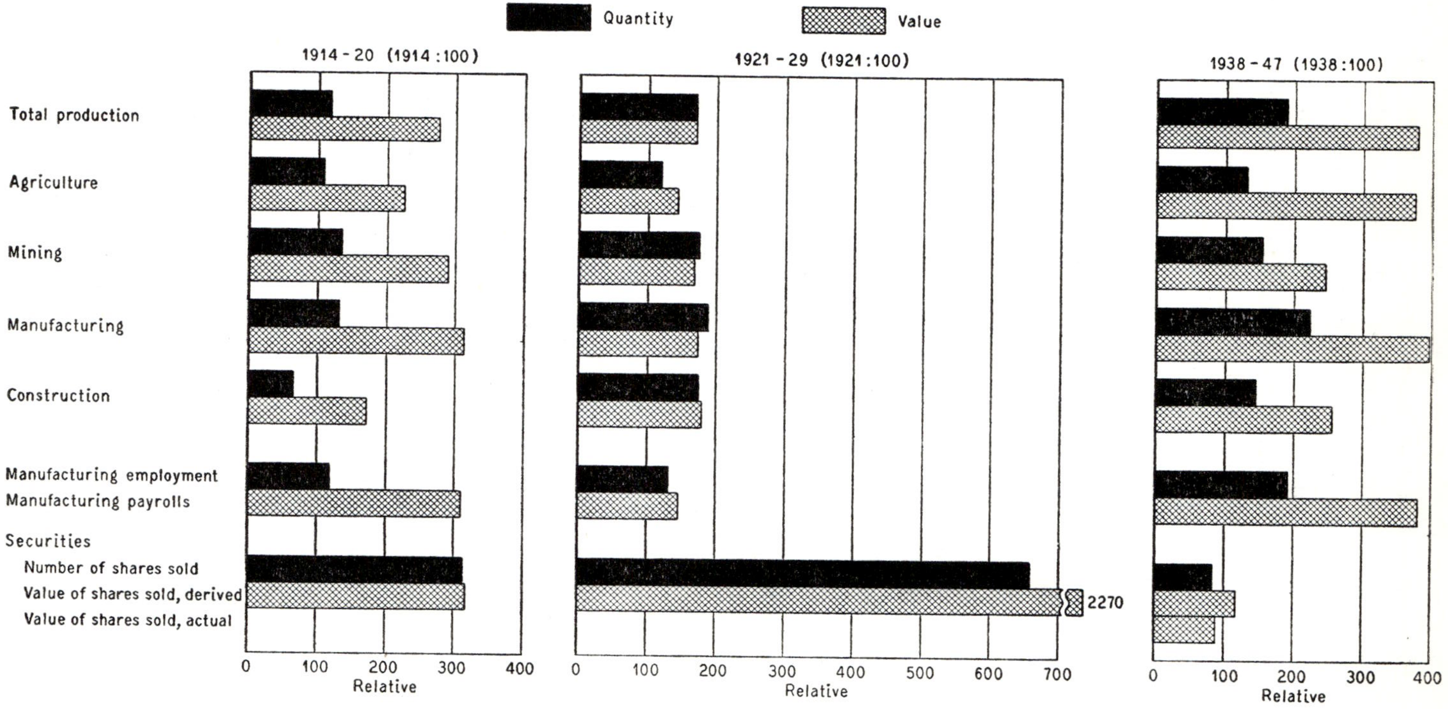

market normally sluggish. The advances in the labor market were greater. Manufacturing employment, measured in aggregate manhours, was 18 percent higher in 1920 than in 1914; payrolls were 210 percent larger. Here, again, unit prices advanced; average hourly earnings of manufacturing labor were 163 percent higher in 1920 than in 1914. Clearly the inflationary pressure of 1914-20 impinged most sharply on commodities—agricultural and mineral, raw and manufactured—and on the services of labor.

Between 1921 and 1929 we turned out goods in a stream that swelled steadily, with only minor interruptions. The production of commodities increased about 70 percent, as against 17 percent between 1914 and 1920. Yet their aggregate value increased only 70 percent, materially less than the gain of 175 percent in the earlier period. The explanation, of course, lies in average unit commodity prices, which rose sharply from 1914 to 1920 and remained level during the 'twenties. We find a similar contrast in the labor market. Total employment in manufacturing (aggregate manhours worked) was 31 percent higher in 1929 than in 1921. This exceeded the 1914-20 increase of 18 percent. But payrolls increased only 46 percent, as against 210 percent in the earlier period. The price of a unit of labor (one manhour) increased only 11 percent from 1921 to 1929, as against 163 percent from 1914 to 1920. It was not in commodity or in labor markets that the pressures of credit expansion were felt.[24]

Notes to Table 16 concluded:

h For 1914-29 the quantity index measures the number of shares sold on the New York Stock Exchange, excluding odd lots and stopped sales, as computed by the *New York Times*. For 1938-47 the quantity index measures the number of shares sold on the New York Stock Exchange, as compiled by the Securities and Exchange Commission. The price index is the combined index of 402 stocks computed by Standard and Poor's Corporation. The segment for 1914-18 was computed by the Cowles Commission for Research in Economics and spliced to Standard and Poor's index.

For each period the value series is derived from the price and quantity measures. The record of value changes, thus derived, would coincide with the actual change in the aggregate value of shares traded only if the composition of the volume of shares traded remained unchanged. If there is a shift in composition (such as would result from a swing to low-priced shares) the quantity, price, and value measures would not be mutually consistent. Such shifts undoubtedly occurred in all three periods here covered. For the final period actual value figures are shown in italics below the derived measures of value changes. Since in this period there was a definite shift to low-priced shares, the actual value relative is well below the derived figure. Although the derived value figures are formal, they are given here as indications of the degree to which changes in the prices of securities cause divergent movements of quantities and values in securities markets.

[24] This statement and the figures do not tell the whole story of monetary movements and commodity production between 1921 and 1929. Manufacturing productivity increased greatly in this period (output per manhour went up about 43 percent), but there was no corresponding reduction in prices. (The average unit selling price of manufactured goods went down about 8 percent. The average cost, per unit of product, of the services

Yet pressure was manifest in two major areas in the 'twenties—urban real estate values and the values of securities. For the first we have no systematic measures of comprehensive coverage.[25] For securities, as represented by common stocks, we have records that indicate the dimensions of the expansion between 1921 and 1929. Trading in 1929, as measured by the number of shares sold, was six and one-half times as great as in 1921; the aggregate value of shares sold increased more than twenty-fold. Chart 7 gives an inadequate picture of this gain, for the horizontal scale has to be broken if changes in other elements are to be appreciated. The index of average unit prices, the direct measure of the volume-value differential, was 345 in 1929 (1921:100).

The expanding force of purchasing power that could not be constrained within the limits of available physical quantities was felt primarily in commodity and labor markets between 1914 and 1920, and within these markets its influence was pervasive. In the 1920's similar pressures were not directly manifest in commodity markets (although we should note that commodity prices did not reflect the great productivity advances of this decade). Upward pressures were strong, however, in the markets for equity shares. Realty values in special areas (e.g., Florida) were also affected. With these two experiences of the fairly recent past we compare the records of 1938-47.

The over-all gain in physical output in the most recent period exceeds that recorded in either earlier period. (The most recent period is longer than the other two; on an average annual basis recent gains were about equal to those of the 'twenties.) Manufacturing industries were the major factor in the dominance of recent gains; increases in construction volume from 1938 to 1947 were well below those of the 'twenties; and mineral output, although gaining notably, advanced less than in 1921-29. The increase in em-

---

of agents of fabrication fell only 4 percent.) In good part advancing fabricational costs and profits absorbed the productivity gains.

[25] Statistics on the assessed valuation of real property (land and improvements) provide some evidence on changes in the value of real estate, which increased 62 percent from the fiscal year ending June 30, 1922 to the fiscal year ending June 30, 1930 (*Financial Statistics of States,* Department of Commerce). In some degree this gain represents new structures, but increased unit prices of existing property contributed substantially to the advance in total values. This is a very considerable increase, occurring over an eight-year period during which commodity prices held level.

The average price per acre of farm real estate declined 32 percent between 1920 and 1930.

ployment in manufacturing (here measured in total manhours worked) was materially bigger than in either earlier period. Activity in the securities markets (measured by shares traded) declined from 1938 to 1947, in contrast to the notable gains of 1914-20 and of 1921-29.

In the differentials between volume and value changes—the most immediate indicators of inflation (or of deflation)—1938-47 stands, of course, much closer to 1914-20 than to 1921-29. In the 'twenties substantial volume increases were accompanied by modest price advances, or by none; volume and value movements were of the same general order of magnitude. But in the last nine years volume increases were outrun by needs and by purchasing power. The pressures that generate price advances were strongest in the markets for agricultural products. For the services of labor, manufactured goods, mineral products, and the products of the construction industry price advances were lower, but still considerable. Realty prices lagged in the early stages of this expansion, but both urban and farm land prices moved rapidly forward in the later stages.[26] Equity shares rose some 40 percent in price between 1938 and 1947—an appreciable gain, but far below the extraordinary advances of the 'twenties.

In the expansion that spanned the first World War physical volume gained moderately, and price advances swelled total values quite disproportionately to the volume gains. For equity shares alone were the net price advances from 1914 to 1920 low. The expansion of the 'twenties was marked by notable gains in physical volume, by slight advances, or no advances, in commodity prices. Prices of securities and realty values in certain areas reflected strong speculative pressures. The last nine years resemble the 'twenties in respect of gains in output (except in construction); they resemble the years covering the first World War in the general character of inflation in commodity and labor markets. The years spanning World Wars I and II were, of course, marked by rapidly expanding demands, both domestic and foreign. Output increased much more in the later period, but supplies still fell far short of effective demand; price advances were an inevitable consequence.

The absence, in the latest period, of advances in equity values at all corresponding to those of the 'twenties is another distinctive feature of the recent record. Changes in unit prices and in the vol-

---

[26] Estimated price per acre of farm land increased 69 percent from 1940 to 1946.

ume and aggregate value of shares traded were small in comparison with other economic developments of these years.

In the three periods here reviewed we have one case of commodity inflation with small advances in physical volume, one of substantial increases in the volume of commodities without inflation, one of large advances in volume with inflation. Monetary factors and fundamental needs, which immediately determine the pressures upon available supplies, differed, of course, in the three periods; output alone provides but one of the strands in the developing record. The story of the latest expansion is unfinished. If further considerable increases in the over-all output of the economy are to be recorded, substantial advances in manhour output must occur; however, the mere maintenance of production at present levels would represent a major accomplishment in the absence of such productivity gains. There was no net increase in general wholesale prices after the middle of January 1948, although there have been some indications that industrial prices may take the leadership from agricultural prices in a new advance.

Prices during Two World Wars

Historical analogies are as dangerous in dealing with economic phenomena as they are in appraising other aspects of human behavior, but they are often illuminating and suggestive. The comparison of price movements during and immediately following the two great wars of recent times is too inviting to neglect. There are interesting and revealing resemblances between these periods, although fundamental underlying differences bar the facile drawing of analogies. With these limitations in mind it will be helpful to compare the patterns of price change during these two periods.

Direct comparison is difficult because the periods of actual fighting were of unequal length. The earlier war lasted slightly more than four years, the later slightly less than six years. For present purposes we shall modify the time scales so that the four years between 1914 and 1918 are made equal to the six years between 1939 and 1945. This treatment of the two periods of actual warfare as though they were equal time intervals puts the price movements in suitable perspective, and facilitates the comparison of postwar changes.

Changes in the general level of wholesale prices and in living costs are shown in Chart 8, the indexes in Table 17. During the first halves of the periods of fighting, average prices at wholesale

TABLE 17
Prices during Two World Wars

WORLD WAR I

	1914	1915	1916	1917	1918	1919	1920	1921
Wholesale prices (BLS)	100	102	126	173	193	204	227	143
Consumers' prices (BLS)	100	101	108	127	150	172	199	178
Farm prices (BAE)	100	98	117	173	202	213	209	123
Nonagr. products, wholesale (NBER)	100	107	143	176	193	195	237	166
Goods entering into capital equip., wholesale (NBER)	100	108	146	189	203	205	255	178
Human consumption goods, wholesale (NBER)	100	103	126	169	198	209	224	144

WORLD WAR II

	1939	1940	1941	1942	1943	1944	1945	1946	1947
Wholesale prices (BLS)	100	102	113	128	134	135	137	157	197
Consumers' prices (BLS)	100	101	106	117	124	126	129	140	160
Farm prices (BAE)	100	105	131	167	202	205	213	245	293
Nonagr. products, wholesale (NBER)	100	102	109	116	118	120	122	133	168
Goods entering into capital equip., wholesale (NBER)	100	103	108	114	115	116	118	130	166
Human consumption goods, wholesale (NBER)	100	103	117	137	145	146	149	173	219

rose about 26 percent in both wars. They diverged sharply in the second halves. Between 1916 and 1918 average annual prices rose 53 percent; between 1942 and 1945, only 7 percent. Effective price control in the second World War is, of course, reflected in the stability of the price level during the last three years of fighting, stability that is the more notable because of the much more extensive mobilization of resources in this war. The two years following the end of fighting in both wars were marked by advances, but the increases were distinctly greater in the second war. An explosive postwar advance is the outstanding feature of the 1945-47 record. The general drop in wholesale prices after 1920 has, as yet, no counterpart in the record for the recent period.

Living costs followed much the same path during the first three-quarters of the two periods of fighting. Over-all increases amounted to something less than 30 percent. Thereafter there was divergence, less sharp than for wholesale prices and with the important difference that from 1918 to 1920 living cost advances were greater than from 1945 to 1947. The retention of rent controls in the recent period was the chief reason for this difference; foods rose more sharply in price from 1945 to 1947 than from 1918 to 1920. For living costs, as for wholesale prices, the force of the rise generated during the first World War had spent itself by 1920. Early 1948 witnessed a check to living cost increases, but more recent months have brought an additional advance.

CHART 8
Prices during Two World Wars

- - - - World War I (1914:100)
——— World War II (1939:100)

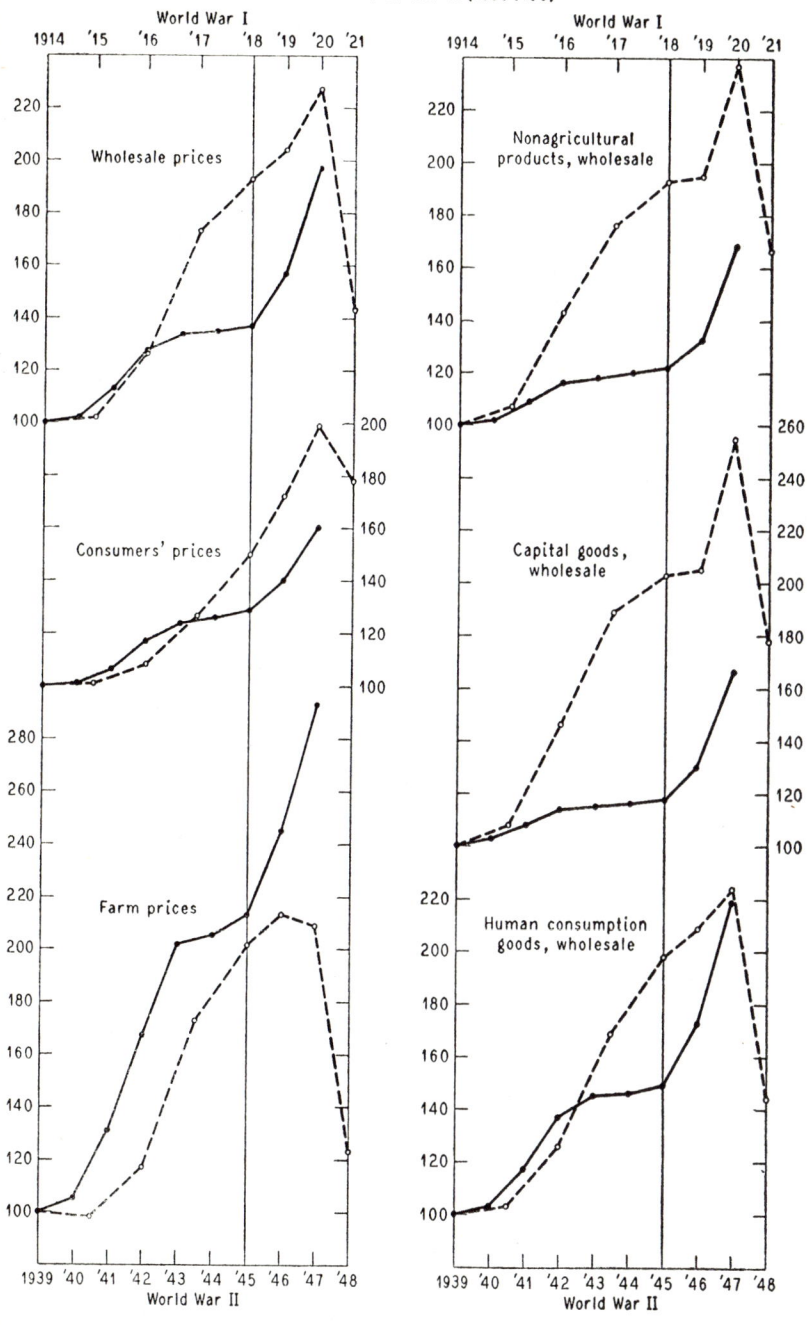

When farm price movements in the two wars are compared on a time scale thus modified to equalize the two periods of actual fighting (Chart 8), striking differences are revealed. The rise came earlier in World War II; it was at a more rapid rate during the first two-thirds of World War II; the sharp postwar advance from 1945 to 1947 departed significantly from the pattern of change between 1918 and 1920. The fact that farm prices were relatively depressed in 1939 while 1914 was a year of good prices has a bearing, of course, on the behavior of farm prices during the early parts of the two wars; the postwar divergence reflects the persistence of fundamental world shortages in recent years and the sustained, high-level demand of domestic consumers. Recovering world production of farm products promises to alleviate the former condition. Anticipations of this improvement have already affected the level of farm prices in the United States.

Differences of another sort are revealed when the behavior of farm prices is contrasted with the behavior of the prices, at wholesale, of all goods of nonfarm origin. In the first World War the course of the latter did not diverge greatly from that of farm prices, although the initial advance was a little sharper for nonfarm products, and the ultimate peak came somewhat later. The pattern for World War II diverges, early in the period of fighting, from that for the first war. Prices of the heavier goods that predominate in the nonfarm group rose little until 1945. Only belatedly, after the close of fighting and the end of controls, did they join in the general advance.

This contrast is brought out markedly when the movements of capital goods and of human consumption goods are compared (Chart 8). Except for a lag during the era of price control, movements of the prices of consumption goods followed similar paths in the two periods. By 1947 the level, with respect to the prewar base, was about equal to that of 1920. Capital goods felt the impact of inflationary forces later. The rise in these prices became rapid only with the end of general price controls in 1946. It is, indeed, in the markets for these goods that the immediately critical problems appear to be. Better world crop prospects were in early 1948 lessening tensions in farm markets. The prices of heavy goods may play a decisive role in the economic developments of the next twelve months.

Patterns of Price Expansions and Contractions

We may illuminate some of the characteristic features of the price expansion that came with the second World War and its aftermath by comparing the patterns of this advance with those occurring in peacetime cycles, and in two earlier war periods. It is clear that the period 1939-48 does not span the precise interval between cyclical turning points in wholesale prices; the date of the peak is still to be determined. But if we treat the rise from August 1939 to January 1948 as a phase of expansion, and set off stages similar to those employed in analyzing the expansion phase of a business cycle,[27] important characteristics of the rise are revealed (Table 18 and Chart 9).

Price expansion during a peacetime specific cycle is typically marked by a relatively sharp initial advance in average wholesale prices; the rate is close to 1 percent a month (the base of the percentage is the average monthly value of the price index for the cycle in question). The typical pattern is marked by deceleration from period E1 to E2, then constancy of rate of change.

Price increases in war periods have been distinctly greater; moreover, they have followed a markedly different pattern. The initial rise was at a lower rate than the succeeding rises. In the Civil War and World War I there was sharp acceleration in the second interstage period (E2), no acceleration in World War II. The acceleration continued into period E3 in the Civil War; was checked in E3 in World War I; continued in World War II, but at a modest rate.

---

[27] The National Bureau procedure for specific cycle analysis involves the identification of cyclical turning points in given economic series. The date of the initial low point in a given specific cycle is stage I, the date of the high stage V, and the date of the terminal low stage IX. Observations covering three months centering at each turning point are averaged to obtain measures of the standing of the series at each stage. Standings at stages II, III, and IV are obtained by dividing the expansion into thirds, and averaging corresponding monthly figures. Standings at stages VI, VII, and VIII are similarly obtained for three subdivisions of the contraction. The final measures of stage standings are relative numbers, the base of the relatives being the average of all monthly observations for the specific cycle in question.

For convenience, the four interstage periods (i.e., intervals between midpoints of successive stages) making up the expansion are designated E1, E2, E3, and E4 (the first relating to interstage period I-II, the second to period II-III, etc.); the four interstage periods making up the contraction are designated C1, C2, C3, and C4.

In getting the base of the relatives used in determining interstage rates of change in the index of wholesale prices in the rise from 1939 to 1948, all monthly indexes from April 1937 to January 1948 were averaged. This is an approximation to an average of monthly figures extending from high to high of a given specific cycle, although the date of the terminal high is still to be established.

TABLE 18

Monthly Rates of Change in Wholesale Prices during Expansions in Peace and War, Specific Cycles

Interstage Period	Av. 18 Peacetime Cycles	1861-64	1914-20	1939-48
E1	+0.9	+1.0	+0.6	+0.5
E2	+0.6	+1.6	+1.8	+0.5
E3	+0.6	+2.2	+1.0	+0.7
E4	+0.6	+5.4	+2.0	+2.1

The rates here given are for interstage movements in specific cycles in wholesale prices, i.e., cycles marked off by turning points in the wholesale price index itself. For the purposes of this study I have treated the period July 1861 to September 1864 as an expansion in a single specific cycle extending from July 1861 to August 1871; the minor drop in prices from March to September 1863 was not regarded as a cyclical recession. Similarly, December 1914 to May 1920 was regarded as an expansion in a single specific cycle extending from December 1914 to January 1921; the drop in prices from September 1918 to February 1919 was not regarded as a cyclical recession.

The index is that computed by the Bureau of Labor Statistics, spliced to the Warren-Pearson index for years prior to 1891.

The price rise in the final period, between stages IV and V, was in all three cases explosive. The monthly rate of advance reached 5.4 percent in the Civil War and 2.0 percent in the first World War. (In the specific price cycle here defined period E4 of the first World War expansion came after the phase of fighting.) The 1939-48 rise (which is merely an approximation to a cyclical expansion since the dating of the peak is still uncertain) brought the same violent terminal increase. Indeed, this terminal increase is sharply distinguished from preceding movements by reason of the very modest increases in the level of wholesale prices through periods E1 to E3.

As was mentioned above, the pattern of internal shifts in price relations during the price advance from 1939 to 1948 differs notably from that characteristic of peacetime expansions (note 8). Deceleration marks the course of price expansions in peacetime cycles; sharp terminal acceleration distinguishes wartime price expansions. Regarded as part of a pattern of wartime increase that began in August 1939, the advance of wholesale prices from August 1946 to January 1948 at a rate exceeding 2 percent a month is the counterpart of similar explosive movements during the wartime expansions of 1861-64 and 1914-20.

Peacetime contraction in wholesale prices conforms, in reverse, to the preceding expansion (Table 19). The initial rate of fall is greatest; thereafter decline proceeds at a decelerating rate. The record of price declines following wartime expansions is here confined to two periods—1864-71 and 1920-22. In both, the initial rate of decline exceeded that characteristic of peacetime cycles. This

CHART 9
Wholesale Prices during Expansions in Peace and War Specific Cycles
Percentage Change per Month

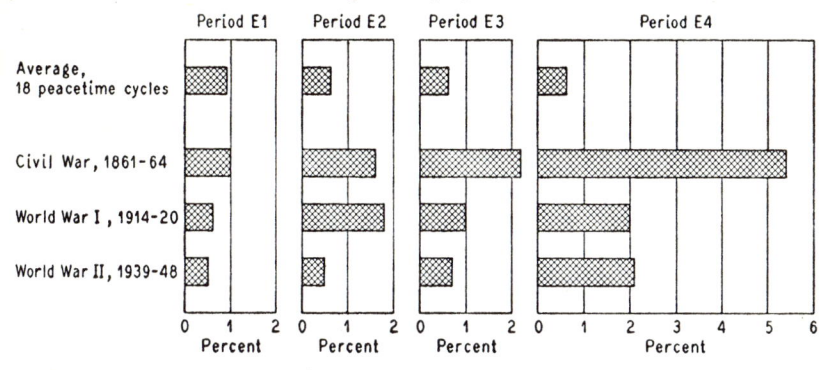

[Bar chart with rows: Average, 18 peacetime cycles; Civil War, 1861-64; World War I, 1914-20; World War II, 1939-48. Columns: Period E1, Period E2, Period E3, Period E4. Scales in Percent.]

abrupt initial drop, following the explosive advances of the final period of price expansion, was subject to progressive retardation in the protracted decline that continued to 1871; in the briefer 1920-22 decline there was violent acceleration through the second period of contraction, then retardation.

TABLE 19
Monthly Rates of Change in Wholesale Prices during
Contractions in Peace and War, Specific Cycles

Interstage Period	Av. 18 Peacetime Cycles	1864-71	1920-22
C1	−1.0	−1.7	−3.0
C2	−0.6	−0.6	−6.9
C3	−0.5	−0.5	−1.5
C4	−0.6	−0.5	−0.3

For definitions and source see note to Table 18.

Reference has been made to the dangers of analogy, but past experience provides some indications of possible prospective developments. To date, we have had the same accelerating price advance that has characterized previous wartime expansions. Some price decline from a postwar peak is, of course, to be expected. The magnitude of the decline and the precise pattern of change will be affected by the special circumstances of the present period, and by institutional changes that have occurred since the two previous experiences were recorded (e.g., government support of farm prices; increased strength of labor organizations). The past record of peacetime declines, as well as of postwar recessions, suggests the possibility of a sharp initial drop in prices when the peak has been passed, perhaps accelerating in the early stages of the decline. Thereafter retardation of the rate of decline is suggested, with stabilization as the forces of revival gather strength. Of course, if price movements should follow this pattern, the more swiftly the price realignments were effected and the more rapidly concurrent readjustments were made elsewhere in the economy, the smaller would be the disturbances of productive and distributive processes.

V Summary

The economy of the United States has been operating at full stretch for five years, with only a modest and temporary interruption during the readjustment that followed the end of fighting. Today it stands as the one major center of industrial production in the world, unharmed by war and capable of producing goods at a level well above that of prewar days. Currently it is feeling the full impact of heavy domestic demand for consumption and capital goods and of the urgent needs of a devastated Europe for food, clothing, and productive equipment. The pressures of these demands, amply implemented by a volume of money and credit that has expanded more rapidly than the physical volume of production, are manifest in a continuing upward push of prices. With these pressures have been associated steadily rising unit costs.

This paper has dealt with various aspects of the price situation in the United States at the beginning of 1948. In summary, and in general conclusion:

1) Prices in wholesale markets have doubled and living costs have risen two-thirds since 1938-39. Because of these advances in unit prices, dollar gains in production and trade substantially overstate the actual increases in physical volume.

2) Uneven advances in the unit prices at which goods and services are sold have altered the terms on which different producing and consuming groups exchange their products and have materially modified the domestic structure of costs and prices.

3) Farmers have gained substantially, in the sense that their aggregate physical rewards have increased much more than their aggregate physical contributions. This is true whether the base of comparison be recent or far removed. The relative gain of farmers in aggregate terms (i.e., the excess of gains in aggregate purchasing power, in terms of goods and services, over gains in aggregate farm output) may be estimated at 47 percent since 1938-39, 28 percent since 1924-

27. The per capita real income of farmers from 1939 to 1947, reflecting gains in output as well as price and subsidy factors, increased about 100 percent.

4) Among other primary producers, those turning out forest products gained at about the same rate as farmers. The terms of exchange (measured in this instance by the ratio of the index of wholesale prices of the commodity group in question to the index of prices of all commodities, at wholesale) moved against producers of metals and anthracite coal. This is true whether the standard of reference be 1938-39 or 1924-27.

5) Manufacturing labor, as a broad group, increased its total input of working time about 80 percent between 1939 and February 1948; its aggregate rewards (in terms of goods and services purchasable with wages received) were more than doubled. The increase in rewards, relative to the increase in time input, i.e., gain in real hourly earnings, was about 21 percent. The real per capita gain of manufacturing labor was about 34 percent.

The gains of manufacturing labor since 1939 were superimposed on prior gains. Between 1924-27 and 1939 these gains (expressed as increases in real hourly earnings or as differential gains in aggregate rewards over increases in aggregate manhours worked) amounted to about 50 percent. Thus the gains in real hourly earnings from 1924-27 to February 1948 were 85 percent.

6) The gains of nonmanufacturing labor from 1939 to the beginning of 1948, in real hourly wages, exceeded those of manufacturing labor for only four groups (of 18 covered in this survey): bituminous coal miners, workers in hotels and in quarrying and nonmetallic mining, and common labor in road building (App. Table 6). For three groups (telephone, electric light and power workers, and skilled labor in construction) real hourly wages declined.

7) The over-all price advance of 1939-47 was most pronounced in the consumption sector of the economy. The prices of foods and of consumption goods not yet finally processed were in the van. Worldwide shortages and high purchasing power of many domestic consumers were factors in this upward movement of prices. Consumer expenditures more than kept pace with rising prices. The flow of goods into actual consumption appears to have been from 40 to 50 percent greater than in 1939 (App. Table 7). Practically all components of the family budget shared in this general elevation of living standards; expenditures for food, clothing, and durable consumer goods rose most. In the terminal months covered by this

record, volume increases had been checked in some lines; for the broad field of consumer goods they were tapering off. Increases in expenditures reflected, mainly, rising selling prices, a situation that had its close counterpart in the 1919-21 cycle.

8) Material and labor costs were high for manufacturing enterprises. Such direct costs, indeed, constituted a larger percentage of the total value of product in 1947 than in any earlier year for which records are available.

9) Industrial profits were high, in the aggregate and per unit of physical product. High volume, the lagging advance of depreciation charges and other elements of overhead costs, and substantial gains due to rising inventory values made possible the maintenance of high profit figures in the face of rising direct costs.

10) The growth of industrial productivity, which contributed to the great industrial advance of the 'twenties, has been retarded in spite of such technical gains as may have been scored in the industrial effort of the war years. The rate of increase in industrial efficiency since 1939 has been well below the rate prevailing during the last quarter century. Under these conditions high wage rates mean high labor costs.

11) Major elements in the present cost and price system are protected today against declines, as they were not in earlier years. Price supports will tend to maintain farm prices when the pressures of present world-wide needs lessen. Wage rates and associated labor costs will be defended by strong labor organizations. To these resistances is added the continuing power of large industrial producers to support the prices of their products in the face of a general recession.

12) The economic expansion in the United States between 1939 and 1947 has no exact historical parallel. The 'twenties brought volume increases of an order resembling those of the recent period, but the general level of commodity prices suffered merely minor shifts. The first World War witnessed similar price advances, but with less notable gains in production. Joint increases of considerable magnitude in both prices and production are a distinctive feature of the latest expansion. The gain in industrial output between 1939 and 1947, a gain partly due to increased capacity, has been one of our major defenses against unbridled inflation.

13) The retarded advance in prices, notably in industrial prices, distinguished the price movements during World War II from those during World War I, and constituted a point of strength in the

period immediately following the end of fighting in 1945. The monthly rate of advance in general wholesale prices between August 1945 and January 1948, however, exceeded the monthly rate from November 1918 to the peak of prices in May 1920. This was not true of the prices of building materials, which had a relatively sharper rise in 1919-20 than in 1945-48.

14) In peacetime business cycles prices increase most rapidly during the first stages of expansion. Wartime price rises, in American history, have been marked by acceleration, the most rapid rises coming in the terminal stages of expansion. The pattern of price change in 1939-48 accords with that of wartime movements. The most explosive upward movement came in the closing months of this period.

The changes in price relations in the United States since 1939 will not necessarily be reversed in the years immediately ahead. Some may have accompanied enduring alterations in underlying conditions. But others are due to passing shortages and temporary shifts. In many of its aspects the price structure that exists in the spring of 1948 is a very recent creation. As transitory shortages are corrected and as conditions of supply and demand are stabilized under peacetime conditions modifications of elements of the system will occur. These modifications may be expected to bring agricultural and industrial prices somewhat nearer to the relations of the interwar period; to reduce, relatively, the prices of soft consumer goods and of material costs to manufacturing producers; to reduce labor costs and to raise overhead costs, per unit of manufactured product. Such corrections may be effected through declines in prices, wages, and production, with widespread unemployment and numerous business failures. This type of readjustment would be difficult and perhaps protracted today, since strong barriers would be placed in the way of a major downward readjustment of prices and wages.

The readjustment may take this form. It is, of course, the usual method of reshuffling relations that have been pulled out of line by war or by business booms. In the existence of a vast vacuum of unfilled wants abroad and of the continuing needs of high living standards at home there is, however, hope of effecting a more gradual amelioration of existing economic stresses. If production can be maintained, giving labor and enterprise opportunity to raise the efficiency of productive processes,[28] time would be given for the

[28] Productivity is usually a long-term rather than a short-term factor in economic processes. In the recovery of the early 1920's, however, the increase in manhour output in manufacturing industries averaged no less than 11 percent a year between 1920 and

working out of correctives for some of the chief difficulties we face. Costs can be lowered through such enhanced efficiency; the continuance of high level production would permit business restraint in pricing; high output would help to equalize the volume of goods and the volume of money and credit, provided the latter does not expand unduly; the burden of domestic living costs can be lightened and the existing gap between agricultural and industrial prices reduced as foreign production of foodstuffs and textiles picks up.

The cumulative movements of prices that we term inflation or deflation do not result from the working of vast, impersonal forces for which there are no personal responsibilities; they reflect a diversity of individual judgments and actions. Under the conditions existing in early 1948 the roles of industrial producers and of industrial labor are strategic. The industrialist operates in an area in which conscious price policy plays a major role in economic processes. During a portion of the period from 1939 to 1948 federal controls kept such prices down. Later, conscious constraints held prices in check over parts of this area. The result has been an increase of industrial prices much less rapid than in 1914-20, and well below the advance in agricultural prices in recent years. If labor costs and industrial prices do not give a further fillip to the general price level, and thus in a widening circle to wages, salaries, and a host of services, there is hope that the needed and inevitable internal readjustment of prices may be effected less painfully than it was in 1920-21.[29] Maintained high production, with the productivity gains that are potential in the present situation, can provide an umbrella under which some of the most necessary of these corrections may be effected. Under these conditions, and with restraint in the areas where deliberate policy shapes price and cost movements—industrial pricing and wage settlement—amelioration with modest strains may be possible. In the present world situation there is an accentuated need to achieve such amelioration without a major check to productive processes.

1922. This extraordinary advance helped to provide the foundation for the sustained prosperity of the 'twenties. In the scope of technical improvements during the recent war, and the unusual retardation of productivity gains to date, lies hope of a similar, rapid short-term enhancement of industrial efficiency that would reduce costs without wage reduction, and facilitate needed price readjustments.

[29] This readjustment may be deferred and further maladjustments created by the pressures of a new preparedness program. The character of this program is not now well enough defined to permit its dimensions or its probable incidence on prices to be estimated.

Director's Comment

The figures in Mr. Mills' paper and other evidence indicate an important feature of the inflation in 1946-47 which in my judgment should receive emphasis, since it is often overlooked. This inflation was characterized by large increases in key prices (particularly farm and food items, building materials, coal and other basic materials) and key wages, (coal, steel, and others) which intensified a cost-of-living-wage-price spiral and stimulated a general inflationary psychology. Subsequent price and wage advances at other points in the economy have in part represented a process of adjustment, supported by liberal use of credit and war-time savings, to those advances in business costs and living costs at key points.

A large armament program similarly produces strong inflationary tendencies at particular key points in the economy, although the focus of impact is, of course, quite different.

These facts emerging from analysis of the process of inflation in different types of situation are important in relation to the question of remedies. They cast doubt on the effectiveness of monetary and fiscal controls by themselves in a situation in which heavy inflationary impacts are at first concentrated on particular key segments in the economy. Could restrictive monetary and fiscal controls have held within moderate limits the increases in prices of grain, meat, milk, and coal, and the increases in key wages in 1946-47? If so, would they have produced a serious depression in the process?

D. H. WALLACE

Appendices

The text of this monograph deals with selected aspects of the complex price and wage movements of the last eight years. For the benefit of those who may wish to study these movements in greater detail, or to trace changes not here discussed, various price index numbers are brought together on a common base in Appendix Tables 1 to 7. Appendix Table 8 contains monthly indexes of prices from July 1943 to March 1948 for the various groups entering into the commodity classifications of the National Bureau of Economic Research.

APPENDIX TABLE 1

Wholesale Prices, Commodity Classifications of the National Bureau of Economic Research, Selected Dates, 1939-1948

	9/1938-8/1939	March 1942	June 1946	March 1947	May 1947	Feb. 1948	March 1948
All commodities	100	129.6	151.8	199.9	197.0	215.8	216.4
Raw materials	100	140.2	180.2	235.1	230.2	253.4	253.6
Manufactured goods	100	123.4	135.4	180.1	178.2	194.9	195.6
Nondurable goods, total	100	138.4	165.7	225.5	219.3	237.3	237.6
Raw	100	153.0	203.0	265.8	257.0	276.7	277.0
Processed	100	130.4	144.5	202.4	197.8	214.7	215.1
Producer	100	150.1	184.2	256.7	248.6	263.8	263.5
Consumer	100	130.1	152.2	202.6	197.8	217.8	218.6
Durable goods, total	100	116.0	129.0	161.1	163.3	179.0	180.0
Raw	100	122.7	144.7	203.1	204.3	224.6	225.0
Processed	100	113.9	123.5	146.9	149.5	163.7	164.8
Producer	100	113.9	130.1	163.4	165.8	183.0	184.3
Consumer	100	122.5	125.4	154.3	155.9	167.2	167.2
Producer goods, total	100	130.0	154.6	203.7	201.4	220.7	221.2
Raw	100	139.8	176.5	239.0	235.0	256.3	256.1
Processed	100	120.0	132.3	168.2	167.4	184.9	185.6
Consumer goods, total	100	129.0	147.9	195.0	191.1	209.7	210.3
Raw	100	141.1	193.9	219.9	210.5	241.5	243.4
Processed	100	126.4	138.5	189.8	187.0	203.2	203.5
Goods destined for use in human consumption, total	100	136.9	162.2	219.1	213.8	232.0	232.3
Raw	100	150.8	199.7	263.0	254.9	274.9	275.2
Processed	100	129.4	142.0	195.7	191.7	209.1	209.3
Goods destined for use in capital equipment, total	100	110.8	120.0	144.3	145.7	158.8	160.1
Raw	100	116.3	124.0	162.0	162.8	177.6	177.8
Processed	100	109.3	118.7	138.8	140.4	152.9	154.3
Building materials, total	100	118.1	141.7	183.7	186.1	202.1	202.9
Raw	100	130.6	162.5	235.6	235.0	259.4	259.9
Processed	100	113.2	130.8	162.1	166.0	178.5	179.5
Producer fuels, total	100	108.3	125.1	141.9	145.3	181.8	182.0
Raw	100	111.4	134.2	151.4	154.9	195.7	195.7
Processed	100	102.8	109.0	125.3	128.2	157.7	157.8
Producer goods destined for human consumption, total	100	150.4	186.3	259.8	252.0	269.7	269.5
Foods	100	152.0	198.1	294.1	277.0	295.7	295.3
Nonfoods	100	148.4	173.6	227.2	228.3	244.8	245.1
Consumer goods, processed Foods	100	127.8	143.4	214.1	205.8	221.8	223.4
Nonfoods	100	125.1	134.0	169.8	171.5	187.9	187.4

APPENDIX TABLE 1 (concluded)

	9/1938-8/1939	March 1942	June 1946	March 1947	May 1947	Feb. 1948	March 1948
Crops, total	100	148.3	190.0	248.0	245.1	253.3	254.0
Raw	100	170.3	249.7	314.1	310.2	316.2	320.0
Producer	100	172.6	248.7	325.5	320.0	323.4	326.4
Consumer	100	163.7	251.7	281.3	281.7	295.8	301.5
Processed	100	136.3	157.6	212.2	209.6	219.0	218.3
Animal products, total	100	139.2	159.0	233.7	220.7	245.3	245.3
Raw	100	146.7	178.5	249.7	232.1	259.3	256.6
Producer	100	151.0	178.7	270.8	253.9	270.3	266.6
Consumer	100	138.0	177.5	207.4	188.6	236.9	236.6
Processed	100	133.8	144.7	222.3	212.3	235.4	237.4
Metals, total	100	111.9	121.1	149.5	150.4	165.3	166.4
Raw, producer	100	111.6	121.5	160.9	163.4	176.9	177.4
Processed	100	112.0	120.9	146.2	146.7	161.9	163.3
Nonmetallic minerals, total	100	108.0	120.5	137.8	141.0	170.1	170.4
Raw	100	111.1	132.2	151.3	154.5	192.8	192.8
Producer	100	111.3	131.2	151.7	156.1	198.6	198.8
Consumer	100	110.0	137.2	148.6	145.0	160.9	161.1
Processed	100	105.5	111.0	127.1	130.2	152.1	152.4
Minerals, total	100	110.0	120.6	143.7	145.8	167.7	168.3
Raw	100	111.2	128.6	154.5	157.4	187.4	187.6
Producer	100	111.3	127.5	155.2	158.8	190.5	190.7
Consumer	100	110.0	137.2	148.6	145.0	160.9	161.1
Processed	100	109.2	116.6	138.5	139.9	157.9	158.8
Forest products, total	100	136.2	168.1	224.9	231.3	256.5	257.1
Raw, producer	100	152.5	199.8	299.6	302.6	337.2	337.5
Processed	100	123.7	142.2	166.5	176.4	194.1	195.2
American farm products, total	100	143.5	176.0	240.3	232.8	249.2	249.9
Raw	100	156.4	211.7	277.6	267.5	284.4	285.5
Producer	100	162.1	215.8	301.9	291.1	300.2	300.8
Consumer	100	141.7	201.3	216.7	207.9	244.2	246.7
Processed	100	135.8	153.7	217.4	211.8	227.6	228.1
American nonfarm products, total	100	116.7	129.6	163.0	164.1	185.7	185.8
Raw	100	123.1	146.6	191.0	191.3	221.2	220.6
Producer	100	120.7	142.3	185.6	187.7	219.1	218.4
Consumer	100	139.6	176.8	228.2	217.5	235.5	235.5
Processed	100	113.5	121.0	148.6	150.1	167.5	168.1
Other than raw American farm products	100	123.5	138.1	182.5	181.1	200.6	201.1
Foods, total	100	140.1	174.3	247.0	235.0	255.1	256.3
Raw	100	151.1	205.7	277.2	263.7	288.2	287.9
Processed	100	130.2	146.4	220.1	209.6	225.8	227.9
Nonfoods, total	100	123.9	139.5	174.9	176.8	195.2	195.4
Raw	100	130.9	158.4	199.6	202.0	224.1	224.9
Processed	100	121.0	131.5	164.5	166.1	182.9	182.9

APPENDIX TABLE 2

Wholesale Prices, Commodity Classifications of the
Bureau of Labor Statistics, Selected Dates, 1939-1948

	9/1938-8/1939	March 1942	June 1946	March 1947	May 1947	Feb. 1948	March 1948
All commodities	100	127.4	147.4	195.2	192.0	209.8	210.7
Raw materials	100	140.9	181.2	234.1	227.5	250.9	250.6
Semimanufactured articles	100	123.4	141.3	195.1	193.7	207.5	206.0
Manufactured products	100	121.9	133.8	178.7	176.7	192.5	194.1
All commodities other than farm products	100	121.8	135.1	179.9	178.0	196.3	197.2
All commodities other than farm products and foods	100	118.3	131.2	162.9	163.9	183.1	183.5
Farm products	100	156.1	212.8	277.3	266.8	281.4	282.5
Grains	100	172.7	279.6	374.4	372.7	405.2	401.5
Livestock and poultry	100	152.3	183.9	289.2	266.0	281.1	280.3
Other farm products	100	157.4	221.1	250.5	246.8	257.1	260.8
Foods	100	135.2	158.8	235.7	224.8	242.5	244.4
Dairy products	100	140.3	189.4	234.5	206.5	275.0	267.6
Cereal products	100	122.9	138.0	204.1	205.8	217.4	215.2
Fruits and vegetables	100	143.5	222.7	231.6	236.2	237.0	239.4
Meats	100	136.0	137.1	258.2	252.8	256.8	270.4
Other foods	100	138.6	152.6	237.6	215.2	228.1	224.4
Hides and leather products	100	126.3	132.5	189.0	184.8	208.7	200.9
Shoes	100	123.2	128.3	170.0	170.7	193.0	191.9
Hides and skins	100	152.6	159.0	251.6	232.6	271.2	243.7
Leather	100	120.7	131.6	218.4	209.6	237.7	222.2
Other leather products	100	118.3	120.0	143.4	144.1	149.8	149.8
Textile products	100	145.3	164.2	209.9	208.9	222.0	224.1
Clothing	100	130.7	147.5	163.1	164.2	171.6	173.8
Cotton goods	100	175.1	216.8	305.8	300.2	333.7	339.5
Hosiery and underwear	100	116.5	126.5	168.3	168.3	175.3	176.0
Rayon	100	106.3	106.0	129.8	129.8	142.8	142.8
Silk	100	a	a	194.2	180.1	123.1	123.1
Woolen and worsted goods	100	144.2	149.5	169.1	171.4	189.4	192.6
Other textile products	100	152.1	174.0	271.3	272.8	279.2	270.6
Fuel and lighting materials	100	105.0	118.6	136.1	139.6	176.6	176.9
Anthracite coal	100	110.1	137.2	148.5	145.1	160.8	161.1
Bituminous coal	100	110.8	135.8	146.8	148.4	181.8	181.9
Coke	100	117.2	128.1	148.9	149.4	182.9	182.9
Electricity	100	81.1	83.5	79.9	79.6	82.7	a
Gas	100	90.5	93.4	99.6	99.8	100.7	104.1
Petroleum and products	100	111.9	122.8	156.8	166.6	233.6	233.8
Metals and metal products	100	110.0	118.9	148.2	149.8	164.5	165.8
Agricultural implements	100	103.4	114.2	124.7	125.7	137.6	137.9
Farm machinery	100	103.2	114.1	124.4	125.5	137.6	137.9
Iron and steel	100	101.0	114.6	132.0	133.8	152.9	154.9
Motor vehicles	100	120.4	126.3	159.4	159.5	172.0	172.6
Nonferrous metals	100	113.8	131.9	184.8	191.4	195.2	195.2
Plumbing and heating	100	124.3	134.2	149.2	151.9	175.6	175.6
Building materials	100	123.5	145.1	198.3	197.8	215.1	215.6
Brick and tile	100	106.0	132.4	144.5	146.8	165.0	165.5
Cement	100	101.0	110.7	121.1	123.0	137.2	137.4
Lumber	100	147.7	195.3	298.9	299.0	337.2	337.4
Paint and paint materials	100	124.0	133.6	216.6	208.1	196.3	192.7
Plumbing and heating	100	124.3	134.2	149.2	151.9	175.6	175.6
Structural steel	100	100.0	111.9	119.0	119.0	139.2	145.2
Other building materials	100	115.5	131.7	159.6	161.1	177.3	179.5

54

APPENDIX TABLE 2 (concluded)

	9/1938-8/1939	March 1942	June 1946	March 1947	May 1947	Feb. 1948	March 1948
Chemicals and allied products	100	128.3	127.3	174.6	167.9	177.8	179.8
Chemicals	100	113.5	115.4	134.9	139.8	149.0	149.4
Drug and pharmaceutical materials	100	162.0	140.1	233.9	222.3	197.6	197.7
Fertilizer materials	100	118.8	123.6	152.2	153.2	171.6	171.7
Mixed fertilizers	100	113.3	118.5	131.7	132.3	140.6	141.0
Oils and fats	100	237.6	222.9	505.5	392.8	440.0	461.6
Housefurnishing goods	100	119.7	128.8	146.8	150.3	165.7	165.8
Furnishings	100	119.8	127.4	146.2	152.3	160.6	161.2
Furniture	100	120.0	130.7	147.8	148.2	172.2	171.7
Miscellaneous	100	122.2	134.2	157.1	158.2	163.4	164.6
Automobile tires and tubes	100	119.3	122.7	122.7	122.7	106.6	106.6
Cattle feed	100	178.6	256.5	309.2	307.9	339.8	368.6
Paper and allied products	100	127.2	142.9	179.4	190.7	206.6	206.4
Rubber, crude	100	135.8	135.5	155.1	133.7	125.2	124.0
Other miscellaneous	100	114.9	124.4	150.5	150.4	160.6	160.3

[a] Data not available.

APPENDIX TABLE 3
Prices Received and Prices Paid by Farmers
Selected Dates, 1939-1948

	9/1938-8/1939	March 1942	June 1946	March 1947	May 1947	Feb. 1948	March 1948
Farm prices	100	160.3	231.4	297.2	288.7	296.2	300.4
Crops	100	177.4	286.6	341.9	344.5	330.3	336.8
Food grains	100	194.7	311.5	440.8	429.9	391.0	405.0
Feed grains and hay	100	174.0	297.7	323.7	332.8	398.5	433.6
Tobacco	100	135.5	219.8	231.7	231.7	222.2	221.0
Cotton	100	215.0	309.3	378.5	397.6	365.2	377.0
Oil-bearing crops	100	200.2	249.1	409.5	370.8	378.8	385.7
Fruit	100	140.5	386.1	318.0	328.4	201.2	207.1
Truck crops	100	177.0	200.9	324.6	310.5	347.4	320.3
Livestock and products	100	148.8	195.6	268.1	252.5	275.5	277.3
Dairy products	100	141.1	192.2	249.8	223.8	285.1	276.7
Poultry and eggs	100	128.5	175.9	196.6	200.6	215.4	209.5
Meat animals	100	158.5	203.7	305.6	289.6	293.2	302.9
Prices paid by farmers incl. interest and taxes	100	120.1	152.5	183.4	185.0	201.2	200.4
All commodities	100	124.8	163.1	199.7	201.3	218.8	218.0
Commodities used in living	100	125.2	167.8	210.4	212.0	225.4	222.9
Commodities used in production	100	122.3	156.0	183.9	185.6	209.4	209.4

Source: Bureau of Agricultural Economics.

APPENDIX TABLE 4

Construction Costs, Selected Dates, 1939-1948

	9/1938-8/1939	March 1942	June 1946	March 1947	May 1947	Feb. 1948	March 1948
Aberthaw Construction Co.[a]	100	116.0	143.6	161.7	159.6	164.9	164.9
American Appraisal Co.[b]	100	118.9	159.1	202.7	210.2	238.3	239.8
Asso. Gen. Contractors of America[c]	100	110.0	134.2	150.2	154.4	170.9	170.9
Engineering News-Record[d]	100	115.8	150.8	168.8	171.8	186.8	186.8
Composite of construction costs[e]	100	115.2	146.9	170.8	174.0	190.2	190.6

[a] The indexes of the Aberthaw Construction Company, constructed quarterly, are based upon the cost of constructing an 8-story reinforced concrete industrial structure by the company in Connecticut. The index does not include data for home-office overhead or for profit on the job, but is confined to the cost of labor, materials, plant, tools, insurance, etc., actually required for the construction of the building. The data cited refer to quarters in which the selected dates fall.

[b] The indexes of the American Appraisal Company are based on a detailed bill of quantities of material and labor required for typical frame, brick-wood frame, brick-steel frame and reinforced concrete buildings, with allowances for contractor's overhead and profit, in 30 representative cities throughout the United States.

[c] The measurements of the Associated General Contractors of America, Inc. combine indexes of wages and materials in the proportion of 40 percent for the former and 60 percent for the latter. Wages used in computing this index are for hod-carriers and common laborers; material prices are for sand, gravel, crushed stone, Portland cement, common brick, lumber, hollow tile and structural and reinforcing steel. Wages and prices are reported by 12 district offices of the Association.

[d] The indexes of the *Engineering News-Record* include: the base price of structural steel shapes at Pittsburgh, wt. 24; consumers' net price of cement exclusive of bags, f.o.b. Chicago, wt. 3; lumber 2 x 4 S4S pine and fir (ENR 20 cities average), wt. 29; common labor rate (ENR 20 cities, average of wage rates in force), wt. 44.

[e] The composite index is an unweighted arithmetic average of the four construction cost indexes in this table.

Appendix Table 5
Average Hourly Earnings, Manufacturing Industries Selected Dates, 1939-1948

	1/1939-8/1939	March 1942	June 1946	March 1947	May 1947	Feb. 1948	March 1948
All manufacturing	100	128.7	172.1	187.3	191.6	204.7	204.9
Durable goods	100	129.5	167.9	178.1	184.1	195.4	195.5
Iron & steel and their products	100	122.9	164.0	172.5	181.2	191.6	192.0
Electrical machinery	100	123.8	162.4	171.4	178.8	190.7	191.1
Machinery, except electrical	100	123.0	163.7	173.8	178.6	189.7	190.4
Transportation equipment, except automobiles	100	132.9	172.0	173.5	175.3	188.9	187.5
Automobiles	100	124.4	145.2	150.4	157.7	166.9	165.6
Nonferrous metals & their products	100	127.6	170.8	180.0	185.0	196.5	197.4
Lumber & timber basic products	100	124.7	187.2	202.7	211.3	222.7	220.6
Furniture & finished lumber products	100	123.5	180.0	200.2	203.1	218.8	218.8
Stone, clay, & glass products	100	118.4	163.9	180.2	184.7	197.5	198.3
Nondurable goods	100	119.9	172.8	192.8	194.7	210.0	210.0
Textile-mill & other fiber products	100	125.4	191.5	224.1	224.3	249.0	249.5
Apparel & other finished textile products	100	119.6	181.1	199.0	188.2	209.1	207.8
Leather & leather products	100	125.3	181.0	195.8	197.1	209.9	210.9
Food	100	115.8	159.2	178.2	181.8	193.4	194.4
Tobacco manufactures	100	114.4	178.7	197.9	199.8	203.8	205.5
Paper & allied products	100	121.4	168.3	188.0	192.0	211.0	211.7
Printing, publishing, & allied industries	100	111.4	148.1	167.2	172.2	186.1	188.2
Chemicals & allied products	100	125.3	167.7	182.1	187.2	203.7	203.6
Products of petroleum & coal	100	114.3	150.3	157.1	161.6	176.6	177.2
Rubber products	100	118.3	170.5	176.7	188.2	188.8	186.3
Miscellaneous industries	100	117.4	166.5	181.9	184.2	196.0	195.8

Source: Bureau of Labor Statistics.

APPENDIX TABLE 6

Average Hourly Earnings, Nonmanufacturing Industries
Selected Dates, 1939-1948

	1/1939-8/1939	March 1942	June 1946	March 1947	May 1947	Feb. 1948	March 1948
Mining							
Anthracite coal	100	107.0	168.6	176.5	172.3	196.5	192.1
Bituminous coal	100	120.3	166.9	168.1	166.5	206.8	209.2
Metal	100	123.0	168.8	177.5	182.8	196.0	195.3
Quarrying & nonmetallic	100	125.8	180.4	194.0	198.2	215.2	220.0
Crude petroleum production	100	113.9	152.0	163.3	166.4	188.3	184.5
Public utilities							
Telephone	100	103.0	139.7	136.9	144.8	150.8	149.0
Electric light & power	100	111.5	146.9	154.5	156.5	164.5	161.4
Street railways & buses	100	111.5	147.7	166.1	167.6	181.6	181.6
Trade							
Wholesale	100	118.1	160.5	172.4	173.8	188.1	186.8
Retail	100	108.2	159.0	174.2	178.8	190.6	189.7
Service							
Hotels, year-round	100	114.5	186.6	200.3	200.6	216.8	216.8
Power laundries	100	112.9	171.0	182.0	181.3	192.3	193.0
Cleaning & dyeing	100	110.7	174.6	179.5	183.2	189.1	190.6
Construction							
Private building	100	116.6	153.9	171.6	176.4	192.5	193.0
Wage rates							
Common labor	100	114.3	151.5	163.8	167.9	186.4	188.0
Skilled labor	100	106.9	125.0	133.3	134.7	149.3	149.3
Road building, common labor	100	120.2	207.2	214.8	225.1	232.7[a]	
Transportation, class I railways	100	115.4	156.5	157.4	156.6	181.6	177.7
Consumers' price index	100	115.3	134.5	157.7	157.4	169.0	168.4

Source: Bureau of Labor Statistics except for construction wage rates (*Engineering News-Record*), common labor in road building (Public Roads Commission), and railway wages (Interstate Commerce Commission).

[a] January 1948.

APPENDIX TABLE 7

Consumer Expenditures, Retail Prices, and Estimates of
Volume of Consumer Purchases, Selected Periods, 1939-1947

	1939	II 1942	II 1946	IV 1946	IV 1947
Consumer expenditures	100	131	205	230	256
Prices of commodities and services at retail[a]	100	122	143	162	174
Derived estimate of volume of consumer purchases	100	107	143	142	147

[a] This index is an average of the consumers' price index of the Bureau of Labor Statistics and the retail price index of the Department of Commerce. The more broadly based Bureau of Labor Statistics index which includes rents and other service items is given a weight of two, that of the Department of Commerce a weight of one. The latter index includes some components of the Bureau of Labor Statistics index, but omits the service items, and adds prices of building materials, farm machinery, and a few other commodities. The coverage of neither index is as broad as that of the consumer expenditure compilations, but the average of the two is believed to give a measure of the course of prices paid by all classes of consumers somewhat more accurate than is either index by itself.

For the purposes of the 'deflation' account has been taken of the "hidden increase in the cost of living . . . due to quality deterioration, disappearance of cheaper goods, decrease of special sales, and increase in under-reporting of prices actually charged" to which attention was called by the President's Committee on the Cost of Living. (See mimeographed release by the Bureau of Labor Statistics on the Consumers' Price Index, January 15, 1947.) Three points have been added to the index for the second quarter of 1942, five points for the second quarter of 1946, and three points for the fourth quarter of 1946. No correction was assumed to be necessary for the fourth quarter of 1947.

APPENDIX TABLE 8

Wholesale Prices, Monthly Indexes, 1943-1948
Commodity Classifications of the National Bureau of Economic Research
1939:100

The index numbers, currently constructed by the National Bureau, are based on price quotations compiled by the United States Bureau of Labor Statistics. They were originally published in *Economic Tendencies in the United States* (1932) and, in greater detail, in *Prices in Recession and Recovery* (1936). In an appendix to *Occasional Paper 12*, Prices in a War Economy (Oct. 1943), revised monthly indexes from November 1927 to June 1943 were published. The National Bureau takes this occasion to bring through March 1948 these wholesale price series. The user will realize that the great economic changes since December 1941 lessen the accuracy of measurements of price movements. Indexes for products of the heavy industries and for other groups containing commodities markedly influenced by the transition from peace to war and war to peace are most seriously affected.

	ALL COMMODI-TIES	RAW MATE-RIALS	MFD. GOODS	PRODUCER GOODS Raw	Processed	Total	CONSUMER GOODS Raw	Processed	Total	PERISHABLE GOODS Raw	Processed	To
1943												
Jul	109.3	115.6	104.7	115.5	103.5	110.1	115.2	105.8	108.0	118.6	100.5	10
Aug	109.2	115.4	104.5	116.0	103.7	110.4	112.8	105.5	107.2	118.0	100.7	10
Sep	109.3	115.7	104.7	116.8	104.0	110.9	111.7	105.5	107.0	118.3	101.1	10
Oct	109.1	115.2	104.6	116.2	104.1	110.7	111.4	105.3	106.8	117.8	101.2	10
Nov	109.2	115.1	104.8	115.2	104.3	110.3	114.3	105.4	107.5	118.2	101.3	10
Dec	109.6	115.8	104.9	116.0	104.6	110.8	114.5	105.5	107.6	118.9	101.5	10
1944												
Jan	109.8	115.9	105.3	116.8	104.8	111.3	112.7	105.8	107.5	118.6	101.8	10
Feb	110.0	116.7	105.3	117.7	105.1	112.0	112.7	105.7	107.4	119.4	101.5	11
Mar	110.3	117.3	105.3	118.4	105.1	112.4	113.0	105.7	107.4	120.1	101.5	1
Apr	110.4	117.4	105.5	118.2	105.3	112.3	114.0	105.8	107.8	120.0	101.8	1
May	110.5	117.5	105.5	118.2	105.3	112.4	114.5	105.8	107.9	120.1	101.8	1
Jun	110.9	118.5	105.5	118.1	105.4	112.3	119.2	105.8	109.0	121.5	101.8	1
Jul	110.6	117.7	105.6	117.7	105.4	112.1	117.1	105.9	108.5	120.1	101.7	1
Aug	110.3	116.8	105.6	117.5	105.4	112.0	113.9	106.1	107.9	118.8	101.7	1
Sep	110.5	116.8	105.9	118.1	105.8	112.6	111.8	106.1	107.5	118.8	101.7	1
Oct	110.6	117.2	105.9	118.7	106.0	113.0	111.3	106.1	107.4	119.4	101.6	1
Nov	110.9	117.7	106.0	119.0	106.0	113.1	112.6	106.1	107.7	120.1	101.7	1
Dec	111.2	118.2	105.9	119.4	106.0	113.3	113.8	106.1	108.0	120.9	101.7	1
1945												
Jan	111.5	118.8	106.1	120.7	106.5	114.3	112.1	106.1	107.6	121.8	101.8	1
Feb	112.0	119.5	106.4	121.6	106.7	114.9	112.4	106.4	107.9	122.8	102.1	1
Mar	112.1	119.8	106.5	122.2	106.7	115.2	111.4	106.5	107.8	123.0	102.3	1
Apr	112.5	120.5	106.5	122.3	106.8	115.2	114.5	106.6	108.5	124.0	102.5	1
May	112.8	121.5	106.6	122.3	106.9	115.3	118.1	106.6	109.4	124.6	102.5	1
Jun	113.0	121.8	106.5	122.3	106.8	115.3	119.6	106.8	109.8	125.1	102.1	1
Jul	112.7	121.1	106.5	121.8	106.8	115.0	118.3	106.6	109.5	124.1	102.0	1
Aug	112.2	119.7	106.6	120.7	106.9	114.5	115.7	106.6	108.9	121.8	102.1	1
Sep	111.7	118.5	106.5	120.3	107.1	114.4	112.1	106.4	107.8	119.7	101.8	1
Oct	112.5	120.1	107.0	121.9	107.6	115.6	113.6	106.6	108.4	121.9	102.2	1
Nov	113.6	122.1	107.4	123.3	108.1	116.4	117.5	107.2	109.7	124.4	102.9	1
Dec	113.9	122.5	107.6	123.1	108.2	116.3	119.8	107.4	110.3	124.6	103.1	1
1946												
Jan	114.0	122.1	107.9	123.7	108.5	116.7	116.3	107.8	109.9	123.7	103.8	1
Feb	114.7	122.9	108.7	124.7	109.5	117.9	116.2	108.5	110.4	124.1	104.4	1
Mar	116.5	125.0	110.2	126.7	111.4	119.8	118.6	109.6	111.8	126.0	105.1	1
Apr	118.0	126.7	111.5	128.2	112.2	120.9	121.2	111.1	113.7	127.8	106.2	1
May	118.9	128.0	112.3	129.7	113.3	122.3	122.3	111.8	114.2	130.1	106.9	1
Jun	121.0	131.4	113.9	133.6	114.6	124.9	123.7	113.7	115.8	132.1	108.6	1
Jul	132.4	144.0	124.4	147.1	119.1	134.4	133.3	128.6	129.7	148.6	130.4	1
Aug	136.2	146.3	129.1	150.4	120.6	136.9	132.1	135.6	135.0	150.4	138.1	1
Sep	132.2	143.3	124.6	146.1	122.0	135.1	133.6	126.7	128.3	144.4	124.2	1
Oct	141.9	150.2	136.1	152.9	127.5	141.3	140.5	142.9	142.4	156.7	144.1	1
Nov	148.0	156.6	142.1	159.4	134.0	147.7	146.6	148.4	148.1	166.6	151.2	1
Dec	150.0	159.1	143.7	163.6	136.3	151.1	143.7	149.3	148.2	164.9	149.9	1
1947												
Jan	151.5	160.5	145.6	166.5	139.8	154.2	140.5	149.8	148.0	162.4	147.1	1
Feb	154.0	163.1	148.1	170.5	141.4	157.2	138.6	153.2	150.2	165.6	151.5	1
Mar	159.3	171.4	151.5	180.9	145.7	164.6	140.3	155.8	152.7	176.3	157.8	1
Apr	157.7	169.3	150.2	178.2	145.5	163.2	140.0	153.5	150.8	171.8	153.9	1
May	157.0	167.8	149.9	177.9	145.0	162.7	134.3	153.5	149.6	169.2	151.9	1
Jun	157.8	169.7	150.2	179.1	144.3	163.1	138.9	154.5	151.3	171.9	152.8	1
Jul	160.7	173.1	152.6	183.4	146.2	166.2	139.2	157.5	153.7	174.2	157.0	1
Aug	163.8	176.3	155.7	186.6	148.2	168.9	142.0	161.3	157.3	178.2	161.2	1
Sep	167.5	179.9	159.6	191.1	152.0	173.0	143.3	165.2	160.6	185.2	167.2	1
Oct	169.4	183.9	160.1	195.2	153.9	176.2	146.8	164.6	160.9	189.8	166.6	1
Nov	170.9	185.0	161.8	196.0	156.1	177.6	148.8	166.0	162.5	188.6	168.5	1
Dec	174.6	190.6	164.2	203.1	158.6	182.6	149.4	168.4	164.5	194.8	170.8	1
1948												
Jan	177.1	192.8	167.0	205.3	162.5	185.6	152.0	170.3	166.5	198.6	174.6	1
Feb	172.0	184.7	163.9	194.0	160.1	178.3	154.1	166.8	164.2	186.9	166.2	1
Mar	172.5	184.9	164.5	193.9	160.7	178.7	155.3	167.1	164.7	186.7	167.4	1

| URABLE GOODS | | NONDURABLE GOODS | | | DURABLE GOODS | | | NONDURABLE GOODS | | DURABLE GOODS | |
Processed	Total	Raw	Processed	Total	Raw	Processed	Total	Producer	Consumer	Producer	Consumer
111.1	108.2	115.4	104.5	109.0	114.5	108.6	110.4	111.9	106.9	108.9	115.7
110.6	107.6	114.8	104.4	108.7	116.3	108.6	110.9	112.2	106.0	109.5	115.7
110.5	107.5	115.0	104.6	109.0	116.9	108.6	111.0	113.0	105.7	109.7	115.6
110.3	107.0	114.3	104.6	108.7	117.0	108.5	110.9	112.5	105.6	109.8	114.9
110.5	106.3	114.1	104.7	108.6	117.2	108.6	111.1	111.3	106.4	110.0	115.0
110.5	106.4	114.8	104.8	109.0	117.2	108.7	111.1	112.0	106.7	110.1	115.0
110.5	106.8	114.8	105.0	109.1	117.1	109.2	111.6	112.6	106.3	110.3	115.7
110.6	107.4	115.7	104.9	109.4	117.3	109.2	111.6	113.5	106.2	110.4	115.6
110.7	107.8	116.5	104.9	109.8	118.0	109.3	111.9	114.1	106.3	110.8	115.6
110.7	107.7	116.3	105.1	109.8	118.9	109.3	112.1	113.8	106.7	111.1	115.6
110.7	107.8	116.5	105.1	109.9	119.0	109.4	112.2	113.7	106.8	111.3	115.6
110.8	108.1	117.8	105.1	110.5	119.0	109.4	112.2	113.6	108.0	111.3	115.6
111.1	108.5	116.7	105.1	110.0	119.0	109.5	112.3	113.3	107.5	111.3	115.8
111.5	108.2	115.5	105.3	109.6	119.1	109.5	112.3	113.1	106.9	111.3	115.8
112.3	109.0	115.5	105.6	109.8	118.9	109.7	112.4	114.1	106.3	111.3	116.0
112.6	109.4	116.0	105.6	110.1	118.7	109.9	112.5	115.0	106.1	111.5	116.0
112.5	109.5	115.7	105.6	110.4	118.8	109.9	112.5	115.2	106.5	111.5	116.0
112.4	109.6	117.5	105.6	110.7	119.0	109.9	112.6	115.5	106.9	111.6	116.1
112.5	109.7	118.3	105.7	111.1	119.1	110.5	113.0	116.9	106.3	112.2	116.1
112.6	109.7	119.1	106.0	111.7	119.7	110.7	113.4	117.6	106.8	112.6	116.1
112.6	109.9	119.4	106.2	111.8	120.2	110.7	113.5	118.2	106.7	112.8	116.1
112.5	110.3	120.4	106.3	112.4	120.2	110.8	113.6	118.4	107.5	112.9	116.1
112.5	110.7	121.2	106.3	112.7	120.4	110.9	113.7	118.0	108.4	113.0	116.1
112.5	110.7	121.6	106.0	112.8	120.3	111.3	114.0	117.6	108.8	113.4	116.1
112.5	110.4	120.6	106.0	112.3	120.4	111.4	114.0	117.0	108.4	113.5	116.1
112.4	110.1	118.6	105.9	111.4	120.4	111.4	114.1	115.9	107.8	113.5	116.1
112.9	110.6	116.9	105.9	110.7	120.1	111.6	114.1	115.6	106.7	113.5	116.1
113.8	111.8	119.2	106.5	112.0	120.5	111.7	114.2	117.6	107.3	113.8	116.2
114.0	112.7	121.7	106.9	113.4	121.1	111.9	114.6	118.9	108.7	114.1	116.2
114.1	113.1	122.0	107.1	113.6	121.9	111.9	114.9	118.6	109.5	114.5	116.2
114.2	113.2	121.3	107.5	113.6	122.6	112.2	115.2	119.1	108.9	114.9	116.5
114.9	114.8	122.3	108.2	114.4	123.0	113.5	116.3	120.2	109.5	116.2	116.5
117.4	117.4	124.5	109.5	116.1	126.1	115.6	118.7	122.0	111.0	119.2	116.7
120.0	119.9	126.4	111.2	117.7	127.8	116.2	119.6	123.2	113.3	120.5	116.8
120.9	120.5	128.1	112.0	118.8	128.1	117.3	120.5	124.9	113.8	121.5	117.0
122.8	123.0	130.7	113.9	120.8	132.4	118.3	122.3	127.3	115.7	124.0	116.9
127.8	131.2	147.0	129.6	136.8	135.7	118.5	123.2	143.0	131.8	125.5	116.2
131.8	135.2	149.1	136.0	141.3	136.9	119.5	124.3	145.9	137.7	126.7	116.8
136.1	138.9	144.9	128.8	135.4	137.1	120.1	124.8	142.3	129.8	127.1	117.6
138.2	139.7	154.2	142.1	147.0	137.4	129.7	132.0	151.0	143.9	131.9	132.2
147.8	144.9	160.8	150.1	154.4	146.9	131.9	135.9	159.8	150.2	136.4	134.3
151.3	148.6	160.3	150.6	154.5	163.7	135.7	143.2	161.2	149.2	143.7	141.7
158.9	155.8	159.5	151.6	154.8	173.5	139.1	148.4	162.5	148.6	150.1	143.2
160.8	157.2	161.8	155.1	157.9	178.6	140.1	150.5	166.1	151.2	152.6	143.8
162.4	159.4	171.2	159.6	164.4	185.8	140.7	152.7	177.4	154.0	155.7	143.8
162.2	159.0	167.5	157.1	161.4	187.8	141.3	153.8	172.7	152.1	157.6	141.9
162.5	159.3	165.5	156.0	159.9	186.9	143.2	154.8	171.8	150.3	158.0	145.3
162.1	160.0	168.4	156.4	161.4	185.2	142.9	154.2	172.4	152.4	157.6	143.8
163.2	161.5	170.7	159.5	164.1	187.3	144.2	155.7	175.2	155.1	159.7	144.1
162.5	159.0	172.5	161.8	166.2	192.0	148.9	160.4	175.3	158.8	164.7	147.5
164.1	158.5	176.9	166.1	170.5	194.9	151.7	163.3	181.0	162.1	167.0	151.6
165.9	161.2	181.5	166.5	172.7	196.6	152.5	164.3	185.5	162.3	168.3	152.6
168.7	165.6	182.2	168.7	174.3	198.5	153.1	165.2	187.0	164.0	169.3	153.0
172.2	169.4	188.2	171.4	178.4	201.7	154.1	166.8	193.6	166.1	170.9	154.3
173.9	168.3	189.5	174.5	180.7	206.2	155.9	169.1	196.0	168.3	173.9	155.2
174.3	165.8	178.2	169.3	173.0	205.5	156.8	169.7	182.3	165.5	174.4	155.8
172.9	165.4	178.4	169.6	173.2	205.9	157.9	170.6	182.1	166.1	175.6	155.8

	ALL GOODS DESTINED FOR HUMAN CONSUMPTION			GOODS DESTINED FOR USE IN CAPITAL EQUIPMENT			BUILDING MATERIALS			CAP. EQUIP. AND BLDG. MAT.	PRODUCER FUE	
	Raw	Processed	Total	Raw	Processed	Total	Raw	Processed	Total	Total	Raw	Processed
1943												
Jul	115.4	105.6	109.8	101.2	108.2	106.3	127.2	103.8	110.5	108.3	119.2	89.1
Aug	114.9	105.4	109.6	101.2	108.2	106.3	130.2	103.8	111.5	108.7	119.2	88.6
Sep	115.2	105.6	109.8	101.2	108.2	106.3	131.2	104.0	111.9	108.8	119.1	88.9
Oct	114.5	105.5	109.4	101.2	108.3	106.3	131.3	104.2	112.1	108.9	119.2	89.2
Nov	114.3	105.6	109.4	101.2	108.3	106.3	131.8	104.6	112.5	109.2	119.5	90.0
Dec	115.0	105.7	109.7	101.2	108.4	106.4	131.8	104.8	112.6	109.3	121.4	91.2
1944												
Jan	115.0	105.9	109.9	100.8	108.4	106.3	131.9	105.5	113.2	109.5	121.9	91.7
Feb	115.9	105.8	110.2	100.4	108.4	106.3	132.3	105.6	113.4	109.6	122.0	93.2
Mar	116.7	105.8	110.5	100.4	108.5	106.3	133.6	105.9	114.0	109.8	122.4	92.8
Apr	116.6	106.0	110.6	100.4	108.5	106.3	135.2	105.8	114.4	110.0	122.5	93.2
May	116.8	106.0	110.7	100.3	108.5	106.3	135.5	106.2	114.9	110.2	122.5	92.9
Jun	118.1	106.0	111.2	100.1	108.3	106.1	135.5	106.4	115.0	110.1	122.4	93.1
Jul	117.0	106.0	110.8	100.1	108.5	106.2	135.7	106.4	115.0	110.2	122.5	93.2
Aug	115.8	106.2	110.4	100.2	108.5	106.2	135.7	106.5	115.1	110.2	122.5	92.6
Sep	115.8	106.6	110.6	100.1	108.5	106.2	135.5	106.7	115.1	110.2	122.5	93.1
Oct	116.3	106.6	110.8	99.8	108.8	106.3	135.4	107.3	115.5	110.5	122.5	92.5
Nov	117.0	106.6	111.1	100.0	108.8	106.3	135.3	107.4	115.6	110.6	122.6	92.5
Dec	117.7	106.6	111.4	100.4	108.8	106.6	135.4	107.5	115.6	110.6	122.6	92.2
1945												
Jan	118.5	106.6	111.7	100.9	109.1	106.9	135.4	108.6	116.5	111.3	122.6	92.3
Feb	119.4	106.9	112.4	101.5	109.3	107.2	135.8	108.9	117.0	111.6	122.6	92.8
Mar	119.6	107.0	112.5	102.1	109.3	107.3	136.0	109.1	117.2	111.8	122.6	92.1
Apr	120.6	107.1	113.0	102.1	109.3	107.3	136.1	109.3	117.3	111.8	122.6	92.0
May	121.4	107.1	113.3	102.1	109.6	107.5	136.4	109.3	117.5	112.0	124.9	91.7
Jun	121.8	106.9	113.4	102.0	110.4	108.1	136.4	109.4	117.5	112.4	125.4	92.1
Jul	120.8	106.9	113.0	101.9	110.5	108.1	136.6	109.4	117.6	112.4	125.4	92.1
Aug	118.9	106.8	112.2	101.8	110.5	108.1	136.8	109.6	117.8	112.5	126.1	93.3
Sep	117.3	106.8	111.4	101.3	110.5	107.9	136.7	110.1	118.0	112.6	126.1	92.3
Oct	119.4	107.3	112.7	101.8	110.6	108.2	136.9	110.2	118.1	112.7	126.2	92.6
Nov	121.9	107.7	113.9	102.4	110.6	108.4	137.4	110.7	118.5	113.0	126.2	94.0
Dec	122.3	107.8	114.2	102.4	110.6	108.4	138.6	110.9	119.1	113.2	126.3	93.8
1946												
Jan	121.6	108.3	114.2	103.1	110.6	108.5	139.6	111.0	119.5	113.5	126.4	93.8
Feb	122.7	109.1	115.0	102.6	112.3	109.7	140.5	112.4	120.7	114.7	126.4	94.3
Mar	124.9	110.2	116.7	103.2	114.0	111.1	145.8	115.9	124.8	117.3	126.5	94.2
Apr	126.8	111.8	118.3	103.6	114.5	111.6	148.4	117.2	126.4	117.8	127.9	94.6
May	128.5	112.4	119.3	103.6	115.4	112.2	149.0	119.0	127.9	119.3	128.4	94.3
Jun	131.2	114.3	121.2	107.4	115.9	113.6	153.4	121.1	132.1	121.3	134.6	94.2
Jul	147.0	128.2	136.0	109.7	116.1	114.4	156.2	123.2	133.0	122.8	138.0	97.1
Aug	149.0	134.1	140.3	111.6	116.9	115.4	156.3	124.8	134.1	123.7	142.2	101.1
Sep	145.1	127.5	134.8	111.6	117.4	115.8	156.6	126.2	135.2	124.5	142.5	100.6
Oct	154.2	141.4	146.8	111.2	127.9	123.3	156.8	127.2	136.0	129.0	142.8	100.7
Nov	160.8	148.1	153.4	120.7	130.3	127.6	167.4	134.7	144.2	135.1	143.2	100.9
Dec	161.2	149.5	154.3	129.2	130.6	130.1	190.9	139.8	154.6	141.1	145.3	102.6
1947												
Jan	160.9	150.2	154.6	133.0	134.6	134.0	206.3	146.1	163.8	147.4	148.7	104.6
Feb	163.4	153.4	157.5	134.2	134.9	134.6	215.2	148.1	167.8	149.5	149.1	105.1
Mar	172.8	157.5	163.7	140.3	135.5	136.6	222.4	150.1	171.2	152.2	151.9	108.3
Apr	169.3	154.8	160.7	141.8	135.4	136.8	224.4	154.0	174.5	153.9	155.2	110.9
May	167.5	154.3	159.7	141.0	137.1	137.9	221.8	153.7	173.4	154.0	155.4	110.8
Jun	170.3	154.7	161.0	138.8	137.2	137.4	219.9	152.5	172.2	153.1	156.1	111.9
Jul	172.6	157.6	163.7	140.6	138.9	139.2	222.4	153.8	173.8	154.8	167.9	113.1
Aug	174.5	160.5	166.2	143.6	143.1	143.1	228.0	156.2	177.1	158.4	177.8	117.0
Sep	178.9	165.0	170.7	144.2	144.3	144.1	233.2	158.7	180.4	160.5	178.2	120.3
Oct	183.4	165.3	172.7	145.8	144.9	145.0	235.7	160.5	182.4	161.9	181.1	121.5
Nov	184.1	167.2	174.1	147.2	146.2	146.3	238.8	161.0	183.7	163.2	183.1	123.7
Dec	190.1	169.7	178.0	147.8	146.7	146.8	243.6	163.0	186.5	164.6	189.3	129.7
1948												
Jan	191.5	172.7	180.2	153.1	148.2	149.3	246.9	164.7	188.6	167.0	195.4	135.5
Feb	180.6	168.3	173.3	153.8	149.3	150.3	244.9	165.3	188.4	167.4	196.3	136.3
Mar	180.8	168.5	173.5	154.0	150.7	151.5	245.3	166.2	189.1	168.4	196.3	136.4

PRODUCER GOODS DESTINED FOR HUMAN CONSUMPTION			CONSUMER GOODS, PROCESSED		PRODUCER GOODS, RAW			FOODS			NONFOODS	
ds	Nonfoods	Total	Foods	Nonfoods	Foods	Nonfoods	Raw	Processed	Total	Raw	Processed	Total
.9	103.2	112.1	102.0	109.0	123.2	110.2	120.9	102.9	112.5	109.7	105.4	107.0
.9	103.1	112.6	102.0	108.4	124.0	110.5	120.3	103.2	112.3	110.0	105.2	106.8
.2	103.4	113.4	102.1	108.4	125.3	110.6	120.6	103.4	112.6	110.1	105.3	107.0
.6	103.0	112.9	102.2	107.9	124.6	110.3	120.0	103.5	112.3	109.9	105.1	106.7
.4	102.1	111.8	102.2	108.0	123.1	109.6	120.4	103.5	112.5	109.3	105.3	106.7
.4	102.2	112.4	102.3	108.2	124.3	110.2	120.9	103.6	112.8	110.2	105.6	107.2
.1	102.7	113.0	102.8	108.4	125.0	110.7	120.6	104.0	112.9	110.7	105.8	107.5
.1	103.6	113.9	102.1	108.6	126.2	111.5	121.1	103.5	112.9	111.6	106.1	107.9
.8	104.3	114.7	102.4	108.6	127.0	112.3	121.9	103.5	113.3	112.2	106.1	108.1
.2	104.3	114.3	102.3	108.7	126.0	112.5	121.8	103.8	113.4	112.5	106.1	108.2
.1	104.3	114.3	102.5	108.8	126.0	112.7	121.9	103.9	113.5	112.6	106.2	108.3
.4	104.8	114.2	102.2	108.8	125.0	113.0	123.6	103.8	114.3	112.8	106.2	108.4
.5	104.9	113.7	102.2	109.0	124.1	113.1	122.0	103.7	113.4	112.9	106.3	108.6
.7	104.4	113.6	102.5	109.2	124.3	112.7	120.7	103.9	113.0	112.5	106.4	108.4
.9	105.1	114.7	102.3	109.5	125.6	112.8	120.6	103.9	112.9	112.5	106.8	108.8
.1	105.3	115.4	102.3	109.4	127.1	112.8	121.2	103.9	113.3	112.6	106.8	108.8
.4	105.5	115.6	102.5	109.4	127.4	113.0	122.0	104.0	113.7	112.8	106.8	108.9
.9	105.7	116.0	102.6	109.2	128.0	113.3	122.9	104.1	114.2	113.0	106.7	108.9
.4	106.0	117.4	102.6	109.2	131.0	113.4	124.0	104.1	114.8	113.1	107.1	109.1
.9	106.1	118.2	103.0	109.3	132.8	113.6	125.2	104.5	115.7	113.3	107.3	109.3
.8	106.5	118.7	103.5	109.3	133.8	114.0	125.3	104.9	116.0	113.8	107.2	109.4
.4	107.1	118.9	103.7	109.2	133.3	114.5	126.5	105.1	116.7	114.1	107.3	109.5
.2	107.6	118.5	103.8	109.2	131.9	115.5	127.1	105.3	117.1	115.1	107.3	109.9
.6	107.6	118.3	103.8	109.2	131.8	115.6	127.6	104.6	117.2	115.4	107.5	110.2
.9	107.3	117.7	103.7	109.2	130.9	115.3	126.2	104.5	116.3	115.5	107.5	110.2
.7	107.0	116.4	103.6	109.0	128.3	115.3	123.5	104.5	114.9	115.5	107.6	110.3
.6	107.5	116.2	103.6	108.7	126.9	115.4	121.0	104.5	113.5	115.6	107.5	110.3
.7	108.4	118.2	103.6	109.4	130.1	116.2	123.6	105.0	115.1	116.2	107.9	110.7
.2	109.5	119.5	104.4	109.6	132.0	117.1	126.5	105.7	116.9	117.2	108.2	111.2
.2	109.9	119.2	104.6	109.7	130.6	117.7	126.7	106.0	117.1	117.8	108.2	111.4
.8	110.6	119.8	105.4	109.7	131.4	118.1	125.5	106.7	116.9	118.2	108.4	111.8
.7	112.2	121.1	106.0	110.4	132.3	119.2	126.1	107.3	117.4	119.3	109.4	112.7
.3	114.6	123.2	107.0	111.6	134.2	121.2	128.2	108.2	119.1	121.1	111.1	114.5
.4	116.6	124.5	108.5	113.6	134.8	123.5	129.8	109.5	120.5	123.2	112.5	116.0
.9	117.1	126.1	108.8	114.3	137.9	123.9	132.1	110.2	121.9	123.6	113.4	116.7
.9	119.8	128.9	110.5	116.2	140.5	128.5	134.3	112.3	123.6	128.0	114.8	119.0
.9	128.5	144.8	139.2	118.4	164.0	135.7	152.2	140.6	146.7	135.5	117.0	123.1
.5	132.8	147.8	150.9	121.1	166.8	139.3	153.5	150.3	152.0	138.8	119.4	125.7
.9	136.3	143.9	130.4	123.0	154.0	140.6	146.4	131.6	139.3	140.0	121.4	127.4
.4	137.1	152.8	157.7	128.7	171.9	140.0	160.4	157.6	159.1	139.4	126.3	130.7
.1	140.7	160.8	163.8	133.8	185.5	141.7	171.4	164.0	167.8	141.0	132.2	135.1
.2	145.7	162.9	159.9	139.6	184.2	149.8	169.3	160.6	165.1	148.6	136.1	140.1
.4	151.2	164.3	155.0	144.8	181.1	156.7	165.8	156.1	161.2	154.9	140.6	145.1
.5	152.3	168.2	160.7	146.1	188.4	158.5	169.3	161.9	165.7	156.6	141.9	146.5
.7	156.8	179.8	165.0	147.2	206.3	163.6	181.0	168.8	175.1	161.3	143.6	149.2
.3	157.7	175.3	160.1	147.4	196.8	165.7	175.2	162.7	169.2	163.2	144.3	150.3
.8	157.5	174.4	158.6	148.7	196.0	165.7	172.2	160.8	166.6	163.2	145.0	150.8
.9	158.2	175.3	160.8	148.5	197.6	166.6	175.2	162.4	169.1	163.9	144.5	150.7
.5	160.6	178.4	166.7	148.9	201.2	171.4	177.4	168.1	172.9	168.6	145.6	152.9
.8	159.3	179.2	173.3	150.2	206.7	173.2	181.4	172.9	177.3	170.8	147.9	155.1
.6	159.1	185.3	179.1	152.3	218.7	172.4	189.3	179.9	184.8	170.1	150.3	156.6
.3	162.4	189.7	175.6	154.4	224.3	175.7	194.3	177.7	186.3	173.2	152.0	158.8
.8	167.3	191.0	176.0	156.8	219.9	179.8	192.5	178.9	186.0	177.1	154.0	161.3
.2	172.4	197.7	177.3	160.1	229.3	185.5	198.4	180.5	189.8	182.3	156.8	164.9
.9	172.5	200.6	178.9	162.5	232.6	187.1	201.5	184.0	193.1	183.9	159.2	167.0
.8	168.9	186.6	170.9	162.9	208.9	183.9	188.2	173.2	180.9	181.1	159.7	166.5
.5	169.1	186.5	172.1	162.5	207.7	184.7	188.0	174.8	181.7	181.7	159.7	166.7

	CROPS					ANIMAL PRODUCTS					METALS	
	Raw Producer	Raw Consumer	Raw Total	Processed	Total	Raw Producer	Raw Consumer	Raw Total	Processed	Total	Raw Producer	Processed
1943												
Jul	117.0	134.7	121.9	109.6	115.2	115.7	104.1	111.8	105.5	108.5	101.5	107.5
Aug	116.7	127.1	119.5	110.0	114.3	116.7	105.2	112.8	105.1	108.9	101.5	107.5
Sep	118.0	122.8	119.4	110.2	114.4	117.3	106.2	113.7	105.0	109.3	101.5	107.5
Oct	119.3	120.8	119.7	110.3	114.6	113.8	107.2	111.7	104.9	108.3	101.5	107.6
Nov	119.5	124.7	120.9	110.4	115.2	109.4	110.0	109.8	104.9	107.4	101.5	107.6
Dec	121.7	124.6	122.5	110.5	116.0	108.8	109.0	109.3	104.9	107.1	101.5	107.6
1944												
Jan	123.1	122.5	122.9	110.9	116.4	109.5	106.9	108.9	104.9	107.0	101.2	107.8
Feb	124.0	124.9	124.3	110.4	116.8	111.3	104.3	109.1	104.9	107.1	101.1	107.8
Mar	124.2	128.0	125.3	110.5	117.2	113.1	103.3	109.8	104.9	107.4	101.1	107.9
Apr	124.1	132.0	126.2	110.9	117.9	111.6	102.2	108.5	105.0	106.8	101.0	107.9
May	124.7	133.3	127.1	110.8	118.2	110.9	101.9	107.9	105.0	106.5	100.9	107.9
Jun	123.1	145.1	129.1	110.9	119.2	112.1	102.8	109.0	104.9	107.0	100.8	107.9
Jul	122.4	137.5	126.4	110.9	118.0	111.5	104.4	109.3	104.9	107.1	100.8	107.9
Aug	120.8	129.2	123.1	111.3	116.7	112.7	104.2	109.9	105.4	107.8	100.8	107.9
Sep	121.3	121.2	121.3	111.9	116.3	114.5	106.0	111.7	105.5	108.8	100.8	107.9
Oct	123.6	118.3	122.1	112.1	116.3	114.4	107.3	112.1	105.6	109.0	100.6	107.9
Nov	123.8	118.8	122.5	112.1	116.9	114.9	109.5	113.2	105.6	109.4	100.7	107.9
Dec	125.2	121.7	124.2	112.1	117.8	114.5	109.9	113.2	105.6	109.4	101.0	107.9
1945												
Jan	126.4	119.5	124.6	112.1	117.9	117.9	107.8	114.6	105.6	110.1	101.3	108.3
Feb	126.9	123.1	125.9	112.3	118.5	120.2	105.8	115.3	106.3	110.9	102.2	108.5
Mar	127.1	121.0	125.5	112.4	118.4	121.9	105.3	116.3	106.7	111.6	102.9	108.5
Apr	126.9	129.5	127.6	112.5	119.4	122.5	105.1	116.5	106.9	111.8	102.9	108.6
May	126.3	139.1	129.8	112.5	120.3	121.7	104.9	116.0	107.0	111.5	102.9	108.7
Jun	126.7	141.8	130.7	111.8	120.7	121.0	105.3	115.7	107.0	111.4	102.8	109.4
Jul	125.5	135.8	128.3	111.8	119.4	120.4	106.0	115.4	106.9	111.3	102.8	109.4
Aug	123.7	127.6	124.7	111.7	117.8	118.1	107.2	114.5	106.7	110.8	102.7	109.5
Sep	123.8	120.7	122.9	112.1	117.2	116.4	104.8	112.5	106.7	109.8	102.4	109.5
Oct	127.2	120.0	125.2	113.5	118.9	118.6	108.6	115.2	106.7	111.2	102.9	109.3
Nov	130.3	127.3	129.5	113.7	121.0	119.5	110.6	116.5	107.6	112.3	103.7	109.5
Dec	131.6	133.0	131.9	114.0	122.2	116.5	110.8	114.7	107.8	111.4	103.7	109.5
1946												
Jan	131.7	129.0	130.9	114.3	122.1	117.8	106.6	114.0	108.3	111.3	104.4	109.5
Feb	134.2	130.1	133.2	115.4	123.6	118.6	105.4	114.1	108.7	111.5	104.1	110.9
Mar	137.7	136.4	137.3	117.9	126.9	119.4	105.5	114.6	109.3	112.2	104.7	113.6
Apr	139.2	142.4	140.1	121.0	129.6	120.1	106.2	115.4	110.5	113.2	105.3	114.2
May	142.9	144.7	143.4	122.8	132.0	120.0	106.6	115.4	110.1	112.9	105.3	114.9
Jun	147.0	138.7	144.8	124.2	133.0	122.6	113.4	119.6	112.9	116.1	110.4	115.8
Jul	165.5	140.3	158.6	133.5	144.3	145.8	129.1	140.4	143.7	142.3	115.0	115.7
Aug	165.3	132.5	156.4	136.9	145.3	152.4	133.2	146.2	155.4	151.3	116.7	116.4
Sep	169.6	128.9	158.4	140.4	148.2	131.4	139.2	134.5	131.3	132.8	116.7	116.6
Oct	173.6	134.5	162.9	146.5	153.6	150.4	149.1	150.4	159.4	155.3	117.0	128.8
Nov	166.8	150.7	162.5	154.8	158.1	173.1	149.1	165.3	167.0	166.3	125.3	131.0
Dec	170.3	145.9	163.7	158.2	160.6	169.5	146.8	162.3	161.8	162.1	133.8	135.1
1947												
Jan	170.2	139.4	161.8	159.8	160.7	171.6	145.0	162.4	162.4	162.4	137.2	139.1
Feb	176.2	144.4	167.6	161.9	164.4	175.2	137.0	162.0	168.9	165.7	137.9	139.6
Mar	192.4	155.0	182.2	167.2	173.6	185.8	132.5	167.3	173.4	170.6	146.3	140.1
Apr	190.5	155.2	180.9	166.8	173.0	173.4	131.7	159.1	165.4	162.6	147.6	139.2
May	189.1	155.2	179.9	165.2	171.6	174.2	120.5	155.5	165.6	161.1	148.5	140.5
Jun	190.5	157.6	181.5	164.3	171.7	177.5	127.9	160.3	167.6	164.3	147.5	140.8
Jul	189.6	152.9	179.6	166.4	172.1	185.4	131.8	166.9	173.2	170.3	149.4	142.1
Aug	187.0	148.2	176.4	164.1	169.4	191.1	138.8	173.0	181.2	177.5	152.9	147.9
Sep	192.1	147.1	179.9	167.6	173.0	198.6	142.0	179.1	188.3	184.1	152.9	151.0
Oct	200.2	148.5	186.2	170.4	177.2	201.1	148.2	182.7	184.1	183.6	153.3	151.5
Nov	206.3	153.5	192.0	173.5	181.5	193.8	148.4	178.1	185.1	182.0	153.6	152.0
Dec	211.4	152.3	195.4	176.1	184.4	204.8	150.4	186.1	187.4	186.9	154.5	152.5
1948												
Jan	211.0	159.1	196.8	178.8	186.5	204.3	150.1	185.6	190.5	188.4	160.0	154.2
Feb	191.1	163.0	183.4	172.6	177.3	185.4	151.4	173.7	183.6	179.1	160.8	155.1
Mar	192.9	166.1	185.6	172.0	177.8	182.9	151.2	171.9	185.2	179.1	161.3	156.4

| NONMETALLIC MINERALS |||| MINERAL PRODUCTS |||| FOREST PRODUCTS ||||
Raw Con-sumer	Raw Total	Processed	Total	Raw Pro-ducer	Raw Con-sumer	Raw Total	Processed	Total	Raw Pro-ducer	Processed	Total
101.0	110.4	92.5	100.2	108.1	101.0	107.3	100.5	102.7	141.4	111.4	124.3
101.0	110.4	92.3	100.0	108.1	101.0	107.3	100.4	102.7	145.9	111.4	126.2
101.0	110.3	92.6	100.2	108.0	101.0	107.2	100.5	102.7	147.2	112.4	127.4
101.0	110.3	92.1	99.9	108.1	101.0	107.3	100.4	102.6	147.6	112.6	127.7
101.9	110.6	92.5	100.3	108.2	101.9	107.4	100.6	102.8	148.3	113.1	128.3
106.2	112.6	93.2	101.6	109.1	106.2	108.7	100.9	103.5	148.4	113.7	128.7
106.3	113.0	93.4	101.9	109.2	106.3	108.8	101.1	103.7	148.5	115.4	129.5
109.4	113.6	94.2	102.5	109.1	109.4	109.2	101.4	104.0	150.2	115.3	130.3
106.9	113.3	94.0	102.3	109.3	106.9	109.1	101.4	103.9	153.1	115.5	131.6
107.4	113.4	94.2	102.5	109.3	107.4	109.1	101.5	104.0	155.4	115.5	132.6
108.0	113.6	94.4	102.7	109.3	108.0	109.2	101.5	104.0	155.9	115.7	132.9
106.7	113.3	94.5	102.5	109.2	106.7	109.0	101.6	104.0	155.9	116.0	133.2
106.6	113.3	94.6	102.7	109.3	106.6	109.0	101.6	104.0	156.0	116.0	133.2
106.6	113.3	94.2	102.4	109.3	106.6	109.0	101.5	104.0	156.1	116.0	133.2
106.6	113.4	94.7	102.7	109.3	106.6	109.0	101.7	104.1	155.8	116.0	132.9
106.6	113.4	94.7	102.8	109.2	106.6	109.0	101.7	104.1	155.3	116.0	132.8
106.6	113.4	94.8	102.8	109.3	106.6	109.0	101.7	104.1	155.5	116.1	132.9
106.7	113.4	94.6	102.7	109.4	106.7	109.2	101.6	104.1	155.6	116.1	133.0
106.7	113.4	95.0	103.0	109.5	106.7	109.2	102.1	104.5	155.5	116.7	133.9
106.7	113.4	95.5	103.2	109.9	106.7	109.5	102.4	104.7	155.8	116.7	134.1
106.7	113.4	95.2	103.0	110.2	106.7	109.7	102.3	104.8	155.7	116.7	134.0
106.7	113.4	95.0	103.0	110.2	106.7	109.7	102.3	104.8	155.8	117.4	134.4
107.0	115.0	94.9	103.6	111.2	107.0	110.7	102.3	105.1	156.2	117.4	134.6
109.5	115.7	95.0	103.9	111.4	109.5	111.2	102.7	105.5	156.2	117.4	134.6
113.8	116.5	95.2	104.3	111.4	113.8	111.7	102.7	105.7	156.5	117.4	134.6
113.9	116.9	95.6	104.9	111.6	113.9	111.9	103.0	106.0	156.6	117.7	135.0
114.4	117.1	94.7	104.3	111.6	114.4	111.9	102.6	105.7	156.3	117.8	134.9
114.4	117.1	95.0	104.5	111.8	114.4	112.2	102.7	105.8	156.5	117.8	135.0
114.4	117.1	95.9	105.0	112.2	114.4	112.4	103.1	106.2	156.8	117.8	135.1
115.8	117.4	95.9	105.1	112.2	115.8	112.6	103.1	106.3	158.7	117.8	135.9
116.3	117.6	96.0	105.3	112.6	116.3	113.0	103.1	106.4	159.3	120.4	137.8
116.4	117.8	96.4	105.6	112.5	116.4	112.9	104.2	107.1	160.7	121.8	139.1
116.4	117.8	96.5	105.7	112.7	116.4	113.3	105.6	108.2	167.8	121.9	142.4
116.4	119.5	96.5	106.5	114.4	116.4	114.6	106.0	108.9	171.6	122.2	144.3
116.6	120.0	96.5	106.6	114.6	116.6	114.9	106.5	109.2	174.7	124.5	146.9
118.8	124.3	96.7	108.6	119.5	118.8	119.5	107.2	111.2	177.6	125.6	148.8
128.9	128.4	98.4	111.4	123.0	128.9	123.8	108.0	113.2	178.7	126.5	149.9
126.9	133.2	101.8	115.3	127.5	126.9	127.4	109.8	115.7	178.9	127.5	150.5
127.0	133.5	102.3	115.6	127.7	127.0	127.7	110.2	115.9	181.4	130.7	153.4
127.0	133.6	102.5	115.9	127.9	127.0	127.8	117.2	120.7	182.5	133.8	155.7
127.0	134.1	103.6	116.7	131.5	127.0	131.0	118.9	122.9	194.3	134.3	160.2
127.2	136.1	105.6	118.7	136.2	127.2	135.2	122.2	126.4	225.7	140.2	176.8
128.4	138.4	107.6	120.9	139.1	128.4	137.9	125.3	129.5	248.9	141.9	188.6
128.6	138.9	108.2	121.4	139.8	128.6	138.5	125.9	130.0	261.3	145.3	195.9
128.7	142.2	110.7	124.2	145.4	128.7	143.5	127.3	132.5	266.3	147.0	199.0
127.5	145.3	113.1	127.0	148.4	127.5	146.0	127.8	133.7	272.0	154.7	205.3
125.6	145.2	113.4	127.0	148.8	125.6	146.2	128.6	134.4	269.0	155.8	204.7
126.3	145.9	113.8	127.6	148.9	126.3	146.3	128.9	134.7	266.2	155.4	203.3
127.8	154.2	115.6	132.2	155.6	127.8	152.4	130.5	137.6	268.5	155.6	204.4
136.3	161.8	118.1	136.8	161.5	136.3	158.6	134.8	142.7	274.9	157.7	208.3
137.2	162.4	120.3	138.4	161.9	137.2	159.1	137.5	144.6	282.5	159.8	212.8
137.5	165.0	121.5	140.2	163.9	137.5	160.8	138.3	145.8	286.5	162.8	216.2
138.1	167.1	123.3	142.1	165.4	138.1	162.3	139.3	146.9	291.0	164.2	219.0
138.2	174.3	127.4	147.6	171.2	138.2	167.5	141.5	149.9	297.6	166.5	223.1
139.2	180.6	131.6	152.6	177.9	139.2	173.5	144.2	153.8	302.4	171.3	227.9
139.3	181.2	132.5	153.3	178.5	139.3	174.1	145.1	154.6	299.8	171.4	227.0
139.5	181.2	132.7	153.5	178.7	139.5	174.3	145.9	155.2	300.0	172.4	227.5

| | PRODUCTS OF AMERICAN FARMS ||||||| PRODUCTS OTHER THAN THOSE ORIGINATING ON AMERICAN FARMS |||||
	Raw Producer	Raw Consumer	Raw Crops	Raw Animal	Raw Total	Processed	Total	Raw Producer	Raw Consumer	Raw Total	Processed	Total
1943												
Jul	118.8	114.0	120.8	114.3	117.5	108.5	112.8	111.2	118.4	112.3	101.6	105.2
Aug	119.1	110.8	118.1	115.4	116.7	108.5	112.4	112.1	118.4	113.0	101.6	105.5
Sep	120.2	109.4	117.9	116.1	117.0	108.6	112.6	112.2	118.4	113.1	101.7	105.6
Oct	119.1	109.0	118.3	114.1	116.2	108.6	112.3	112.3	118.4	113.2	101.6	105.6
Nov	117.1	112.8	119.7	112.3	115.9	108.6	112.1	112.6	118.9	113.4	101.9	105.9
Dec	118.1	112.1	121.5	111.5	116.3	108.6	112.4	113.3	121.3	114.4	102.1	106.4
1944												
Jan	119.1	109.7	122.0	111.1	116.4	108.9	112.6	113.4	121.3	114.7	102.5	106.7
Feb	120.6	109.1	123.6	111.3	117.3	109.0	113.0	113.8	123.1	115.1	102.4	106.8
Mar	121.5	110.0	124.7	112.2	118.2	109.0	113.4	114.3	121.6	115.4	102.4	106.9
Apr	120.8	111.2	125.8	110.8	118.1	109.4	113.5	114.8	122.0	115.9	102.5	107.1
May	120.8	111.7	126.7	110.1	118.2	109.4	113.6	114.9	122.2	116.0	102.5	107.1
Jun	120.5	118.3	129.1	111.2	119.9	109.2	114.3	114.9	121.5	115.8	102.6	107.1
Jul	119.7	115.5	126.1	111.5	118.6	109.4	113.7	114.9	121.4	115.9	102.6	107.1
Aug	119.4	111.2	122.2	112.2	117.1	109.8	113.3	114.9	121.4	115.9	102.5	107.1
Sep	120.6	108.4	120.1	114.1	117.0	110.2	113.6	114.9	121.4	115.8	102.6	107.1
Oct	121.8	107.6	121.1	114.4	117.7	110.3	114.0	114.7	121.6	115.7	102.7	107.1
Nov	122.2	109.4	121.5	115.6	118.6	110.3	114.3	114.8	121.6	115.8	102.7	107.2
Dec	122.8	111.1	123.5	115.5	119.4	110.3	114.8	114.9	121.6	115.9	102.7	107.2
1945												
Jan	125.2	108.7	123.9	117.0	120.4	110.4	115.2	115.0	121.6	116.0	102.9	107.4
Feb	126.5	109.1	125.3	117.8	121.5	110.7	116.0	115.3	121.6	116.2	103.1	107.6
Mar	127.4	107.7	124.9	118.7	121.8	111.0	116.2	115.5	121.6	116.4	103.1	107.6
Apr	127.6	111.9	127.3	119.0	123.0	111.1	116.9	115.5	121.6	116.4	103.1	107.8
May	127.0	116.6	129.8	118.4	124.0	111.2	117.4	116.3	121.9	117.1	103.2	108.0
Jun	126.8	118.3	131.0	118.2	124.4	110.9	117.5	116.5	123.3	117.5	103.4	108.3
Jul	125.9	115.6	128.2	117.9	122.9	110.8	116.7	116.5	125.5	117.9	103.4	108.4
Aug	123.8	112.3	124.1	116.9	120.4	110.7	115.5	116.8	125.6	118.1	103.7	108.6
Sep	122.9	107.3	122.0	114.9	118.4	110.9	114.7	116.7	125.9	118.0	103.4	108.4
Oct	125.9	109.4	124.6	117.7	121.1	111.6	116.3	116.9	125.9	118.2	103.5	108.6
Nov	128.1	114.4	129.5	119.0	124.2	112.2	118.0	117.2	125.9	118.4	103.9	108.8
Dec	127.3	117.3	132.3	117.1	124.5	112.4	118.4	117.5	126.6	118.9	103.9	109.1
1946												
Jan	128.1	112.6	131.2	116.5	123.6	112.9	118.2	118.0	126.9	119.2	104.2	109.4
Feb	130.0	112.4	133.6	116.6	124.9	113.8	119.2	118.1	127.0	119.4	105.1	110.1
Mar	132.3	115.6	138.4	117.0	127.4	115.6	121.4	119.6	127.2	120.8	106.2	111.1
Apr	133.5	119.1	141.6	117.9	129.3	117.9	123.4	121.5	127.3	122.3	106.5	111.9
May	135.5	120.4	145.4	117.8	131.1	118.7	124.6	122.4	127.4	123.1	107.1	112.6
Jun	139.0	122.0	147.0	122.0	134.0	120.8	126.7	126.5	128.5	126.8	107.9	114.3
Jul	161.7	129.6	160.7	144.4	152.3	141.4	146.3	130.1	143.7	132.0	108.9	117.0
Aug	164.7	127.6	157.6	150.3	153.9	149.1	151.3	133.7	144.9	135.3	110.7	119.3
Sep	156.6	129.2	159.9	137.8	148.5	138.4	142.9	133.8	145.9	135.6	111.7	120.0
Oct	168.8	137.2	164.2	154.9	159.5	156.1	157.7	134.6	149.7	136.8	117.5	124.3
Nov	176.1	141.6	160.1	171.2	166.0	163.6	164.7	140.0	160.8	143.0	122.0	129.2
Dec	176.2	137.4	160.0	169.0	164.8	162.9	163.7	149.3	161.4	151.0	125.7	134.5
1947												
Jan	172.4	132.9	156.9	164.0	160.7	161.4	161.1	159.7	162.3	160.1	130.1	140.4
Feb	179.0	129.7	162.9	165.6	164.5	165.9	165.2	160.7	163.9	161.1	130.9	141.3
Mar	194.4	131.3	179.2	172.2	175.7	170.9	173.0	165.0	165.9	165.2	132.5	143.8
Apr	187.1	132.1	178.2	163.8	170.9	167.3	168.9	167.9	162.6	167.1	133.3	145.0
May	187.5	126.0	178.9	160.2	169.3	166.5	167.6	166.9	158.1	165.5	133.8	144.7
Jun	190.2	131.2	180.7	165.3	172.8	167.0	169.5	166.1	160.6	165.3	133.7	144.6
Jul	193.6	131.2	178.1	172.2	175.1	170.6	172.6	171.6	161.8	170.2	135.0	147.1
Aug	194.8	132.9	173.9	178.7	176.5	174.0	175.0	177.2	167.9	175.9	137.3	150.9
Sep	200.8	134.0	176.3	185.1	181.0	179.1	179.9	179.8	169.8	178.3	140.4	153.5
Oct	205.0	138.5	181.5	188.7	185.4	178.7	181.6	183.8	170.3	181.9	141.8	155.6
Nov	203.9	140.7	186.8	183.3	185.1	180.9	182.7	186.9	172.1	184.7	143.2	157.5
Dec	213.5	141.8	192.5	191.9	192.3	183.2	187.2	190.9	171.3	188.1	145.6	160.2
1948												
Jan	214.4	145.2	194.0	193.5	193.8	185.6	189.2	195.0	171.4	191.5	148.9	163.6
Feb	193.3	148.0	178.7	180.8	180.0	178.9	179.4	194.8	171.2	191.3	149.3	163.8
Mar	193.7	149.5	181.9	179.3	180.7	179.3	179.9	194.2	171.2	190.8	149.9	163.9

Officers
(1948)

C. Reinold Noyes, *Chairman*
H. W. Laidler, *President*
W. W. Riefler, *Vice-President*
George B. Roberts, *Treasurer*
W. J. Carson, *Executive Director*
Martha Anderson, *Editor*

Directors at Large

Arthur F. Burns, *Columbia University*
W. L. Crum, *University of California*
Oswald W. Knauth, *New York City*
Simon Kuznets, *University of Pennsylvania*
H. W. Laidler, *Executive Director, League for Industrial Democracy*
Shepard Morgan, *Vice-President, Chase National Bank*
C. Reinold Noyes, *New York City*
George B. Roberts, *Vice-President, National City Bank*
Beardsley Ruml, *Chairman, Board of Directors, R. H. Macy & Company*
Harry Scherman, *President, Book-of-the-Month Club*
George Soule, *New York City*
N. I. Stone, *Consulting Economist*
J. Raymond Walsh, *WMCA Broadcasting Co.*
Leo Wolman, *Columbia University*

Directors by University Appointment

E. Wight Bakke, *Yale*
C. C. Balderston, *Pennsylvania*
Corwin D. Edwards, *Northwestern*
G. A. Elliott, *Toronto*
H. M. Groves, *Wisconsin*
Gottfried Haberler, *Harvard*
Clarence Heer, *North Carolina*
R. L. Kozelka, *Minnesota*
Wesley C. Mitchell, *Columbia*
Paul M. O'Leary, *Cornell*
W. W. Riefler, *Institute for Advanced Study*
T. O. Yntema, *Chicago*

Directors Appointed by Other Organizations

Percival F. Brundage, *American Institute of Accountants*
Arthur H. Cole, *Economic History Association*
Frederick C. Mills, *American Statistical Association*
Boris Shishkin, *American Federation of Labor*
Warren C. Waite, *American Farm Economic Association*
Donald H. Wallace, *American Economic Association*

Research Staff

Arthur F. Burns, *Director of Research*
G. H. Moore, *Associate Director of Research*

Moses Abramovitz
Harold Barger
Morris A. Copeland
Daniel Creamer
Solomon Fabricant
Milton Friedman
Millard Hastay
W. Braddock Hickman
F. F. Hill

Thor Hultgren
Simon Kuznets
Clarence D. Long
Ruth P. Mack
Frederick C. Mills
Wesley C. Mitchell
Raymond J. Saulnier
George J. Stigler
Leo Wolman

Relation of the Directors to the Work of the National Bureau of Economic Research

1. The object of the National Bureau of Economic Research is to ascertain and to present to the public important economic facts and their interpretation in a scientific and impartial manner. The Board of Directors is charged with the responsibility of ensuring that the work of the Bureau is carried on in strict conformity with this object.

2. To this end the Board of Directors shall appoint one or more Directors of Research.

3. The Director or Directors of Research shall submit to the members of the Board, or to its Executive Committee, for their formal adoption, all specific proposals concerning researches to be instituted.

4. No report shall be published until the Director or Directors of Research shall have submitted to the Board a summary drawing attention to the character of the data and their utilization in the report, the nature and treatment of the problems involved, the main conclusions and such other information as in their opinion would serve to determine the suitability of the report for publication in accordance with the principles of the Bureau.

5. A copy of any manuscript proposed for publication shall also be submitted to each member of the Board. For each manuscript to be so submitted a special committee shall be appointed by the President, or at his designation by the Executive Director, consisting of three Directors selected as nearly as may be one from each general division of the Board. The names of the special manuscript committee shall be stated to each Director when the summary and report described in paragraph (4) are sent to him. It shall be the duty of each member of the committee to read the manuscript. If each member of the special committee signifies his approval within thirty days, the manuscript may be published. If each member of the special committee has not signified his approval within thirty days of the transmittal of the report and manuscript, the Director of Research shall then notify each member of the Board, requesting approval or disapproval of publication, and thirty additional days shall be granted for this purpose. The manuscript shall then not be published unless at least a majority of the entire Board and a two-thirds majority of those members of the Board who shall have voted on the proposal within the time fixed for the receipt of votes on the publication proposed shall have approved.

6. No manuscript may be published, though approved by each member of the special committee, until forty-five days have elapsed from the transmittal of the summary and report. The interval is allowed for the receipt of any memorandum of dissent or reservation, together with a brief statement of his reasons, that any member may wish to express; and such memorandum of dissent or reservation shall be published with the manuscript if he so desires. Publication does not, however, imply that each member of the Board has read the manuscript, or that either members of the Board in general, or of the special committee, have passed upon its validity in every detail.

7. A copy of this resolution shall, unless otherwise determined by the Board, be printed in each copy of every National Bureau book.

(Resolution adopted October 25, 1926, and revised February 6, 1933, and February 24, 1941)

Lombard Street
in
War and Reconstruction

BENJAMIN H. HIGGINS

FINANCIAL RESEARCH PROGRAM
NATIONAL BUREAU OF ECONOMIC RESEARCH

LOMBARD STREET
IN
WAR AND RECONSTRUCTION
BENJAMIN H. HIGGINS

Occasional Paper 28: June 1949

FINANCIAL RESEARCH PROGRAM
NATIONAL BUREAU OF ECONOMIC RESEARCH
1819 BROADWAY, NEW YORK 23, N. Y.

Price $1.00
COPYRIGHT, 1949 BY NATIONAL BUREAU OF ECONOMIC RESEARCH, INC.
1819 BROADWAY, NEW YORK 23, N.Y.   ALL RIGHTS RESERVED
MANUFACTURED IN THE UNITED STATES OF AMERICA BY
JOHN N. JACOBSON & SON, INC.

Preface

It is by now abundantly clear that the methods of war finance followed by the several belligerents in World War II have had significant and lasting effects on their economic and financial institutions. In certain respects Great Britain is the most striking case in point, although the causes of her postwar difficulties are far from exclusively economic in nature and their roots are, in some important instances, to be found in circumstances antedating World War II. Professor Higgins' essay, *Lombard Street in War and Reconstruction*, begins therefore with the pre-World War I status of Britain's financial institutions and carries the account through World War II and into the postwar period up to early 1948. While Britain's financial position was grave at that time, the main directions of change in the institutions that comprise Lombard Street—which is the study's focus of interest—were reasonably evident and it seems unlikely that they will be altered materially by the events of the calculable future.

This study complements Professor Higgins' earlier essay, *Canada's Financial System in War,* and together with other Financial Research Program studies that have dealt with wartime developments in the United States and in National Socialist Germany, it completes a closely related series of studies on the impact of war on financial machinery.

The author is Bronfman Professor of Economics at McGill University and has completed the study as a member of the staff of the Financial Research Program. In preparing his essay Professor Higgins has had the benefit of an unpublished National Bureau manuscript on the same subject by Dr. Tibor Scitovszky, and has also profited from the extensive and thoughtful comments of several readers both on the staff of and outside the National Bureau.

The first draft of the manuscript was edited by Donald Dunham and subsequent drafts by Dorothy Wescott, who was assisted by Mary Watkins.

R. J. Saulnier
Director, Financial Research Program

Table of Contents

PREFACE iii
LIST OF TABLES vi
LIST OF CHARTS vii

INTRODUCTION 1

I. LOMBARD STREET IN 1913 3
    BANK OF ENGLAND 3
    JOINT STOCK BANKS 5
    DISCOUNT MARKET 6
    MERCHANT BANKS 7
    CAPITAL MARKET 8
    LOMBARD STREET AND INTERNATIONAL FINANCE 9

II. WORLD WAR I AND ITS EFFECTS ON BRITISH FINANCIAL INSTITUTIONS 10
    EMERGENCY MEASURES 10
    WARTIME BORROWING 11
    FOREIGN BORROWING AND DISINVESTMENT 13
    BANK OF ENGLAND 14
    JOINT STOCK BANKS 18
    DISCOUNT MARKET 20
    MERCHANT BANKS 22
    CAPITAL MARKET 23
    SUMMARY 25

III. GOVERNMENT CONTROLS AND LOMBARD STREET IN WORLD WAR II 26
    TAXATION 27
    PRICE CONTROL 30
    PRODUCTION CONTROL 31
    MANPOWER REGULATIONS 32
    EXCHANGE CONTROL 32
    EFFECTS OF WARTIME CONTROLS ON LOMBARD STREET 34

IV.	LENDING TO FINANCE THE WAR	36
	GOVERNMENT BORROWING	36
	LENDING BY THE BANK OF ENGLAND	41
	LENDING BY THE JOINT STOCK BANKS	43
	LENDING BY THE DISCOUNT MARKET	46
	LENDING BY THE CAPITAL MARKET	47
	GENERAL RESULTS OF BRITISH WARTIME BORROWING	48
V.	EFFECTS OF WAR ON LOMBARD STREET	50
	BANK OF ENGLAND	50
	JOINT STOCK BANKS	51
	MERCHANT BANKS	57
	DISCOUNT MARKET	58
	CAPITAL MARKET	59
	OTHER DEVELOPMENTS IMPORTANT TO LOMBARD STREET	62
	Exports	62
	Shipping	62
	Industrialization of Other Countries	64
	Effects of the War on British Insurance	65
	Loss of Overseas Investments and Increase in Overseas Debt	66
	IMPORTANCE OF BRITAIN'S INTERNATIONAL FINANCIAL POSITION FOR LOMBARD STREET	69
VI.	POSTWAR TRANSITION AND THE FUTURE OF LOMBARD STREET	70
	BANK OF ENGLAND	71
	JOINT STOCK BANKS	73
	Cheaper Money	74
	Asset Structure	77
	End of Window-Dressing	80
	DISCOUNT MARKET	82
	MERCHANT BANKS	85
	CAPITAL MARKET	86
	Finance Corporation for Industry	88
	Industrial and Commercial Finance Corporation	88
	OUTLOOK FOR LOMBARD STREET AS A WHOLE	90
	Exports	90
	Shipping	93
	Insurance	94
	Britain as a Creditor Nation	95
	Britain's Bargaining Position	97
	GENERAL CONCLUSIONS	98

List of Tables

1. Bank of England Return, Selected Dates 4
2. British Debt Structure, End of Fiscal Years 13
3. British National Resources and Their Disposal 27
4. British Government Receipts and Expenditures, by War Years 29
5. Annual Increases in British Debt, by War Years 37
6. Maturity Distribution of Marketable Government Securities at End of Fiscal Years for United Kingdom, United States, and Canada 38
7. Yields (Actuaries Index) of British Securities 49
8. Combined Balance Sheet of the London Clearing Banks 53
9. Net Profits of Joint Stock Banks 57
10. New Capital Issues in the London Market 59
11. Merchant Tonnage (1,000 Gross Tons and Over) Operated by Principal Maritime Countries 63
12. Proceeds of Sales or Repatriation of Overseas Investments of the United Kingdom, September 1939—June 1945 66
13. Estimated Position of United Kingdom on International Capital Account, Selected Dates 67
14. United Kingdom Overseas Receipts and Payments of Dividends, Interest, etc., 1945 68
15. Estimates of Dry-Cargo Tonnage Used by United States Merchant Fleet, 1939, and Suggested Requirements for Postwar Trade 94
16. Drawings on U. S. Credit and Net Spendings from U. S. and Canadian Credits 96

Appendix Tables

A. Bank of England Return 101
B. Selected Balance Sheet Items for Joint Stock Banks of England and Wales 102
C. Composition of British Banks' Advances 103
D. Balance Sheets of Discount Houses 104
E. Balance Sheets of Merchant Banks 106
F. Selected Interest Rates, London Money Market 108

List of Charts

1. New Issues in the London Capital Market 24
2. Indexes of Cost of Living and of Wholesale Prices for United Kingdom, United States, and Canada 28
3. Selected Balance Sheet Items for Banks in the United Kingdom, United States, and Canada 52
4. Growth of Personal and Other Accounts of the London Clearing Banks 55
5. Yields on Selected Government Obligations, United Kingdom 76

vii

Introduction

> I venture to call this Essay "Lombard Street," and not the "Money Market," or any such phrase, because I wish to deal, and to show that I mean to deal, with concrete realities. A notion prevails that the Money Market is something so impalpable that it can only be spoken of in very abstract words, and that therefore books on it must always be exceedingly difficult. But I maintain that the Money Market is as concrete and real as anything else; that it can be described in as plain words; that it is the writer's fault if what he says is not clear.

This introductory passage from Bagehot's 70-year-old classic[1] expresses the objective of the present essay. It, too, deals with "concrete realities." It considers problems connected with the functioning of the British financial system in war and reconstruction, and with the effects of war and its aftermath on British financial institutions.

The institutions comprising the London money market are much the same today as they were 70 years ago. "The objects which you see in Lombard Street, and in that money world which is grouped about it," Bagehot stated, "are the Bank of England, the Private Banks, the Joint Stock Banks, and the bill brokers."[2] These institutions have a long and venerable history, and they have played a prominent part in the shaping of world affairs. Before World War I, London was the undisputed center of world finance; when World War II broke out, she was sharing this distinction, and the accompanying privileges and responsibilities, with New York.

In Britain, perhaps even more than in other countries, conditions in the money market reflect conditions in the British economy as a whole. British prosperity, power, and prestige are founded upon international trade and finance. The London money market has grown and flourished through the financing of foreign trade and investment. A distinguished French economist has stated, "The complete significance of the banking system cannot be properly realized unless we keep constantly before our eyes the body which this blood stream of money and credit is continually nourishing. Behind the City of London, it is

---

[1] Walter Bagehot, *Lombard Street* (London, revised edition, 1909) p. 1. The study was first published in 1873.
[2] *Ibid.*, p. 21.

necessary always to imagine The Port of London, Great Britain, the whole Empire."[3]

During the period between the two World Wars, the growth of economic nationalism retarded the expansion of international trade and finance on which Britain is so dependent. Consequently, British prosperity is increasingly dependent upon economic policies undertaken elsewhere. If conditions in other countries are such as to threaten the recapture by Britain of her position as a major exporter of goods or services, and of capital, Britain will almost certainly think it necessary to rely more heavily on policies of economic nationalism and self-sufficiency. What happens in the United States is especially germane to developments in Britain. Nothing is feared more there than American policies that would perpetuate a "chronic shortage of American dollars," or bring about an American depression. There is no lack of recognition on the far side of the Atlantic of the importance to Britain of American economic policy, or of the importance of Anglo-American cooperation for the success of new adventures in international finance.

For the six years of World War II the activities of the British financial system, and of the British economy as a whole, were concerned not with foreign trade but with war. Now that war is over, will Britain regain her position as a leading foreign trader and lender? Upon an answer to this question depends not merely the future of Lombard Street, but the future of the whole British economy, and of the entire international economic structure.

The primary concern of the present essay is with the institutions of Lombard Street during World War II, the effect of the war upon them, and their possible future role in reconstructing Great Britain and the world. To scrutinize developments with the proper perspective, however, it is necessary to know something of the organization and significance of the London money market before World War I, and of how the market was affected by that war and by the Great Depression of the thirties.

[3] R. J. Truptil, *British Banks and the London Money Market* (London, 1936) p. 20.

Chapter 1
Lombard Street in 1913

BANK OF ENGLAND

THE DOMINANT institution in Lombard Street in 1913 was, of course, the Bank of England. Many writers have pointed to the curious nature of England's Central Bank. A private corporation, organized in 1694 for purposes of war finance, it was subject to virtually no legal controls except that a limit was imposed on its note circulation, and it was debarred from engaging in merchandising operations;[1] yet this private corporation controlled the credit policy of the nation—one could almost say of the world. It had a monopoly of the note issue in England and Wales, and Bank of England notes comprised nearly two-thirds of the note circulation of the entire United Kingdom. Notes of and deposits with the Bank constituted the basic reserves of the joint stock banks and the private banks. The discount houses, bill brokers, merchant bankers, some insurance companies and stock brokers, and many foreign banks kept deposits with the Bank of England.

Nominally, the operations of this powerful institution were controlled by a Court, comprising a governor, a deputy governor, and 24 directors. The shareholders elected the directors, and the latter elected the governor and deputy governor. In practice, new directors were recommended by the Court itself and approved by the shareholders, and the Court consulted the Treasury on matters of national policy. Indeed, the Issue Department was a *de facto* government department; its liabilities consisted solely of notes issued, and its assets of gold, funded government debt, and other securities (Table 1). The fiduciary issue against government debt was fixed by law; issues against other securities were permitted only as a consequence of the replacement of the notes of other banks by the notes of the Bank under the Act of 1844. Otherwise, notes had to be backed one hundred percent by gold.[2]

The nature of the operations of the Banking Department is indicated in Table 1. On the liabilities side, the "proprietors' capital" represented the original capital of the Bank (£1.2 million) and additions per-

---

[1] See *Report of the Committee on Finance and Industry* (henceforth called the "Macmillan Report") Cmd. 3897 (London, 1931) p. 25.
[2] The Bank had the right to constitute a fourth of its metallic reserve in silver. Since silver coins were not full legal tender, this provision was not effective.

Table 1—BANK OF ENGLAND RETURN, SELECTED DATES[a]
(in millions)

	December 31, 1913	July 29, 1914	November 27, 1918
Issue Department			
Liabilities			
Notes issued	£52.32	£55.12	£93.71
Assets			
Government securities	11.02	11.02	11.02
Other securities	7.43	7.43	7.43
Gold coin and bullion	33.87	36.67	75.26
	52.32	55.12	93.71
Banking Department			
Liabilities			
Proprietors' capital	14.55	14.55	14.55
Rest	3.25	3.49	3.19
Public deposits[b]	10.26	12.71	30.43
Other deposits	61.09	54.42	143.75
Seven-day and other bills	0.01	0.01	0.01
	89.16	85.19	191.93
Assets			
Government securities	13.20	11.01	62.63
Other securities	52.14	47.31	100.99
Notes	22.72	25.42	27.72
Gold and silver coinage	1.11	1.46	0.59
	89.16	85.19	191.93

[a] From *The Economist*, January 3, 1914, p. 33; August 1, 1914, p. 249; November 30, 1918, p. 753. In some cases totals do not agree with the sums of the items because of rounding.
[b] Include Exchequer, Savings Banks, Commissioner of National Debt, and Dividend Accounts.

mitted by subsequent legislation up to 1844. The "rest" was really undistributed profits and reserves. "Public deposits" constituted the accounts of the British government. "Other deposits," the largest item on the liability side, consisted mainly of deposits of joint stock and private banks, but also, in part, of deposits of merchant banks, discount houses, foreign banks, Indian and colonial governments, and a few large commercial and financial concerns. The "seven-day and other bills," which were promises to pay on seven-days' notice, were introduced in 1738, to provide a means of payment by mail safer than notes, and to give the owners time to notify the Bank in case of a highway robbery of the mails.[3] On the asset side, "government securities" consisted of long- and intermediate-term obligations of the British government, and British Treasury bills purchased for the Bank's own

[3] The bills were originally for three days, but this proved to be insufficient time for making notifications. Cf. W. M. Acres, *The Bank of England from Within* (London, 1931) pp. 158-59, and Sir John Clapham, *The Bank of England* (New York, 1945) Vol. I, p. 144.

account. The "other securities" were commercial bills and Treasury bills discounted for customers, advances to bill brokers and other customers of the Bank, foreign and colonial government securities, and commercial bills purchased for the Bank's own account. The "notes" consisted of currency issued by the Issue Department but not yet in circulation. The "gold and silver coinage" was in fact mostly silver.

The chief instrument of central bank control was the rediscount or Bank rate. Short-term interest rates were, for the most part, directly related to the Bank rate: the rate paid by commercial banks on their deposits was usually $1\frac{1}{2}$ to 2 percent under the Bank rate; the rate paid by discount houses on their deposits was usually $\frac{1}{4}$ percent higher than that paid by commercial banks; the rate on advances from the clearing houses to the discount market was usually 1 percent under the Bank rate; the rate on prime bills was accordingly slightly higher than the clearing house rate on advances; the rate on ordinary commercial loans was the Bank rate plus a variable amount. Thus a change in the rediscount rate would alter the entire complex of short-term money rates in the same direction. In addition, the Bank utilized "open market policy" (purchase or sale of securities and bills) to increase or decrease the basic reserves of the financial system. Moreover, the British financiers had what R. J. Truptil has called "a remarkable sense of discipline," and "hints" received from the Bank were "followed by the market."[4]

Before World War I, England was the guardian of the gold standard, and the Bank was the institution primarily concerned with its control. An outflow of gold from the Bank in response to an unfavorable balance of payments was the signal for a rise in the Bank rate, designed to attract foreign funds, and perhaps also to reduce British export prices through monetary contraction and so to reverse the gold flow. For this reason, the "ratio" of the Bank of England—the ratio of gold and silver coin and notes to deposits—was anxiously watched by the British money market and the entire financial world.

Joint Stock Banks

Next in importance among British financial institutions on the eve of World War I were the joint stock banks. After the crisis of 1825 and the accompanying large-scale failures of "private banks" (banks with no more than six partners, each carrying unlimited liability), the commercial banking business of the United Kingdom was gradually taken over by the large banking corporations, or joint stock banks. In

[4] R. J. Truptil, *British Banks and the London Money Market* (London, 1936) pp. 212-17. See also Macmillan Report, *op. cit.*, pp. 32-33, 92-106, and 155.

1913, only a few private banks remained, and the dozen or so joint stock banks that were members of the London Clearing House dominated the field. These banks had no legal reserve requirements, but in practice they retained reserves of currency and balances with the Bank of England equivalent to 9 to 11 percent of their deposits.[5] It is generally presumed that the hidden assets of the larger banks were nearly as great as their published capital and reserves.[6]

Money at call amounted to almost as much as cash reserves. The investments of the joint stock banks were government securities, mostly Treasury bonds of intermediate and short maturity, and constituted some 10-15 percent of total assets. Bills discounted included both Treasury and commercial bills, with the latter predominating. The chief asset, reflecting the character of the major business done by the banks, consisted of advances or commercial loans, and amounted to roughly half of total assets; they were made mainly to industrial and commercial firms, for three to six months. Deposits were by far the largest liability of the joint stock banks.[7]

Discount Market

Truptil attributed the "pleasing harmony in the 'City'" and the "absence of sudden jars in the delicate machinery of the monetary markets" largely to "the unique institution of discount houses."[8] The discount market consisted of discount houses and bill brokers specializing in the purchase of Treasury and commercial bills on their own account, using their own capital and the deposits of clients to some extent, but relying mainly on day-to-day loans from the joint stock banks with the bills as security. About half the market's capital resources was held by the three largest discount houses (Alexanders, National, and Union), which were organized as public companies and which published regularly complete balance sheets. In addition, there were in 1913 four private limited companies, ten private companies with unlimited liability, and a few "running brokers" who served as intermediaries between commercial houses and banks wishing to invest

---

[5] The published statements show a reserve ratio averaging close to the upper limit of this range, but these statements involve a certain amount of "window dressing" —that is, temporary withdrawal of cash from the money market for the day for which the weekly statement is published. The banks publish statements on different days of the week. Consequently, the actual average reserves of the clearing banks, as a whole, differ from those shown in the published statements. See R. J. Truptil, *op. cit.*, pp. 93-94, and Macmillan Report, *op. cit.*, p. 36, paragraph 79, and pp. 156-57. See also "End of Window Dressing," Chapter VI below.

[6] Truptil, *op. cit.*, p. 86.

[7] Selected balance sheet items for joint stock banks are given in Appendix Table B.

[8] Truptil, *op. cit.*, p. 192. See also Macmillan Report, *op. cit.*, p. 161.

in bills and willing to pay a small commission for the special knowledge of the brokers as to the reliability of various firms whose names appeared as acceptors and endorsers.

Loans and deposits were the main liabilities of the three principal discount houses, and bills discounted were the main asset. Most of the bills, however, were Treasury bills or prime commercial bills, readily discountable at the Bank of England. Cash reserves and investments—the latter comprising high-grade securities of British and foreign governments, of short or intermediate maturity—amounted to only a small percentage of total assets.[9]

The discount market provided the London banker with an ever-present outlet for surplus liquid funds, permitting him to earn a small return on them and still to be in a position to recall them whenever needed. It also provided expert knowledge of the relative safety and liquidity of the commercial bills offered in the market; the business of the discount bankers and bill brokers was to know everything possible about the firms whose paper they handled. The discount market thus permitted a day-by-day—indeed, hour-by-hour—adjustment of the supply of short-term money to the demand for it, with a speed and precision matched by no other money market. The discount houses were important also as a buffer between the joint stock banks and the Bank of England. Unlike commercial banks in most countries, the joint stock banks in England did not go to the central bank when they wished to improve their cash position; instead, they called in loans made to the discount market and so compelled the discount houses to go to the Bank of England for whatever rediscounting was necessary.

Merchant Banks

The merchant banks, or acceptance houses, were firms originally engaged in trade, and especially foreign trade. Most of them were established early in the nineteenth century by continental merchants. Their banking function consisted mainly of accepting foreign trade bills, and thus making them discountable at the banks. In addition, some of the larger houses made loans to foreign governments and firms. By 1913, most of them had abandoned merchandising and had evolved into bankers specializing in international finance; they were accepting deposits, making loans, floating and underwriting new capital issues, and investing in securities.[10] The majority of the houses were organized as partnerships, with unlimited liability for each partner.

[9] Balance sheet statements of discount houses are given in Appendix Table D.
[10] Balance sheet statement for Baring Brothers, 1913, is given in Appendix Table E.

The merchant bankers were by no means restricted to financing British trade with the rest of the world. Through their acceptance functions, they financed much of the trade between countries far from English shores. Indeed, so common was this kind of transaction that the pound sterling was, for all practical purposes, the international medium of payment.

Capital Market

As ordinarily used, the term "Lombard Street" refers only to the institutions in the City of London providing short- and intermediate-term credit. In fact, however, a hard and fast line cannot be drawn between the short- and long-term money markets. The merchant banks —surely as indigenous to Lombard Street as any institution—engaged in long-term foreign lending before World War I. Moreover, the joint stock banks provided long-term capital indirectly, since the facilities they offered enabled their clients to economize in the amount of long-term capital which they employed. Therefore, although this study is concerned primarily with the market for short-term funds, the long-term capital market cannot be ignored altogether.

Certain institutions in the capital market, in 1913 as well as today, were quite distinct from those already discussed. The most obvious were the stock exchange and the stockbrokers. In addition, there were syndicates formed occasionally for the flotation of a particular new issue. Conspicuously absent from the London capital market were large industrial banks of the Continental type, or investment banking houses of the American type.

Actually, much of the long-term financing of British industry was provided directly by private individuals and nonfinancial concerns. A large proportion of British industry consisted of private companies and partnerships. Such concerns were unable to borrow from the general public, and relied chiefly on family savings or on the accumulation of their own profits. If they borrowed long-term funds at all, they went directly to the lender and not to the organized capital market. Loans from friends and acquaintances, safeguarded only by common-law contracts, were the chief sources of outside long-term capital for domestic enterprise. Prior to World War I, new issues in the capital market were primarily for overseas borrowers, with railways the largest single category of such borrowers; domestic issues amounted to about 20 percent of the total floated on the London market, even when issues of central and local government authorities are included.

Lombard Street and International Finance

The financial institutions of Lombard Street in 1913 formed a complicated, delicate, but highly efficient machine, and this machine was without rival in its scale of operations. International trade and finance centered in London. The activities of the City were based to a large extent on trade between countries producing manufactured goods (such as Great Britain) and countries producing raw materials and foodstuffs (such as countries of the British Empire). Britain's foreign lending went a long way toward financing her own exports and developing raw materials markets. So widely accepted was sterling as an international means of payment that Lombard Street financed much of the trade between non-British countries as well.

W. A. Brown has presented a convincing case for the contention that the period of British pre-eminence in international trade and finance coincided with the period of successful operation of the international gold standard; and that the international gold standard was successful chiefly because it was in fact a "sterling exchange standard system."[11] This system provided an efficient distribution of credit and gold, a common medium of payment (sterling), and an international clearing house and foreign exchange market, all organized and operated through London. London was the center for distributing newly mined gold, and world markets were bound together by movements of gold and capital through London.

Even before World War I, there were signs that this sterling exchange standard system was beginning to break down. The industrial basis of Britain's international trade position was dangerously narrow. Over half her exports consisted of textiles and iron and steel, but the development of efficient industries for manufacturing these products in other countries, notably the United States, Germany, and Japan, was threatening Britain's superiority in these fields. Her share in world trade was declining, and the deterioration of Britain's terms of trade, which was to be an important factor in Britain's international problems at a later date, was already making its appearance. The positions of New York, Paris, and Berlin as financial centers, while still subsidiary to London's, were nevertheless assuming greater importance. World War I accelerated these basic trends, and disrupted both national and international trade and finance in a manner that left a permanent imprint on Lombard Street.

[11] William Adams Brown, Jr., *The International Gold Standard Reinterpreted, 1914-1934* (National Bureau of Economic Research, 1940) Vol. I, p. xiii. The discussion in this section is based primarily on Professor Brown's study.

Chapter 2
World War I and Its Effects on British Financial Institutions

GREAT BRITAIN'S effort in World War I was on an incomparably greater scale than that of the United States or Canada, and was sizable even on present day standards. Total government expenditures in the war years amounted to £9.5 billion, which, judging from national income estimates for 1913 and 1924, was possibly one-third of total national income for the period. Total government expenditures at their peak in the fiscal year 1918 exceeded the entire national income of 1913.

Considerably less use was made of taxation than in World War II, and the proportion of total outlays covered by taxes was smaller in Great Britain than in the United States or Canada. In the five fiscal years from April 1, 1914 through March 31, 1919, 25 percent of the government's financial resources was derived from taxes. Monetary expansion and borrowing from the public were the chief forms of war finance, and Lombard Street was heavily involved in both.

EMERGENCY MEASURES

Three factors influenced the Treasury's policy at the beginning of the war. First was the lack of any real precedent for its task. Second was the general belief that the war would be short, which seemed to justify short-run policies such as meeting war costs by credit creation. Third, when war broke out the City was on the verge of financial panic, and the Treasury felt obliged to create money market conditions that would prevent a crisis.

To this end, the government undertook a series of emergency measures. The Bank rate was raised from 3 percent on July 29, 1914 to 10 percent on August 1. On July 30 the government closed the stock exchange. On August 2 it declared a moratorium on bills of exchange, which was subsequently extended. On August 6 it passed the Currency and Bank Notes Act, which gave the Bank permission to extend its fiduciary issue without additional gold reserves. In addition, the Act authorized the Treasury to issue £1 and 10s. notes as legal tender, made postal orders legal tender until the Treasury notes could be printed and circulated, and permitted the Scotch and Irish banks to meet their obligations with their own notes. The Treasury currency, an innovation in British finance, was issued through the Bank of England to the banks, and by December 31, 1918 had reached a circulation of £323 million.[1] The government underwrote shipping insurance up to 80 percent, and the Treasury agreed to guarantee the Bank of England against loss on bills discounted for banks and brokers.

WARTIME BORROWING

These emergency measures forestalled panic, but they simultaneously set the stage for credit inflation, and they became the basis for heavy reliance on credit-supported short- and intermediate-term loans for financing the war. The whole structure of debt was sustained by increased credit from the commercial banks, based in turn upon the Treasury's issues of currency notes. In view of the Bank of England's readiness to discount bills, it is not surprising that the Treasury found a ready market for its own bills; the banks could buy them and still provide the discount market with ample funds. Influenced by the success of its first big issue of bills, the Treasury subsequently made liberal use of short-term finance, in the form of Treasury bills and ways-and-means advances. Although Treasury bills were held mainly by the discount market, on day-to-day money from the commercial banks, the banks themselves held substantial quantities. Before the war, ways-and-means advances consisted of advances by the Bank of England to the Treasury on those rare occasions when the government found it difficult to renew its bills. During the war, however, this form of borrowing assumed a much more extensive role, and included borrowing "through" the Bank as well as "from" the Bank; that is, the Treasury borrowed spare balances of the commercial banks and of foreign depositors, in addition to borrowing directly from the Bank.[2]

The Treasury also borrowed the spare balances of Public Departments. In England, certain departments of the government with their own sources of funds and some degree of autonomy in their administration, such as the Post Office Savings Bank, the Trustee Savings Banks, the Post Office Fund, the National Health Insurance Fund, the Unemployment Insurance Fund, the Treasury Pensions Fund, etc., and (later) the

[1] The Treasury received a deposit credit with the Bank of England for the amount of currency deposited with it, and the Bank distributed the currency to the commercial banks, more or less in response to the banks' need for currency, up to a limit of 20 percent of each bank's liabilities on deposit accounts (savings or time deposits) plus current accounts. At the beginning of the scheme, the banks were charged interest on the currency distributed to them. Cf. Henry F. Grady, *British War Finance, 1914-1919* (New York, 1927) pp. 13-17.

[2] Cf. U. K. Hicks, *The Finance of British Government, 1920-1926* (London, 1938) pp. 320-21. See also A. W. Kirkaldy, *British Finance During and After the War, 1914-21* (London, 1921) p. 47.

Exchange Equalization Fund, are important subscribers to government securities.[3] These departments play a particularly useful role in smoothing the market for new issues, by disposing of Treasury bills, building up their balances with the Bank, buying enough of the new loan to guarantee its success, and then gradually disposing of their holdings of the longer-term issues to the general public, through the government broker, in order to replete their portfolio of Treasury bills.

The floating debt was reduced during the war period by three issues of long-term bonds.[4] The first of these, in November 1914, consisted of 3½ percent, fourteen-year war stock, issued at 95 to yield 3.97 percent. The bonds could be paid for in instalments. The public response was disappointing, and the banks were called upon to take nearly a third of the total cash subscriptions, which amounted to more than £330 million. The Second War Loan of June 1915 was hardly more successful. While the proceeds were larger, reaching about £600 million, there were only 597,000 subscribers and the banks again took about a third of the cash subscriptions.

A more intensive effort was made to sell the Third War Loan of January 1917 to the public. The issue was offered in two forms, both highly attractive. One was a 5 percent bond sold at 95, maturing in 1929-47, and so yielding 5.58 to 5.34 percent, depending on the year of retirement. The other was a tax-free 4 percent bond maturing in 1929-42 and issued at par. The Treasury embarked upon a widespread propaganda campaign, and even threatened compulsory purchases of Treasury securities if voluntary purchases proved inadequate. In addition, it encouraged the banks to grant liberal advances to potential subscribers. The loan yielded approximately £1 billion, with bank advances being kept down to one-fifth of cash subscriptions. The number of subscribers amounted to over two million.

Three- and five-year Exchequer Bonds bearing interest of 3 to 6 percent were used to reduce the volume of floating debt between major loan drives, and a few war savings certificates and war expenditure certificates were issued. Starting in October 1917, however, the Treasury abandoned tender issues for the duration, and tap issues[5] of

[3] According to U. K. Hicks (*op. cit., pp.* 165-70), the Unemployment Insurance Fund in 1936 held 36.2 percent of the outstanding 1 percent Treasury bonds.

[4] A fourth was issued in June 1919.

[5] "Tap issues" consisted of obligations sold by the Treasury at any time, as distinct from "tender issues," which consisted of obligations sold only on stipulated dates. There were four types of tap issues: 5 percent 5-year bonds redeemable at 102; 5 percent 7-year bonds redeemable at 103; 5 percent 10-year bonds redeemable at 105; and a tax-free 4 percent of 10-year maturity redeemable at par. For a summary table of British borrowing in World War I, see *The Economist,* October 4, 1919, p. 531.

"National War Bonds" became the chief form of government borrowing. Nevertheless, over the whole war period, Treasury bills accounted for 17.2 percent and ways-and-means advances for 8.3 percent of the total increase in internal debt. Altogether, about 25 percent of the debt contracted was short-term. The structure of debt was radically altered (Table 2); the funded debt (obligations with no specified maturity date, but subject to recall) shrank from 90 percent to about 5 percent of the total; the floating debt (less than one year's maturity) rose from 2 to 23 percent; and the unfunded debt (mostly 1 to 10 years' maturity) from 8 to 72 percent. Interest rates in this period rose sharply.

Table 2—BRITISH DEBT STRUCTURE, END OF FISCAL YEARS[a]
(pound figures in millions)

	March 31, 1914 Amt.	%	March 31, 1919 Amt.	%	March 31, 1920 Amt.	%	March 31, 1926 Amt.	%
Floating debt[b]	£13	2	£1,412	23	£1,264	19	£704	11
Unfunded debt[c]	50	8	4,413	72	4,974	76	4,728	72
Intermediate-term	50	8	2,268	37	2,089	32	1,593	24
Long-term	—	—	2,145	35	2,885	44	3,135	48
Funded debt[d]	587	90	318	5	315	5	1,074	17
TOTAL	650	100	6,143	100	6,553	100	6,505	100
External debt	0	—	1,292	—	1,279	—	1,111	—

[a] Based on data in *Appendices to the Report of the Committee on National Debt and Taxation* (1927) pp. 14-17.
[b] Obligations of less than one year's maturity.
[c] Obligations of specified maturity over one year.
[d] Obligations with no specified maturity.

FOREIGN BORROWING AND DISINVESTMENT

Before the United States entered the war, British domestic policy was somewhat hampered by a belief that the pound sterling must be supported on the foreign exchange market. The desire to attract United States funds for this purpose was no doubt one reason for keeping up interest rates.

At the outbreak of war, there was a scramble for sterling which drove the pound to a temporary premium; but by the middle of February 1915 heavy British buying in the United States had forced it back to $4.79, which was the lowest figure on record since the 1870's. Despite substantial transfers of gold and a $500 million loan in New York, the pound had sagged to $4.50 by September 1915. In December of that year the Treasury announced its "dollar security" plan, under which it borrowed or bought British-held American and other securities selling on the New York exchange, and either sold them in New York or used them as collateral for dollar loans.[6]

The original plan was on a purely voluntary basis. The first element of compulsion was introduced in May 1916 in the form of a penal additional income tax of 2 shillings on the pound on securities listed by the Treasury as eligible under the plan. Of the $4½ billion of American securities held in the country, $2 billion had been deposited by January 1917 when deposit of a selected list of eligible securities was made compulsory. The exchange yielded by the plan, together with proceeds from the sale of $250 million of Exchequer Bonds, $300 of 3- to 5-year bonds, and $250 million of 1- to 2-year bonds, was sufficient to maintain the pound at $4.75-$4.77, although the list of eligible securities had to be extended until it finally included 900 items. Altogether, some £900 million of foreign investments were liquidated, mostly American railway securities. After the United States entered the war, direct loans to the British government made it possible to withdraw certain securities from the list.

Bank of England

The Bank of England's first wartime task was to help the Treasury stave off panic in the London money market. During the summer and autumn of 1914, the Bank announced that it would make loans to the acceptance houses, backed by a Treasury guarantee, discount bills without recourse to the holder, and make advances to lenders to the amount of 60 percent of the value of securities held by the lenders against any loan outstanding on July 29. The discount rate was lowered from 10 to 5 percent, and kept between 5 and 6 percent for the duration of the war.

As the government's banker, the Bank assisted in the flotation of

---

[6] Under the original plan, the Treasury paid ½ of 1 percent of the face value of securities borrowed, as well as dividends accruing while the stocks were in Treasury hands. If the Treasury found it necessary to sell borrowed securities, it paid the lender the New York price plus 2½ percent. In August 1916 the plan was elaborated considerably. Under this broader plan securities were deposited with the Treasury for a period to expire by the end of March 1922, subject to the right of the Treasury to return them to the lender at any time on or after March 31, 1919. The lender received ½ of 1 percent as before; but if the stocks were sold, the lender received all payments he would have obtained from them in the five-year period, and at the end of that time the Treasury replaced them with similar securities or repaid the deposit value plus 5 percent.

war loans, serving as an agent for their sale. It also provided the joint stock banks with funds to meet temporary drains resulting from the marketing of these loans. For example, in the First War Loan, the Bank offered to make loans to the joint stock banks against war loan stock at the attractive rate of 1 percent below the Bank rate. Since the banks took nearly a third of this loan directly, and probably acquired more of it in the open market, this offer afforded a cheap and convenient means for the banks to borrow from the Bank of England. In early 1916, the Bank inaugurated the practice of borrowing the spare cash of commercial banks and holding it in the form of deposits withdrawable at three days' notice and bearing 3 to 5 percent interest; against this cash the Bank made advances to the Treasury. Indeed, the most striking wartime change in the Bank's weekly return was the rise in the banking department's portfolio of government securities, from £11.0 million on July 29, 1914 to £62.6 million on November 27, 1918, or from 13 percent of total assets to 33 percent. The Bank's note circulation increased in the same period from £55.1 million to £93.7 million.[7]

Superficially, little of the close relationship of the Bank to the Treasury and to the joint stock banks survived the reconstruction period. Such wartime innovations as direct lending to banks, borrowing from the banks and making ways-and-means advances "through" the banks, paying interest on deposits, and the special interest rate on foreign deposits, were scrapped within a year of the cessation of hostilities. The Treasury notes, another war phenomenon, were taken over by the Bank as part of its fiduciary issue, and its monopoly of the note issue was thus restored. However, despite the Treasury's heroic and partially successful efforts to consolidate its debt (see Table 2), government securities remained a much larger share of the assets of the Banking Department than they were before the war. Between June 30, 1919, when they reached their peak, and March 31, 1920, ways-and-means advances from the Bank of England and Public Departments were cut from £774 million to £205 million, and were further reduced to £139 million by March 31, 1926; but the Bank's holdings of government securities dropped only from an average of £58 million in April 1920 to an average of £41 million in April

---

[7] In view of the expansion of bank deposits and the availability of Treasury currency, the growth of Bank of England note circulation requires explanation. The suspension of the gold requirement for Bank of England notes seems to have been used for only two days after passage of the Currency and Bank Notes Act, to fill the need until the new Treasury currency could be printed. It seems likely that the increased stamp duty led to increased use of cash in general, and that the £1 and 10s. Treasury notes became inconveniently small as prices rose.

1926. Assistance with government finance in general continued to be an important aspect of the Bank's operations. Such being the case, it seems likely that the Bank's actual relationship with the Treasury was much closer in the decade following the war than in the decade before it.

The war reduced the power of the Bank in a number of subtle but significant ways. First, the relative displacement of sterling trade bills by Treasury bills in the portfolios of banks and discount houses diminished the effectiveness of the Bank's discount policy in controlling domestic credit. The supply of Treasury bills was dictated by considerations of public finance rather than by conditions of the money market; and, unlike the supply of commercial bills, it was not affected by changes in the Bank rate. On the other hand, the discount rates on commercial bills were inevitably influenced by rates on Treasury bills. While the Treasury no doubt consulted the Bank concerning its bill policy, the demands of war finance inevitably shifted some measure of monetary control from the Bank to the Treasury.[8]

In addition, the substitution of Treasury bills for commercial bills reduced the effectiveness of foreign exchange control through changes in Bank rate. Whereas a change in the rediscount rate could influence the flow of foreign funds into and out of London through borrowing and repayment under sterling acceptances, it did not influence the flow of Treasury bills. This development was only partially offset by the growth between 1920 and 1931 of deposits by foreigners, which were relatively responsive to changes in Bank rates.

This weakening of the Bank's control of international capital movements had four aspects, according to W. A. Brown: the Treasury bill did not broaden the market for sterling exchange in the same degree as the sterling acceptance did; it did not draw deposits to London; it did not multiply the effectiveness of changes in the Bank rate on the exchange market; and the decline in the volume of bankers' acceptances, together with an expansion of the volume of Treasury bills

---

[8] According to Lord Bradbury, the postwar situation was such "as to render the task of the Bank of England in controlling the supply (as distinct from the price) of the basis of credit extremely difficult. The main cause of this has been the enormous amount of Treasury bills. This has resulted not only in increasing the dimensions of the bill market (and so making larger scale operations necessary to produce a given effect) but also in altering its character. When the holdings of the market were mainly commercial bills drawn on London on foreign account, a rise in bank rate diminished the supply of these bills. Now that the market holdings are largely Treasury bills . . . a restriction in the volume of bankers' cash, followed by a reduction of their market money, merely . . . drives the 'market' 'into the Bank,' i.e., forces the Bank of England to recreate the credit it has previously withdrawn . . ." *Report of the Committee on Finance and Industry* (the Macmillan Report) Cmd. 3897 (London, 1931), Memorandum of Dissent by Lord Bradbury, p. 274.

outstanding, transferred some of the initiative in the control of sterling exchange from the grantors of sterling acceptance credit to foreign investors in British Treasury bills.[9]

There were other difficulties. The war led to such widely varying degrees of inflation in different countries that stabilization of foreign exchange rates through gold flows, price changes, and money market adjustments alone was impossible. Stabilization was eventually accomplished on the basis of various domestic policies, arrived at independently. The distribution of the world's monetary gold stocks was inconveniently uneven.[10] Mainly because of political insecurity, international capital movements did not proceed in an orderly manner through the London banking system, but were large and erratic. Sterling was not unchallenged as an international currency.[11]

Moreover, industrialization of other countries was stimulated, while Britain's peacetime industries lost ground. Britain's merchant marine dwindled 10 percent between 1910 and 1920, while the United States' merchant fleet expanded 50 percent and that of Japan more than doubled. New York established itself as a strong competitor in the international money market. During the war the sterling bill lost its unique position as the most acceptable means of payment for American imports, and dollar bills of exchange grew in volume and importance. The telegraphic transfer tended to reduce the volume of sterling acceptances. Embarrassing balances of Dominions and neutrals accumulated in London. Wartime controls over the London and other European stock markets made New York the chief trading center for securities. New York supplanted London as the world's main source of credit.

In the entire period between World War I and World War II, the chief problem of Central Bank policy was the British balance of payments and the pound-dollar relationship. After World War I, opinion in both the United States and Britain turned against the wartime system of pegging the pound by American loans. Early return to the gold standard was considered desirable, and the general opinion was that return to the old rate of £1 = $4.87 was a matter of honor and essential to the

[9] William Adams Brown, Jr., *The International Gold Standard Reinterpreted, 1914-1934* (National Bureau of Economic Research, 1940) Vol. I, pp. 643-54. See also A. T. K. Grant, *A Study of the Capital Market in Postwar Britain* (London, 1937) pp. 90-98, and N. F. Hall, *The Exchange Equalization Account* (London, 1935) pp. 85 ff.

[10] Even when an international gold exchange standard was eventually restored in 1928, it no longer had a single center but a "nucleus" of several leading money markets.

[11] The development of the "sterling bloc" in the early thirties clearly demonstrated that the sterling exchange standard was no longer an international gold standard.

recovery of prestige by the City.[12] Consequently, from 1919 to 1925 financial policy was dominated by efforts to bring the pound close enough to $4.87 to warrant return to gold at that rate. The instrument chosen was the classical one of endeavoring to affect price levels and capital movements by alterations of the Central Bank discount rate. British policy had perforce to be deflationary *relative to* the American. It was wishfully thought that American prices would rise so that relative deflation would require no reduction of British prices, but this hope was frustrated by the collapse of American prices in 1920-21. At last, in response to a number of factors,[13] the pound reached $4.84, the gold export point, toward the end of April 1925, and a month later the Gold Standard Act was passed, requiring the Bank to sell gold for 77s. 10½d. per ounce.[14]

JOINT STOCK BANKS

In World War I the joint stock banks had the dual role of providing the Treasury with funds and financing wartime industry and trade. Deposits doubled, investments grew from 13 percent of total assets in 1913 to 20 percent in 1918, while discounts and advances fell in the same period from 56 percent to 48 percent, and acceptances shrank from 6 percent to 3 percent. Moreover, the ratio of bills discounted to advances rose from around 20 percent to more than 60 percent, mainly because of the acquisition of a large volume of Treasury bills.

Over the war period as a whole, the banks took only some 5-10 percent of the increase in long-term government debt. Loans to customers under the "borrow-to-buy" policy introduced in the Third War Loan of January 1917 contributed more than direct purchases by banks to the success of long-term issues. The banks advertised their willingness to lend against War Loan stock at 1 percent below the Bank rate to all purchasers of the Loan; and, as noted above, about one-fifth of total cash subscriptions to the Loan were financed in this manner.

Investments as a percentage of assets reached their peak in 1915. In the late years of the war, purchases of Treasury bills and indirect loans through Bank of England ways-and-means advances were a more

---

[12] According to W. A. Brown (*op. cit.*, Vol. I, p. 221), Britain's decision to return to gold at the old parity was made on the very day that she departed from the gold standard in 1914.

[13] For a full discussion of these factors, see W. A. Brown, *op. cit.*, Vol. II.

[14] The extent to which "overvaluation" of the pound was responsible for the lack of prosperity in Britain between 1925 and 1929 is not easily determined, but it clearly was a contributing factor. In sharp contrast to the prewar period, when the average annual rate for the pound tended to run above par, the pound was below par in every year between 1925 and 1931. There was a persistent tendency for gold to flow out, and British interest rates were kept relatively high throughout the entire period.

important form of financial assistance than purchases of long-term bonds. Altogether, the banks probably took 20 percent to 25 percent of the increase in debt directly, and perhaps financed as much again indirectly. By the close of 1918 investments of the banks were three times their 1913 figure; and the proportion of bills discounted that consisted of Treasury bills was much higher than before the war.

The prewar trend toward amalgamation, which had lowered the total number of British banks from 155 in 1895 to 77 in 1914, was accelerated during the war period. The most spectacular amalgamations occurred among the London joint stock banks; the 12 largest of these amalgamated into 5. In the same period the total number of London clearing banks was reduced from 17 to 11.[15] As for the private banks, only six survived the war. The concentration of banking power arising from amalgamation fostered a fear of monopoly in the financial field, and led to the introduction of the Joint Stock Banks (Amalgamations Control) Bill of April 1919. This Bill would have made consolidation subject to approval of the Treasury and the Board of Trade. The Bill was never passed, but the mere discussion of it was enough to check the movement toward concentration of banking.

In the early postwar years, interest rates on government securities were lower than rates on commercial loans, and the wartime growth of government obligations in bank portfolios brought a lower average return on bank assets. Such a development is not inconsistent with a rising rate of return on bank capital, when, as in this case, assets are rising relative to capital. The spread between rates on government securities and those on commercial loans may explain the increased competition for commercial paper after the war, both among the joint stock banks themselves and between those banks and other financial institutions. The competition among the banks took the form of an increase in the number of branch offices and bidding for deposits through the interest allowance.

Prior to the war the banks had acted merely as agents in the marketing of new issues, but after the war they acted increasingly as principals. They also invaded the acceptance market, arguing that with the growth of corporate organization in trade the personal contacts of the merchant bankers were less essential to the business of accepting bills. During the twenties, advances generally formed a somewhat higher proportion of

---

[15] Bank amalgamations, which usually resulted in the writing down of capital, are a partial explanation of the decline in the ratio of capital to deposits from 10 percent at the beginning of the war to 6 percent at the end, and the concomitant rise in the ratio of deposits to total liabilities from 84 percent in 1913 to 91 percent in 1918. However, the simple fact that deposits increased without a commensurate increase in capitalization for banks in general is undoubtedly the major factor in these relationships.

deposits than before the war, probably as a result of the gradual displacement of commercial paper by bank overdrafts.

In the thirties, there was a decline in bank advances relative to total assets. This decline can be explained in part by the efforts of the acceptance houses to reintroduce acceptances as a credit instrument in domestic trade, and partly by the increasing importance of self-finance in British industry. Postwar reconstruction in England brought greater use of the corporate organization, and greater concentration of industrial enterprises. The new giant corporations relied more and more on self-finance, building up their liquid funds out of undistributed profits. This tendency toward self-finance becomes more noticeable still when the composition of the bank's advances is analyzed.[16] The most striking feature is the small percentage figures for such important industries as textiles, "heavy" industries, leather, rubber, and chemicals, and the decline of these figures over the period 1930-38. Most of what they lost, however, was gained by the item "other advances," which are primarily personal and professional loans.

In order to recover some of the lost market for advances, the banks departed somewhat from their policy of making only short-term self-liquidating loans of moderate size, by occasionally granting large advances for capital expansion, in the expectation of repayment out of subsequent capital issues. In general, however, the banks continued to adhere to their traditional principles.

Investments declined somewhat during the twenties, both in absolute volume and as a share of total assets; at the same time Treasury bills averaged higher than commercial bills, despite the reduction of the floating debt and the consequent contraction of banks' holdings of Treasury bills. With the onslaught of the great depression, the volume of Treasury bills in bank portfolios rose, while commercial bills dropped sharply and investments began to increase again.

Discount Market

The outbreak of war in 1914 caused a great dislocation in the London bill market, mainly because of the importance of England's trade with Germany, and also because of the market's complete unpreparedness for the war. In addition to the emergency measures outlined above, the Bank of England relieved the market of bills whose normal liquidation was rendered impossible by the war.[17]

When the foreign bills outstanding had been liquidated, the market

---

[16] For figures on bank advances see Appendix Table C.
[17] For a brief description of the measures taken, see W. A. Brown, *op. cit.*, pp. 21-23.

was left with ample resources but little normal business for their employment. Its liquid funds, however, were soon taken up by Treasury bills; and for the duration of the war the market's main function was the financing of the floating debt. The result was a somewhat increased margin, which varied from $\frac{1}{2}$ to 1 percent, between the bill rate and the money rate, and financial strengthening of the discount companies. The ebb and flow of the market's normal activities subsided almost completely, however; arbitrage was rendered impossible by the pegging of exchange rates; and there never was any need for rediscounting with the Bank of England. The Treasury, as the market's main customer, acquired complete control over the "open market rate," especially from 1916 onward, when it issued Treasury bills "on tap," in unlimited quantities at fixed rates.

The replacement of commercial bills by Treasury bills hit the discount market more directly than the joint stock banks. Not that the discount houses and merchant banks lacked outlets for their funds; Treasury bills served perfectly well for that purpose. But discount houses were no better equipped for handling Treasury bills than were other financial institutions. This fact, together with the growth of public corporations whose relative merits could be more easily judged by non-specialists than was the case for individual enterprises and partnerships, exposed the discount houses to increased competition from the joint stock banks.[18]

While the partial funding of the floating debt and the revival of international trade after the war brought the discount market closer to its normal activities, the market was less important than in prewar years. Other financial centers, especially New York, competed with London in international finance. The internal bill virtually disappeared from the London market, and domestic trade was increasingly financed by the joint stock banks, in the form of overdraft facilities or discounts. Treasury bills became a permanent feature of the discount market; and throughout the period between the two World Wars, Treasury bills made up more than half the total volume of bills held by the London market.

The discount houses were never in serious danger during the depression of the thirties. The Bank of England stood ready to discount bills affected by the German and Austrian standstill agreements, thus remov-

---

[18] As W. A. Brown put it, "The growth in the number of acceptances bearing the names of the joint stock banks (as distinct from merchant banks) seemed to the discount houses to improve the quality of bills. At the same time, however, this change in names together with the predominant importance of the treasury bill was gradually taking from the discount houses their genuine economic function of making a market for, maturing, and judging bills." *Op. cit.*, Vol. I, p. 649.

ing illiquidity of continental bills; and help was given to the discount houses when gilt-edged securities depreciated in 1931-32. However, the discount market was adversely affected by the decline in interest rates in the thirties, especially since (judging from the accounts of the "big three") their portfolios showed little over-all expansion. The partial replacement of bills by short-term bonds in the discount houses' portfolios was no doubt a response to the declining rate on the former, and may explain the rise in net profits of the "big three" after 1933. The depression also resulted in further contraction of international trade, and further substitution of Treasury for commercial bills.

Merchant Banks

Most seriously affected by changes in the position and operations of the London discount market were the merchant banks. These houses, more than other financial institutions in Lombard Street, traded upon their personal knowledge of commercial concerns; accordingly, when the importance of this knowledge diminished, their loss was considerable. Similarly, the merchant banks relied heavily on the supremacy of London in international finance, and therefore they suffered the greatest loss from the growing competition and competence of other financial centers and from the decline in international trade during the twenties and thirties.

Not only did the volume of trade bills decline after World War I; their quality deteriorated. Bills drawn by the foreign seller of goods were increasingly replaced by bills drawn by an importer or a bank, representing goods not yet sold. The line of demarcation between trade bills and finance bills became less clear-cut. Moreover, the wartime disruption of trade with the continent, and the loss of direct contact with continental traders, diminished the confidence of the merchant banks in their own judgment of continental firms.

The uncertainty introduced by the war and reconstruction into the acceptance market had two direct consequences. One was the innovation of granting acceptance credits to foreign bankers, as distinct from foreign traders. Another was the tendency for the acceptance houses to reorganize as limited liability corporations; partnerships were becoming too risky for the acceptance business. This revised form of organization probably diminished, rather than enhanced, the reputations of the acceptance houses.

The merchant banks suffered further blows during the depression. From 1928 to 1933, British foreign trade was so sharply contracted that the market for acceptance credit was cut approximately in half; and the expansion of the discount market facilities which had taken place in the twenties, in response to the opportunity for profitable investment in Treasury bills, proved to be excessive. Moreover, during the financial crisis of 1931 acceptance credit granted to continental bankers for short-term financing was used for long-term investment in industry, to the misfortune of the London discount houses. Abandonment of the gold standard in the same year restricted merchant-bank operations abroad. The scale of their operations in the long-term capital market also diminished. Their attempt to recoup losses by reviving the domestic bill market was thwarted by slack business and by a reduction of minimum rates for bank credit below the traditional 5 percent.

Capital Market

During the war years, restrictions were imposed on new issues in the capital market. In 1915, issues were permitted only with the approval of the Treasury; a committee was appointed "'to consider and advise upon applications received by the Treasury for approval of fresh issues of capital.'"[19] The committee, which included the Governor of the Bank of England and a representative of the Board of Trade, was to bar all issues on behalf of foreign borrowers, and to authorize issues on behalf of borrowers at home and within the Empire only when they appeared to be in the public interest. No restrictions were imposed on home investment through private channels, except by urging the purchase of war bonds, but the government had direct control over home investment through allocation of raw materials.

There was widespread recognition that the regular sources of long-term capital for domestic purposes would be unable to meet the greatly increased demands of the reconstruction period. A parliamentary "Committee on Financial Facilities for Trade" was appointed in 1916 to consider this problem; and on recommendation of this committee the British Trade Corporation was founded in an effort to introduce in England the continental system of industrial banking. In 1917 a committee appointed by the Exchequer suggested that the joint stock banks should depart from their traditional short-term lending policy and assist reconstruction by lending on long term to domestic enterprises.

No departure from traditional British banking practice proved to be necessary, however, for the problem was finally solved by adjustments in the capital market. The political uncertainty of the twenties and thirties, together with American competition, decreased the attractiveness of foreign investment, which was also discouraged by the authorities. Finding its main outlet blocked, the new issues market turned to the domestic field for new customers. At the same time the resources

[19] *The Economist,* January 30, 1915, p. 185.

of the capital market were increased. Many investors who before the war lent directly to private firms learned to appreciate the convenience of marketable securities during the war, and looked to the capital

Chart 1—New Issues in the London Capital Market[a]

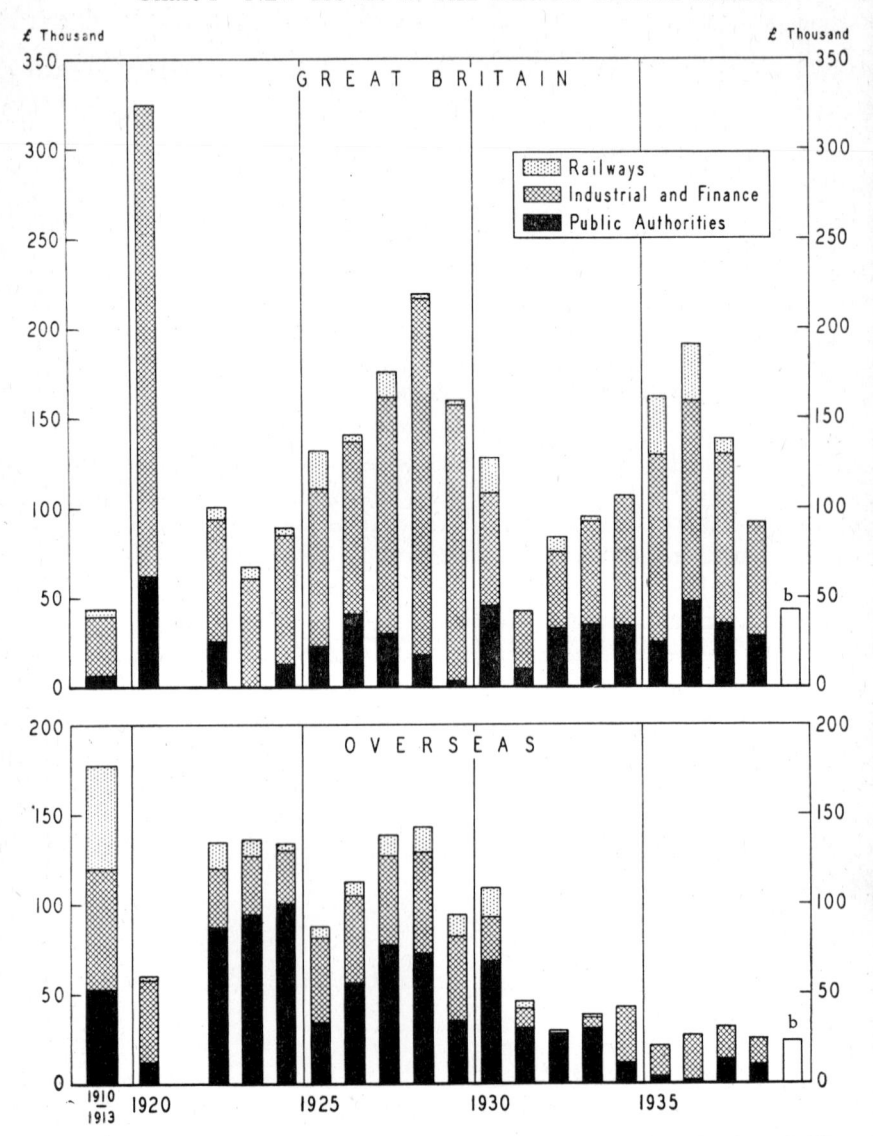

[a] Based on data from *The Statist* and reports from the Midland Bank, Ltd. The data for 1910-13 are an average of annual totals; for 1920 and subsequent years, they are annual totals.

[b] Total figures only are available.

market for investment opportunities when the war-loan campaigns came to an end.

The discrepancy between the geographic distribution of the demand for capital and of the supply of loan funds, arising out of changes in industrial location, led naturally to increasing reliance on the stock exchange, as distinct from personal relations, for the financing of industry. The growth of building societies, insurance companies, and investment trusts for the mobilization of small savings further increased the market's resources, because the funds of these institutions were available for investment in marketable securities. Higher death duties, which increased the importance of having investments in liquid form, may also have played some role in the expansion of domestic security markets.

The London capital market ceased to be primarily an organization for overseas lending and became the main channel for long-term investment at home. The investment houses, specializing by industries, made closer contacts with domestic enterprises; and the industries that came into existence in this period were usually established on a corporate basis. Subsidiary changes in the nature of British long-term lending during the twenties and thirties were the sharp decline of overseas railroad financing compared with prewar years, and the growing scale of borrowing by local public authorities and by local industrial and financial concerns (Chart 1).

It is interesting to note that between the return to the gold standard and the crisis of 1929, Britain regained some of the foreign investment market from the United States.[20] British new foreign lending as a percentage of American rose from 36 in 1925 to 52 in 1928.

Summary

By 1914, Lombard Street had enjoyed half a century of stability and prosperity, interrupted only by minor crises. By 1939, the British financial system had been shaken by 25 years of almost unceasing uncertainty and varying degrees of depression. In view of the enormity of the problems it faced, Lombard Street showed great strength and considerable flexibility in the interwar period; but changes came so fast that the adjustment of the financial organization to these changes necessarily lagged somewhat. At the beginning of World War II the British money market was considerably less secure than it was on the eve of World War I.

---

[20] See W. A. Brown, *op. cit.,* Vol. I, p. 618.

Chapter 3

Government Controls and Lombard Street in World War II

WARTIME economic policy changed the scope and character of Lombard Street's activities in three ways. First, the huge scale of government borrowing resulted in greatly increased investment in government securities by financial institutions; this effect is discussed in Chapter 4. Second, the position of Lombard Street in the British economy was affected by the changed pattern of resource use, brought about by greatly expanded government expenditures, tax policy, direct controls of prices, production, manpower, foreign exchange, etc. Third, the banking system was accorded some new administrative functions in connection with war finance. Government policies related to the second and third of these effects are outlined in the present chapter.

The broad outlines of the changes in the structure of the British economy brought about by wartime policies are indicated in Table 3. Between 1938 and 1945, the proportion of total resources devoted to meeting personal consumption fell from 77.4 percent to 51.8 percent, and the proportion devoted to investment for nonwar purposes fell from 6.5 percent to 1.3 percent. On the other hand, the share utilized in government activities rose from 16.1 percent to 46.9 percent. Net imports of goods and services (which are paid for by borrowing abroad and by the sale of foreign assets) rose over twelvefold, reflecting a contraction of exports in excess of a concurrent decline in imports.

Government expenditures on goods and services in 1944 constituted about half the total value of production ("gross national product"); this was also true in the United States and Canada. Two conditions, however, distinguished the British war effort from the Canadian or American, as far as the magnitude of the financial task was concerned. First, as early as 1940 government expenditures on goods and services exceeded 40 percent of gross national product, whereas this figure was not reached until 1942 in Canada and the United States. Second, because Britain suffered more destruction of plant and more disruption of production throughout the war period, and because she entered the war with less unemployment, less excess capacity, and smaller stock piles than the United States or Canada, the problem of controlling

Table 3—BRITISH NATIONAL RESOURCES AND THEIR DISPOSAL[a]
(in millions)

	1938	1939-44 Average	1945	1946
National income of United Kingdom	£4,671	£7,027	£8,340	£8.200
Borrowing from abroad and sale of assets to foreigners	70	645	875	380
Total resources available for use at home	4,741	7,672	9,215	8,580
National cost of Personal consumption	3,668	4,033	4,777	5,500
Government	765	3,838	4,320	2,330
Net nonwar capital formation at home	308	—199	118	750
Total resources used at home	4,741	7,672	9,215	8,580

[a] From *National Income and Expenditure of the United Kingdom, 1938-1946*, Cmd. 7099 (London, April 1947) p. 5.

inflation was more acute than it was on this continent. In the United States and Canada, fighting a "total war" involved no reduction in the volume of civilian consumption as a whole; but in Britain, civilian consumption declined by about 20 percent.[1] While complete prevention of inflation in the United States and Canada would have involved merely recapturing or sterilizing *increases* in money income, in Britain it would have been necessary to *reduce* disposable income in the hands of civilians. As Chart 2 shows, none of these countries succeeded in preventing wartime inflation altogether; but to achieve even the degree of success she did, Britain was compelled to use heavier taxation and more rigorous direct controls than her North American allies.

TAXATION

From the standpoint of fiscal policy, taxation is generally considered the most desirable instrument for absorbing increases in income.[2] In the six years ending August 31, 1945, Britain met about 46 percent of total central government expenditures by taxes (Table 4)—less than

[1] Combined Production and Resources Board, *The Impact of the War on Civilian Consumption in the United Kingdom, the United States, and Canada* (Washington, September 1945) Table 13, p. 21.
[2] Cf. William Leonard Crum, John F. Fennelly, and Lawrence Howard Seltzer, *Fiscal Planning for Total War* (National Bureau of Economic Research, 1942) Chapters 5, 6, and 7, and especially pp. 137-44.

Chart 2—INDEXES OF COST OF LIVING AND OF WHOLESALE PRICES FOR UNITED KINGDOM, UNITED STATES, AND CANADA[a]
(*August 1939 = 100; logarithmic vertical scale*)

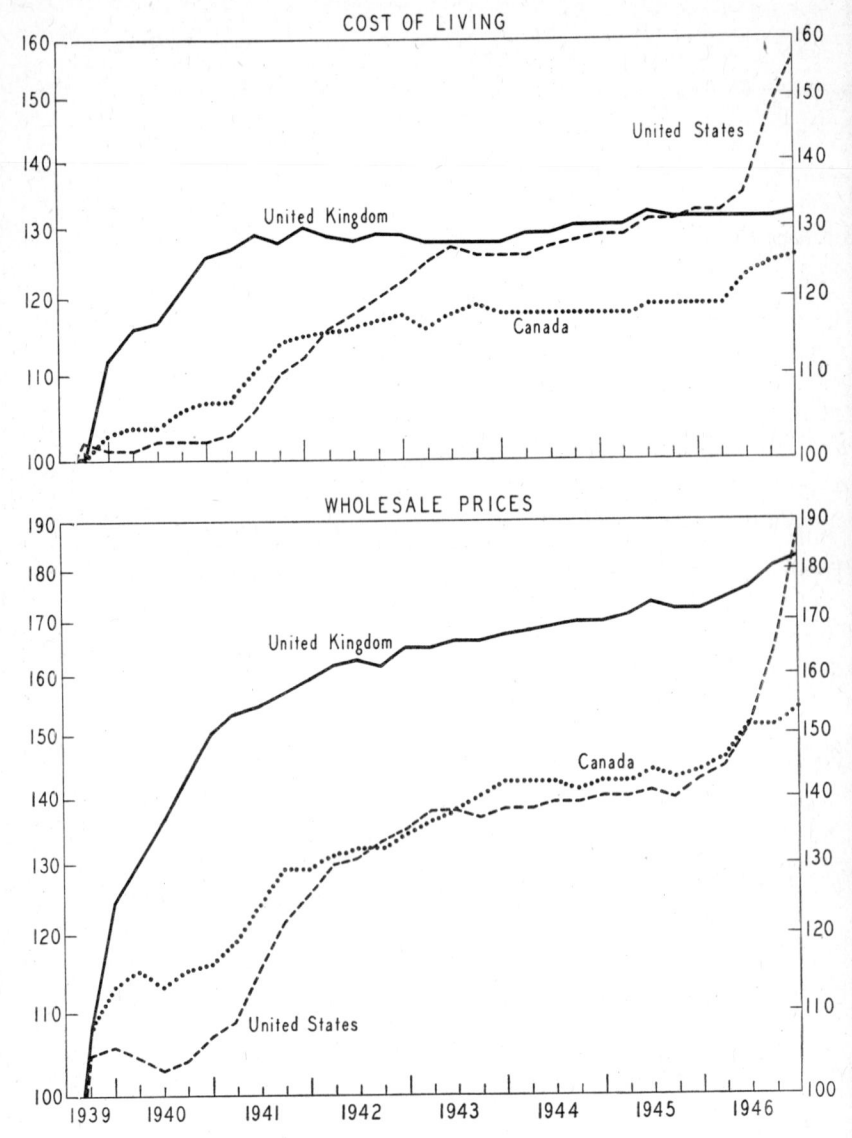

[a] Sources: United Kingdom: *Ministry of Labor Gazette* and *Board of Trade Journal;* United States: *Monthly Labor Review;* Canada: Dominion Bureau of Statistics Reports and Bank of Canada, *Statistical Summary.* Data plotted are for the last month of each quarter.

Table 4—BRITISH GOVERNMENT RECEIPTS AND EXPENDITURES, BY WAR YEARS[a]
(pound figures in millions)

	\multicolumn{6}{c	}{Years Ending August 31}	Total
	1940	1941	1942	1943	1944	1945	
Expenditure							
Interest	£222	£229	£281	£325	£376	£424	£1,856
Supply services	2,368	4,139	4,801	5,409	5,439	5,438	27,594
Other items	17	17	17	16	17	18	101
TOTAL	2,607	4,384	5,099	5,750	5,831	5,880	29,551
Receipts							
Taxation	1,105	1,575	2,166	2,664	3,001	3,130	13,641
Canadian government contribution	....	....	141	83	....	....	225
Other items, including War Damage Fund	43	82	137	104	88	177	631
Net borrowing	1,459	2,727	2,655	2,899	2,742	2,572	15,054
TOTAL	2,607	4,384	5,099	5,750	5,831	5,880	29,551
Taxation as percent of total expenditure	42%	36%	42%	46%	51%	53%	46%

[a] From *The Economist*, Banking Supplement, October 27, 1945, p. 2. In some cases totals do not agree with the sums of the items because of rounding.

Canada but more than the United States. Since taxes in Britain at the beginning of the war period were somewhat heavier than those in the other two countries, the increase in tax revenues was less striking. Tax collections increased less than 200 percent from the first full year of war to the sixth, while American tax collections rose nearly 700 percent and Canadian over 400 percent. In 1944, British central government tax revenues were some 37 percent of national income, while both Canadian and American federal revenues were about 27 percent.[3] When state or provincial and local taxes are added in, the differences among the three countries in this respect are less marked.[4]

[3] Figures for Britain are based on years ending August 31, 1940-45; for the United States, on fiscal years ending June 30, 1940-45; for Canada, on fiscal years ending March 31, 1940-45.
 National income taken at market prices. This figure, which is the income out of which taxes can be paid without capital consumption, is the most relevant one for measuring the burden of taxation.
[4] Cf. R. A. Musgrave and H. L. Seligman, "The Wartime Tax Effort in the United States, the United Kingdom, and Canada," *Federal Reserve Bulletin*, January 1944, p. 18.

Price Control

In contrast to American and Canadian practices in World War II, Britain did not have a single agency to administer price control, or an over-all price ceiling. With few exceptions, the same agency that controlled the supply of a commodity also regulated its price. The original Prices of Goods Act (or POGA) of 1939 was found to be ineffective, and the continued price increases led to a new Goods and Services (Price Control) Act in July 1941. Clothing, furniture, and about 90 percent of the average housewife's expenditure on foods were subject to specific price ceilings by October 1943.

Rationing was much more extensive and much more stringent in Great Britain than it was in either Canada or the United States. It began with foods, under the Rationing Order of December 1939, and spread to a wide range of essential civilian commodities. Clothes rationing was introduced in June 1941, and was applied to virtually all clothing. To facilitate administration of the system, all dealers, except a few small retailers, were required to conduct their ration coupon transactions through coupon accounts held with their banks.

Subsidies also were a more important part of the price control system in Britain than in Canada, and much more important than in the United States. The greatest proportion of direct subsidies was applied to foods which constituted 60 percent of the Ministry of Labor's cost-of-living index;[5] however, prices of certain raw materials also were subsidized. In October 1942, subsidy payments amounted to nearly 10 percent of expenditures on food,[6] and by June 1945, they had risen to nearly 17 percent.

Consumer credit restrictions were less severe than in the United States or Canada, probably because instalment buying is less important in Great Britain and because many consumer durables were very difficult to get under any circumstances. Consumer instalment credit extended by banks was virtually eliminated by the government's request to limit credit to purposes essential to the war effort.

No wage ceiling was imposed in Great Britain. The government felt that stabilization of the cost of living would limit the need for wage increases, and relied upon trade unions and employers not to raise wages unduly. The dangers of an upward wage-price spiral were fully recognized, but the government hesitated to interfere with the normal mechanism of wage negotiation and determination. Many trade unions made use of their wartime bargaining position; average earnings of wage

[5] See *Food Control in Great Britain* (International Labour Office, 1943).
[6] *Bulletin of the Oxford Institute of Statistics,* October 13, 1945.

earners rose about 70 percent and wage rates around 50 percent in six years of war, considerably more than the cost of living, although less than wholesale prices.

Production Control

The policy for reducing the use of plant and materials in civilian production went through three stages. In the first stage many industries producing for the domestic civilian market and some producing for export were designated "controlled industries" and were restricted as to the volume of deliveries they could make to retailers. In some cases, output was prohibited altogether, while in others production was permitted only under license from the Board of Trade.

Limitation led logically to concentration. Reduced output of controlled industries meant that many of them were operating part time or with only part of their plant. In order to check inefficient use of resources, the Concentration of Production Plan was introduced in March 1941. Originally applied to only 30 industries, the coverage was later broadened to include some 70 industries. It is estimated that these measures closed 3,294 factories by August 1943, and released 260,000 workers and 70 million square feet of floor space for war production.[7]

The third step, sometimes labeled "concentration of products," involved stripping production specifications of unnecessary details and reducing the number of grades or types of particular commodities produced. The final development in this branch of industrial regulation was the "utility product," which consisted of "goods sufficiently clearly defined for their prices to be fixed, designed to meet essential needs in a sensible manner, and produced in the most economic manner possible."[8]

Like Canada and the United States, Britain experimented with various types of war contracts. By the end of the fourth year of war, cost-plus-a-percentage-of-cost and cost-plus-a-fixed-fee contracts had been largely abandoned, even when subject to a maximum price, and the "target price" contract (fixed price plus shared excess profits or losses) was also considered unsatisfactory by British authorities. "None [of these types of contract] offered any real incentive to efficient, and therefore, cheap production," reports the British Information Services. All methods suffered "from the difficulties inherent in any attempt to

[7] British Information Services, *Concentration of Consumer Industries and Trade in Britain,* I.D. 279 (December 1943) p. 6.
[8] British Information Services, *"Utility" Production in Britain,* I.D. 404 (April 1943) p. 2.

determine actual and proper costs for specific jobs."[9] Therefore, fixed price contracts were made whenever possible. Critical materials were allotted when contracts were let, and thus the producer was spared the necessity of applying for supplies after an order was received.

Special efforts were made to utilize small concerns, usually as subcontractors. In the months immediately following the great loss of British equipment at Dunkirk, it was considered particularly desirable to take advantage of the ready capacity of small plants, rather than to wait for construction of larger ones which might ultimately be more efficient. These efforts seem to have been attended by considerable success, probably because in Britain small concerns normally play a large role in those industries so important for war production.

Manpower Regulations

Although in Great Britain shortages of manpower caused more concern than shortages of raw materials, it was not until the spring of 1940, when the Emergency Powers (Defense) Act was passed, that manpower regulation was effectively organized. By an amendment to this Act the Minister of Labor and National Service was empowered to "direct any person in the United Kingdom to perform such services in the United Kingdom as may be specified . . . , being services which that person is, in the opinion of the Minister, capable of performing." Under the Essential Work (General Provisions) Order of April 1941, permission of the Ministry was required before a worker could quit or be removed from a job listed in the Minister's Schedule of Reserved Occupations.

Exchange Control

A major financial problem for Britain was to obtain, with a minimum strain on her productive resources, foreign exchange (especially dollars) to pay for vital imports. Britain entered the war with an Exchange Equalization Fund already established, and with several years of experience in operating it. When war seemed inevitable, diminished exports and increased imports were expected to make it difficult to support the pound at the then current rate of $4.68. Accordingly the official sterling rate was allowed to drop for several weeks, and then was established at $4.03. British holders of gold and foreign exchange were required to offer them to the Treasury; the Treasury was authorized to acquire foreign securities held by residents; and export of capital from Britain was forbidden. The Bank of England's gold reserves were

---

[9] British Information Services, *Industrial Mobilization of Great Britain*, I.D. 328 (April 1943) p. 8.

transferred to the Fund, so that all gold in the country could be used to meet an adverse balance of payments.

For several months after the war began, transactions in sterling between residents of other countries were subject to no restrictions, and a considerable spread developed between the "official" and the "free" rate. It was gradually realized, however, that the disposition of sterling balances acquired at free market rates by residents of other countries was a matter of some importance. If such balances were held idle, no strain would be placed on British productive resources; if balances were used to buy British exports, resources would be diverted from war production while relatively few dollars would be provided.[10] On March 26, 1940, foreign holders of sterling balances were forbidden to use them in payment for six major Empire exports: whiskey, furs, tin, rubber, jute, and jute products. These commodities had henceforth to be paid for in foreign currencies or in sterling bought at the official rate. The immediate effect of these provisions was to reduce the demand for free sterling, which fell in price from $3.96 in February to $3.27 in May. In June, restrictions on the use of free sterling were extended to all exports to the United States and Switzerland, but at the same time sales of sterling securities by foreigners were limited. The reduced supply of sterling, and the rush of speculators to cover their positions, brought the free pound up sharply. After September 1940 it remained very close to the official rate.

Exchange control was supplemented by the direct regulation of exports and imports. In the early months of the war, exports were encouraged as a means of obtaining foreign exchange, but insufficiently high priority ratings for men and materials, and shortage of shipping space, made severe inroads into the export trade. A British Export Council was organized with advisory powers, and together with the Board of Trade and the Ministries of Supply and Labor, the Council undertook to confine exports to goods demanded by friendly countries whose exchange was in turn needed by Britain for essential imports. The Ministry of Economic Warfare obtained power to prevent exports altogether if their destination or some other cause made them inexpedient or injurious to the war effort. Imports were under the direction of an Executive Committee for Imports, composed of the President of the Board of Trade, the First Lord of the Admiralty, and the Ministers of Food, Supply, and Aircraft Production. This Committee limited imports to essential goods and services, regulated the placing of orders, and arranged for shipping space.

[10] See F. W. Paish, "The Free Sterling Rate," *Memorandum No. 82 of the Royal Economic Society*, May 1940, p. 11.

Britain's most difficult wartime period with regard to foreign exchange was from the beginning of the war until early in 1941. From September 1, 1939 to December 31, 1940, Britain lost £575 million in gold and dollar resources, primarily to the United States, Canada, and Newfoundland.[11] Substantial amounts of Canadian and American securities held by British investors were requisitioned and sold. Net borrowing abroad plus net sales of foreign assets and financial claims in 1939 and 1940 amounted to more than £1 billion.[12]

During 1941, the sterling area deficit of Canadian dollars was financed largely by the accumulation of sterling balances, and in March of that year Lend-Lease began to operate. A year later came the Canadian billion dollar gift; at the same time, Canadian sterling balances were converted into a $700 million interest-free loan;[13] and with the United States in the war, Lend-Lease was in full swing. Obtaining foreign exchange then was not a major problem of British war finance, although the means of obtaining it had serious postwar implications.

Effects of Wartime Controls on Lombard Street

Fiscal policy, price and exchange controls, and production and manpower regulations inevitably altered the functioning of the money market; their net effect was to reduce the usual demands for credit. Higher taxes in themselves diverted income from other uses—consumer spending, saving, and private investment—and reduced net return on capital; they therefore tended to restrict the demand for both consumer and commercial credit. Production and manpower regulations, by limiting the resources available for nonwar production, had a still more forthright effect on credit requirements of companies concerned with normal peacetime pursuits. The bulk of war construction and of war production was financed directly by the government. Price ceilings and rationing, and consumer credit restrictions, directly diminished the demand for consumer credit, and indirectly contracted the demand for commercial credit by reducing the volume of business transactions. Direct procurement and distribution by the government tended in itself to reduce the credit needs of distributors. The sharp contraction in physical volume of foreign trade and the greatly expanded role of

---

[11] "Gold and Dollar Resources of the United Kingdom," *Federal Reserve Bulletin*, February 1941, pp. 99-101.

[12] *National Income and Expenditure of the United Kingdom, 1938-1945* (Cmd. 6784, April 1946) p. 8.

[13] Canadian aid to Britain is discussed more fully in Benjamin H. Higgins, *Canada's Financial System in War* (National Bureau of Economic Research, Financial Research Program, Occasional Paper 19, April 1944) pp. 32-33.

governments in financing foreign trade, greatly reduced the demand for private finance from this quarter. Exchange control limited the volume of foreign lending.

True, wartime controls gave Lombard Street some new jobs, notably coupon-banking and administration of exchange control regulations. These new jobs were important in the administration of Britain's wartime economy, but from the banks' point of view they hardly offset the effects of the contraction in normal banking operations. However, war finance had another and more powerful effect on banking activities; it resulted in a huge demand for credit from the government itself.

Chapter 4

Lending to Finance the War

IN BRITAIN, as in other warring countries, lending institutions found themselves more and more heavily involved in government finance as the war progressed. As outlined in Chapter 3, financial concerns assisted the government with exchange control, credit restrictions, and rationing, and provided short-term credits to meet swelling tax payments. They also participated in the financing of war industries by making direct loans. Their chief wartime function, however, was to make loans to the government and to help it borrow from the public.

GOVERNMENT BORROWING

The government's demand for funds to finance war industries and military operations in part replaced normal peacetime demands, but in part was superimposed upon them. The net effect was to raise the total demand for credit, and to concentrate it in the hands of the government. Lending institutions accordingly had to adapt their operations to the larger volume and changed nature of the demand.

The growth and composition of the British government's wartime borrowing are shown in Tables 5 and 6. Short-term obligations (less than one year) were the chief instrument of new indebtedness, providing more than half the increase in total marketable securities. At first sight it appears that Britain made less use of intermediate-term (1 to 5 years) and long-term obligations, and greater use of short-term borrowing than did the United States and Canada; at the end of the fiscal year 1946, 53 percent of the increase in British marketable public securities [1] consisted of obligations maturing within one year, compared with 38 percent in the United States and 15 percent in Canada. However, much of the increase in British floating debt comprised "ways-and-means advances" and Treasury bills. Ways-and-means advances consisted partly of loans to the Treasury from other government departments, and the tap issue of Treasury bills was held almost entirely by government departments, government insurance funds, the Exchange Equalization Account, and overseas governments, holding sterling balances. Altogether, nearly half of the floating debt was intra-

[1] Including Treasury deposit receipts.

Table 5—Annual Increases in British Debt, by War Years[a]
(in millions)

	\multicolumn{6}{c}{Years Ending August 31}	
	1940	1941	1942	1943	1944	1945	Total
War Loans Raised							
Bonds							
3% War loan	£302.5	....	....	....	....	....	£302.5
3% Defense bonds	146.5	£181.0	£151.4	£127.1	£113.8	£73.5	793.3
3% National defense loan[b]	....	121.9	....	123.6	....	....	245.5
3% Funding loan[b]	....	....	242.5	....	....	....	242.5
3% Terminable annuity[b]	....	....	....	120.0	474.1	342.3	936.4
2½% National war bonds	186.0	750.3	534.3	686.8	651.1	262.3	3,070.7
3% Savings bonds	....	291.0	545.1	501.5	391.2	385.4	2,114.2
1¾% Exchequer bonds	....	....	....	....	....	326.8	326.8
Tax reserve certificates	....	....	346.9	203.7	98.2	108.3	757.1
National saving certificates	124.5	185.4	213.4	272.6	247.1	126.4	1,169.5
"Other debt"	18.8	57.0	259.2	37.3	5.5	Dr 16.9	361.1
Total	778.3	1,586.6	2,292.8	2,072.6	1,981.0	1,608.1	10,319.6
Floating Debt							
Ways-and-means advances							
Public departments	11.5	153.2	40.5	58.8	77.7	188.6	530.3
Bank of England	....	1.0	Dr 1.0	....	....	0.8	0.8
Treasury bills							
Tender	336.0	134.0	5.0	195.0	260.0	260.0	1,190.0
Tap	424.3	482.7	143.0	224.0	306.6	86.0	1,666.6
Treasury deposit receipts	30.0	483.0	182.5	349.5	433.5	707.0	2,185.5
Total	801.8	1,253.9	370.0	827.3	1,077.8	1,242.4	5,573.2
Grand Total	£1,580.1	£2,840.5	£2,662.8	£2,899.9	£3,058.8	£2,850.5	£15,892.8

[a] From *The Economist*, Banking Supplement, October 27, 1945, p. 2. In some cases, totals do not agree with the sums of the items because of rounding.
[b] Invested by National Debt Commissioners on behalf of savings banks.

Table 6—Maturity Distribution of Marketable Government Securities at End of Fiscal Years for United Kingdom, United States, and Canada[a]
(pound and dollar figures in millions)

Maturity	United Kingdom	United States	Canada
Within 1 Year			
1939	£992	$5,094	$679
1946	7,126	62,091	2,499
Increase as percent of increase in total public marketable debt	53%	38%	15%
1 to 5 Years			
1939	£353	$13,394	$1,024
1946	1,343	35,055	4,738
Increase as percent of increase in total public marketable debt	9%	14%	27%
Over 5 Years			
1939	£5,476	$20,927	$2,735
1946	9,896	92,501	10,078
Increase as percent of increase in total public marketable debt	38%	48%	58%

[a] From compilations prepared for the National Bureau of Economic Research by the Board of Governors of the Federal Reserve System and the Bank of Canada. Although non-marketable, Treasury deposit receipts are included for the United Kingdom and Treasury deposit certificates for Canada, because of their similarity to Treasury bills. Fiscal years for the United Kingdom and Canada end on March 31 and for the United States on June 30.

governmental, and exclusion of the intra-governmental debt would reverse the relative positions of Britain and the United States and bring Britain and Canada much closer together. It should also be noted that when war broke out the share of total debt consisting of obligations with maturities of five years or less was much smaller in Britain than in the other two countries. By the end of fiscal 1946, however, the proportion had increased so that such obligations were 46 percent of the British marketable debt, compared with 42 percent in Canada and 51 percent in the United States.

Treasury bills—tender and tap—were the main instrument of floating indebtedness, constituting over half of the total wartime floating debt. After the third year of war, however, increases of floating debt consisted chiefly of Treasury deposit receipts ("TDR's"), just as the growth of Canadian short-term debt was composed mainly of Treasury deposit certificates. This new form of government security was introduced in Great Britain in July 1940, bore interest at the rate of $1\frac{1}{8}$ percent per annum for six months, compared with 1 percent per annum for three months on Treasury bills, and was issued only to English and Scottish banks.[2] The Treasury stated its requirements of Treasury deposits every week, and allotment was made by agreement among these banks. The TDR's were non-negotiable. They could be redeemed prior to maturity "in case of emergency," subject to a discount at Bank rate, but it probably would have required a substantial "emergency" to induce the banks to use this privilege. Furthermore, TDR's could be tendered in payment for purchases of government obligations other than Treasury bills, whether on the bank's own account or on their customers' accounts, and after the first year or so this privilege was exercised frequently and substantially, especially during war loan campaigns.

From the Treasury's viewpoint, there were several reasons for the substitution of TDR's for Treasury bills. The new system enabled the Treasury to borrow directly from the banks for six months, at a rate only about $\frac{1}{8}$ of 1 percent higher than the 3-month Treasury bill rate, and perhaps permitted more exact adjustment of revenues to outflows. Since the TDR's were non-negotiable, and the penalty on encashment prior to maturity for purposes other than conversion to government long-terms was a deterrent to liquidation, they afforded the Treasury control over its balances. At the same time, the prior encashment facility meant that if necessary the banks could draw on the Treasury's own balance at the Bank of England, and thus avoid undue pressure on the money market which would result from the transfer of public loan subscriptions to the Exchequer.

The tax reserve certificate was another new short-term credit instrument which grew in importance. It performed much the same function as the United States tax certificate,[3] being designed to divert to the Treasury deposits held idle in anticipation of tax payments. However, the British certificates, the income from which was tax-free, bore 1 percent interest if used for taxes, while the United States certificates, taxable as regards income, bore interest of from $\frac{1}{2}$ of 1 percent to 2 percent. Since under the British income tax the standard rate was 50 percent of taxable income, a tax-free 1 percent was equivalent to a taxable minimum of 2 percent gross. For someone in the 80 percent tax bracket, the tax-free 1 percent was equivalent to 5 percent gross. Thus the tax certificates were an attractive investment, particularly for businesses and for people in the upper income groups, and sub-

---

[2] Cf. W. T. C. King and Paul Bareau, *The London Money Market and Banking System in the Second Eighteen Months of War* (National Institute of Economic and Social Research, London, 1942) and Charlotte Muller, "British War Finance and the Banks," *The Journal of Business of the University of Chicago,* April 1943, p. 86.

[3] Issues of American tax certificates were discontinued in June 1943, when Treasury tax savings notes of Series A were discontinued, and Treasury notes of Tax Series C were redesignated Treasury savings notes of Series C.

scriptions to them may not have been entirely from otherwise idle. funds. The tax-free feature was attacked on the grounds that for individuals in the 47½ percent surtax bracket, the return on tax certificates was equivalent to 40 percent on any taxable security, while for those liable only to the standard income tax rate it was equal to just 2 percent.

In marketing long-term issues, the British attempted to provide securities suitable for "large" and "small" savings, and special emphasis was laid on the latter. The distinction was based on the size of the individual subscription expected and on the income group that the obligation was meant to reach. The chief differences between the two types of security were their tax status and denomination. National savings certificates and national defense bonds were small in denomination, and therefore regarded as particularly suitable for small investors. The 15s. savings certificates yielded a tax-free 3.17 percent if held to maturity and were freely redeemable; holdings were limited to 500 certificates. The £1 savings certificates yielded only 1.41 percent free of taxes, were cashable only after 90 days, and were limited to holdings of 250 certificates. The 3 percent defense bonds were subject to tax, were cashable at 6 months' notice, and were limited to holdings of £1,000. The £1 issue of savings certificates and the 3 percent national defense bonds were designed for small savers who had acquired their full quota of 15s. savings certificates. All issues intended for small savers were sold through Post Offices, Trustee Savings Banks, and Savings Groups. For statistical purposes, the government also considered increased balances in Post Offices and Trustee Savings Banks as small savings.

The obligations aimed at large investors consisted of the tap issues of 3 percent savings bonds, 2½ percent war bonds, and 1¾ percent Exchequer bonds, which were sold through the Bank of England and on the Stock Exchange by existing holders. These were available in large denominations (£50-£100) at the Bank of England and smaller denominations (£10-£25) at the Post Offices and Trustee Savings Banks.

Needless to say, any individual investor, whatever his income, probably obtained his quota of tax-free obligations before buying others; for taxpayers, the 3.17 percent tax-free yield on 15s. savings certificates was equivalent to a minimum of 6 1/3 percent on other securities. Because of the restricted quota on issues designed for small savers, and the greater inconvenience of the smaller denominations, institutions and people with high incomes no doubt invested mainly in other issues. It does not follow automatically that the bulk of "small" savings came from families with small incomes. Statistical inquiries conducted in 1942 suggest that less than half of small savings up to that time came from the lower income groups. However, as working class earnings continued to rise, and medium and large investors reached the statutory limit to holdings of savings certificates and defense bonds, it seems likely that the proportion of these issues held by the lower income groups was somewhat higher in the later years of the war.[4]

The stimulation of public saving was entrusted mainly to the National War Savings Committee, an outgrowth of the Savings Movement which was launched in 1916 and which continued throughout the interwar period. The Committee, set up in November 1939, consisted of members appointed by the Treasury, representing interested agencies and organizations, and eighteen members elected by the Local Savings Committees, one for each of the twelve regions and each of the six great cities. There was an official staff of 1,600, including a Commissioner for each of the twelve regions, supplemented by some 600,000 voluntary workers. As the British Information Services put it, the local savings groups were the "cells" of the movement.[5] These groups were organized by industries, schools, neighborhoods, and branches of the Armed Forces. The number of such groups grew from 41,500 before the war to over 320,000 in July 1944, at which time their membership covered one-third of the total population. The Committee relied mainly on a steady flow of reminders of the need for saving, and except for the War Loan of March 1940, all long-term issues were on tap. However, the Committee did organize a series of special drives, similar to the American and Canadian war loan campaigns.

Lending by the Bank of England

War brought closer collaboration between the Treasury and the Central Bank in all belligerent countries. The Treasury in Great Britain, as in the United States and Canada, adopted a deliberate policy of "pegging" the interest structure at a low level,[6] and the cooperation of the Central Bank was essential to this policy in all three countries.

In accordance with traditional practice in time of crisis, the Bank

---

[4] Cf. M. Kalecki, "The Problem of 'Small' Savings," *Bulletin of the Oxford Institute of Statistics,* Vol. 5, No. 16, November 20, 1943.

[5] British Information Services, *The British War Savings Campaign,* I.D. 395 (April 1943).

[6] In a statement to the House of Commons on April 12, 1943, Sir Kingsley Wood remarked, "During this war we have stabilized the general complex of interest rates at a level so low as would have been thought impossible by anyone who merely based himself on the experience of the last war."

of England raised its Bank rate shortly before the outbreak of hostilities —from 2 to 4 percent. However, in keeping with the Treasury policy of maintaining a low rate of interest, the Bank rate was reduced to 3 percent on September 28, 1939, and to 2 percent on October 29, 1939, where it was held throughout the war. With world conditions as they were, it is unlikely that a higher Bank rate would have increased the supply of foreign exchange, either by attracting capital or by increasing exports.[7] In any case, responsibility for controlling foreign exchange rates was taken over by the Treasury's Exchange Equalization Fund, and the Bank served merely as the principal agent for operation of the Fund. During the war, central banking policy was determined mainly by domestic considerations.

In war as in peace, the Bank acted as the government's agent in the flotation of loans. It also lent directly to the government through ways-and-means advances and purchases of government obligations. However, since the Treasury in World War II borrowed from the commercial banks directly by means of TDR's, Bank ways-and-means advances were an insignificant aspect of war finance, and total Bank lending to the government was small.

By far the most important function of the Bank was to provide reserves to the joint stock banks, to help them buy government obligations, and to carry on as much of their traditional task of financing trade and industry as was compatible with a maximum war effort. In the years between the two World Wars, the Bank altered the volume of bank reserves according to the demand for credit from the commercial banks and to the Bank's own canons of sound finance, including its judgments regarding the proper balance between protecting the gold standard and reducing unemployment. During the war, the commercial banks lent to the government according to Treasury needs, and to industry, commerce, and consumers according to Treasury advice; the necessary reserves for these operations were provided by the Bank of England, by buying Treasury bills. As a rule the commercial banks met any stringency resulting from an exceptionally large issue of TDR's, or from heavy revenue payments to the Treasury, by calling funds from

---

[7] In World War I, likewise, the Bank consulted the Treasury when changes in the rate were made. The preponderance of Treasury bills in the discount market weakened the Bank's control of the open market rate on bills, and transferred much of the power over market rates to the Treasury. As stated in Chapter 2, shortly after the outbreak of war the Bank rate was reduced from its crisis peak of 10 percent to 5 percent, and it remained between 5 and 6 percent for the duration of the war. Had the financial authorities been concerned only with domestic policy and felt no need to use the discount rate to assist in supporting the pound, the rate might have been reduced further.

the discount houses, which were in turn compelled to sell Treasury bills to the Bank of England. Sometimes, however, the Bank bought bills directly from the commercial banks, usually at the market rate. In either case, the cash that the Bank paid for bills found its way into the commercial banks' tills or into their deposits with the Bank of England, thus increasing reserve ratios.

In September 1939, virtually all of the Issue Department's gold reserve (£279 million) was transferred to the Exchange Equalization Account. "Lending" by the Issue Department in connection with currency increases constituted nearly 87 percent of the Bank's wartime lending to the government. The increase in the Banking Department holdings of government securities was only £159 million to the end of the war period, less than 1 percent of the rise in national debt. Holdings by the Issue Department, on the other hand, rose by £1,054 million, just 7 percent of the increase in national debt. Thus, total central bank loans to the government were only 8 percent of the increase in debt. Over the fiscal years 1939-45, the Federal Reserve Banks absorbed 9 percent of the increase in the United States national debt, and the Bank of Canada 14 percent of the Canadian.

Lending by the Joint Stock Banks

The role of the joint stock banks in war finance was threefold: to buy government obligations themselves, to assist in the sale of government securities to institutional and other investors, and to make direct advances to war industries. The banks served as agents for the sale of war bonds, and they did much to stimulate and facilitate public subscriptions. Rates of interest paid on bank deposits were reduced below the prewar level early in the war, and were subject to a maximum of 1 percent. The banks likewise refrained from lending for personal purposes and nonessential undertakings. The embargo on new capital issues applied to borrowing from banks with the intention of repaying the loan out of proceeds from a subsequent issue of securities; and while the law applied to the borrower's action and not to the lender's, the banks undertook to scrutinize the purposes of loans and to refuse them if they were not satisfied with their legality.

The commercial banks absorbed only 15 percent of the wartime increase in national debt; this percentage was moderately lower than that in Canada and less than half as much as in the United States. Commercial bank holdings of governments included intermediate- and long-term as well as short-term securities. During the war years, holdings of intermediate- and long-term governments increased markedly, both absolutely and relative to total assets, and when the war ended they comprised 22 percent of assets of the London clearing banks. This increase was largely the result of the banks' subscription of about £300 million to the first two loans. Since the Treasury, with the co-operation of the Bank of England, provided the banks with reserves and at the same time limited lending to business, the banks needed no direct urging to induce them to buy government securities during the war. During the last three years of the war, however, the banks' portfolios of long-terms were virtually constant, reflecting the government's continually increasing success in placing war loans with the general public.

In the first year of war, the banks followed the pattern of World War I by increasing their bill holdings considerably. After August 1940 bills were largely replaced by TDR's, which in August 1945 comprised 39 percent of the commercial banks' total assets, contrasted with 4 percent for Treasury bills. The banks' holdings of bills represented less than 5 percent of total Treasury bills outstanding at that time.

As mentioned above, TDR's had somewhat limited liquidity. They could be redeemed prior to maturity, subject to the penalty of discounting at Bank rate, in case of emergency; but discounting a $1\tfrac{1}{8}$ percent security at the 2 percent Bank rate would, according to *The Economist,* "be too expensive, and perhaps too undignified, a procedure to commend itself to the banks, except on very abnormal occasions." [8] Bills were therefore a better reserve against such contingencies as tax payments by depositors. On the other hand, the TDR's had the advantage of being redeemable at par to pay for longer-term governments bought by a bank itself or by a customer. Consequently, subscriptions to war loans by depositors could be met by temporary depletion of the banks' TDR holdings instead of by temporary decreases in reserves; and the yield on TDR's was slightly higher than that on Treasury bills.

At the outbreak of war, it was an open question whether or not the Treasury's request that the banks curtail advances for "nonessential purposes" covered borrowing for the purchase of war loans. When the March 1940 war loan was tendered, the banks offered to grant facilities to their customers for subscribing to the issue, but such facilities were to be granted only for a very short period and only after careful consideration of each case. It is believed that very little use was made of the banks' offer, and by February 1942 the Treasury had expressly requested the public not to borrow for the purpose of buying war bonds.

[8] Quoted by Donald F. Heatherington in "British Banking and Finance," *Foreign Commerce Weekly,* July 24, 1943, p. 6.

However, the banks helped to finance the discount market's holdings of Treasury bills. Most of these were held on day-to-day money loaned from the commercial banks. The bulk of Treasury bills was held by government departments and various official and semi-official bodies, such as government insurance agencies, the Bank of England, and Dominion and other sterling-area central banks.

The banks not only assisted the Treasury with war finance but they also had their usual task of providing trade and industry with short-term credit. The traditional policy of the banks was one of making "self-liquidating" advances and of "not interfering in their clients' business affairs" by keeping most of their loans down to "average size."[9] When the war began the banks were asked by the government to extend short-term credit liberally to government contractors and subcontractors, even if this meant relaxation of peacetime standards of "sound finance." In order to aid the banks in this part of their contribution to the war effort, and to provide them with ready means of verifying the existence and exact status of their customers' war contracts, liaison officers were appointed by the banks to the supply ministries, and by the supply ministries to the banks. They served as a channel for informal discussion; and this system enabled the joint stock banks to extend overdraft facilities to war-essential industries very much in excess of what would normally be considered safe.

The government undertook to finance directly a large part of war industry. A good share of the armaments production was carried on by Royal Ordnance Factories entirely owned and operated by the government.[10] Other war plants were government owned but privately operated. In some cases the government supplied the fixed capital to these concerns, the private contractors receiving a "reasonable profit" on the working capital that they provided. In other cases the government supplied all the capital, and paid the contractors a fee for construction based on cost, and a fee for management based on output. From the beginning of the war to the end of 1942, the government extended capital assistance amounting to nearly £293.6 million.[11] Ex-

---

[9] According to evidence before the Macmillan Committee in 1930, the average overdraft of Lloyds Bank was £10,900 to £15,600 for industrial credits, £561 for personal and professional loans, and £1,151 for advances as a whole. (*Minutes of Evidence Taken before the Committee on Finance and Industry*, London, 1931, Vol. I, p. 128.)

[10] These plants turned out 60 or 70 percent of the explosives and 66⅔ percent of the guns produced in Great Britain (Report of the Minister of Supply to the House of Commons, August 5, 1942, House of Commons *Debates*, 1942, Cols. 1071-83).

[11] Select Committee on National Expenditures, Sixteenth Report, Session 1942-43, *State-owned Assets*, pp. 4-6.

cept for armaments, however, most war plants were privately owned and operated. The government aided long-term financing of these private firms by permitting them to raise money in the capital market, and by allowing generous rates of amortization for tax purposes.

The rapidity of expansion, the special risks of war operations, and the novelty of type and size of war contracts, created short-term credit requirements of a sort not easily met by traditional banking procedures. Accordingly, the supply ministries made increasing use of monthly progress payments, whereby the government extended funds, monthly, on work in progress under war contracts. Such payments ran as high as 90 percent of total expenditures incurred by a contractor during a month. The payments were made against "progress certificates," which testified to the exact expenditures incurred in connection with a government contract, and were signed by the firm's auditor or accountant.

Government short-term finance through progress payments was so general as to leave little scope for bank credit. Bank loans were used mainly for tiding over firms between the actual outlay and the next monthly progress payment. The wartime decline in advances indicates that the banks financed only a small fraction of the war industries' short-term credit requirements, and that this was insufficient to offset the diminishing requirements of civilian industries.

Lending by the Discount Market

The diminishing importance of the commercial bill in the London discount market during the twenties and thirties helps explain the market's smooth transition to war conditions. The war was anticipated, and as it drew nearer the acceptance houses required customers importing through German ports to have ample sterling funds in their accounts. Nevertheless, the government took stringent precautions on the day that war was declared to prevent a repetition of the panic that occurred in the exchange market at the outbreak of World War I. A government War Risks Insurance Office was opened, and the Treasury instructed the Bank of England to accommodate acceptance houses that might be called upon to meet their liabilities while deprived of the necessary remittances from their clients. This accommodation was offered at the punitive cost of 2 percent above Bank rate, with a minimum of 6 percent.

After the outbreak of war, the market's commercial business declined steadily, owing partly to Germany's occupation of the continent, partly to bulk purchases by government departments, and partly to the Lend-Lease Agreement, which took care of a large portion of Great Britain's trade with the United States. Defense regulations modified the nature of some acceptances by forbidding loans to nonresidents. This necessitated the replacement of acceptance credits by sight credits, or acceptances fully covered by sterling accounts. As in World War I, Treasury bills assumed paramount importance in the discount market, and the Treasury again acquired a large degree of influence on the open market bill rate.

After a short flurry when war broke out the rate on three-month Treasury bills was held virtually constant at about 1.01 percent, compared with the rate on day-to-day loans, which was around 1 percent, leaving a slender margin for the market. However, on short- and intermediate-term bonds, which comprised an ever-growing share of discount market investments during the war, the profit margin was considerably greater.

Lending by the Capital Market

An embargo was imposed on new capital issues under "Defense (Finance) Regulations" at the very beginning of the war. Issues in excess of £5,000 in any one year were made illegal, except when specifically approved by the Treasury. "Issue" was defined broadly, to include mortgages and bank loans to be repaid from the proceeds of public issues, as well as public offerings of securities for sale or subscription. Blanket exemptions included issues involving no new cash subscriptions (such as those made only to amalgamate two or more companies or to rearrange a firm's capital), issues to any government department, and issues to provide direct security for bank advances. Otherwise "the issue of new securities other than Government war loans" had to be confined to "issues to raise money for essential services and enterprises or to provide for obligatory repayments of maturing debt",[12] as determined by the Treasury. Issues by firms operating in the United Kingdom or the Empire were allowed only if they were "advisable in the national interest," while issues for undertakings outside the Empire were permitted only "in special circumstances in cases of urgent necessity."

A Capital Issues Committee, composed of representatives of the business organizations most concerned with the capital market, reviewed applications for permission to float an issue, and made recommendations to the Treasury based on its findings. The majority of actual applications (as distinct from inquiries) were approved. The concerns allowed to go to the market for capital were mainly engineering and public utility enterprises.

[12] Quoted by W. F. Crick in *An Outline of Wartime Financial Control in the United Kingdom* (London, 1941) p. 11.

In November 1942, a new regulation was added prohibiting agreements to do, at some future date (when regulations would be relaxed), anything that was then illegal under the Defense (Finance) Regulations.[13] Special regulations were also issued at various times during the war to prevent payment of interest on capital items to enemy interests. Disposal of securities in which there was a nonresident interest was made subject to license in the spring of 1940, and later additional controls were imposed on collection of both income and capital items on securities belonging to residents of such neutral countries as Switzerland, Sweden, Spain, and Portugal.[14]

General Results of British Wartime Borrowing

Like the United States and Canada, Britain was able to carry through its huge wartime borrowing operations and at the same time to reduce interest rates. The decline in the average interest cost of the war debt, which fell from 3.1 percent in March 1939 to 2.4 percent in March 1945, was mainly a result of the change in debt structure.[15] The latter figure compares with 1.9 percent in the United States and 2.6 percent in Canada.

Despite the reductions in British interest rates after 1931 (Table 7), Britain entered the war with both short- and long-term rates on government debt somewhat higher than in Canada and considerably higher than in the United States. Prices of British long-term securities were then abnormally low, however, and they subsequently recovered to levels midway between the American and Canadian. Except for an initial flurry when war broke out, and for a brief period in the spring and summer of 1943 when allied military successes led to some shifting from government to other securities, the yields on long-terms followed a downward course throughout the war. As Table 7 shows, yields on corporate bonds and industrial securities moved in sympathy so far as wartime trends are concerned. Short-term rates rose sharply at the very beginning of the war, but promptly fell again and remained quite stable throughout the balance of the war period.

---

[13] Order-in-Council S. R. & O. 1942, No. 2096.

[14] Cf. *The Banker,* November 1940, pp. 84 ff.; April 1940, pp. 139 ff.; June 1940, article by J. Mead, "Bank Lending and the Capital Issues Control," pp. 9-18; April 1941, article by C. J. Shimmins, "Securities Work in Wartime"; January 1944 and August 1944, *passim.*

[15] The basis of this statement is a computation of the average interest cost that would have prevailed on the debt shown for 1945 in Table 7, at the interest rates prevailing for the three main categories of debt in 1939.

A second major feature of Britain's fiscal policy was the large proportion of the wartime increase in debt in Britain which was placed outside the banking system. Approximately 75 percent of the increase in debt from 1938 to 1945 was sold outside the Bank of England and the joint stock banks; comparable figures for Canada and the United States are approximately 77 and 60 percent, respectively. The reasons for these differences, in terms of the inducements offered and the preferences of investors to place funds in government securities, and the effects of the loan campaigns on the relative degree and timing of inflation in the three countries, are interesting and important subjects for analysis but lie outside the scope of this paper. There can be little doubt, however, that sales of government obligations to the public rather than to the banks helped to limit private expenditures during the war, and that the success of the loan campaigns was a factor in the relative stability of British prices after 1941.

Table 7—YIELDS (ACTUARIES INDEX) OF BRITISH SECURITIES[a]

Date[b]	Treasury Bills	2½ Percent Consols	Home Corp's	Industrial Debentures	Industrial Preference	Industrial Ordinary
1931	5.60%	4.57%	5.01%	6.18%	6.75%	6.94%
1938	.93	3.56	3.64	4.15	4.65	6.13
1943	1.017	3.16	3.30	3.91	4.34	4.43
1944	1.004	3.08	3.28	3.82	4.20	4.16
1945, Sept.	1.010	2.83	3.21	3.80	4.23	4.27

[a] Data on Treasury bills for 1931 are from *Banking and Monetary Statistics* (Board of Governors of Federal Reserve System, 1943) p. 660; for 1938-45, from *Statistical Summary, Bank of Canada*. Data on other securities are from *The Economist*, October 6, 1945, p. 494.
[b] End of period indicated.

Chapter 5

Effects of War on Lombard Street

CHAPTER 4 has indicated clearly that war brought unusual activity to Lombard Street, and that the activity was limited almost entirely to transactions with one customer—the government. So drastic a departure from the normal functioning of British financial institutions necessarily produced changes that may have far-reaching implications.

BANK OF ENGLAND

The most pronounced changes in the Bank of England's return during the six years of war were the virtual disappearance of the Issue Department's gold holdings, the decline in the Banking Department's reserve ratio, the 150 percent rise in note circulation, and the accompanying 370 percent increase in the Issue Department's holdings of government securities (Appendix Table A).

The growth of the Bank's note circulation, and the corresponding increase in holdings of governments by the Issue Department, was fairly steady throughout the entire war period. The expansion of about 165 percent in total active currency circulation, which in World War II consisted almost entirely of Bank of England notes, seems moderate when compared with the 700 percent rise during World War I, or even with the 340 percent rise in the Canadian and 280 percent rise in the United States active currency circulation during World War II.

In so far as the Bank's profits were concerned, developments in the Issue Department were of no importance. As mentioned in Chapter 1, gold and government securities were the Issue Department's chief assets, notes its sole liability, even before the war; and since profits of the Issue Department reverted to the government, the replacement of gold by interest-earning government securities added nothing to dividends.[1]

In the Banking Department, total assets expanded considerably, and earnings probably rose more than costs, although no official information is available on this point. However, throughout the war period dividends were held at 6 percent, as they had been ever since

---

[1] Profits of the Issue Department for various fiscal years were published in the House of Commons *Debates* (July 21, 1943), as follows (in millions of pounds sterling): 1940, £6.1; 1941, £8.9; 1942, £7.6; 1943, £9.1.

1923. When the dividend for 1943 was declared, this rate, which is the same as the first dividend of the Bank, declared in 1695, provided a yield on current value of shares about equal to the yield on consols. Possibly the Bank accumulated undistributed profits not shown in its return, but, on the whole, its position in respect to earnings (which for many generations has not been a major consideration in the operation of the Bank) was not profoundly altered by the war.

The Bank's position as a world institution, however, was affected significantly by developments in both departments. The substitution of government securities for the Issue Department's gold holdings, and the drop in the Banking Department's reserve ratio (or "proportion") far below the traditional 30 percent, constituted a profound change in British banking. For at least a century before 1931, the Bank of England's reserve ratio was the primary index of the credit situation in the whole money market—not for England alone, but for virtually the whole financial world. No substitute for this easy guide to probable developments in the money market has been provided. Henceforth, monetary policy will be guided less by the state of the Bank's return, and more by a whole complex of criteria, including such factors as the volume of unemployment and the balance and terms of trade. The very ease with which the Bank's gold holdings were removed and the ratio of reserves to deposits reduced without the slightest flurry in the money market shows how far the world has moved away from a monetary system in which major decisions were based on purely banking considerations.

Joint Stock Banks

As in the United States and Canada, the most obvious effect of war finance on the balance sheets of commercial banks was the increased holdings of government securities on the one hand and the growth of deposits on the other (Chart 3).[2] The importance among total assets of government securities of all kinds—both short-term and long-term—grew considerably. At mid-1945 they amounted to 61 percent of total assets compared with 58 percent for the United States and 52 percent for Canada. "Investments"—i.e., medium- and long-term securities—doubled (Table 8); as a percent of total assets, however, they declined from 24 percent to 22 percent, and as a percent of total deposits from 27 percent to 23 percent. More important was the port-

---

[2] Since detailed balance sheet statements for all joint stock banks combined are not available, the figures in this section are based on data for London clearing banks. A comparison of the data in Appendix Table B and those in Table 8 indicate that the percentage changes for the two groups of banks differ only slightly.

Chart 3—Selected Balance Sheet Items for Banks in the United Kingdom, United States, and Canada[a]

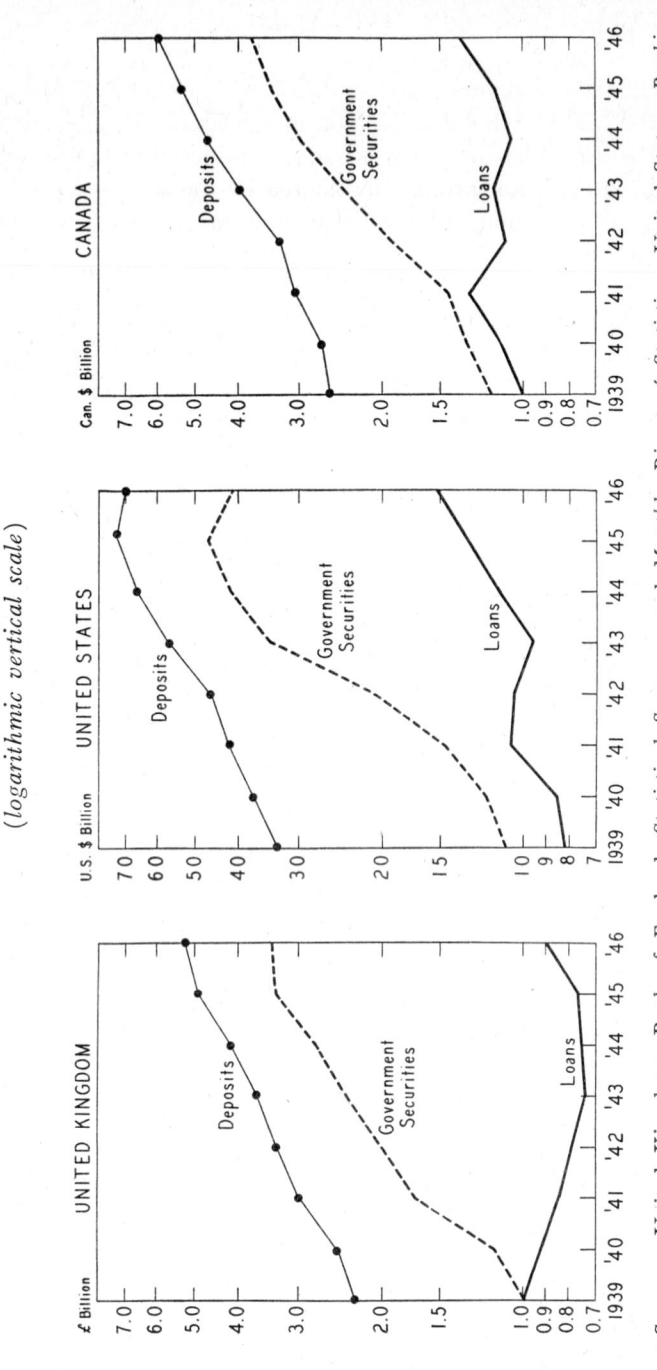

(*logarithmic vertical scale*)

[a] Sources: United Kingdom: Bank of England, *Statistical Summary* and *Monthly Digest of Statistics;* United States: *Banking and Monetary Statistics* and *Federal Reserve Bulletin;* Canada: Bank of Canada, *Statistical Summary.* Figures as of August each year. Data cover eleven London Clearing Banks, Reporting Member Banks of Federal Reserve System, and Canadian Chartered Banks.

Table 8—COMBINED BALANCE SHEET OF THE LONDON CLEARING BANKS[a]
(pound figures in millions)

	August 1939[b]		August 1945[c]	
	Amount	%	Amount	%
Assets				
Coin, notes, and balances with Bank of England	£233	9.3	£511	10.0
Balances with other banks[d]	68	2.7	128	2.5
Money at call and on short notice	147	5.8	233	4.5
Acceptances and endorsements	132	5.2	[e]	[e]
Advances to customers and other accounts	985	39.1	756	14.8
Bills discounted	279	11.1	195	3.8
Investments	599	23.8	1,126	22.0
Treasury deposit receipts	....	....	1,993	38.9
Miscellaneous assets	75	3.0	177	3.5
TOTAL[f]	2,518	100.0	5,119	100.0
Liabilities				
Current accounts	1,239	49.2	3,236	63.2
Deposit and other accounts	1,007	40.0	1,638	32.0
Total deposits	2,245	89.2	4,875	95.2
Other liabilities	273	10.8	244	4.8
TOTAL[f]	2,518	100.0	5,119	100.0

[a] From Bank of England, *Statistical Summary,* June 1940, p. 46, and December 1945, p. 96. Data are for 11 banks.
[b] Averages of weekly balances.
[c] Balances on a day, varying from bank to bank, toward the end of the month.
[d] Balances with, and checks in course of collection on, other banks in Great Britain and Ireland.
[e] Data not available.
[f] In some cases totals do not agree with sums of items because of rounding.

folio of Treasury deposit receipts, which grew from nothing to 39 percent of total assets. Finally, "bills" at the close of the war consisted almost entirely of Treasury bills, and amounted to slightly less than 4 percent of total assets. Advances during the war period dwindled from 39 percent to 15 percent of total assets; in fact, they declined even in absolute terms.

The rise in investments and the drop in bank advances reversed the customary relationship among bank earning assets.[3] Investments, consisting mainly of government securities, had increased substantially during the years 1929-33, but were fairly stable during the later thirties; the rapid rise since 1939 can be regarded as essentially a wartime phenomenon. Advances, however, showed a tendency to fall off relative to other assets even in the thirties, and the wartime decline may be merely an acceleration of this prewar trend. *The Economist* has stated, "Before the war 44 percent of the banks' resources (taking the clearing banks as a whole) were employed in advances to industry and private borrowers, while 46 percent represented direct and indirect loans to the Government—excluding cash, which is really a further, interest-free, loan. Now the corresponding proportions are 17 percent for private borrowers and 70 percent for public."[4]

Total monetary expansion in Britain was considerably less than in the United States, about the same as in Canada, but somewhat more than British monetary expansion in World War I, when the money supply approximately doubled. When clearing bank deposits are added to currency in circulation, British money supply increased somewhat more than 115 percent in the six years of World War II, while the Canadian money supply rose by approximately the same amount, and the American supply by more than 165 percent. The bulk of deposit expansion was in current accounts; by August 1945 total deposits had risen 117 percent while current accounts had increased 161 percent. Direct loans to customers played a relatively small role in deposit expansion; for the most part, the increase in deposits (as in Canada and the United States) represented growth of business accounts (Chart 4).

[3] The "ideal" asset structure was presented to the Macmillan Committee on Finance and Industry in 1930 by Frederick Hyde, then managing director of the Midland Bank. A comparison of the current asset structure with this "ideal" shows that, while the broad outlines are unchanged, the banks have departed considerably from the "ideal" structure in so far as the detailed assets are concerned (figures are ratios to assets):

	"Ideal" Asset Structure		London Clearing Banks August 1945	
Cash items				
Cash, etc.	10.0		12.5	
Money at call	6.3	16.3	4.5	17.0
Earning assets				
Advances	49.5		14.8	
Bills discounted	14.5		3.8	
Investments	10.8		22.0	
Treasury deposit receipts	....	74.8	38.9	79.5
Other assets	8.9		3.5	
Total	100.0		100.0	

[4] *The Economist*, January 26, 1946, p. 140.

Chart 4—GROWTH OF PERSONAL AND OTHER ACCOUNTS OF THE LONDON CLEARING BANKS[a]
(*logarithmic vertical scale*)

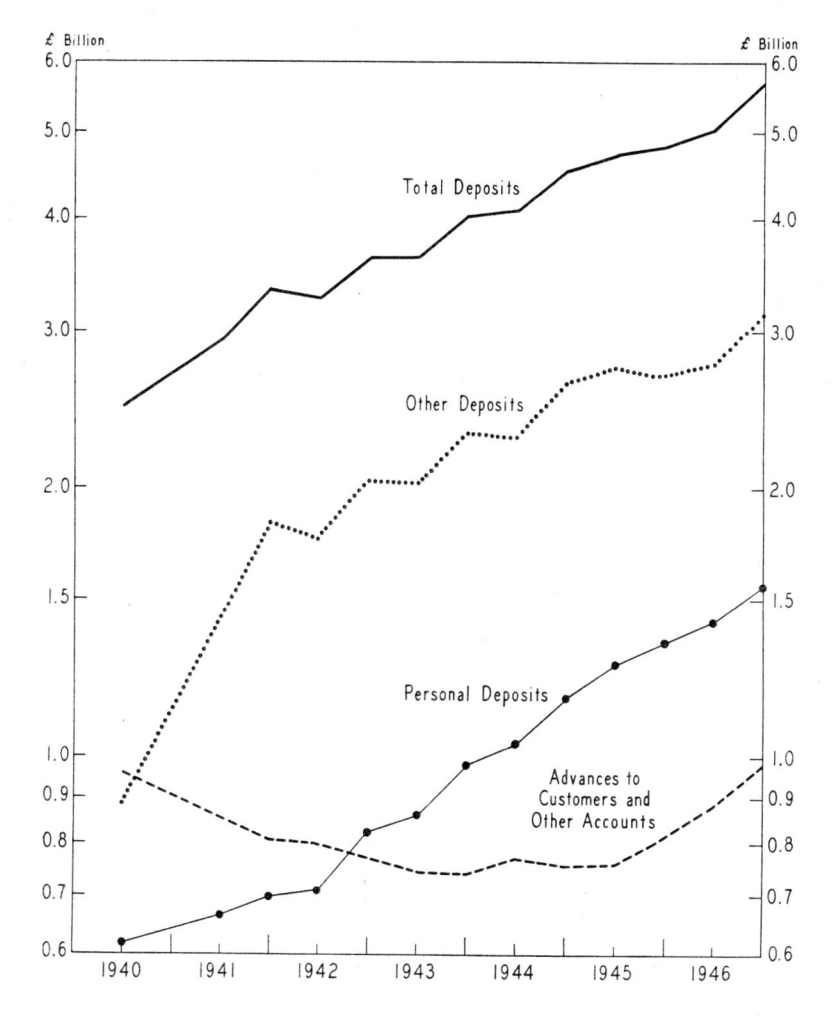

[a] Source: British White Papers on *War Finance, National Income and Expenditure* (Cmd. 6520, April 1944, and Cmd. 6438, April 1943); *Monthly Digest of Statistics*, March 1947, Table 126.

Net personal deposits exclude the accounts of businesses, financial institutions, public authorities, and also those of individual traders, shopkeepers, farmers, and professional men where the accounts are known to be used for the purpose of business.

55

Cash reserves kept pace with deposits, so that the reserve ratio was maintained between 10 and 11 percent.[5]

Published figures of bank profits are not very satisfactory,[6] but it seems clear that war did not injure bank prosperity. While the composition of earning assets changed, the ratio of earning to total assets increased, and total assets doubled. Replacement of advances carrying 4 or 5 percent with government obligations bearing 3 percent on long-term and 1 to 2 percent on short-term, inevitably lowered the rate of earnings on total bank assets. According to various financial writers, National War Bonds bearing 2½ percent comprised a large share of bank investments. Nevertheless, total profits apparently increased as a result of over-all expansion. *The Economist* estimated that gross earnings of the London clearing banks rose from £67 million for the year ended June 1939 to £84 million for the year ended June 1944.[7] Apparently no bank became subject to excess profits taxation, and there was considerable speculation as to why this was the case. Several reasons were suggested: Profits in the base year were high because of advantageous security sales. The banks were allowed to write off their German standstill balances against profits for tax purposes. Low profits in the early war years reduced the taxable average of later years.

[5] It will be noticed that the rate of deposit expansion dropped after the second year of war. This deceleration has been attributed to the introduction of tax reserve certificates in December 1941. Individuals and businesses which had previously held cash balances to meet tax payments preferred to hold tax certificates once these were made available.

[6] *The Banker,* February 1943, p. 93, speaking of bank profit figures, asked: "What are we to make, in the circumstances, of the Banks' published profits? Not a great deal, evidently. 'It is not always easy,' says Lord Wardington, 'to decide whether any item in a particular year is likely to be of a recurring nature, and therefore to be reasonably included in our Profit and Loss, or whether, on the other hand, it would be wiser to consider it as exceptional and more suitable to be placed to reserve for contingencies in a less favorable year. All these, and many other factors, make a scientifically accurate comparison of profits one year with another a matter of considerable difficulty. To show these differences year after year by a closely detailed analysis of our Profit and Loss would be impracticable in any statement short enough to be intelligible. The whole matter seems to resolve itself into a question of sound banking judgment...'"

[7] July 22, 1944, p. 117. The basis of the calculation is as follows, with volume and earnings figures given in millions:

	1939			1944		
Assets	Volume	Yield	Earnings	Volume	Yield	Earnings
Call money	£150	1¼%	£1.9	£184	1%	£1.8
Bills	249	1⅝	4.0	202	1	2.0
Treasury deposit receipts				1,246	1⅛	14.0
Investments	600	3⅝	21.7	1,169	3⅛	36.5
Advances	988	4	39.5	770	3⅞	29.8
Gross Earnings			£67.1			£84.1

Costs rose on several counts. The banks paid full salary less soldiers' pay to members of their staffs who entered the Armed Forces. Interest paid on deposits rose a little in absolute terms, but as a percentage of deposits it declined, since most of the increase in deposits was in current accounts on which relatively little interest was paid.

Table 9 suggests that bank profits rose substantially but tells us nothing about profitability of banking as a business enterprise. Mr. McKenna, late Chairman of the Midland Bank, quoted bank earnings on "the shareholders' true capital" at about 4 percent; but *The Economist* believed that, if this figure was correct, the banks must have had substantial reserves in excess of those reported.

Table 9—NET PROFITS OF JOINT STOCK BANKS[a]
(in millions)

	1943	1944	1945	1946	Profits "Grossed-Up"[b] Change, 1939-1946	Change, 1929-1946
Barclays	£1.6	£1.7	£1.7	£1.7	+10.8%	+10.0%
Lloyds	1.5	1.7	1.6	1.6	+17.4	− 4.9
Midland	2.0	2.0	2.1	2.0	+ 7.0	+13.7
National Provincial	1.3	1.3	1.4	1.3	+28.5	+10.0
Westminster	1.3	1.4	1.4	1.4	+24.3	− 3.3
TOTAL	7.7	8.0	8.2	7.9	+13.5	+ 5.2

[a] From *The Banker,* February 1947, p. 104.
[b] "The year 1943 was the first in which comparisons in published profits between the several banks was possible, as in earlier years some banks computed 'net' profits after deducting tax on their dividends while one bank showed the dividends gross. This difference is eliminated, however, if published profits are 'grossed-up' by adding back income tax at the standard rate (and N.D.C. for war years), thus making comparisons possible over a longer period." *Loc. cit.*

MERCHANT BANKS

Because of their unfortunate experiences during and after World War I (as outlined in Chapter 2), the position of the merchant banks was none too strong when World War II broke out. During World War II their normal operations were again restricted by the virtual disappearance of bills of exchange and acceptances, by suspension of new issue business, and by their omission from the list of authorized dealers in foreign exchange. Little of the expansion noted for the joint stock banks was evidenced by merchant banks.[8] (See Appendix Table E.)

[8] Since few of the merchant banks publish complete statements, it is not possible to give a picture of the effects of the war on merchant banks as a whole.

Indeed, S. Japhet suffered a net contraction of total assets between 1939 and 1945; advances were reduced sharply, while investments showed only a slight increase. Baring Brothers and Hambros also added to their portfolios of "other securities." The net effect on earnings of the merchant banks is not easy to ascertain; but it seems possible that those firms which expanded their total assets were able to increase their total earnings as well.

Discount Market

The discount houses, while hardly showing the expansion of the joint stock banks, were not held in check so much as the merchant banks. Bills discounted and investments, in particular, rose substantially.[9] The growth of this latter item, which consisted largely of increased holdings of short-term government bonds, constituted what *The Economist* termed "a silent revolution in Lombard Street." In the late thirties, the discount market "did indeed deal substantially and increasingly in short bonds," but this break with tradition was "tolerated simply as a means of keeping discount market machinery in working order until its bill-dealing functions revived." Because of their key role as go-between for the Bank of England and the joint stock banks, the disappearance of the discount houses would have required considerable reorganization of the British financial system. During the war, bond dealing became "legitimized, and, if not yet the primary function of the discount market, . . . certainly as important as its bill-dealing function."[10] It is questionable, however, whether the over-all growth and the shift to bonds were sufficient to offset entirely the reduction in earnings resulting from the substitution of Treasury bills for commercial bills. The figures of the three major houses indicate that it was not.

It may have been considerations such as these that persuaded the Bank of England to express openly in 1941 its long-felt wish to see the discount market consolidated into fewer and stronger units. In the first four years of World War II, seven discount houses disappeared, leaving a total of eleven concerns. By the spring of 1944, the resources of each remaining concern (except Seccombe, Marshall, and Campion[11]) were at least £500,000, and the eleven combined had resources of £14.4 millions.[12]

The interesting feature of this wartime consolidation, however, is that it took the form of absorptions and mergers rather than with-

---

[9] See Appendix Table D.
[10] "Short Bond Problems," *The Economist*, November 24, 1945, p. 756.
[11] Brokers for the Bank of England in transactions with the market.
[12] "Consolidation of the Discount Market," *The Banker*, May 1944, pp. 79-84.

drawals from the market. Only two concerns retired altogether, and during the sixth year of war there was actually a net inflow of capital to the discount market. The reason lies in the opportunity for profitable investment in government obligations that developed during the war and which was expected to remain when the war was over. "It can be taken for granted," wrote a correspondent to *The Banker* in 1944, "that [the actual] method of achieving the desired consolidation would not have been permitted had the authorities not been convinced that the market after the war will have an important function to perform in the gilt-edged sphere."[13]

CAPITAL MARKET

The effectiveness of the embargo on new capital issues is apparent from Table 10. The immense capital expansion necessitated by the war was not financed through the regular channels of the capital market.

Table 10—NEW CAPITAL ISSUES IN THE LONDON MARKET[a]
(in millions)

	1938	1939	Total 1940-44	1945	1946
Home					
Public bodies	£27.6	£12.1	£3.7	.0	.0
Production	48.3	19.0	17.6	£13.1	£73.5
Trade	11.0	3.4	1.3	2.9	26.5
Transport	.5	7.4	.1	.2	.4
Finance	5.4	1.5	.4	.8	11.3
TOTAL[b]	92.7	43.3	23.1	17.0	111.7
India and Ceylon					
Public bodies	.0	.0	.0	.0	.0
Companies	.5	.9	.2	.1	.1
TOTAL	.5	.9	.2	.1	.1
Other British Countries					
Public bodies	10.1	12.6	.0	.0	.0
Companies	10.7	4.8	1.7	2.4	16.7
TOTAL	20.8	17.4	1.7	2.4	16.7
Foreign Countries					
Public bodies	.0	.0	.0	.0	.0
Companies	4.1	4.6	1.6	1.0	2.3
TOTAL	4.1	4.6	1.6	1.0	2.3
TOTAL OVERSEAS[b]	25.4	23.0	3.4	3.5	19.1
ALL ISSUES	118.1	66.3	26.5	20.5	130.8

[a] From Midland Bank special report on new capital issues, released January 1, 1947. Figures for years ended December 31.
[b] In some cases sums of items do not agree with totals because of rounding.

[13] *Ibid.*, p. 84.

This development is not surprising, for, while the Capital Issues Committee would probably have authorized public issues by war industries, such securities would hardly have appealed to the investing public. War plants are specialized investments subject, on the one hand, to profit limitations and, on the other, to special risks because of the nature of the market and the high rate of obsolescence of war equipment. It is for such reasons that a large part of Britain's war machinery was built up by the government on its own account.

The war and the financial difficulties of reconstruction, inherent in war on so vast a scale, finally brought action to meet the problem of providing small and medium-sized British concerns with investment capital, and of providing intermediate-term credit for British industry. This problem is one of long standing in England. During the fifty years prior to 1945, every person and every parliamentary committee concerned with financial problems of British industry and trade emphasized the need for new machinery to meet it. The joint stock banks were frequently criticized for their policy of restricting themselves to short-term advances representing only a small proportion of the funds in use by a specific business, and their "noncommittal" attitude toward their customers. Some critics lauded the American investment bank and the continental industrial bank financing of industry as examples that might be followed. Others, however, pointed to the failure of the German industrial banks, and emphasized the drastic revision in the nature of British banking that would be entailed in expansion of its industrial business to the German scale. It was also argued that, whereas German industry had always been short of capital, there might not exist in Britain a sufficient long-run demand for intermediate-term industrial credit to warrant a transformation of the banking system.[14]

Certain relatively small organizations had been set up to assist with industrial financing: Credit for Industry, Ltd., owned by the United Dominions Trust; the Charterhouse Industrial Development Company, controlled by the Charterhouse Investment Trust; and the Bankers' Industrial Development Company, set up during the early 1930's under the joint auspices of the Bank of England and the joint stock banks to assist large or basic industries with reconstruction. The combined resources and operations of these organizations, however, were not adequate to meet the need for intermediate-term credit, and for capital of small and medium-sized concerns.

In the spring of 1945, with the European war in its final phase, the

[14] Cf. G. Eberstadt, "Industrial Banking Reconsidered," *The Banker*, April 1944, pp. 15-19.

Chancellor of the Exchequer announced in the House of Commons that two new financial institutions would be set up to meet this vexatious problem. One was the Finance Corporation for Industry, owned by the Bank of England, the insurance companies, and the trust companies, which held respectively 30, 40, and 30 percent of the total capital of £25 million. It had power to borrow up to an additional £100 million, bringing its total potential resources to £125 million. The stated purpose of the Corporation was "the provision of temporary or longer period finance for industrial businesses of the country with a view to their quick rehabilitation and development in the national interests, thereby assisting in the maintenance and increase of employment." It was to take no initiative in the reorganization of industry and to confine its activities to the provision of finance. It was intended to supplement, and not to displace, previously extant channels through which industrial concerns obtained finance. The Board of the Company was chosen from the business world, but "the appropriate Departments" of the government were to be "kept informed" of "developments of major importance."[15]

The second institution, the Industrial and Commercial Finance Corporation, had capital of £15 million, one-third subscribed by the Bank of England, the balance by the London Clearing Banks and the Scottish banks. It had authority to borrow another £30 million from its shareholders. Its function was "to provide credit and finance by means of loans or the subscription of loan or share capital or otherwise for industrial and commercial businesses or enterprises in Great Britain particularly in cases where the existing facilities provided by banking institutions and the Stock Exchanges are not readily or easily available." This statement of purpose was interpreted to mean that the corporation would make loans mainly within the range of £5,000 to £200,000—loans too big for the joint stock banks and too small for the capital market.

Like the Finance Corporation, the Industrial and Commercial Finance Corporation was designed to supplement, and not to compete with, other banking facilities and particularly to meet the capital needs of small and medium-sized businesses. The directors were appointed by the share-holding banks, and the first chairman was named by the Bank of England. In keeping with British tradition, no *legal* limitations were placed on the powers of the Corporation in regard to the size of loans it could make.

---

[15] See "Finance for Industry and Commerce," *Journal of the Institute of Bankers,* April 1945, p. 72.

Other Developments Important to Lombard Street

Other wartime developments of significance to Lombard Street were, for the most part, similar to those during World War I: a decrease in exports, loss of shipping, industrialization of other countries, loss of continental insurance and short-term credit business, liquidation of foreign assets, and accumulation of sterling balances.

Exports

Commercial exports of the United Kingdom shrank from £471 million in 1938 to £258 million in 1944. In terms of physical volume, exports in 1944 were only 30 percent of their 1938 level. Indeed, the demands of the armed forces and war industries imposed a greater relative reduction of employment in the direct export industries than in any other major group of industries. However necessary or advantageous this re-allocation of manpower may have been in terms of allied war strategy, it left Britain with a particularly difficult task in attaining her postwar objectives of maintaining full employment and providing a high standard of living for her people, while meeting her needs for foreign exchange. The achievement of these goals depended upon the export industries.

Shipping

Income from shipping was a large factor in Britain's prewar balance of payments. The insurance of shipping and the financing of transoceanic trade was an important prewar source of revenue to Lombard Street. The City therefore has a double interest in the fate of British shipping: one immediate and one indirect. While the correlation between nationality of ships and nationality of the firms insuring them and financing their cargoes is by no means perfect, there is some relation. Other things being equal, it is reasonable to suppose that the share of Lombard Street in insuring and financing world trade will vary directly with Britain's share in world oceanic shipping. In addition, since shipping contributes heavily to British prosperity, especially through helping to balance foreign payments without restrictive or deflationary policies, it contributes indirectly to the general activity of Lombard Street.

During World War II, as in World War I, Britain's relative position as a world shipper deteriorated (Table 11). Before the war, Britain had the world's largest merchant fleet, amounting in June 1939 to more than 18 million gross tons, or more than one-quarter of the world's merchant fleet. During the European war, Britain's loss was

Table 11—MERCHANT TONNAGE (1,000 GROSS TONS AND OVER) OPERATED BY PRINCIPAL MARITIME COUNTRIES[a]

Country	June 30, 1939 (gross)	June 30, 1945 (gross)
United States (nonmilitary)	8,672,090	27,959,000
United States (military)		8,254,000
British Empire (except Canada)	18,179,020	14,934,00[b]
Canada	654,786	892,000
Belgium	374,575	241,000[b]
Brazil	419,962	445,000
Denmark	1,069,937	748,000
France	2,745,884	1,113,000[b]
Germany	3,973,893	1,068,000
Greece	1,727,931	697,000[b]
Netherlands	2,728,381	1,576,000[b]
Italy	3,245,670	350,000
Japan	5,255,627	1,526,000
Norway	4,552,895	2,813,000[b]
Spain	775,828	850,000
Sweden	1,364,683	1,389,000
Other countries	4,865,360	4,462,000
WORLD TOTAL	60,606,522	69,335,000

[a] From Knute E. Carlson and Geraldine Lytzen, "Postwar Shipping," *Foreign Commerce Weekly*, February 23, 1946, p. 4. The 1939 data were taken from Lloyd's Register of Shipping, Vol. II (1939-40) Table 5. Except for the United States, for which data were supplied by the U. S. Maritime Commission, the figures for 1945 were developed by adding construction and other acquisition to 1939 figures and subtracting losses.

[b] United States owned tonnage under lend-lease has been reported as part of the tonnage of the countries operating it. Thus Great Britain had 1,997,448 gross tons under lend-lease; U.S.S.R., 613,950; Norway, 181,923; Greece, 100,771; France, 93,445; Belgium, 50,327; Netherlands, 28,202; Poland, 16,529; and China, 14,386. Great Britain's figure also includes approximately 620,000 gross tons turned over to Great Britain by Canada.

considerable. Moreover, after the entry of the United States into the war, Britain diverted resources from merchant shipbuilding to other fields of war production, leaving merchant shipbuilding mainly to the United States, and to a lesser extent to Canada. During the whole period of the European war, Britain built less than 9 million tons of merchant shipping; captures and non-returnable acquisitions amounted to some 2 million tons. In sum, Britain's merchant fleet in June 1945 was less than 15 million tons, some 80 percent of the prewar fleet. Moreover, in quality and age the merchant fleet in 1945 was "immeasurably inferior" to the prewar fleet.[16]

Meanwhile, world tonnage of merchant shipping had increased

[16] "Shipbuilding Problems Now," *The Economist*, March 6, 1948, p. 386. See also "British Shipping in the New World," *ibid.*, February 7, 1948.

about 14 percent, with the increase concentrated mainly in the United States. Canada also enjoyed a substantial growth, and Spain, Sweden, and Brazil slight increases. All the rest of the world suffered losses; but while the Axis countries lost the highest percentages of their fleets, the net loss of tonnage in absolute terms was much higher for Britain than for any other country except Japan.

Britain therefore entered the postwar period at a considerable disadvantage so far as competing for postwar shipping business was concerned. Not only had her merchant fleet dwindled, both relative to the rest of the world and absolutely, but her shipyards were operating below prewar capacity, while the yards of the United States and Canada were operating well above prewar rates.

Industrialization of Other Countries

Britain's problem of expanding exports has been complicated by the wartime industrialization of countries that formerly provided markets for British manufactured goods.

In Canada, World War II accelerated the trend, already discernible in the interwar period, for that country to become an essentially manufacturing, rather than an essentially agricultural, country. During 1919, agriculture contributed 44 percent of the total net value of Canadian production, and manufacturing 33 percent. When World War II began, agricultural production had already shrunk to 22 percent of the total, while manufacturing had grown to 39 percent. In 1943, well over half the net value of Canadian production consisted of manufactured goods, and agriculture, despite a 60 percent increase in the value of agricultural production, accounted for only 20 percent of the total. The Canadian export situation has been well described by Homer S. Fox, Commercial Attaché of the United States Embassy in Ottawa. "Prior to World War I . . . exports of raw materials were nearly double the total exports of fully and semi-manufactured goods. . . . By 1944, . . . exports of manufactures were nearly three times those of raw materials, although the latter were in turn more than three times the corresponding exports in 1930."[17]

In Australia, wheat acreage was reduced during the war, acreage of some coarse grains expanded, and manufacturing output greatly increased. Factory employment rose from 542,000 in 1938-39 to 724,000 in 1944-45. Output of industrial metals, machinery, implements, and conveyances nearly doubled.

The war also led to acceleration of industrial development in such

[17] H. S. Fox, "Canada's Economy in 1945," *Foreign Commerce Weekly,* January 19, 1946, p. 6.

relatively unindustrialized countries as China and India. There is good reason to suppose that some of these wartime gains will be maintained. India has certain raw materials, such as cotton and leather, in abundance. Its labor is as yet relatively cheap, and with training can be made just as efficient as the British labor force. Moreover, India's new industries are not handicapped by established labor and managerial procedures, and are in many cases equipped with the most up-to-date machinery.

Some of the fields of Indian industrial expansion compete directly with former British exports. Mill production of cotton, for example, rose 90 percent between 1921-25 and 1934-38, and another 10 percent from 1938-39 to 1944-45. The value of production of woolen and worsted cloth rose during the war from £7.3 million per year to £27 million, and output of woolen clothing increased over 300 percent. Output of army footwear rose over sixfold. The iron and steel industry grew substantially, and two new aluminum plants were established. The engineering industry also expanded; whereas before the war only 10 percent of hand tool requirements were met by domestic production, by 1944 domestic production met virtually all Indian needs. The chemical, fertilizer, and drug industries also grew considerably.

There is, of course, no incompatibility between world-wide industrialization and a high level of world trade. A fact frequently cited is that the bulk of international trade takes place among the advanced industrial countries. It is equally clear, however, that *all* countries cannot export *all* types of manufactured goods. World-wide industrialization must be accompanied by increased geographical specialization within the field of manufacturing if world trade is to grow at the same time. In this process, Britain may find it necessary to abandon some of her traditional fields of export and to develop new ones.

Effects of the War on British Insurance

Insurance of foreigners was a significant source of income to the British money market before the war, and payment of insurance premiums by foreign policyholders was an important source of foreign exchange. "The overseas business of British insurance companies and underwriters at Lloyd's," *The Economist* has said, "is a national asset of substantial importance." Aggregate annual premiums were estimated at £100 million, and the net contribution to the balance of payments at £12 million to £15 million.[18]

Much of this business had been derived from countries in Europe and Asia which fell under the Axis domination during the war. Years

[18] "The Export of Insurance," *The Economist,* August 25, 1945, p. 272.

of enemy occupation resulted in dispersal of prewar portfolios. In Japanese-occupied cities such as Shanghai, not only portfolios but records and staffs disappeared, making it necessary, at the war's end, for British insurance firms to start from scratch to rebuild their shattered business in the Far East.[19] In Europe, the Germans had made not altogether successful attempts to transfer the British business to German concerns. A nucleus of perhaps 10 percent of prewar business in France was available at the war's end as a basis for rebuilding, as a result of a German regulation which permitted French policyholders to continue British policies already in force, provided the policies were reinsured in full with German companies.

Loss of Overseas Investments and Increase in Overseas Debt

Assistance provided by the United States, Canada, and other United Nations under the Lend-Lease and Mutual Aid Agreements was "too little and too late" for Britain to avoid liquidation of overseas investments on a scale even larger than in World War I. Total sales and repatriations of British foreign investments up to VE day, most of which took place before the Agreements were negotiated, are itemized in Table 12.

Table 12—PROCEEDS OF SALES OR REPATRIATION OF OVERSEAS INVESTMENTS OF THE UNITED KINGDOM, SEPTEMBER 1939 - JUNE 1945[a]

(in millions)

Sterling Area	
Dominions (Australia, New Zealand, South Africa, and Eire)	£201
India, Burma, and Middle East	348
Colonies and other sterling area countries	15
Total, Sterling Area	£564
North America	
United States	203[b]
Canada	225
Total, North America	428
South America	96
Europe	14
Rest of world	16
TOTAL	1,118

[a] Estimates from *Statistical Material Presented During the Washington Negotiations,* Cmd. 6707 (December 1945) p. 9.
[b] Does not include collateral for Reconstruction Finance Corporation loan.

[19] *The Economist,* September 22, 1945, pp. 424-25.

At the same time that the debts of foreigners to Britain were reduced, the debts of Britain to foreigners were increased. British external liabilities, most of which consist of short-term sterling balances accumulated by foreign banks, increased from £476 million on August 31, 1939 to £3,355 million on June 30, 1945.

The Lend-Lease agreement involved an increase in British net foreign obligations, not definitely stipulated at the time but later settled at $650 million. Finally, the financing of wartime imports involved a substantial depletion of the United Kingdom's gold and dollar reserves. Between August 31, 1939 and June 30, 1945, those reserves were reduced from £605 million to £453 million.

The effect of the war on the estimated international capital account position of the United Kingdom is summarized in Table 13. The figure for prewar long-term foreign assets, is, of course, only an estimate in so far as direct investments are concerned.

Table 13—Estimated Position of United Kingdom on International Capital Account, Selected Dates[a]
(in millions)

Foreign Assets 1939		Foreign Indebtedness,	
Gold and foreign exchange	£700	September 1939	£476
Long-term investments[b]	3,900	*Plus*: Creation of debt,	
	4,600	Sept. 1939—June 1945	2,879
Less: Sales of Foreign Assets,		*Equals*: Foreign Indebt-	
Sept. 1939—June 1945		edness, June 1945	£3,355
Gold and foreign exchange	152		
Long-term investments	1,118		
	1,270		
Equals: Foreign Assets,			
June 1945[b]	£3,330		

[a] Data on foreign assets are from *The Economist*, November 10, 1945, p. 688; other data are from *Statistical Material Presented During the Washington Negotiations*, Cmd. 6707 (December 1945) pp. 11, 12.
[b] Estimated nominal value.

Figures of foreign assets and foreign debts, even if completely accurate, would provide no clear-cut indication of the relationship between interest and dividends received and paid. The net income on capital account obviously depends not only upon the relative magnitudes of assets and debts, but also upon the rate of return paid on each. By and large, since the foreign assets liquidated have not consisted, to any significant extent, of direct investments upon which the highest returns are earned (at least in prosperous years), and since the debts acquired are short-term obligations upon which the rate of interest, even after conversion into long-term debt, is not likely to be high, it would seem that Britain's position at the end of the war had deteriorated considerably less in terms of net income from foreign investment than in terms of net long-term capital position.

The figures presented in Table 14 substantiate this view. In 1945, despite the fact that Britain was probably a slight net debtor on capital account, she enjoyed a net income of £97 million from foreign investment. On the other hand, it should not be forgotten that this figure was less than half that received in 1938, and that this decline in net income from foreign investment involved a serious deterioration in Britain's balance of payments position as a whole.

Table 14—UNITED KINGDOM OVERSEAS RECEIPTS AND PAYMENTS OF DIVIDENDS, INTEREST, ETC., 1945[a]
(in millions)

Area	Gross Receipts[b]	Gross Payments[b]	Net Receipts
Sterling Area			
Dominions (Australia, New Zealand, South Africa, and Eire)	£45	£16	£29
India, Burma, and Middle East	11	22	—11
Colonies and other sterling area countries	17	12	5
Unallocated, sterling area	22	[c]	22
TOTAL	95	50	45
North America			
United States	9[d]	13[e]	—4
Canada	14	3	11
TOTAL	23	16	7
South America	28	1	27
Europe	12[f]	6	6
Rest of world and unallocated	12	[c]	12
TOTAL	170	73	97

[a] Data are partly estimated. From *Statistical Material Presented During the Washington Negotiations,* Cmd. 6707 (December 1945) p. 10.
[b] Gross receipts and payments include certain collections of interest on external securities remitted to holders overseas. This does not, of course, affect the figures of net receipts.
[c] Less than £1 million.
[d] Includes income on investments (other than insurance holdings) pledged to RFC.
[e] Includes interest charges on RFC loan.
[f] Includes nonrecurring payments of arrears arising in the war years.

Importance of Britain's International Financial Position for Lombard Street

Apart from the dependence of Lombard Street for its prosperity on the general economic and financial health of the nation that it serves, the British balance of payments problem is important to Lombard Street because it leads to replacement of private by public lending. The money market of a debtor nation can still be active; the City could make money from commissions on foreign borrowing just as well as on foreign lending. However, concern for the safety of the pound will limit the volume of private lending to Britain; and Lombard Street cannot make money out of inter-governmental loans, or from the operations of the International Monetary Fund and the International Bank for Reconstruction and Development. In addition, some of the foreign assets liquidated to meet Britain's wartime needs for dollars were presumably held by financial houses. Others were held by clients of these houses. It is at least questionable whether domestic lending to replace these lost assets could be expected to yield returns equal to those formerly earned on the liquidated assets. Indeed, there is a strong likelihood that it could not.

On the other hand, in so far as the British international financial position leads to a successful program of expanding exports, the position of Lombard Street will be improved to the extent that the increased exports are financed by British houses. How successful Britain will be in expanding foreign trade, and what the share of the City in its financing will be, are among the major factors that will determine the future of Lombard Street.

Chapter 6

Postwar Transition and the Future of Lombard Street

THE ANALYSIS in the foregoing chapters indicates that what has happened to the various institutions comprising the British money market cannot be regarded merely as the results of World War II, or even exclusively as the results of wars and depressions in the past 35 years. Events in these years have merely accelerated changes that were appearing before World War I. Sooner or later, some of the changes in the structure and operations of Lombard Street would probably have occurred anyway, if only because of changes in Britain's position in the world as producer and trader.[1]

At time of writing, the war has been over for nearly two and one-half years, and some evidence is available of the extent to which a reversal of wartime trends can be expected. The postwar picture has been complicated, however, by the election in 1945 of a labor government committed to financial reforms of various kinds. It is difficult to distinguish the effects of war and reconstruction from the effects of the election. Of course, a good case could be made for the argument that the election of a labor government was itself the result of the events of the two world wars and of the reconstruction period between them. As the editor of the *Midland Bank Review* has put it, "before the war the trend was already set towards more extensive and more positive Government intervention in economic affairs. What happened in July last year gave a sharp upward turn to a curve that was already rising."[2] However, support of this thesis would require much more than economic analysis and cannot be provided here. Suffice it to say that some of the labor party legislation relating to the operations of Lombard Street was proposed by the previous government, and that it is at least to some extent the direct outcome of the long process of development since 1913.

---

[1] "Of course, it had been perfectly evident long before [1919] that British pre-eminence could not persist. By 1875 she was seriously challenged; by 1913 she was probably no longer the world's leading or even second industrial nation, and others were not far behind her. But it was not until after the war that the impact of these long-run factors was fully felt and the need for drastic readjustment made perfectly clear." Alfred E. Kahn, *Great Britain in the World Economy* (New York 1946) p. 65.

[2] "Three Aspects of Transition," *Midland Bank Review,* May 1946, p. 1.

Bank of England

The nationalization of the Bank of England, under the Bank of England Act of February 1946, illustrates this point. The necessities of war and reconstruction brought the Bank and the Treasury into closer relationship, and the operations of the Bank were guided to an increasing extent by the demands of national fiscal policy. Nationalization of the Bank consequently became an easy step, and for a labor government a rather obvious one.

The main provisions of the Act are set forth in Sections one (compensation of the Bank's stockholders), two (Court of Directors), and four (Treasury directions to the Bank and relations of the Bank with other banks). In effect, the bargain made with the stockholders was such as to maintain for twenty years the income received on their investment. They received for their bank stock an equivalent amount of government stock which "shall bear interest at the rate of three percent per annum; and the equivalent amount of Government stock shall, in relation to any person, be taken to be such that the sum payable annually by way of interest thereon is equal to the average annual gross dividend declared during the period of twenty years immediately preceding the thirty-first day of March, nineteen hundred and forty five, upon the amount of Bank stock of which that person was the registered holder immediately before the appointed day" (March 1, 1946). However, the government stock may be redeemed at par by the Treasury on or any time after April 5, 1966.

Under Section two, the number of directors was reduced from 24 to 16, appointed by the Crown for four years. The term of office of the governor and of the deputy-governor was extended to five years, subject to renewal.

Section four was the only one that really perturbed the City. Under this section, "The Treasury may from time to time give such directions to the Bank as, after consultation with the Governor of the Bank, they think necessary in the public interest"; and "The Bank, if they think it necessary in the public interest, may request information from and make recommendations to bankers, and may, if so authorized by the Treasury, issue directions to any banker for the purpose of securing that effect is given to any such request or recommendation."

According to *The Economist*, "there is no denying that the City is disturbed about the breadth of these powers." On the other hand, "it is doubtful whether this clause does anything more than formalise a state of affairs that already exists. Requests from the Bank have never been lightly ignored in the City, and the whole structure of monetary control might collapse if the unwritten conventions on which it is based . . . could not be enforced in the last resort." Similarly, "it is widely recognised that, although the Government seeks wide legal powers, it does not really intend to do much (if anything) more than has been done less formally in the past few years . . . Hence the whole case against this subsection rests on the argument that it could be abused by a future and less discreet Government . . . But if a Government wants to do what the City might regard as unreasonable things . . . it will do them whether there is a pre-existing legal power or not . . ."[3]

On the whole, nationalization leaves the Bank's position in the British money market, and in the world, unchanged. It is merely a formal recognition of what the Bank had clearly become and in a sense always was: a government institution and agent.

The Bank has not resumed stewardship of the nation's monetary gold, and it seems unlikely that it will do so in the near future. The separation of exchange funds from central bank reserves has administrative advantages that commend themselves to British financial officials. It also gives internal monetary policy a greater degree of independence from the foreign exchange position, although the mere establishment of a separate foreign exchange institution will certainly not provide the British economy with a cushion deep enough to prevent outside shocks from having internal repercussions. The reserve ratio of the Banking Department rose considerably throughout 1947 and early 1948. However, it is unlikely that the Bank's reserve ratio will regain its earlier significance as an index of the liquidity and safety of the Bank, and as a guide to monetary policy.

Apparently the rediscount rate also has lost much of its significance in the British money market. In March 1948, Bank rate was the same as at the end of October 1939—2 percent—and while it may be changed at some time in the future it is difficult to attribute significance to a discount rate that has remained unchanged for so long a period. England has depended more on fiscal policy, price policy, direct control of foreign exchange, etc., than on the traditional central banking measures for control of economic and financial conditions.

It is perhaps not even too much to say that "central bank policy" will become a meaningless phrase in England. The highly skilled personnel of the Bank will be consulted, and their advice will be seriously considered, when general economic and financial policy is formulated; but the Bank itself will be merely one of several government agencies which contribute to policy determination and through which policies

[3] *The Economist,* October 13, 1945, p. 514, and October 20, 1945, p. 570.

are executed. Its executive role will be limited largely to providing joint stock banks with whatever reserves are needed to permit lending to government and business in the volume considered appropriate to general economic policies for maintaining full employment, preventing inflation, stimulating exports, and so forth.[4]

The rate of monetary expansion promoted by (or through) the Bank fell off after the war. In the first postwar year the note circulation of the Bank rose by about £42 million and notes held by the Banking Department by £8 million; thus total notes issued were less than the amount issued in any war year and less than one-third of the increase in the last year of war. From September 1946 to September 1947, the note circulation rose only £25 million; notes held by the Banking Department also increased by £25 million, reflecting a £50 million increase in the fiduciary issue during this period. In the six months following, notes in circulation actually fell, while notes held in the Banking Department rose to a peak in January 1948 and then decreased sharply. During this period the amount of the fiduciary issue was cut by £150 million. In the first postwar year the increase in bankers' deposits was around £70 million, about twice that of the previous year; in the second postwar year such deposits decreased £15 million; and in the following six months they fluctuated somewhat but ended the period with an increase of about £25 million. The net effect was a small expansion of bank reserves over the two and one-half year period. It seems likely that, while consumers' goods remain scarce, the lifting of the pressure of war finance and the fact that the budget is approaching balance will result in a British monetary policy which for some time will be considerably less expansionary than that of the war period.

Joint Stock Banks

Postwar legislation has not fundamentally altered the position of the joint stock banks. As indicated above, Section 4 of the Bank of England Act provides the government with greater formal control over the operations of the commercial banks, but it has not created any truly new relationship of the banks to the central bank or to the Treasury. There has been no suggestion thus far that the clause will be used so as to interfere with the confidential nature of the relationship of banks to their clients. It is not clear that the Treasury intends to control the allocation of credit among particular clients, although the determination of certain priorities for credit among various types of enterprise would

[4] See the previous government's White Paper, *Employment Policy*, Cmd. 6527 (May 1944), especially Chapters IV and V. This White Paper has not been officially retracted by the labor government, and probably represents their view to a large extent.

seem to be implicit in government policy.[5] On the whole, the Act leaves the day-to-day transactions of the joint stock banks much as they were.

Cheaper Money

More directly significant for the prosperity of the joint stock banks was Chancellor Dalton's drive for still cheaper money. In Britain, the "costless credit" controversy has been of real significance, and now that Britain is governed by a party whose intellectual leaders have often pressed for costless credit,[6] the controversy is much more than academic. The nationalization of the Bank of England, and of the leading banks of France, might be regarded as examples to be followed in the case of all British banks. Moreover, just as the problems of war and reconstruction have led to closer relationship between the Treasury and the Bank of England, so the banking system as a whole has become more and more the agent of government policy.

So far, there is no indication that the present British government has plans for nationalizing the British banking system as a whole. Instead, the government seems to be striving to achieve "costless credit" through reduction in short-term interest rates. An announcement that the Chancellor was "studying the possibility of cheaper money and lower rates of interest" was made in September 1945, on the eve of a loan campaign. It seems likely that a desire to create an active market for the new obligations to be issued during this campaign played some role in the government's decision to reduce interest rates still further below the level of September 1945. In addition, however, three considerations seem to have influenced the government in its interest policy: (1) the desire to minimize the debt service, in view of the enormous wartime growth of national debt and the possibility that the problems of reconstruction would result in still further increases; (2) the hypothesis that, to the extent that the policy succeeds in reducing those interest rates which enter into investment decisions, the govern-

[5] In Parliamentary debates on the Bill, the Chancellor of the Exchequer made statements indicating that the Treasury has such a procedure in mind: " . . it is essential that we should be able, in the last resort, to establish priorities in the disposal of short-term funds in the same manner as we shall, in a later measure . . . assure priorities of national interest in regard to long-term credit . . . it may be desirable, in certain circumstances, to urge the banks to devote their resources to one or other form of investment, which it was felt by the Government and by the Bank of England was necessary in the interests of a planned priority, with a view to securing full employment in the country and building up our export trade and other necessary elements in our economy" . . . Quoted in *The Economist,* February 16, 1946, p. 260.

[6] See, for example, the Fabian Society pamphlet, *The Prevention of General Unemployment* (Research Series No. 79, London, 1944), and "Costless Credit: The Fabian Reply," *The Banker,* May 1944, p. 84.

ment would be aided in its avowed aim of maintaining a high and stable level of employment; (3) the wish of the government to finance its huge housing program at interest rates as low as possible.

To launch the cheap money policy, the rate on Treasury deposit receipts was reduced on October 22, 1945 from $1\frac{1}{8}$ percent to $\frac{5}{8}$ of 1 percent (Chart 5). The Treasury bill rate was accordingly adjusted to a $\frac{1}{2}$ of 1 percent basis. In response to these reductions in the return on short-term earning assets, the London Clearing Banks gave notice that after November 30, 1945 no interest would be paid on current accounts, and the maximum rates on deposit accounts would be cut from 1 percent to $\frac{1}{2}$ percent. Moreover, deposit accounts were henceforth to be left for a minimum of fourteen days instead of seven days.

The government's method of launching an attack on the general pattern of interest rates was a novel one, and was clearly an outgrowth of wartime experience. As the editor of *The Economist* put it, the Chancellor in "harmonising the banks" chose for his "tonal system . . . not the classical scale, but something more modern—and to many ears, more dissonant. For he has begun, not by establishing a lower and effective Bank Rate, but by operating on one particular rate which, owing to the technical characteristics of the great expansion of wartime finance in Britain's closed economy, offers the least resistance to changes in terms imposed by the borrower."[7]

At time of writing, the fate of the cheap money policy itself seems uncertain. In May 1947, Chancellor Dalton began to have qualms about the growth of the floating debt, and called for consolidation, while still aiming at $2\frac{1}{2}$ percent on long-term issues.[8] In the following month, for the first time since the war began, a government issue (Southern Rhodesia) was offered through normal city channels instead of official channels; and it was offered at a price 1 point less, and with five years' shorter life, than the previous important new long-term issues (Cities of Derby and Newcastle). These actions represented the

---

[7] *The Economist*, October 27, 1945, p. 601.

[8] Chancellor Dalton justified his indifference to the rise in floating debt a year earlier, "because we were then carrying through the cheap money drive with the object of arriving at a basis of $2\frac{1}{2}$ per cent long-term. We have got that. Later, we may advance towards other objectives, but at the moment we are consolidating the $2\frac{1}{2}$ per cent long-term.

. . . If we are in position to consolidate $2\frac{1}{2}$ per cent long-term and also gradually to reduce the floating debt through a Budget surplus, then, indeed, we are getting the best of both worlds, and we are very well content. Therefore, we have now reached a point where a reduction in the floating debt is a very desirable subsidiary process to what we have been carrying on in the reduction of long-term interest rates. I hope that by the end of this financial year we shall have seen both a firming-up of the $2\frac{1}{2}$ per cent long-term rate and also a reduction of the floating debt." (Quoted in *The Economist*, May 24, 1947, p. 812.)

Chart 5—YIELDS ON SELECTED GOVERNMENT OBLIGATIONS, UNITED KINGDOM[a]

(*monthly averages of daily yields*[b])

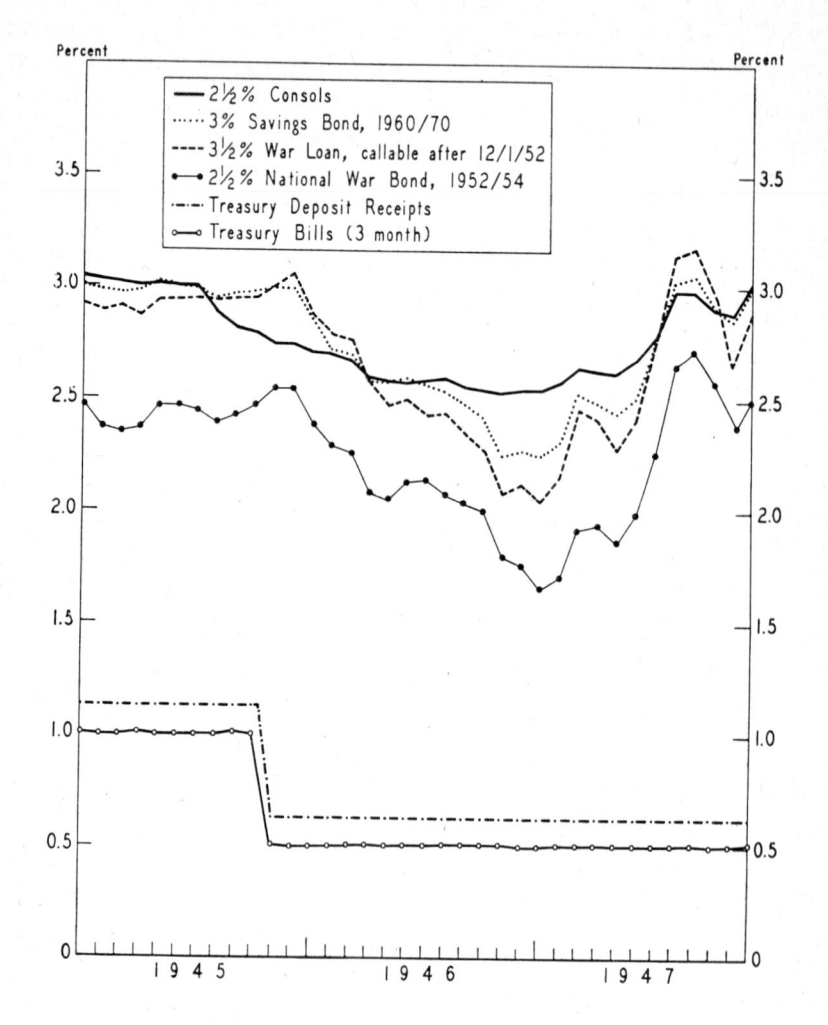

[a] Sources: Bank of Canada, *Statistical Summary;* Bank of England, *Statistical Summary; Monthly Digest of Statistics* (London).

[b] For 2½ percent Consols, a flat yield is taken irrespective of price. For 2½ percent National War Bond (1952/54) and 3 percent Savings Bond (1960/70), redemption is assumed in 1954 and 1970, respectively, if price is below par, and in 1952 and 1960, respectively, if price is above par. For 3½ percent War Loan, a flat yield is taken if price is below par, and redemption is assumed in 1952 if price is above par. Income tax is neglected in calculating the yields. For Treasury Bills, a tender rate is taken as close as possible to the fifteenth of the month.

Chancellor's "awakening to realities" in the capital market, which had begun to weaken in February. The fuel crisis, unfavorable City reaction to the terms of the rail nationalization bill, and other immediate incidents are part of the explanation of the decline in long-terms; but the more basic difficulty, of "deliberately engineering a further reduction in interest rates in a period of acute postwar scarcity of capital, when the physical controls which are the only substitute for financial controls were inevitably growing steadily weaker,"[9] was perhaps a more important part. At the end of the second postwar year, yields on consols and most other government bonds were above the level of October 1945. In the six months following, yields on consols continued to rise, but yields on other governments steadied. However, the announcement of the "deflationary budget" for 1949, with its special levy on investment income, led to a further fall in prices of fixed interest securities, despite the Chancellor's assurance that the levy ("special contribution") would be a "once-for-all" affair.

Some observers hailed the issue by Chancellor Dalton's successor, Sir Stafford Cripps, of a 1978-88 stock at 3 percent as evidence of official abandonment of the cheap money policy;[10] but it would be hazardous at this time to regard recent increases in yields on government securities as a reversal of the long-term downward trend.

The general scarcity of "real" reserves of capital, in the form of inventories and plant and equipment in good condition, combined with heavy borrowing for government undertakings, is likely to continue in England for several years.[11] Bank holdings of government securities will probably continue to expand. Provided growing portfolios of government obligations are accompanied by a corresponding growth of total assets and do not require displacement of higher-yield assets, bank profits (as distinct from the average rate of return on assets) will tend to rise as long as interest rates are above zero. If, however, banks should expand their holdings of government securities at the expense of advances to private customers, or should replace earlier issues of government securities with new issues bearing lower rates of interest, bank profits will tend to fall unless total assets expand fast enough to offset the decline in average rate of return on assets.

Asset Structure
In contrast to the Bank of England statement, the balance sheets of

---

[9] *The Economist,* July 5, 1947, p. 25.
[10] Cf. "End of Cheaper Money," *The Banker,* February 1948, p. 61.
[11] See International Labour Office, Report II, 1945, *Maintaining High Levels of Employment in the Period of Industrial Rehabilitation and Reconversion,* Chapter 2, and literature there cited.

the joint stock banks have shown some reversal of wartime trends, especially with regard to the structure of assets. The first two and one-half postwar years saw a notable expansion of advances, both in absolute and relative terms. In 1947 their volume surpassed their peak prewar level, but as a percentage of total assets, advances remained far below prewar figures. Investments reached a new peak in October 1947 and declined slightly in the following months; relative to total assets, however, they showed no great change. The most striking change was in the relationship of bills discounted to Treasury deposit receipts. Bills ceased to dwindle and expanded rapidly, while TDR's stopped expanding rapidly and began to dwindle.

The increase in Treasury bill holdings and the decrease in holdings of Treasury deposit receipts reflect a change in Treasury policy rather than in joint stock bank policy. Not that the banks were averse to the shift of short-term government financing from TDR's to bills; bills have certain advantages that recommend them to the banks. They are somewhat more liquid than TDR's since they have a shorter average life and can be cashed without penalty. However, the banks are still in the position of having to take whatever short-term obligations the government offers them; and the altered structure of bank assets is the result of a change in the relative supply of, rather than the relative demand for, bills and TDR's. Starting in September 1945, the Treasury began retiring TDR's, and in the two years following reduced the outstanding volume in nearly every month. From August 11, 1945 to August 16, 1947, the volume of TDR's outstanding was reduced by £749 million, while the outstanding volume of Treasury bills was increased by £618.5 million.[12] In the next six months the banks' holdings of bills and TDR's showed little change.

The expansion of bank investments in the first postwar years, at a rate faster than during the war itself, was due to several factors. First, since the retirement of TDR's roughly offset the expansion of Treasury bills, the short-term debt available to the banking system was more or less stable; any significant net increase in holdings of government securities had accordingly to take the form of longer-term investments. Second, the first year of reconversion failed to bring about a significant expansion of advances. Third, the first months of the Chancellor's cheap money campaign produced anomalies in the structure of interest rates,

[12] *The Banker,* September 1946, p. 176 and September 1947, p. 191. Closing the "tap" for 2½ percent Savings Bonds in July 1946, redeeming the unconverted portion of the National War Bonds 1946-48, and meeting heavy day-to-day expenditures, required a net expansion of TDR's in the summer of 1946; but "this reliance upon T.D.R.'s" at that time "could not properly be regarded as a reversal of policy" (*The Banker,* October 1946, p. 6).

particularly in short-dated bonds, that made investments particularly attractive to the banks from the point of view of yield. Fourth, as a result of lower yields and the expectation of increased supplies of consumers' goods, raw materials, and equipment, the "liquidity preference" of the general public, and especially of business, increased after the war, leading to a smaller net absorption of gilt-edged securities by the public, and necessitating the absorption of a larger share of new government issues by the banks and by government departments. Finally, the banks were provided with additional reserves to enable them to expand their portfolios of government securities.

Prognosis of future developments of bank advances is aided somewhat by analysis of the postwar composition of bank lending.[13] In August 1947, "other advances," consisting mainly of personal and professional loans, were the largest single category, as they had been before the war. Financial loans, which include advances to banks, insurance companies, and a small amount of lending to stockbrokers, fell in relative terms but their absolute amount was slightly more than in 1938 and considerably greater than in August 1946. Loans to the building trades were almost the same in absolute amount as in 1938 although they had dropped from fourth to eighth place. Increases were registered in the majority of categories, with the greatest expansion in loans to heavy industry. Although these changes in the composition of bank advances reflect to a considerable degree the special financial needs of reconstruction and reconversion, there is no evidence in the developments to August 1947 that further expansion of advances after the transition period are not possible.

The volume of bank deposits continued to rise in the first two postwar years. After an initial contraction from September 1945 to February 1946, deposits increased for several months at a more rapid rate than at any time during the war, the expansion being mainly in business, financial, and local authority accounts, rather than in personal accounts. W. T. C. King attributed the rapidity of the rise in large measure to an unusually heavy "concealed absorption" of government securities by government departments, in support of the cheaper money policy.[14] He estimated this "concealed absorption" for the eleven months from the beginning of the cheaper money drive to the end of August 1946 at £529 million, compared with £421 million in the same period in 1945.[15] The approach to budget balance in 1947 produced a fairly stable volume of deposits.

[13] See Appendix Table C.
[14] *The Banker,* October 1946, pp. 7-8.
[15] *Ibid.,* p. 15. See also "Cheap Money and Unfunding," *The Economist,* September 7, 1946, pp. 382-84.

The ratio of published capital and reserves to total liabilities continued to fall after the war, dropping well below the customary prewar level. Some of the banks apparently contemplated new issues. But, as *The Economist* had very rightly pointed out, "The exact role which 'capital' plays in modern banking is difficult to define." [16] True, "in the old days, the capital account was an additional security for the depositor, since it defined the proportions in which unfortunate subscribers could be compelled to contribute, to the limit of their fortunes, in the event of failure. But with the spread of limited liability, this function has long disappeared." It is highly doubtful in view of the changing structure of bank assets "whether orthodox principles ought now to be regarded as a proper guide to bank capitalization policy. If the banks increase their capital in order to buttress their expanding gilt-edged position, the very object of that expansion will be to some extent frustrated, because the additional earnings will need to be spread over larger shareholders' resources. The justification, as distinct from the need, of this fresh plunge into gilt-edged securities must be that the banks acknowledge both the determination and the technical competence of the authorities firmly to maintain cheap money. So long as that assumption holds good, the risk of capital loss on a gilt-edged portfolio of £1,400 million will not be greater, and may even be less, than it was with a prewar portfolio of one-third that size."[17]

End of Window-Dressing

One of the most interesting postwar developments in Lombard Street has been the end of window-dressing, a practice which British banks have followed at least since the Baring crisis of 1890. The reform was announced in a simple communiqué:

> The Committee of London Clearing Bankers give notice that on and from December 31, 1946, the Monthly Statements of Balances of London Clearing Banks will be aggregated on common dates synchronizing with the weekly Return of the Bank of England and compiled on the third Wednesday in each month, except in the months of June and December when the Statements will be made up as at the 30th and 31st respectively.
>
> They further announce that taking into account the general disposition of Bank assets now ruling it has been agreed in consultation with the Bank of England that the daily ratio of cash balances will be maintained on the basis of 8 per cent.[18]

Thus ended the curious institution that has long attracted comment

[16] *The Economist*, February 10, 1945, pp. 184-85.
[17] *The Economist*, August 31, 1946, p. 342.
[18] "The Truth about Bank Cash," *The Banker*, January 1947, p. 19.

by observers both within and without the country. In elaborating the importance of this reform, *The Banker* expressed itself as follows:

> The ark of the covenant for the banks, with one lofty dissentient in former times, was the 10 per cent cash ratio, classical basis of the 'one-in-ten' principle of credit creation. Nor—paradox within paradox—was its sanctity dimmed by the fact that the cherished figure always was a myth. It had reality in but one of the large banks, and in the others took tangible shape only rarely, and then by accident. Yet it was immutable.
>
> This is the standard by which last month's decision must be measured. To end the rite of window-dressing, the banks have had to recant the primary article of faith that has guided them for half a century. The mystique 10 per cent has been swept away. In future the cash ratio will be 8 per cent; and that will be a real, not a mythical, figure . . . In the past twenty years or so, revolutionary changes have occurred in the shape of the banking system and in the role it plays, but principles and conventions have scarcely altered. Now that the cardinal principle has gone, the others one by one will have to be justified on their merits, and honest criticism will find an audience. It is a heartening thought.[19]

The time chosen for the passing of window-dressing was opportune, since in the late years of the war the degree of window-dressing had reached unprecedented heights. According to *The Banker's* calculations, the excess of the published cash ratio over the true cash ratio fell from 16.7 percent in 1929 to 9.7 percent in 1934, rose again to 12.6 percent in 1937, and contracted to 8.3 percent in 1939; but during the war it rose steadily until it reached 27.6 percent in 1945.[20]

The transition to an 8 percent reserve basis seems to have caused few technical difficulties for the banks. The computed ratio of reserves to deposits in October-November 1946 was 7.75 percent, just under the 8 percent regarded as the figure at which the banks should aim on the average. True, if the calculation is adjusted to exclude the two banks regularly keeping 10 percent, the average for the other banks was around 7 percent for those months; but the additional cash needed by these banks was approximately balanced by the surplus cash of the other two, and much of that surplus was released to the money market on the morning after the new regulation was announced.[21]

The abandonment of window-dressing is an added reason for substituting Treasury bills for Treasury deposit receipts in the short-term borrowing of the Treasury; such a shift would assist the banks in obtaining the precise daily cash adjustments that the new system requires. Also, it becomes more important than before that Treasury bills should

[19] *Ibid.*, p. 13.
[20] *Ibid.*, p. 15.
[21] *Ibid.*, p. 19.

be available which will mature on every day of bank business, account being taken of future Sundays and holidays when the bills are first issued.

Discount Market

For the discount houses, as for the joint stock banks, the first two and one-half postwar years brought a continued expansion of the role of government borrowing in day-to-day activities. The recovery of foreign trade and of domestic acceptance credit was not sufficient to restore the relative importance of commercial paper in discount house portfolios; government finance provided profitable outlets for the funds of the discount market.

The effect of the labor government's cheap money policy on the discount market differed from that on the joint stock banks. The rates at which the discount houses obtained funds, as well as the rates at which they lent them, were reduced. After October 1945 the discount market was able to obtain call money against bills at $\frac{1}{2}$ of 1 percent, compared with the former 1 percent, and advances against bonds at $\frac{3}{4}$ of 1 percent, compared with the former $1\frac{1}{4}$ percent from the banks or $\frac{5}{8}$ of 1 percent from the outside market. In order to maintain earnings it was necessary only to expand the scale of operations, which the discount houses did cheerfully. Weekly allotments of Treasury bills to the discount market reached unprecedented heights in November 1945, and continued high thereafter.[22] As *The Economist* put it, "At present the discount houses are doing very well out of Mr. Dalton." Operations in the short-term bond market were particularly profitable; in the first months of the cheap money drive, yields on short-term bonds actually rose (Chart 5), which, with the reduced loan rates on bond money, meant that "the handsome margins available . . . through the war period" were "increased at both ends," and "the running profit on bonds" became "very handsome."[23]

This happy state of affairs, however, did not continue. The rise in yields on short-dated bonds resulted from the expectation that some of them would be called for refunding on a lower yield basis. Starting in December 1945, these expectations began to be fulfilled, as the Chancellor called in two short-dated issues for conversion. The strategy employed at that time set the pattern for later conversions. First, the "tap" for $2\frac{1}{2}$ percent National War Bonds of 1954-56 and 3 percent Savings Bonds 1965-75 was turned off. Second, it was announced that

[22] In some weeks, indeed, the allotment was somewhat in excess of the discount market's wishes, since money pressure obliged it to dispose of earlier issues still bearing the higher yield.

[23] *The Economist*, November 3, 1945, p. 649, and November 24, 1945, p. 757.

the 2½ percent Conversion Loan of 1944-49 would be called on April 1, 1946, and the 2½ percent National War Bonds on July 1, 1946; holders were given the option up to February 25 of that year of converting into 1¾ percent Exchequer Bonds of 1950. Third, the limit on holdings of 3 percent Defense Bonds was raised from £1,500 to £2,000. In May 1946, these bonds were replaced by a 2½ percent bond, identical except for a limit on holdings of £2,500. "Unfunding" tactics of this sort were successful in bringing most short-bond yields below 2 percent by the end of the first postwar year,[24] but the rise in yields had, by the end of 1947, restored a 2½ percent rate for short-dated bonds.

As more and more of the outstanding "shorts" come due for conversion, there will be fewer and fewer opportunities for the discount market to maintain its rate of return on investments of this sort. The fact is that the net profits of the "Big Three," which had risen from £628.2 million in 1945 to £830.6 million in 1946, fell to £621.3 million in 1947.[25] The question naturally arises, therefore, as to the likelihood of the discount market achieving greater independence of government finance in the future.

It does not seem very probable that the 1913 volume of foreign bills will be restored in the London discount market. Foreign trade may well revive, but over the near future both international investment and the financing of foreign trade may involve a larger measure of government participation, including government bulk purchases, exchange control, and government international lending. The more rapid turnover of foreign trade will tend to reduce the average term of acceptance credit and thus its total volume. The role of private enterprise in continental finance has been greatly curtailed and its future is uncertain at best. Likewise, it hardly seems possible that London's share in financing the world's international trade and investment will be greater than it was before the war. The trend of international finance toward New York and Washington was accelerated by the war; Canada and the other Dominions have outgrown much of their former financial dependence upon Britain; Britain has lost a large share of her foreign assets, while acquiring substantial foreign debts; Switzerland has emerged as a rival in the financing of continental commerce and industry.[26]

---

[24] See "Cheap Money and Unfunding," *The Economist,* September 7, 1946, pp. 382-84, and "Gilt-Edged Yield Comparisons," *The Economist,* October 26, 1946, p. 679.

[25] *The Banker,* February 1948, p. 119.

[26] These matters are discussed more fully in Chapter 5 above. See also "London or New York—World Money Market," *The Statist* (British Banking Section), July 20, 1946, pp. 3-6.

Domestic bills may receive more attention than before the war because of these factors, but it is unlikely that they can play a prominent enough part in themselves to keep the discount houses alive. Much depends, too, on the willingness of the joint stock banks to leave this field open to specialists. Certainly, if the role of the discount houses is to be reduced to one of government finance, the need for specialized institutions to deal in bills is much less apparent. It requires little special knowledge to judge the acceptability of Treasury bills.

No doubt, the discount houses will continue to operate in their traditional sphere, and in new ones as well. Not only are these institutions essential to the smooth operation of the British money market as now constituted, but also, through experience extending over several generations, they have built up a knowledge and prestige in the field of international finance, together with an acquaintance with the organization and personnel of foreign financial centers, that British authorities consider precious. In view of Britain's professed desire to recapture her position as a leading lender and trader, she is naturally reluctant to see these venerable institutions replaced by untried organizations.

Judging from the capital expansion of the discount market in the first postwar year, both the discount houses themselves and the Capital Issues Committee took a favorable view of the future of the discount market. In January 1946, Cater Brightwen and Company, fourth largest of the discount houses, undertook an expansion; Alexanders followed suit shortly thereafter; and somewhat later Smith St. Aubyn, Jessel Toynbee, and others did likewise. By the spring of 1947, the number of houses was one-third lower than in prewar years, but the aggregate resources of the discount market were 70 percent higher than prewar.[27]

This optimism may prove well founded; but even if it does, the activities of the discount market will be very different from what they were in 1913. In the next few years at least, the market's major operations will not be in private bills but in short-term government bonds. Since the discount houses are professional dealers for tax purposes, they can charge the amortization of premiums on bond purchases against profits when calculating their tax liability. Consequently, they can bid higher than nonprofessional investors for short bonds, relieving institutional holders of bonds as they approach maturity and keeping them until they can be turned over to the government authorities. Thus the discount market "is both qualitatively and quantitatively a more important unit in the financial structure than it has been for many

[27] W. T. C. King, "The Changing Discount Market," *The Banker,* March 1947, p. 185.

years." But "it is a new Lombard Street, which serves above all the needs of a Treasury wedded to cheap money."[28]

W. T. C. King also stressed the change in the discount market:

> Although the whole mechanism of Lombard Street has been enlarged, the purpose of this inflow of capital is to expand, not the discount mechanism, but the new mechanism in the short bond market which the discount houses have grafted on to their traditional bill-dealing apparatus. Lombard Street, which in the pre-war decade often found cause to wonder whether it was doomed to eventual extinction, has during the war acquired a new and important function, the function of making and smoothing the market in a huge block of short-term Government securities.[29]

By the end of 1945, he pointed out, the "Big Three" companies were financing a bill-and-bond portfolio twice as large in relation to their resources as before the war.

These are the facts that induced Professor D. H. Robertson to ask, in an after-dinner address to the Lombard Association in London,

> And what about your esteemed satellites, the bill-brokers? Will they ever be called on to do an honest day's work again, distinguishing by smell and touch a good trade bill from a bad one? Or are they, too, doomed to remain for evermore an all but functionless appendage of the Exchequer, never handling any two objects more different than the Chancellor's promise to pay in three months and the same gentleman's promise to pay in twelve? It seems a dull end to a long and not inglorious history.[30]

Merchant Banks

The composition of assets of the merchant banks is even less likely to assume the pattern of 1913, since the granting of international acceptance credit will probably not recapture its prominent position in merchant bank activities, and the merchant banks have no special competitive advantage in the short-term market for domestic credit. Government financing and long-term financing of trade and commerce appear to be the two main areas of possible expansion.

One line of development is suggested by the activities of Hambros Bank. As reported in *The Statist*, Hambros Bank "was faced with the likelihood that a quick postwar resumption of acceptance business was hardly possible, and therefore prepared to participate in Anglo-United States trade on a basis more intimate than is usual for banks."[31] This "departure" was followed by another: the granting of £1 million of

---

[28] *The Economist*, February 15, 1947, p. 292.
[29] *Ibid.*, p. 171.
[30] D. H. Robertson, "Is There a Future for Banking?" *The Banker*, November 1946.
[31] *The Statist*, March 30, 1946, p. 268. Cf. also *The Economist*, March 30, 1946, p. 503.

commercial acceptance credit to nationalized industries in Czechoslovakia, for imports of raw materials from the sterling area. The loans presumably are to be liquidated ultimately by Czechoslovakian exports to the United Kingdom and other countries, and are renewable year by year. The credits were arranged through leading Czech banks (also nationalized) and were guaranteed by the National Bank of Czechoslovakia. This credit is quite different from the acceptance of ordinary trade paper representing transactions already undertaken. The Czech importing firms will draw on Hambros Bank, and the resultant bills will be discounted in the London market. *The Statist* added, "It is natural to hope that this credit may prove to be the prototype of many others granted by our merchant banks, but the number of directions in which substantial credit risks on private account may at present be safely undertaken is still very limited." *The Economist* also notes "significant credit lines . . . in other directions," notably with Scandinavia, and hopes that "Hambros' action will serve *pour encourager les autres.*" The new departures seem to have been profitable for Hambros; foreign acceptances increased during 1946 from £2.5 to £6.9 million, while holdings of cash, Treasury bills, and government stocks also rose. So pleased was the bank with its expansion that it called for new capital in May 1947.[32]

There have been numerous suggestions that the merchant banks may expand their investment banking activities.[33] The composition of the Issuing Houses Association, organized since the war, lends support to this view. This new body has the same chairman, secretary, and office address as the old Accepting Houses Association. Of the twenty-four members of the new body, seventeen are members of the old. *The Economist* explained the establishment of the new association, when the Accepting Houses Association already provided a means for coordinating operations of the merchant banks, in terms of the decline of acceptance business and of overseas lending, and of the increasing share of domestic long-term finance in the business of the older merchant banks.

Capital Market

With regard to the capital market, the legislation of the labor government has done little more than carry out the promises of its predecessor to continue wartime regulations. The Investment (Control and Guaranties) Act of 1946 retained wartime controls of the capital market, and provided for a Treasury guarantee of industrial loans up to £50

[32] *The Economist,* May 24, 1947, p. 819.
[33] See, for example, "The Merchant Banks," *The Economist,* Banking Supplement, October 28, 1944, pp. 1 and 2.

million per year.[34] The act was not considered startling in financial circles. Indeed *The Economist* criticized it for its conservatism: "The Investment Bill seeks to perpetuate existing methods of control, and is at least as solicitous about established industries as it is about the development of new ones. It exhibits in almost every line Treasury habits of thought, and Treasury conceptions of control, rather than the views of progressive economists and enterprising industrialists."[35]

Even these controls were relaxed somewhat in May 1947. Wholly unsecured and stock market loans repayable in six months were exempted from regulation, and Treasury permission for new issues of stocks and shares was limited to offers by "bodies which have, within two years of the offer, made any issue under one or other of the exemptions conferred by the Capital Issues Exemptions Orders."[36]

The end of the war and the election of the labor government caused a temporary recession of the stock market, but during 1946 the market was buoyant, and the average price for industrials in August 1946 was considerably above that of August 1945. The first budget of the new government was enthusiastically received in Lombard Street. The reduction in the excess profits tax, the relief from taxation of expenditures on research, the increase in tax allowances for obsolescence and for investment in parts and equipment, were probably responsible for this attitude. Even the difficulties of the first six months of 1947 failed to produce a lasting downward revision of share prices. The *Financial Times* index shows a break in prices of ordinary shares early in the year, followed by almost complete recovery. Although the dollar crisis of August was accompanied by a sharp decline on the London stock exchange, recovery set in quickly, and continued throughout the rest of the year, despite the doubling of profits taxes in November. The grim picture painted by the *Economic Survey for 1948,* however, was quite understandably reflected in a break of security prices. Less understandable was the recovery after the "deflationary budget" for 1949 was announced; the "Special Contribution" from investment income was one of its main features; and the budget did little to offset the impact of this feature on the outlook for shareholders except to confirm expectations that it would include no further increase in profits taxes and would impose no formal limitations on dividends, in view of the Federated British Industries' proposal for voluntary dividend limitations.

---

[34] A "National Investment Council" has taken over the work of the Capital Issues Committee and the Public Works Loan Board, and has continued to reserve access to the new issue market for those industries considered most essential, with national development and reconversion in mind instead of prosecution of war.

[35] *The Economist,* January 26, 1946, p. 124.

[36] *The Economist,* May 31, 1947, p. 867.

The vitality of the capital market is also illustrated by new capital issues, which in 1947 amounted to £151.1 million; £117.6 million were United Kingdom issues and £33.5 million for overseas. These figures may be compared with £17.0 million and £3.5 million for United Kingdom and foreign issues, respectively, in 1945. Although the share of home issues in the total has shown some fluctuation since the end of the war, it has continued to be the largest, with the public particularly receptive to industrials; new issues of this type have for the most part been greatly oversubscribed.

Finance Corporation for Industry

During the first postwar year, the new finance corporations made only insignificant inroads into the capital market. The first annual report of the Finance Corporation for Industry was submitted in May 1946, and covered the first ten months of operations, ending March 31, 1946. As the Chairman pointed out in his accompanying statement "it was naturally some months before the organization of the Corporation was completed and its first loans arranged," and the report is of limited value as an indication of the probable effect of the Corporation on the British capital market. Organization costs ate up £126,008 of the initial £500,000 of called-up share capital, £125,000 of which went for stamp duties.[37] The Corporation also suffered an operating loss of £16,085. It had made advances of only £254,500.

The Corporation was a good deal more active during its second year. Total loans outstanding on March 31, 1947 amounted to £1,862,051. One of the larger items in this total was a loan of £210,600 to a concern for which the Corporation was later appointed a receiver, and to which it later extended further accommodation. The FCI's losses were reduced to £9,142 for fiscal 1947. Its commitments for the fiscal year 1948, however, far exceeded its earlier activities; one loan alone, to the Steel Company of Wales, amounted to £35,000,000.[38]

Industrial and Commercial Finance Corporation

The first report of the Industrial and Commercial Finance Corporation covered the period July 20, 1945, when it was incorporated, to September 30, 1946. Its preliminary expenses were somewhat less than those of the Finance Corporation for Industry (£76,300, of which £75,000 went for stamp duties), but its operating losses were larger (£29,175). Loans actually disbursed in the period amounted to a little less than £1,250,000, but commitments had been made for £1,600,000. In

---

[37] England has a high and progressive stamp tax on legal documents, including marketable securities. (Cf. 53 and 54 Victoria C. 39 and amendments.)

[38] *The Economist,* August 2, 1947, p. 213.

addition, "£2.4 million was in process of completion, while £1 million was in a slightly earlier stage of tying up."

The range of actual and prospective borrowers was very wide, with no marked concentration in any single industrial category, although mechanical engineering trades as a group took one-quarter of the total.[39] Analysis of a sample of £7,000,000, including excess profits tax refunds and new capital supplied from other sources, as well as I. C. F. C. advances, showed that £4,250,000 was for fixed assets, and £2,750,000 for working capital. Half the number of loans made was for relatively small amounts, £5,000 to £20,000; less than 10 percent was for more than £100,000. The interest rates were described by the Chairman in his statement as "the lowest . . . which are commercially possible, . . . normally from 4 percent to 5 percent" when loans are made for medium or long term and on good security.

In presenting the report, the Chairman made several interesting observations on the relation of the Industrial and Commercial Finance Corporation to the capital market as a whole.

> Our function is not new. It is the supply of capital to concerns which find it necessary to raise capital for development from outside sources, concerns, more precisely, whose requirements fall within the limits of £5,000 and £200,000. Our customers are mainly private Limited Companies engaged in manufacture, but we do not exclude any type of business, industrial or commercial, from our scope, nor, of course, do we restrict our facilities to private Limited Companies. At 30th September we had examined 840 applications having definite outline; and of 703 conclusively dealt with, we had been able to grant facilities in 133 cases, or about 20 percent.
>
> Bank accommodation is complementary to the class of facilities we offer, which is of the nature of a long-term, or maybe a permanent, addition to the customer's capital resources. In general, the facilities extended by us make the customer a better customer for the Bank. In a sample of 89 cases of a straightforward kind, customers who had enjoyed previously overdraft limits aggregating £1,900,000 were granted new limits aggregating £2,890,000, based on their now increased resources. There are cases, on the other hand, where Banks have provided exceptional facilities on a temporary basis, and here what is required is a reduction of limit. In three such cases which I have in mind, overdrafts amounting roughly to £627,000 were brought down to new limits aggregating £495,000. I do not stress these figures, which are based upon an experience not yet very wide. They serve, however, to illustrate the complementary character of our facilities and those of the Banks, and the advantage of this to eligible customers.

Like the FCI, the ICFC expanded its activities during its second

[39] Includes producers of agricultural machinery, machine tools, prime movers, printing and paper-making machinery, textile machinery, cooking, heating and ventilation machinery, and "all other machinery."

fiscal year. By September 31, 1947, it had approved proposals amounting to £10,501,000, of which £5,716,000 had been taken up. However, there was some question as to whether this expansion represented the kind of financing for which the Corporation was organized. Less than 12 percent of the number and 5 percent of the amount of all loans made in the Corporation's second fiscal year were for amounts between £5,000 and £10,000. Moreover, loans of amounts exceeding £100,000 rose during the year from 7 to 22 percent of the number, and from 28 to 56½ percent of the amount, of all loans made.

Outlook for Lombard Street as a Whole

This essay has stressed the close relationship of the prosperity of Lombard Street to the prosperity of the British economy as a whole, and especially to British foreign trade and finance. If Britain ultimately achieves her stated objective of expanding physical exports to a volume of 75 percent above the prewar level, and consequently solves her balance of payments problem without restricting the ratio of imports to national income below the prewar level, Lombard Street will prosper along with the rest of the British economy.

Exports

At time of writing, the outlook for the achievement of Britain's objectives in international trade is very dim. Early optimism has been dispelled by the fuel crisis, growing competition in export markets, labor difficulties, the burden of overseas military obligations, and rising American prices. During the first postwar year, British exports showed a rapid recovery. By the second quarter of 1946, the value of exports of British manufactured goods was three and one-half times the quarterly average of 1943, and the value of total exports was back to the 1938 level. In May 1946, employment in manufacturing for export was 30 percent above the prewar level, and so cautious an economist as R. G. D. Allen felt safe in predicting that an increase in exports of 50 percent would be achieved by the end of 1946, and that the full 75 percent increase would be reached by the spring of 1947.[40] For 1946 as a whole, the physical volume of exports was approximately at the 1938 level, exports of manufactured goods rose more than 10 percent, while imports were held to 69 percent of the 1938 volume.

The early success in increasing exports was based largely on unusually heavy demands from devastated countries, where keen international

[40] R. G. D. Allen, "A Year of Reconversion," Royal Economic Society, *Memorandum No. 107*, pp. 9-10.

competition for markets had not yet developed. By the spring of 1947, this advantageous situation was rapidly disappearing. The President of the Board of Trade, Sir Stafford Cripps, stated in June 1947, "From everywhere we receive the warning that the sellers' market is disappearing—it has already disappeared as far as some commodities are concerned—and we are right on the verge of a period when we shall have to rely not only on the quantity and quality of our production, but also upon the power of our salesmanship."[41]

The fuel and transport crisis arising out of the adverse weather conditions of early 1947 not only interrupted the expansion of exports but led to an absolute decline. The index of volume of exports fell from 110.8 (1938 = 100) for the last quarter of 1946 to 100.5 in the first quarter of 1947. Despite rapid recovery in the second half of the year, the volume of exports for 1947 as a whole was only 8 percent above the 1938 level. The critical situation, together with rising American prices, also necessitated an unplanned increase in the value of imports. The original program laid down in the *Economic Survey for 1947*[42] called for imports in 1947 of £1,450 million (exclusive of films), which was already £350 million above 1946; but the revised estimates for mid-1947 to mid-1948 were £235 million higher still. Even this expansion would not have provided any improvement in the British standard of living. In volume, imports would have been only 80 percent of prewar imports, and a large share would have had to be reserved for incorporation into exports. At time of writing, however, even this modest import target had been abandoned and new restrictions on imports had been imposed. Actual imports for 1947 were £1,574 million, equivalent in volume terms to 77 percent of the 1938 level.[43]

While the reverses of early 1947 constituted a serious setback to British plans for increasing exports, these reverses do not weigh heavily in an assessment of long-run prospects. The outcome of the export drive will depend ultimately upon the ability of the government, in cooperation with employers and workers, to reduce costs in the export industries. Professor MacDougall has demonstrated in convincing fashion that achievement of the export target will require foreign sales of British manufactures *double* the prewar level; and that since world trade in manufacturers is unlikely to reach a volume twice as high as before the war, this requirement really means that Britain must enlarge her share of the world market in manufactures.[44] In other words, Britain must

---

[41] Quoted in *The Economist,* June 28, 1947, p. 1036.
[42] Cmd. 7046 (London, February 21, 1947).
[43] *Economic Survey for 1948,* Cmd. 7344 (London, March 1948).
[44] G. D. A. MacDougall, "Britain's Foreign Trade Problem," *The Economic Journal,* Vol. LVII, March 1947, especially pp. 91-110.

outsell her competitors, especially the United States; and the only way to do this and to raise the British standard of living at the same time is to increase the productivity of the British economy.[45]

The disparity in productivity between British and American industry appeared long before the war, and became increasingly obvious during it.[46] Early in 1944, a Cotton Textile Mission was sent to the United States to study differences in British and American productivity in that industry. In its Report,[47] the Mission stated that with normal staffing British production per man-hour was below American by 18 to 49 percent in spinning, by 80 to 85 percent in winding, by 79 to 89 percent in beaming, and by 56 to 67 percent in weaving. The Mission found a variety of factors in the American industry to account for these disturbing disparities: high-draft, high-speed, automatic machinery; up-to-date plant; scientific methods of labor-utilization; concentration on high operative efficiency rather than on high machine efficiency; lower age of operatives; integration of industry; continuous, standardized production; lack of long-standing conventions in the methods of labor utilization; and the fact that "American mill managers, generally, are young and analytical and progressive in their outlook."

It is not unreasonable to suppose that similar conditions affect other industries where British efficiency falls far below American.[48] In any case, the broad lines of policy adopted by the government have been the same for other industries as for cotton, except for coal and transportation, which are being nationalized. In October 1945, the Board of Trade set up a "Working Party" consisting of four employer representatives, four trade union representatives, four independent members, and a Chairman appointed by the Board of Trade; the employer and worker representatives were selected by the Board from panels nominated by the associations and unions. This Working Party studied the deficiencies of the cotton industry and considered such remedies as re-equipment of the mills, double-shifts, amalgamations and "nationalization," integration, and joint consultation in the industry. It presented its report in May 1946, and recommended a compre-

[45] Cf. Alfred E. Kahn, "The British Balance of Payments and Problems of Domestic Policy," *The Quarterly Journal of Economics,* Vol. LXI, May 1947, especially pp. 372-74.
[46] Cf. P. S. Brown, "Prospective National Income and Capital Formation in the United Kingdom," *The American Economic Review,* Vol. XXXVI, No. 4, Part 1, p. 555.
[47] *Report of the Cotton Textile Mission to the U.S.A. March-April 1944* (commonly known as the "Platt Report," London, 1944).
[48] The Reid Committee Report (Cmd. 6610, March 1945) on the coal industry showed British coal output per man-shift to be lower than in Poland, Holland, and the Ruhr, and far below the United States.

hensive survey of existing plant and its suitability for modernization, group operation of mills, new loan facilities, and the building up of a fund to aid re-equipment from a levy on yarn offset by a higher controlled price. The government accepted these recommendations in general and offered grants of 25 percent of the cost of re-equipment of machinery. Fourteen similar working parties have been established in other industries, and have since published Reports. The Industrial Organization Act of 1947 is in large measure a response to the proposals in these Reports. The Act provides for the establishment of Development Councils, with representatives of employers, workers, and experts, in industries operated by private enterprise. These Councils will endeavor to raise productivity by improving equipment and layout, introducing incentive schemes, etc.[49]

Shipping

It is not yet certain that Britain will recapture her position as the world's leading merchant shipper. Construction of merchant shipping, both in terms of tonnage completed and tonnage laid down, averaged little more in 1946 than in 1945, and was well below the wartime peak of 1942. In 1947, there was some expansion. The tonnage launched was greater than in any year since 1930, except for 1942. American production fell in 1947, and British tonnage launched was 57 percent of the world total (excluding Russia, Germany, and Japan), which compares with 58 percent in 1913. Nevertheless, the tonnage registered under the British flag was less in 1947 than in 1939, and the quality was much inferior.

Given a sufficient volume of world trade, Britain might find profitable use for a merchant fleet even larger than her prewar fleet. The American fleet, however, may remain greater than the British, whatever the ultimate development of trade. As indicated in Table 15, the U. S. Maritime Commission planned a postwar merchant fleet nearly 50 percent above that of prewar years, with the greater part of it assigned to the trans-Atlantic and trans-Pacific runs. Canada's merchant fleet, in all likelihood, will also remain above the prewar level, and Norway, France, Belgium, and Holland plan to regain their prewar positions as shippers. All told, it seems quite probable that Britain will suffer a

[49] Cf. United Kingdom Information Office, *Monthly Commentary,* June 1, 1946, p. 4; "Plan for Cotton," *Labour and Industry in Britain,* Vol. V, No. 1, January 1947; and "Efficiency in Privately-Owned Industry," *ibid.,* No. 4, April 1947; "Productivity in Britain," *ibid.,* Vol. VI, No. 1, March 1948.

relative loss in world shipping, and in the world insurance and finance that goes with it.

Table 15—ESTIMATES OF DRY-CARGO TONNAGE USED BY UNITED STATES MERCHANT FLEET, 1939, AND SUGGESTED REQUIREMENTS FOR POSTWAR TRADE[a]

	Dry-Cargo Tonnage Used June 30, 1939		Maritime Commission's Suggestion for Postwar Trade	
	No. of Vessels	Gross Tons	No. of Vessels	Gross Tons
Atlantic	83	528,840	118	770,220
Mediterranean	29	172,485	20	135,432
Caribbean	67	353,046	81	323,334
African	13	81,747	21	135,762
South American	43	302,903	55	453,288
Pacific	24	199,666	93	704,418
Round the world	12	102,124	7	46,200
TOTAL	271	1,740,811	395	2,568,654

[a] From *Foreign Commerce Weekly*, February 23, 1946, p. 6. It should be noted that these figures exclude tankers, harbor craft, river craft, and lake shipping.

Insurance

Rebuilding the British insurance business will be no easy task. In the first place, the British companies must make an almost completely fresh start. In the second place, they face competition from American concerns eager to expand into fresh fields. In the third place, much of the businesses, property, and shipping upon which the insurance business was based has been destroyed, and it will not be quickly restored. In Germany and Japan, and in the areas closely tied to them economically, private enterprise of the prewar type is not likely to be restored for a very considerable period. In the fourth place, there is, in some countries at least, the possibility that as the insurance business is restored it will be nationalized. Even where actual nationalization does not take place, present indications are that government policy abroad will discourage foreign insurance through such devices as discriminatory taxation, "reinsurance banks" with partial or complete monopolies of reinsurance business, requirements of unduly onerous deposits for foreign concerns, and so forth.[50]

The companies themselves are well aware of the complexity of their situation, and have taken steps to deal with it. Missions have been sent to Belgium, Denmark, France, and Greece to survey the field, ascertain the extent of the market, and "recreate goodwill." An advisory committee representing Lloyd's and the other companies has been set up at the request of the Board of Trade to deal with overseas business.

Britain as a Creditor Nation

In 1946, Britain still had a net credit balance of current income from foreign capital, amounting to £60 million. In 1947, it had shrunk to £51 million, and there is no assurance that Britain will remain a "creditor nation" even in this restricted sense. Indeed, the chances are that Britain's capital position will be worse before it is better.

The statistical White Paper (Cmd. 6707) supporting the request for an American loan estimated the deficit in Britain's balance of payments in 1946 at £750 million; a deficit of £500 million was anticipated for 1947-48; a "slight" deficit was expected in 1949 or 1950; and it was hoped that in 1951 equilibrium on current account would be achieved. The 1946 estimate proved unduly pessimistic; "the export drive developed faster than had been expected,"[51] and the actual deficit was around £450 million. It was met in large part by drawing £150 million on the U. S. credits and £130 million on the Canadian. The reverses of the winter and spring of 1947, however, led to much higher deficits than had been anticipated for that period. As shown in Table 16, drawings on U. S. credit, and disbursements out of U. S. and Canadian credits, were very much higher in the first half of 1947 than they were in the second half of 1946. Nevertheless, the British government

---

[50] In a presidential address to the Insurance Institute of London, C. H. Leach said in 1946, "It is not an exaggeration to say that scarcely a week passes in which consideration has not to be given to legislative problems from some parts of the world—threats of restrictive decrees, Government monopolies, State control, increased and discriminatory taxation." (Reported in *The Banker,* December 1946, p. 160.) A correspondent to *The Banker* went on to say, "Company reports show, however, how successfully the companies' representatives have safeguarded British insurance interests in enemy and enemy-occupied countries during the war years, and how speedily business has been resumed in many of the countries that were over-run by the enemy. In Central and Southern Europe, of course, resumption depends upon the solution of complex political questions and economic restoration. Elsewhere, too, financial and economic problems have in many instances hampered the full and free resumption of operations. But it is widely appreciated that the delicate fabric of international trade can be restored only with the help of the protection provided by insurance facilities, and, despite perplexing problems, the re-establishment of British insurance overseas is being actively pursued."

[51] Cmd. 7046, *op. cit.*

proceeded with negotiations for liquidation of sterling balances, and on July 15 restored convertibility for current transactions, in accordance with Article 10 of the "Financial Agreement between the Governments of the United States and the United Kingdom of 6 December 1945." The result was an unprecedented rate of withdrawals on U. S. credit in July and August. Import restrictions introduced early in August had a negligible effect. In the week of August 18 alone, withdrawals amounted to $237 million, leaving only $400 million of the initial $3,750 million U. S. credit.[52] On August 20 convertibility was restricted again, the loan was temporarily "frozen," and a new period of Anglo-American financial negotiations began.[53] At the end of 1947, gold and dollar reserves were down to £680 million, which was not expected to last much beyond the end of 1948.[54]

Table 16—DRAWINGS ON U. S. CREDIT AND NET SPENDINGS FROM U. S. AND CANADIAN CREDITS[a]
(in millions)

Period	Drawings on U. S. Credit	Net Spendings from U. S. and Canadian Credits
1946		
Third quarter	$400	$210
Fourth quarter	200	369
1947		
January	200	137
February	100	224
March	200	323
April	450	307
May	200	334
June	300	308
July	700	538
Total through July	2,750	2,750
August 1-20	600	....
Total through August 20	3,350	....

[a] Based on *The Economist*, August 16, 1947 and *Monthly Letter of the National City Bank of New York*, September 1947.

[52] *Monthly Letter of the National City Bank of New York*, September 1947, p. 99.
[53] In an interesting analysis of the causes of this breakdown, *The Economist* (August 30, 1947, p. 350) showed that the major item in the deterioration of Britain's balance of payments position since 1938 was the huge increase in government overseas expenditures for military and political purposes. World inflation, and the fact that British import prices rose more than export prices, were the next most serious factors. The physical balance of trade was considerably better after the war than it was in 1938 and, except for reduced income from foreign investment, the decline in invisible income was of relatively little importance.
[54] *Economic Survey for 1948, op. cit.*, p. 15.

Britain's Bargaining Position

Britain's bargaining power in world trade and financial negotiations leans heavily upon her self-styled position as "the world's best customer."[55] The argument is a simple one: "Not only is the volume of British purchases higher than that of any other country and, on the whole, more stable; it also consists more largely of those staple primary products that other countries are usually most anxious to sell abroad." Britain "is willing to continue to play this role," but "what is bought must be paid for" and Britain "having spent in the common cause a higher proportion of her substance will have to pay for nearly all her future purchases with exports of her own goods." Accordingly Britain "is preparing to make a great effort to supply the manufactures and the services the world wants": she prefers a system of multilateral trading, but "it is for other countries to say whether they too will cooperate in bringing into existence the conditions in which Britain can continue to be the World's Best Customer."[56]

There are, however, a few weaknesses in this argument. In the first place, it is not at all certain that what the rest of the world wants is a return to the 1913 kind of trade organization, in which Britain exported manufactured goods in exchange for primary products. Two major wars in one generation have greatly accelerated the industrialization of the nations with which Britain trades, and many of these countries are now at least as anxious to export manufactured goods and import primary products and services as to export primary products and services and import manufactures. In the second place, Britain can hope to obtain markets for her manufactures only if she can produce them more cheaply than other countries.

Finally, there is some doubt as to the strength of Britain's position as "the world's best customer." It is true that in 1938 Britain absorbed more imports than any other country—one-fifth of the world's exports. But when these imports are broken down,[57] it is at least questionable whether this fact will be enough to persuade the world to take British exports in preference to cheaper goods and services from other countries. The countries selling more than 20 percent of their exports to Britain were for the most part not countries to which Britain in turn sent anything like an equal share of her total exports. Indeed, two-fifths of total British exports in 1938 went to countries selling one-fifth and less

---

[55] United Kingdom Ministry of Information, *Great Britain—the World's Best Customer* (London, 1945).

[56] *Ibid.*, p. 5.

[57] As has been done, for example, by G. D. A. MacDougall in "Britain's Bargaining Power," *Economic Journal,* Vol. LVI, March 1946, p. 301.

of their exports to Britain.[58] Also, the United States was not far behind Britain as an importer before the war; as Professor MacDougall put it, "If ever we [British] are tempted to use our bargaining power as a large importer to force other countries to take our exports, we would do well to remember that at least one-third of our exports went to countries which depended more on the United States market than on our own."[59]

General Conclusions

Britain's share of the world's financial business is not likely to be so great in the future as it was before World War I. The Bretton Woods agreements themselves give evidence of how little of London's position as a banking center has survived the two World Wars. Basic reserves are gold and American dollars; par values are expressed in gold and American dollars; voting power is determined by the American dollar value of quotas; both the International Monetary Fund and the International Bank for Reconstruction and Development are located in Washington, not London; and both organizations will involve supervision of foreign exchange rates and capital movements by an international organization, not by Lombard Street.

As stated in Chapter 1, one source of Lombard Street's income in the past was the financing of trade between countries far removed from Britain. That type of credit is incompatible with bilateral agreements and the controls of exchange and trade that developed during the war and interwar periods. Its restoration depends upon the relaxation of such controls. In addition, the growth of banking facilities in other trading countries restricts this kind of credit.

Britain's own trade policy must depend considerably upon measures adopted by other countries, particularly the United States. Britain naturally wants stable foreign exchange rates, and is determined that the pound shall be established at a level that does not overvalue it. Whatever its relative importance may have been, overvaluation of the pound was given considerable emphasis in the discussion of Britain's difficulties after 1925, and the error of overvaluation is not likely to be consciously repeated. There is no question this time of pursuing a deflationary internal policy in order to support an overvalued pound. Some persons feel that in order to guarantee an adequate volume of exports, a rate even lower than the present $4.03 must be established; others, attaching as much importance to the *terms* as to the *volume* of trade, have expressed a fear that the pound may be set too low. Determination of the most appropriate exchange rate will require concepts

[58] *Ibid.*, p. 31.
[59] "Britain's Foreign Trade Problem," *op. cit.*, p. 100.

of equilibrium, and techniques for estimating its position, more refined than the "purchasing power parity equation" in vogue after the last war.[60]

The widest difference of opinion, both within the government and outside, appears in regard to the organization of postwar international trade. On one point only is there complete unanimity: no form of organization which threatens full employment will be acceptable.[61] But whether full employment can best be achieved through "omnilateral" trade, through a sterling bloc that would restrict trade with nonsterling countries, or through imperial preference, is still a controversial question.

Much of the free trade tradition remains in Britain. It grew up at a time when Britain, as the leading industrial nation, had a strong bargaining position in buying raw materials and in selling finished goods, and therefore had everything to gain by free access to world markets. British bargaining power may be weaker today than it was before the last war, but it is still strong enough to make the people keenly aware of the advantages of geographic specialization.[62] However, there are grave doubts in Britain as to whether economic policies of other countries will permit a return to free trade policy.

Britain's balance of payments does depend to a considerable extent upon American commercial and employment policies. American imports vary closely with the level of American income, and accordingly the magnitude of the gap in the British balance of payments tends to vary inversely with the level of American income. However, experience after World War I suggests that the level of prices as well as the level of income in the United States is important to the balance of payments. A high, or even rising, national income might not eliminate the balance of payments problem for Britain (and other countries dependent on exports) if accompanied by a slow decline in the American price level, and consequent deterioration of Britain's competitive position in world export markets. On the other hand, price inflation in the United States complicates the British situation by raising raw material and food prices both in the United States itself and in other countries. The only complex of American developments that would make the British

---

[60] Cf. MacDougall, "Britain's Foreign Trade Problem," *op. cit.,* pp. 103-109.

[61] Even so conservative a journal as *The Banker,* while supporting the proposed International Monetary Fund, added that "All these advantages [of the Fund] would admittedly count for very little if they could only be bought at the cost of restraints on our internal freedom of action that would interfere with a policy of full employment" (June 1944, p. 125).

[62] MacDougall estimates that resort to bilateralism would reduce world trade by some 25 percent. ("Britain's Foreign Trade Problem," *op. cit.,* p. 86.)

feel completely safe in embarking on a course of unrestricted "omnilateralism" would be one that maintained a high level of economic activity, with an expanding national income, a reasonably stable price level, and a willingness to promote an import surplus as soon as the time comes for net repayment of American loans. Because the British appear not to expect conditions in the United States to be of the kind necessary for successful "omnilateral" trade, a degree of restriction seems inevitable for some time to come.

The British viewpoint on the necessity for United States recognition of the full weight of its responsibility in determining conditions of world trade is a defensible one. It would surely be unfortunate for both countries if economic disturbances in the United States compelled the British (and the rest of whatever "sterling bloc" ultimately materializes) to continue restrictions against American exports.

Britain's financial outlook is not altogether black. The demand for goods in general may continue high throughout the world. Unless the world degenerates to protectionism and bilateralism in the field of international trade, or suffers another major depression, there will still be a substantial volume of world finance to be handled by Lombard Street.

What Britain needs to attain her stated economic goals of full employment and a rising standard of living is not a restoration of her former *pre-eminence* in international trade, shipping, and finance, but only an adequate increase in *total sales of British goods and services.* Other countries may surpass Britain as exporters of industrial products; other nations may help Britannia rule the waves; other agencies may supersede Lombard Street as the world's bankers. But if Britain narrows the gap between American productivity and her own, and if expansionist policies succeed in bringing the *total volume* of world trade, shipping, and finance to an optimum level, the British economy — including Lombard Street—can still prosper.

Item	Dec. 31, 1913	July 29, 1914	Nov. 27, 1918	Aug. 30, 1939	Aug. 29, 1945	Sept. 3, 1947
			Issue Department			
Liabilities						
Notes issued:						
In circulation	....	....	£93.71	£529.50	£1,325.91	£1,392.41
In banking department	£52.32	£55.12	....	33.51	24.33	57.83
Total[b]	52.32	55.12	93.71	563.01	1,350.25	1,450.25
Assets						
Government debt	11.02	11.02	11.02	11.02	11.02	11.02
Other securities	7.43	7.43	7.43	3.47	.64	.64
Other government securities	....	....	....	284.80	1,338.33	1,438.34
Silver coin	....	....	....	.71	.01	.01
Gold coin and bullion	33.87[c]	36.67[c]	75.26[c]	263.01[d]	.25[e]	.25[e]
Total[b]	52.32	55.12	93.71	563.01	1,350.25	1,450.25
			Banking Department			
Liabilities						
Proprietors' capital	14.55	14.55	14.55	14.55	14.55	14.55
Rest	3.25	3.49	3.19	3.65	3.46	3.92
Public deposits[f]	10.26	12.71	30.43	31.07	16.04	12.49
Other deposits						
Bankers	....	....	....	90.14	238.17	292.30
Other accounts	61.09	54.42	143.75	38.98	54.99	94.27
Seven-day and other bills	.01	.01	.01	....	....	....
Total[b]	89.16	85.19	191.93	178.39	327.21	417.54
Assets						
Government securities	13.20	11.01	62.63	113.13	272.11	319.37
Other securities						
Discounts and advances	....	....	....	6.39	7.18	19.89
Securities	52.14	47.31	100.99	24.63	23.16	17.91
Notes	22.72	25.42	27.72	33.51	24.33	57.83
Gold and silver coin	1.11	1.46	.59	.74	.43	2.54
Total[b]	89.16	85.19	191.93	178.39	327.21	417.54

[a] From *The Economist*, January 3, 1914, p. 33; August 1, 1914, p. 249; November 30, 1918, p. 753; September 2, 1939, p. 468; September 1, 1945, p. 316; January 4, 1947, p. 46; September 6, 1947, p. 193.
[b] In some cases totals do not agree with the sums of the items because of rounding.
[c] At 85s. per oz. fine.
[d] At 158s. 6d. per oz. fine.
[e] At 172s. 3d. per oz. fine.
[f] Including Exchequer, Savings Banks, Commissioners of National Debt, and Dividend Accounts.

Table B—Selected Balance Sheet Items for Joint Stock Banks of England and Wales[a]
(pound figures in millions)

Item	1913	1914	1918	1929	1939	1945	1946
Number of banks	43	38	26	16	13	13	13
Capital and reserves	£82.07	£81.90	£92.90	£141.59	£140.26	£146.77	£148.87
Deposits	809.35	895.56	1,583.41	1,911.01	2,419.33	4,811.93	6,645.40
Acceptances	61.71	47.80	58.85	179.30	117.26	118.50	194.68
Cash in hand, and money at call and notice	235.96	276.05	481.22	481.34	556.20	965.40	1,163.86
Investments	121.24	146.49	347.23	285.18	632.56	1,253.03	1,445.64
Discounts and advances[b]	539.80	553.50	834.67	1,250.76	1,328.39	2,702.63	3,147.57
Total Assets (Liabs.)	963.05	1,034.49	1,742.72	2,238.86	2,682.49	5,082.48	5,994.46

[a] From *The Economist*, Banking Supplement, May 18, 1935, p. 20; October 27, 1945, p. 8; November 16, 1946, pp. 6-7; November 15, 1947, p. 410.
[b] After 1939, includes Treasury deposit receipts.

Table C—Composition of British Banks' Advances[a]
(pound figures in millions)

	1929-30[b]		1938[c]		August 1946[d]		August 1947[d]	
	Amt.	%	Amt.	%	Amt.	%	Amt.	%
Textiles (cotton, wool, silk, linen, jute)	£81.6	8.3	£38.1	4.0	£27.2	3.0	£32.4	2.8
Heavy industries (iron, steel, engineering, and shipbuilding)	63.0	6.4	45.8	4.8	79.5[e]	8.7	105.7[e]	9.0
Agriculture and fishing	68.6	6.9	62.4	6.5	78.3	8.6	95.7	8.2
Mining and quarrying (including coal)	30.0	3.0	15.2	1.6	12.5	1.4	11.8	1.0
Food, drink, and tobacco	63.2	6.4	36.1	3.8	52.8	5.8	68.5	5.8
Leather, rubber, and chemicals	22.0	2.2	14.0	1.5	12.6	1.4	22.6	1.9
Shipping and transport (including railways)	25.2	2.6	26.5	2.8	20.2[f]	2.2	31.0[f]	2.6
Building trades	47.8	4.8	68.1	7.1	51.1	5.6	67.8	5.8
Miscellaneous trades	....	....	69.1	7.2	36.0	4.0	51.7	4.4
Retail trades	146.5	14.8	66.4	7.0	67.8	7.5	109.0	9.3
Total	547.9	55.5	441.7	46.3	438.0	48.2	596.2	50.8
Local government authorities and public utilities (excluding railways)	52.4	5.3	59.2	6.2	77.8	8.5	88.6	7.5
Amusements, clubs, churches, charities, etc.	26.5	2.7	46.6	4.9	37.8	4.2	42.4	3.6
Financial (including banks, discount houses, stock exchange, and building societies)	142.5	14.4	109.0	11.4	87.1	9.6	113.7	9.7
Other advances	218.4	22.1	297.7	31.2	268.8[g]	29.5	333.5	28.4
Total	439.8	44.5	512.5	53.7	471.4	51.8	578.2	49.2
Grand Total[h]	987.7	100.0	954.3	100.0	909.4	100.0	1,174.4	100.0

[a] Figures for 1929-30 are from *Report of the Committee on Finance and Industry* (the "Macmillan Report") Cmd. 3897 (London, 1931) p. 298; they cover data for various dates from October 24, 1929 to March 19, 1930. Figures for 1938 are from the Bank of England, *Statistical Summary*, November 1938, p. 131, and are for various dates between August 3 and October 31, 1938. Figures for August 1946 are from the *Monthly Digest of Statistics* (London), April 1947, Table 127; those for August 1947 are from *Monthly Digest of Statistics*, July 1948, p. 122.
[b] Ten clearing banks. [c] Eleven clearing banks. [d] Members of the British Bankers Association.
[e] Excludes shipbuilding. [f] Includes shipbuilding. [g] Personal and professional entirely.
[h] In some cases totals do not agree with the sums of the items because of rounding.

Table D—Balance Sheets of Discount Houses[a]
(in thousands)

	Dec. 31, 1913	Dec. 31, 1914	Dec. 31, 1918	Dec. 31, 1939	Dec. 31, 1945	Dec. 31, 1946
Alexanders and Company, Ltd.						
Liabilities						
Capital and reserves	£600.0	£620.0	£700.0	£2,000.0	£2,000.0	£3,600.0
Undivided profits	35.1	38.0	56.0	237.0	262.9	446.3
Loans, deposits, and other accounts	10,134.9	9,427.4	13,826.9	31,131.9	68,231.0	102,764.9
Bills rediscounted	1,497.2	281.7	1,912.3	1,037.5	b	b
Rebate on bills discounted	86.3	76.9	124.2	194.7	....	....
Total	12,353.6	10,444.1	16,619.4	34,601.1	70,494.0	106,811.2
Assets						
Cash at bankers	293.7	350.1	420.5	679.7	1,384.1	1,396.0
Investments	944.2	1,341.7	2,235.4	5,835.3	18,661.6	22,971.2
Bills discounted	10,798.7	8,684.2	13,798.2	27,804.8	50,156.5	82,216.5
Loans and sundry accounts	317.0	68.1	165.4	281.3	291.8	227.5
Buildings and sundries	....	....	....	....	....	....
Total	12,353.6	10,444.1	16,619.4	34,601.1	70,494.0	106,811.2
National Discount Company, Ltd.						
Liabilities						
Capital and reserves	1,351.7	1,351.7	1,346.7	2,150.0	2,776.7	3,153.3
Undivided profits	64.0	64.5	82.9	306.0	283.1	321.9
Loans, deposits, and other accounts	15,757.5	13,010.5	17,973.1	43,872.5	87,948.8	116,139.4
Bills rediscounted	5,656.5	2,285.4	8,388.7	7,348.4	c	c
Rebate on bills discounted	178.3	186.6	323.8	....	....	....
Total	23,008.0	16,898.8	28,115.2	53,676.9	91,008.5	119,614.7

Table D—(concluded)

	Dec. 31, 1913	Dec. 31, 1914	Dec. 31, 1918	Dec. 31, 1939	Dec. 31, 1945	Dec. 31, 1946
Assets						
Cash at bankers	£503.3	£427.9	£515.6	£1,229.3	£1,223.0	£1,307.9
Investments	1,851.1	1,851.9	2,369.0	5,678.2	15,591.1	15,559.7
Bills discounted	19,785.4	13,690.5	23,491.4	46,378.6	73,486.8	102,111.3
Loans and sundry accounts	669.5	761.5	1,446.3	290.9	607.6	535.8
Buildings and sundries	198.7	167.1	292.9	100.0	100.0	100.0
TOTAL	23,008.0	16,898.8	28,115.2	53,676.9	91,008.5	119,614.7

Union Discount Company of London, Ltd.

Liabilities						
Capital and reserves	1,549.1	1,759.0	1,830.3	3,750.0	4,750.0	7,700.0
Undivided profits	152.7	172.6	168.3	434.9	647.8	595.6
Loans, deposits, and other accounts	20,662.3	16,223.4	27,577.5	66,779.6	144,650.1	205,037.5
Bills rediscounted	8,966.3	3,113.5	4,823.5	10,031.2	d	d
Rebate on bills discounted	229.8	210.0	243.9	473.9	....	....
TOTAL	31,560.3	21,478.4	34,643.5	81,469.6	150,047.9	213,333.1
Assets						
Cash at bankers	886.3	918.7	1,065.7	1,760.9	2,525.7	3,099.2
Investments	2,213.5	2,786.7	4,249.1	6,498.6	29,731.8	56,561.5
Bills discounted	27,363.4	16,634.9	26,657.0	71,230.3	116,542.3	152,246.0
Loans and sundry accounts	954.5	980.7	2,491.6	1,506.7	489.4	1,091.3
Buildings and sundries	142.5	157.3	180.1	473.1	758.6	335.1
TOTAL	31,560.3	21,478.4	34,643.5	81,469.6	150,047.9	213,333.1

[a] From *The Economist*, Banking Supplements, May 22, 1915, May 20, 1916, May 17, 1919, November 16, 1946, and November 15, 1947.
[b] Contingent liability, excluding Treasury bills (1945) £1,267.7; (1946) £3,692.5.
[c] Contingent liability, excluding Treasury bills (1945) £3,090.9; (1946) £5,886.8.
[d] Contingent liability, excluding Treasury bills (1945) £4,061.7; (1946) £8,974.0.

Table E—Balance Sheets of Merchant Banks[a] (in thousands)

	Dec. 31, 1913	Dec. 31, 1914	Dec. 31, 1918	Dec. 31, 1939	Dec. 31, 1945	Dec. 31, 1946
Baring Brothers						
Liabilities						
Capital and reserves	£1,125.0	£1,125.0	£1,125.0	£3,050.0	£3,050.0	£3,050.0
Acceptances	6,636.6	3,723.7	3,064.0	1,646.2	449.3	2,591.1
Deposit, current and other accounts	8,053.4	11,390.1	19,258.0	16,123.7	20,175.9	22,584.1
Total	15,815.0	16,238.8	23,447.0	20,819.9	23,675.2	28,225.2
Assets						
Cash at hand, at call and short notice	3,029.0	7,378.5	5,386.0	3,320.7	3,075.5	3,834.1
Investments	1,503.5	1,489.3	1,607.3	9,530.3	14,840.2	15,883.9
Bills receivable	2,909.8	1,493.6	11,318.0	2,211.2	3,065.9	3,473.7
Advances, liability of customers on acceptances and other accounts	8,245.6	5,750.5	5,008.7	5,630.6	2,566.6	4,906.5
Premises	127.0	127.0	127.0	127.0	127.0	127.0
Total	15,815.0	16,238.8	23,447.0	20,819.9	23,675.2	28,225.2
Erlangers						
Liabilities						
Capital and reserves	....	....	....	1,925.0	1,925.0	1,925.0
Acceptances	....	....	....	2,475.4	3,795.6	4,406.2
Deposit, current and other accounts	....	....	....	2,174.3	1,894.5	2,269.6
Total	....	....	....	6,574.7	7,615.1	8,600.8
Assets						
Cash at hand, at call and short notice	....	....	....	1,005.4	750.4	966.9
Investments	....	....	....	1,044.7	1,691.1	1,657.6
Bills receivable	....	....	....	....	....	....
Advances, liability of customers on acceptances and other accounts	....	....	....	4,524.6	5,173.6	5,976.2
Premises	....	....	....			
Total						

106

Table E—(concluded)

	Dec. 31, 1913	Dec. 31, 1914	Dec. 31, 1918	Dec. 31, 1939	Dec. 31, 1945	Dec. 31, 1946
S. Japhet						
Liabilities						
Capital and reserves	....	....	....	£1,400.0	£1,300.0	£1,300.0
Acceptances	....	....	....	830.3	....	....
Deposit, current and other accounts	....	....	....	1,121.4	596.5	824.0
Bank loan secured under Currency (Defense) Act of 1939	....	....	....	498.9	271.2	....
TOTAL	....	....	....	3,850.6	2,167.8	2,124.0
Assets						
Cash at hand, at call and short notice	....	....	....	834.2	219.5	374.3
Investments	....	....	....	200.4	289.6	257.3
Bills receivable	....	....	....	10.1	....	....
Advances, liability of customers on acceptances and other accounts	....	....	....	2,625.9	1,478.7	1,452.5
Premises	....	....	....	180.0	180.0	40.0
TOTAL	....	....	....	3,850.6	2,167.8	2,124.0

[a] From *The Economist*, Banking Supplements, May 17, 1919, October 28, 1944, November 16, 1946, and November 15, 1947. In some cases totals do not agree with the sums of the items because of rounding.

Table F—Selected Interest Rates, London Money Market

Year	Bank Rate[a]	Bank Bills, Three-Months Rate[b]	Short Loans, Day-to-Day Rate Against Bills[b]	Yield on 2½% Consols[c]
1913	4.77%	4.38%	..	3.40%
1920	6.71	6.36	..	5.32
1921	6.09	5.20	4.3%	5.21
1922	3.69	2.62	2.0	4.43
1923	3.49	2.78	2.0	4.32
1924	4.00	3.45	2.4	4.38
1925	4.57	4.16	3.5	4.44
1926	5.00	4.48	4.0	4.54
1927	4.65	4.24	3.7	4.55
1928	4.50	4.16	3.6	4.47
1929	5.50	5.30	4.6	4.61
1930	3.42	2.62	2.4	4.49
1931	3.97	3.53	2.9	4.40
1932	3.01	1.94	1.7	3.75
1933	2.00	.71	.5	3.40
1934	2.00	.81	.6	3.10
1935	2.00	.57	.5	2.89
1936	2.00	.61	.5	2.94
1937	2.00	.59	.5	3.28
1938	2.00	.61	.5	3.38
1939	2.27	1.20	.8	3.72
1940	2.00	1.04	1.0	3.40
1941	2.00	1.03	1.0	3.13
1942	2.00	1.03	1.0	3.03
1943	2.00	1.03	1.0	3.10
1944	2.00	1.03	1.0	3.14
1945	2.00	.93	.9	2.92
1946	2.00	.53	.5	2.60
1947	2.00	.53	.5	2.76

[a] From *British Government Securities in the 20th Century,* Pember and Boyle.
[b] From London and Cambridge Economic Service, *Bulletin IV,* Vol. XXIV (1946) p. 118, and Vol. XXVI (1948) p. 102. (Averages for weeks ending the 15th of the month.)
[c] From A. T. K. Grant, *A Study of the Capital Market in Postwar Britain* (London, 1937); *The Economist,* "Trade Supplement," February 27, 1937; Bank of England, *Statistical Summary,* selected issues between September 1932 and January 1944; and *Monthly Digest of Statistics* (London) January 1947 and July 1948.

Officers

C. REINOLD NOYES, *Chairman*
H. W. LAIDLER, *President*
HARRY SCHERMAN, *Vice-President*
GEORGE B. ROBERTS, *Treasurer*
W. J. CARSON, *Executive Director*
MARTHA ANDERSON, *Editor*

Directors at Large

DONALD R. BELCHER, *American Telephone and Telegraph Co.*
OSWALD W. KNAUTH, *New York City*
SIMON KUZNETS, *University of Pennsylvania*
H. W. LAIDLER, *Executive Director, League for Industrial Democracy*
SHEPARD MORGAN, *Vice-President, Chase National Bank*
C. REINOLD NOYES, *New York City*
GEORGE B. ROBERTS, *Vice-President, National City Bank*
BEARDSLEY RUML, *Chairman, Board of Directors, R. H. Macy & Company*
HARRY SCHERMAN, *President, Book-of-the-Month Club*
GEORGE SOULE, *New York City*
N. I. STONE, *Consulting Economist*
J. RAYMOND WALSH, *WMCA Broadcasting Co.*
LEO WOLMAN, *Columbia University*
THEODORE O. YNTEMA, *Vice President - Finance, Ford Motor Company*

Directors by University Appointment

E. WIGHT BAKKE, *Yale*
C. C. BALDERSTON, *Pennsylvania*
ARTHUR F. BURNS, *Columbia*
G. A. ELLIOTT, *Toronto*
H. M. GROVES, *Wisconsin*
GOTTFRIED HABERLER, *Harvard*
CLARENCE HEER, *North Carolina*
R. L. KOZELKA, *Minnesota*
PAUL M. O'LEARY, *Cornell*
ROBERT B. WARREN, *Institute for Advanced Study*

Directors Appointed by Other Organizations

PERCIVAL F. BRUNDAGE, *American Institute of Accountants*
ARTHUR H. COLE, *Economic History Association*
FREDERICK C. MILLS, *American Statistical Association*
STANLEY H. RUTTENBERG, *Congress of Industrial Organizations*
BORIS SHISHKIN, *American Federation of Labor*
WARREN C. WAITE, *American Farm Economic Association*
DONALD H. WALLACE, *American Economic Association*

Research Staff

ARTHUR F. BURNS, *Director of Research*
G. H. MOORE, *Associate Director of Research*

MOSES ABRAMOVITZ
HAROLD BARGER
MORRIS A. COPELAND
DANIEL CREAMER
DAVID DURAND
SOLOMON FABRICANT
MILTON FRIEDMAN
MILLARD HASTAY
W. BRADDOCK HICKMAN
F. F. HILL
THOR HULTGREN
SIMON KUZNETS
CLARENCE D. LONG
RUTH P. MACK
FREDERICK C. MILLS
RAYMOND J. SAULNIER
GEORGE J. STIGLER
LEO WOLMAN

Occasional Papers

1. MANUFACTURING OUTPUT, 1929-1937 (December 1940)
   Solomon Fabricant .... .25

*2. NATIONAL INCOME, 1919-1938 (April 1941)
   Simon Kuznets ....

3. FINISHED COMMODITIES SINCE 1879, OUTPUT AND ITS COMPOSITION (August 1941)
   William H. Shaw .... .25

*4. THE RELATION BETWEEN FACTORY EMPLOYMENT AND OUTPUT SINCE 1899 (December 1941)
   Solomon Fabricant ....

5. RAILWAY FREIGHT TRAFFIC IN PROSPERITY AND DEPRESSION (February 1942)
   Thor Hultgren .... .25

*6. USES OF NATIONAL INCOME IN PEACE AND WAR (March 1942)
   Simon Kuznets ....

*7. PRODUCTIVITY OF LABOR IN PEACE AND WAR (September 1942)
   Solomon Fabricant ....

*8. THE BANKING SYSTEM AND WAR FINANCE (February 1943)
   Charles R. Whittlesey ....

*9. WARTIME 'PROSPERITY' AND THE FUTURE (March 1943)
   Wesley C. Mitchell ....

10. THE EFFECT OF WAR ON BUSINESS FINANCING: MANUFACTURING AND TRADE, WORLD WAR I (November 1943)
    R. A. Young and C. H. Schmidt .... .50

11. THE EFFECT OF WAR ON CURRENCY AND DEPOSITS (September 1943)
    Charles R. Whittlesey .... .35

12. PRICES IN A WAR ECONOMY: SOME ASPECTS OF THE PRESENT PRICE STRUCTURE OF THE UNITED STATES (October 1943)
    Frederick C. Mills .... .50

13. RAILROAD TRAVEL AND THE STATE OF BUSINESS (December 1943)
    Thor Hultgren .... .35

14. THE LABOR FORCE IN WARTIME AMERICA (March 1944)
    Clarence D. Long .... .50

15. RAILWAY TRAFFIC EXPANSION AND USE OF RESOURCES IN WORLD WAR II (February 1944)
    Thor Hultgren .... .35

16. BRITISH AND AMERICAN PLANS FOR INTERNATIONAL CURRENCY STABILIZATION (January 1944)
    J. H. Riddle .... .35

Out of Print

17. NATIONAL PRODUCT, WAR AND PREWAR (February 1944)
    Simon Kuznets .... .50
18. PRODUCTION OF INDUSTRIAL MATERIALS IN WORLD WARS I AND II
    (March 1944)
    Geoffrey H. Moore .... .50
19. CANADA'S FINANCIAL SYSTEM IN WAR (April 1944)
    B. H. Higgins .... .50
20. NAZI WAR FINANCE AND BANKING (April 1944)
    Otto Nathan .... .50
*21. THE FEDERAL RESERVE SYSTEM IN WARTIME (January 1945)
    Anna Youngman ....
22. BANK LIQUIDITY AND THE WAR (May 1945)
    Charles R. Whittlesey .... .50
23. LABOR SAVINGS IN AMERICAN INDUSTRY, 1899-1939 (November 1945)
    Solomon Fabricant .... .50
24. DOMESTIC SERVANTS IN THE UNITED STATES, 1900-1940 (April 1946)
    George J. Stigler .... .50
25. RECENT DEVELOPMENTS IN DOMINION-PROVINCIAL FISCAL RELATIONS IN
    CANADA (March 1948)
    J. A. Maxwell .... .50
26. THE ROLE OF INVENTORIES IN BUSINESS CYCLES (May 1948)
    Moses Abramovitz .... .50
27. THE STRUCTURE OF POSTWAR PRICES (July 1948)
    Frederick C. Mills .... .75

Technical Papers

*1. A SIGNIFICANCE TEST FOR TIME SERIES AND OTHER ORDERED
    OBSERVATIONS (September 1941)
    W. Allen Wallis and Geoffrey H. Moore ....
*2. THE RELATION OF COST TO OUTPUT FOR A LEATHER BELT SHOP,
    by Joel Dean, with a Memorandum on Certain Problems in the
    Empirical Study of Costs by C. Reinold Noyes (December 1941)......
3. BASIC YIELDS OF CORPORATE BONDS, 1900-1942 (June 1942)
    David Durand .... .50
4. CURRENCY HELD BY THE PUBLIC, THE BANKS, AND THE TREASURY,
    MONTHLY DECEMBER 1917 TO DECEMBER 1944 (January 1947)
    Anna J. Schwartz and E. Oliver .... .75
5. CONCERNING A NEW FEDERAL FINANCIAL STATEMENT (December 1947)
    Morris A. Copeland 1.00
6. BASIC YIELDS OF BONDS, 1926-1947: THEIR MEASUREMENT AND PATTERN
    (December 1947)
    David Durand and Willis J. Winn .... .75

*Out of Print

Relation of the Directors to the Work of the National Bureau of Economic Research

1. The object of the National Bureau of Economic Research is to ascertain and to present to the public important economic facts and their interpretation in a scientific and impartial manner. The Board of Directors is charged with the responsibility of ensuring that the work of the Bureau is carried on in strict conformity with this object.

2. To this end the Board of Directors shall appoint one or more Directors of Research.

3. The Director or Directors of Research shall submit to the members of the Board, or to its Executive Committee, for their formal adoption, all specific proposals concerning researches to be instituted.

4. No report shall be published until the Director or Directors of Research shall have submitted to the Board a summary drawing attention to the character of the data and their utilization in the report, the nature and treatment of the problems involved, the main conclusions and such other information as in their opinion would serve to determine the suitability of the report for publication in accordance with the principles of the Bureau.

5. A copy of any manuscript proposed for publication shall also be submitted to each member of the Board. For each manuscript to be so submitted a special committee shall be appointed by the President, or at his designation by the Executive Director, consisting of three Directors selected as nearly as may be one from each general division of the Board. The names of the special manuscript committee shall be stated to each Director when the summary and report described in paragraph (4) are sent him. It shall be the duty of each member of the committee to read the manuscript. If each member of the special committee signifies his approval within thirty days, the manuscript may be published. If each member of the special committee has not signified his approval within thirty days of the transmittal of the report and manuscript, the Director of Research shall then notify each member of the Board, requesting approval or disapproval of publication, and thirty additional days shall be granted for this purpose. The manuscript shall then not be published unless at least a majority of the entire Board and a two-thirds majority of those members of the Board who shall have voted on the proposal within the time fixed for the receipt of votes on the publication proposed shall have approved.

6. No manuscript may be published, though approved by each member of the special committee, until forty-five days have elapsed from the transmittal of the summary and report. The interval is allowed for the receipt of any memorandum of dissent or reservation, together with a brief statement of his reasons, that any member may wish to express; and such memorandum of dissent or reservation shall be published with the manuscript if he so desires. Publication does not, however, imply that each member of the Board has read the manuscript, or that either members of the Board in general, or of the special committee, have passed upon its validity in every detail.

7. A copy of this resolution shall, unless otherwise determined by the Board, be printed in each copy of every National Bureau book.

(Resolution adopted October 25, 1926, and revised February 6, 1933, and February 24, 1941)

Financial Research Program: Committee

In the planning and conduct of all research under the Financial Research Program the National Bureau benefits from the advice and guidance of its Committee on Research in Finance. The functions of this committee are to review and supervise the specific research activities of the Program staff.

RALPH A. YOUNG, Chairman pro tempore — *Associate Director, Division of Research and Statistics, Board of Governors of the Federal Reserve System*

RAYMOND J. SAULNIER, Secretary — *Barnard College, Columbia University; Director, Financial Research Program, National Bureau of Economic Research*

BENJAMIN HAGGOTT BECKHART — *Columbia University; Director of Research, The Chase National Bank*

ARTHUR F. BURNS — *Columbia University; Director of Research, National Bureau of Economic Research*

WILLIAM J. CARSON — *University of Pennsylvania; Executive Director, National Bureau of Economic Research*

GEORGE W. COLEMAN — *Economist, Mississippi Valley Trust Company*

ERNEST M. FISHER — *Columbia University*

E. A. GOLDENWEISER — *Institute for Advanced Study*

F. CYRIL JAMES — *Principal and Vice-Chancellor, McGill University*

WALTER LICHTENSTEIN

WALTER L. MITCHELL, JR. — *Managing Director, Controllers Institute of America*

SHEPARD MORGAN — *Vice-President, The Chase National Bank*

WILLIAM I. MYERS — *Dean, College of Agriculture, Cornell University*

JACK H. RIDDLE — *Vice-President, Bankers Trust Company*

GEORGE BASSETT ROBERTS — *Vice-President, The National City Bank; Treasurer, National Bureau of Economic Research*

HAROLD V. ROELSE — *Vice-President, Federal Reserve Bank of New York*

CASIMIR A. SIENKIEWICZ — *President, Central-Penn National Bank of Philadelphia*

WOODLIEF THOMAS — *Director, Division of Research and Statistics, Board of Governors of the Federal Reserve System*

DONALD S. THOMPSON — *Vice-President, Federal Reserve Bank of Cleveland*

ROBERT B. WARREN — *Institute for Advanced Study*

JOHN H. WILLIAMS — *Graduate School of Public Administration, Harvard University; Economic Adviser, Federal Reserve Bank of New York*

JOHN H. WILLS — *Second Vice-President, Northern Trust Company*

LEO WOLMAN — *Columbia University; Research Staff, National Bureau of Economic Research*

DONALD B. WOODWARD — *Second Vice-President, Mutual Life Insurance Company of New York*

The Rising Trend
of
Government Employment

SOLOMON FABRICANT

OCCASIONAL PAPER 29

NATIONAL BUREAU OF ECONOMIC RESEARCH, INC.

The Rising Trend of Government Employment

SOLOMON FABRICANT

Occasional Paper 29: June 1949
NATIONAL BUREAU OF ECONOMIC RESEARCH, INC.
1819 Broadway, New York 23, N. Y.

THE STUDY UPON WHICH THIS PAPER IS BASED WAS made possible by funds granted by The Maurice and Laura Falk Foundation of Pittsburgh. The Falk Foundation is not, however, the author, publisher, or proprietor of this publication, and is not to be understood as approving or disapproving by virtue of its grant any of the statements made or views expressed herein.

Grateful acknowledgment is also due Belle C. Nathan for aid in assembling the data and to Robert E. Lipsey for checking them; to Martha Anderson for editing the manuscript; and to H. Irving Forman for the charts.

Price: Fifty cents

Copyright, 1949, by the National Bureau of Economic Research, Inc.
1819 Broadway, New York 23, N. Y.
All rights reserved.
Manufactured in the U.S.A. by John N. Jacobson & Son, Inc. N. Y.

ONE OUT OF EVERY EIGHT OR NINE PERSONS EMPLOYED in the United States today is a government worker. Is the proportion merely a hangover from the war, which may be expected in time to diminish substantially, or was it large before the war too? If large before the war, did it reflect a changed concept of government's functions brought into being by the New Deal, or was it part of a trend already established before the great depression? If part of a long-term trend, what accounts for it? In answering these questions I shall omit details. Nor shall I say very much about the statistical basis of the answers, important though it is for appraising their accuracy. These matters will be presented later in a full report, on which this brief Paper is based.

I Number of Government Workers

Total Government Employment
In 1900 governments in the United States employed somewhat more than one million persons. Each decade thereafter saw substantial net increase in the number: over a half million in 1900-10, almost a million in 1910-20, three-quarters of a million in 1920-30, over a million in 1930-40, and over two million in 1940-48. By 1948—and the figure for 1949 is so far about the same—the total exceeded six million. Today's huge government employment, then, is the latest figure in a series with a pronounced upward trend.

The cautious reader—refusing to wait for the full report I have promised—will want to know immediately how reliable this series is. He should look at Chart 1. Estimates based on two quite independent sources show substantially the same expansion in government employment. Whether the estimates are based on workers' reports of the status of their employers or on governments' reports on the length of their payrolls, each decade records an increase in government workers. Both estimates show total net increases, for the last five decades, of well over five million.

CHART 1
Number of Employed Government Workers
(including Military Personnel)
Selected Years

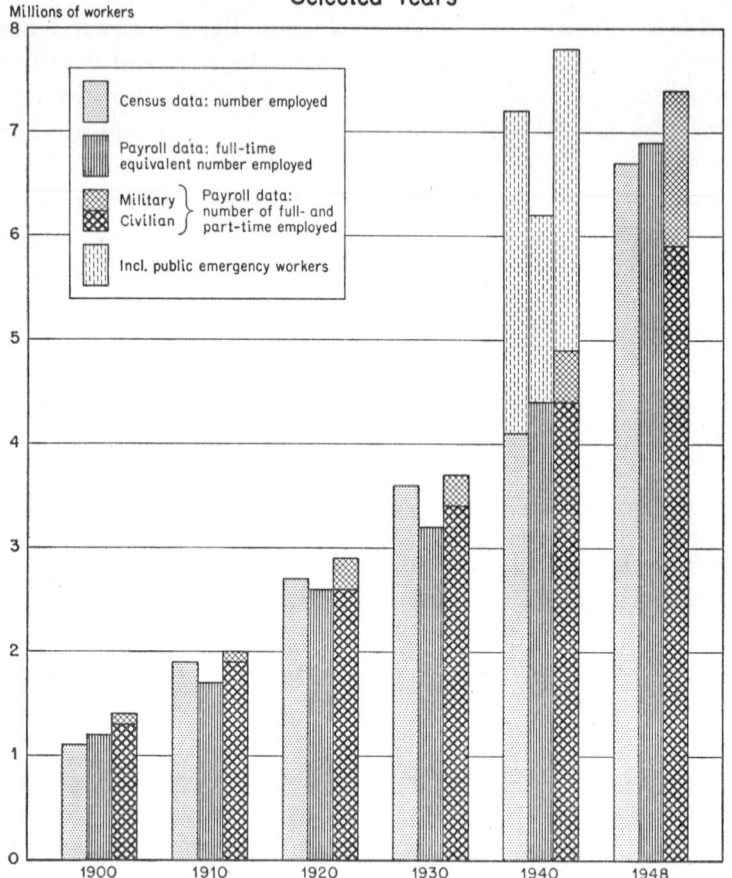

Millions of workers

Legend:
- Census data: number employed
- Payroll data: full-time equivalent number employed
- Military } Payroll data: number of full- and
- Civilian } part-time employed
- Incl. public emergency workers

The figures I have cited include all ordinary employees of all types of governmental unit—federal, state, local, including school and other 'districts', and government enterprises and corporations. Among these employees are members of the armed forces as well as civilians, and unclassified and temporary employees as well as civil service appointees. All part-time workers are covered by the payroll data, in terms of either number or 'full-time equivalent'. The exclusion of many part-time workers from the Census data helps to explain some of the differences in the chart.

The glance at Chart 1 will have disclosed, also, the large number of public emergency employees in 1940, an extraordinary class of government worker I ignored when describing the trend. Hardly any appear in the record for 1930, and none at all for the other years covered by the chart. This fact and the special nature of emergency employment justify showing it separately.

Employees of government contractors are entirely excluded, of course, as is the expanding host of pensioners and recipients of welfare, subsidy, and similar government payments.

Government Employment in Relation to All Employment
In a country where population is at a standstill or changing only slightly, the trend in the absolute number of government workers would be sufficient to give the picture. But our population—and with it, total employment—has been growing rapidly. How do the two trends, of government and total employment, compare?

It will be no surprise to find that the rate of growth in total employment, substantial though it has been, fell far short of the very high rate of growth in government employment. Total employment too rose each decade (on net balance), but each time the percentage increase was less than in government employment. For the 1900-48 period as a whole, total employment increased about 120 percent, government employment 450-500 percent. The contrast is still more striking when the 450-500 percent increase in government workers is compared with the 100 percent increase in privately employed workers.

Another way to describe the changing relative importance of government workers in the total is to compare the proportion with which I opened this Paper with corresponding proportions in earlier years. In 1900 one out of 24 workers was on a government payroll, in 1920, one out of 15, and in 1940, one out of 11. The current ratio, as I have said, is one out of 8 or 9. The upward trend, from 4.2 percent in 1900 to 11.4 percent in 1948, is sharp and clear (Chart 2).

CHART 2
**Employed Government Workers
(including Military Personnel)
as a Percentage of All Employed Workers
Selected Years**

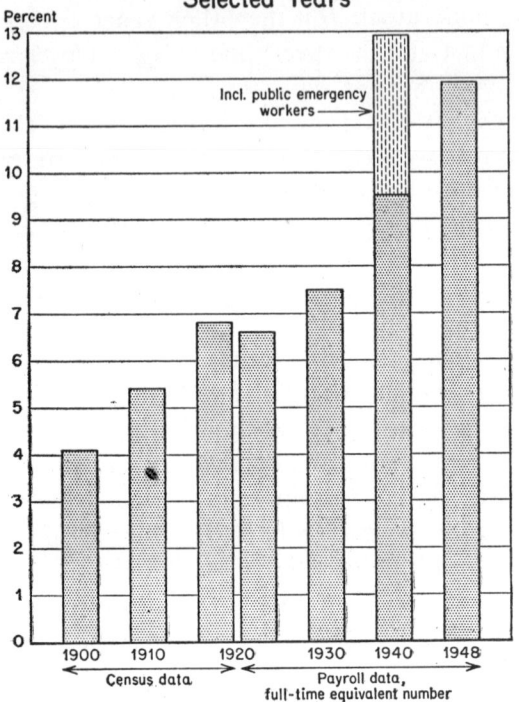

Incl. public emergency workers →

1900 1910 | 1920 1930 1940 1948
← Census data → | ← Payroll data, full-time equivalent number →

Employment by Type of Governmental Unit
The huge federal budget and large volume of federal employment have been discussed widely and often. Some readers may suppose, therefore, that the larger part of today's six or seven million government workers is on federal payrolls and that expansion of federal payrolls accounts for all or most of the five million workers taken on since 1900. The facts show this notion to be exaggerated.

Even today, when the cold war keeps our armed forces at an unprecedented peacetime level, federal employment is no larger than that of state and local governments. Of the 6.7 million full-time equivalent persons on government payrolls, 3.4 million work for state and local governments.

(The proportion before adjusting part-time work to a full-time equivalent basis is even higher because part-time work is largely a local government arrangement.) In 1940, just before the big expansion in national defense activities, state and local governments accounted for almost two-thirds of the 4.4 million regular employees on government payrolls.

Of the increase between 1900 and 1948, about three million workers were additions to federal payrolls; two and a half million, to state and local government payrolls. Counted only until 1940, the increase in state and local personnel, two million, substantially exceeded the increase in federal personnel, 1.2 million. After 1940, the big increase came, of course, in federal employment, 1.9 million; state and local employment rose 600,000.

CHART 3
Percentage Distribution of Government Workers among Main Types of Governmental Unit, Selected Years
(Payroll data, full-time equivalent number; public emergency workers excluded)

Year	Armed forces	Federal civilian	States, nonschool	Cities, nonschool	Counties, townships and special districts, nonschool	School
1900	11.3	15.0	5.9	16.8	10.6	40.4
1910	8.2	20.3	6.4	19.8	11.3	34.0
1920	12.9	23.3	6.9	16.3	10.0	30.6
1930	8.2	17.0	8.6	21.6	10.6	34.1
1940	12.1	22.3	10.4	17.1	10.1	27.9
1948	21.7	27.9	8.7	13.0	7.6	21.2

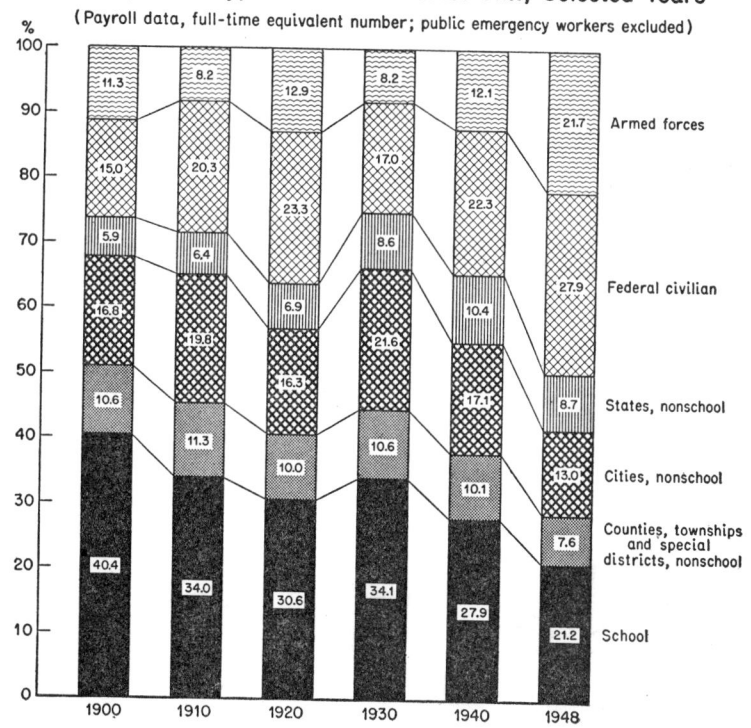

The changes in the distribution of government employees among the various types of unit from 1940 to 1948, and around 1920 as well (Chart 3), largely reflect the effects of war, about which more will be said in a moment. The great depression too is reflected in the chart. If we focus on the net change between 1900 and 1940, we find little change in the relative importance of the armed forces, municipal nonschool employment, and other local nonschool employment. The net change in federal civilian employment was definitely upward. State nonschool employment also expanded relatively. School employment fell rather consistently and very considerably, relatively to other types of government employment.

While some sectors of government show drops in relative importance, all show substantial increases in absolute number. In schools, the slowest growing sector, the number of teachers and other employees more than tripled between 1900 and 1948.

The Impress of Wars and Business Cycles
The two major wars of our time are clearly reflected in the annual series plotted in Chart 4.

As one would expect, federal civilian as well as federal military employment rose to great heights during the wars, then fell sharply. After both wars, the decline halted at a level substantially above the prewar. The post-World War I level of employment was approximately in line with, or even below, the level that would have been reached had prewar trends persisted. The level after World War II, however, is still considerably above the projected prewar trend. Current budgets afford little ground for thinking that federal employment will soon drop to that trend level.

State and local government employment also felt the impact of war. But the effect was, of course, opposite to that on federal employment. During World War II each nonfederal sector cut employment. After the war, each sector restored its personnel to prewar levels and pushed on to new heights. The impact of World War I is less

CHART 4
Number of Government Workers Employed
by Each Main Type of Governmental Unit, Annual Estimates
(Payroll data, full-time equivalent number)

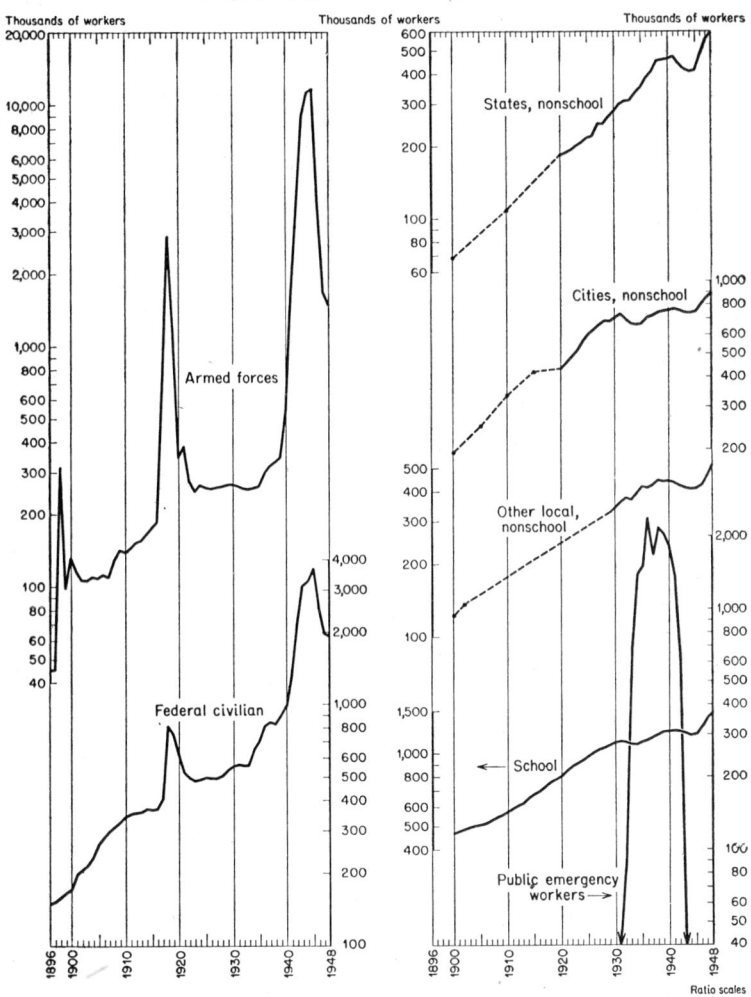

definite, partly because our information is scanty. Municipal employment did not increase from 1915 to 1920, because of the war. The series on state government employment contributes nothing to the question, but scattered information for one or two state governments suggests a similar effect of the war on their employment. School employment, on the contrary, was not affected by World War I; and we do not have any information on employment by other units of local government.

Apart from the war periods, fluctuations in ordinary government employment are few, and none is really large. Employment in the great majority of private industries fluctuates closely and usually substantially with general business conditions, even when measured on an annual basis. Our annual series on government employment—with the notable exception of public emergency employment—shows hardly any such obvious repercussions.

The sharp contractions of 1920-21 and 1937-38, and the mild contractions of 1923-24 and 1926-27 seem to have caused scarcely a ripple in the series. Even the big contraction of 1929-32 made only a modest impression, certainly one much different from that stamped on the line for total employment, including private industry, plotted in Chart 5. All the series except that for the armed forces continued to gain until 1931, some without abating speed significantly. Municipal nonschool employment and total school employment alone declined after 1931 and then only until about 1933 or 1934—presumably a belated effect of the decline in revenues. After 1933 federal civilian and state nonschool employment accelerated sharply, as did the armed forces after 1935.

The most striking reflection of the great depression, and of the 1937-38 contraction as well, is in the count of public emergency workers—those on WPA and similar rolls. Few persons were on work-relief before the New Deal in 1933. All through the preceding severe contraction in employment, additions to work-relief lists were large in percentage terms but small in absolute terms. The big expansion in number came after 1933 and continued through 1936, a period when private employment too was growing. Work-relief did not begin to move counter to regular employment until after 1936. With the onset of the war, and the resulting labor shortages, emergency workers declined, then vanished.

CHART 5
Government and Total Employment, Annual Estimates
(Full-time equivalent number)

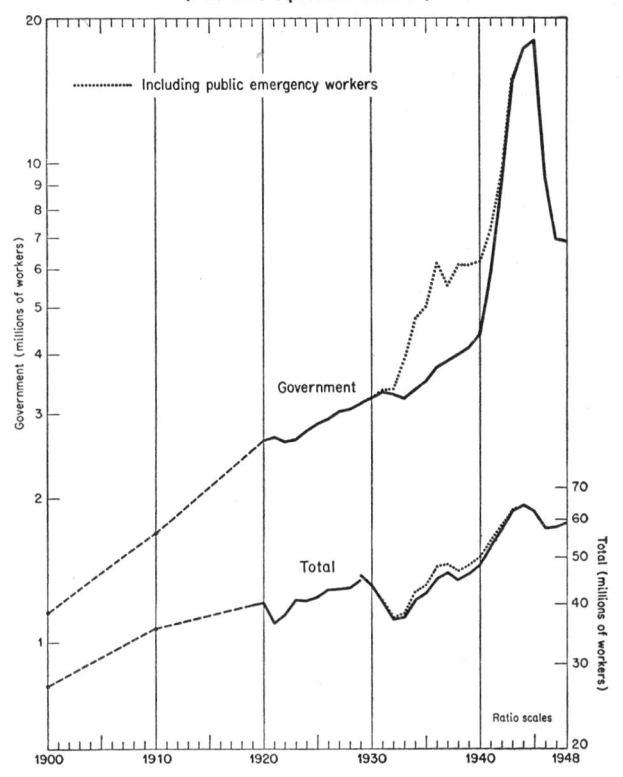

To return to a question posed at the outset of this Paper, it seems clear that the activities government took on under the New Deal were a substantial factor in expanding government employment. After 1933 growth in both federal and state government employment speeded up. Yet the New Deal was not the sole factor determining trends in government employment even in that period. And growth before 1933 is attributable to other factors.

II Functions of Government Workers

To understand the big increase in the number of government workers since 1900 we need to know more about their functions. Government engages in even more diverse activities than housewives, ministers, or handymen. Many are as well known, but the ordinary citizen's notion of the relative importance of the various activities is likely to be shaped by his range of experience with them. To get a more balanced view, let us look at the current functional distribution of all government workers and the major changes during the last half century.

The Prewar Pattern
Two-thirds of all government employees in 1940, though on government payrolls, were working in industries producing goods and services also produced by nongovernmental agencies. (Following the Census, I use 'industry' rather broadly to cover any class of activity employing paid workers.) The most substantial portion was in education, as the reader will have gathered from preceding charts: education itself occupied close to a third of all government workers in 1940. Medical and health services, transport and public utilities (including the postal service), construction, and shipbuilding also occupied considerable numbers of government employees. The rest were scattered over almost all other industries.

Only one-third were in the group labeled, for want of a better title, 'general government' (Chart 6). This group carries on functions rated in this country as peculiarly governmental—protection by the armed forces, police, and fire departments, regulation of business and other social relations, roads, and similar functions.

That 'government' and education are entirely or largely manned by government workers is obvious, of course. That government employees constituted a substantial fraction—over 10 percent—of workers in forestry, medical and health services, construction, and transportation and public utilities, is less well known. In 1940, 21 percent of all workers in health and medical services were on government payrolls; the percentage was 22 for forestry, 17 for construction, 24 for electric and gas utilities, and 37 for shipbuilding (classified under manufacturing).

CHART 6

Industrial Distribution of Government and Total Employment, 1940
(Census data)

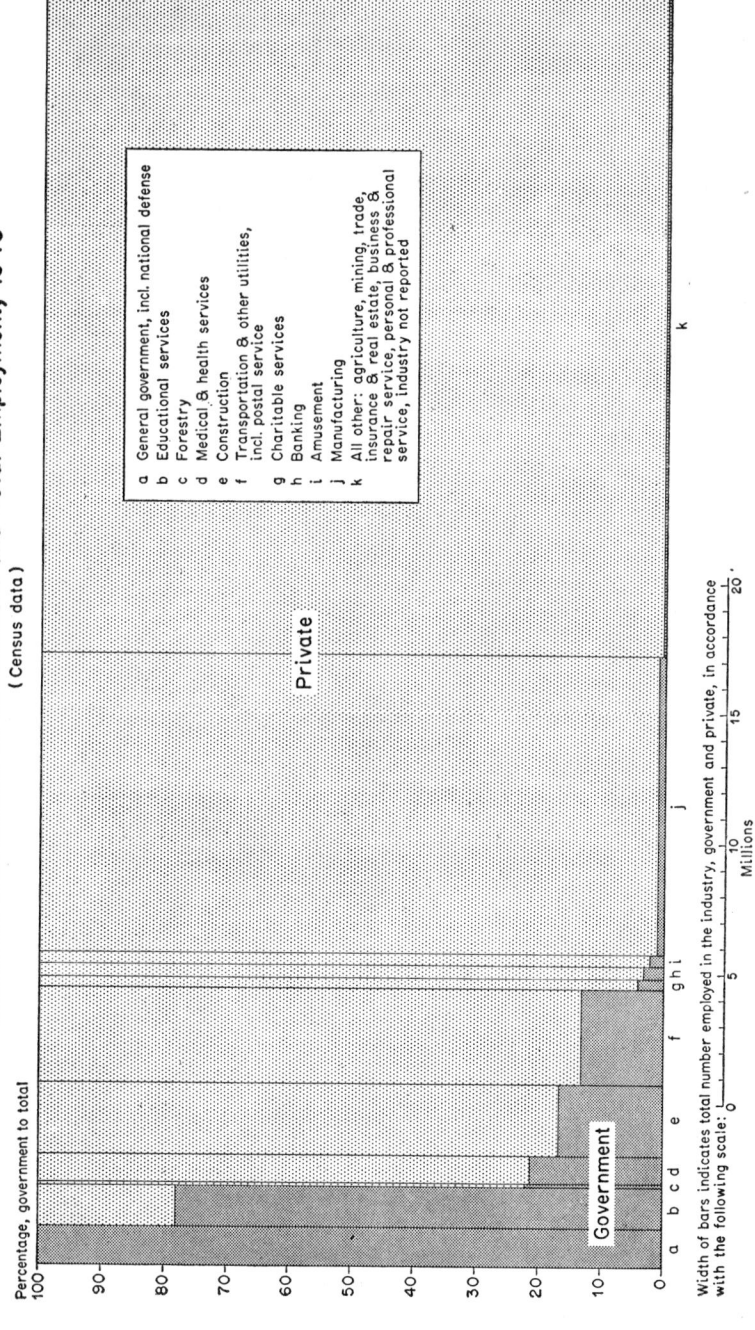

a General government, incl. national defense
b Educational services
c Forestry
d Medical & health services
e Construction
f Transportation & other utilities, incl. postal service
g Charitable services
h Banking
i Amusement
j Manufacturing
k All other: agriculture, mining, trade, insurance & real estate, business & repair service, personal & professional service, industry not reported

Width of bars indicates total number employed in the industry, government and private, in accordance with the following scale:

Such functions of government as are involved in administration, legislation, tax collection, and regulation accounted for only a small fraction of all government workers in 1940, much smaller than the third mentioned above. This is shown by a subclassification of the 'general' government function (Table 1), in accordance with groups more conventional in government statistics. Even the 9 percent or so shown in the table is something of an overstatement. Because 'full-time equivalents' could not be computed for each functional group, the large number of part-time county, township, and village workers inflates the figure.

Something like a 'division of labor' among governmental units is also revealed by the table. The prevalence of federal troops, state hospitals, and county courts has deep historical roots. Rural-urban differences in the populations served help to explain differences between cities and counties with respect to number of policemen, firemen, park workers, and employees in public service enterprises.

Change in the Pattern

Almost ceaseless change in the relative importance of private industries seems to be a characteristic concomitant of economic development. During the last half century relative declines in agricultural employment, relative rises then declines in mining, domestic service, and rail transport, and almost continuous relative rises in electric light and power, insurance, real estate, and personal and business service (other than domestic) reflect some of these changes in the industrial distribution of private employment.

Within government, also, there have been changes. The 1940 pattern is that of a section cut across trends of varying slope (Charts 7 and 8 and Tables 2-4). In few cases was I able to push the figures through to 1948, or to cover identical periods, yet the secular developments in which we are primarily interested are portrayed with reasonable accuracy.) Some activities of government that occupied but small percentages of government workers around 1900 grew to command the labor of much larger percentages in

Functional Classification of Government Workers by Type of Governmental Unit, 1940

	Federal	State	City	County	Sub-total	All Other Local	Grand Total
			PERCENTAGE DISTRIBUTION				
General administrative & financial	5.7	5.9	5.7	24.2	7.7		8.7
Legislative	.2	.3	3.8	...	1.3	4.2	
Judicial	.2	.7	1.0	5.0	1.0		
National defense	44.7	...	...	...	17.7	...	13.9
Law enforcement	.9	4.4	11.9	3.8	5.2	.6	6.6
Fire	...	...	10.6	...	3.1		
Public works							
Highways	0.2						
Waterways & flood control	3.0	23.2	11.2	25.8	12.8	8.3	13.3
Other public works	2.0						
Sanitation & waste removal	...	...	6.4	...	1.9		
Health	.5	2.5	2.2	2.2	1.6		
Hospitals	.1	14.6	4.9	11.2	5.7		12.7
Welfare*	10.5	8.7	2.4	6.5	7.3	1.8	
Correction	.2	3.6	...	2.2	1.1		
Development & conservation of natural resources	2.7	3.9	...	1.0	2.0	...	1.5
Recreation & parks	.2	.4	4.2	...	1.4	...	1.1
Agricultural, industrial, & commercial development	2.9	...	...	...	1.1	...	.9
Regulation	2.9	...	...	...	1.2	...	.9
General information & research	1.1	...	...	...	.4	...	.4
Schools	.05	27.5	16.3	12.5	11.7	84.5	27.4
Libraries & museums	.1	.1	1.5	.8	.6	...	.5
Other general functions	...	2.5	4.0	4.2	2.1	.6	1.8
Postal service	20.3	...	...	...	8.0	...	6.3
Water supply	...	...	6.8	...	2.0	...	1.6
Gas & electric systems	.4	...	1.7	...	.7	...	.5
Other public service enterprises	1.0	2.0	5.3	.2	2.4	...	1.8
Total	100.0	100.0	100.0	100.0	100.0	100.0	100.0
			NUMBER OF WORKERS (1,000)				
Total	1,496	768	1,113	400	3,777	1,039	4,815

Blank spaces indicate either zero or small amounts not shown separately but included in the figures for other functional categories. The federal government figures are for June 1940; the school figures (other than federal), for the school year 1939-40; the other figures, for Oct. 1940. Employment is measured by the total number of full- and part-time workers, with no adjustment to a full-time equivalent basis. Public emergency workers are excluded.

* Includes direct relief, social security, work programs, Veterans' Administration, and Indian affairs.

CHART 7
Federal Government Workers, Major Functional Categories
1896 – 1948

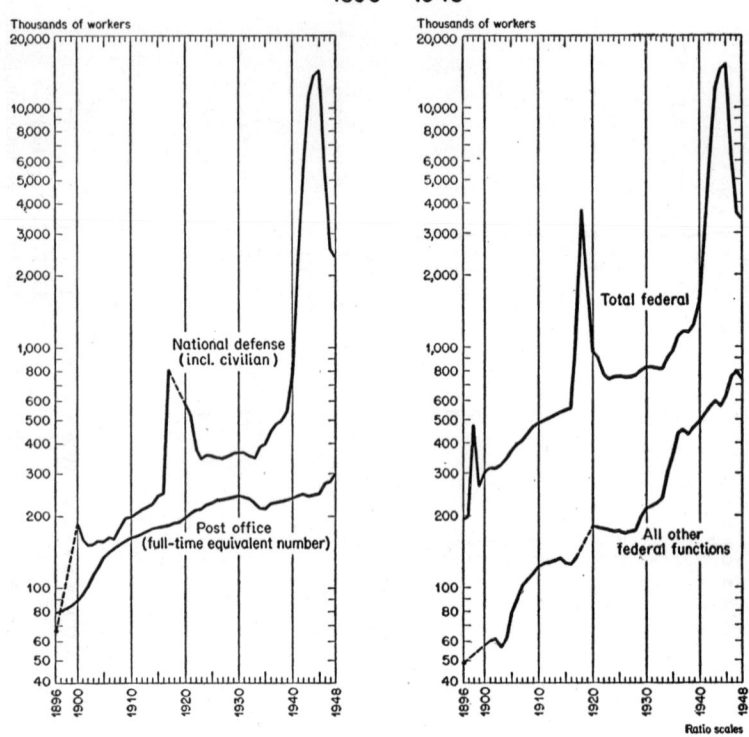

1939 or 1940. Others, of course, declined in relative importance.

That no revolution took place in the patterns needs equally to be emphasized. Important though the changes during the four decades are, the beginning and end patterns bear a distinct family resemblance. The correlation between the percentages at the opening of the century and just before World War II is substantial. Education, which had fallen off, continued to be a major function of state and local government (Table 4). And the postal service, to cite another example of relative decline, was still an outstanding employer of federal personnel in 1939.

These and other functional divisions of government declined in relative importance as employers of labor. Yet in not a single function of the federal government, the cities,

TABLE 2

Functional Classification of Federal Workers, 1896 and 1939

	NUMBER (1,000) 1896	NUMBER (1,000) 1939	% OF TOTAL INCL. POSTAL SERVICE & NATIONAL DEFENSE 1896	% OF TOTAL INCL. POSTAL SERVICE & NATIONAL DEFENSE 1939	% OF TOTAL EXCL. POSTAL SERVICE & NATIONAL DEFENSE 1896	% OF TOTAL EXCL. POSTAL SERVICE & NATIONAL DEFENSE 1939	1939 RELATIVE TO 1896
General government, incl. legislative & judicial	29.9	90.5	15.3	6.9	52.6	18.2	3.0
Law enforcement	1.6	14.0	.8	1.1	2.8	2.8	8.8
Public works	10.1	88.6	5.2	6.8	17.8	17.9	8.8
Conservation & development of natural resources	1.9	34.7	1.0	2.7	3.3	7.0	18.3
Agricultural, industrial, & commercial development	5.2	37.6	2.7	2.9	9.2	7.6	7.2
Regulation	1.1	41.5	.6	3.2	1.9	8.4	37.7
Health	1.1	9.7	.6	.7	1.9	2.0	8.8
Welfare	4.3	151.9	2.2	11.6	7.6	30.6	35.3
Public service enterprises other than postal	0.0	18.6	0.0	1.4	0.0	3.7	*
General information & research	1.2	6.6	.6	.5	2.1	1.3	5.5
Education & reference	.4	2.5	.2	.2	.7	.5	6.2
Subtotal	56.8	496.2	29.1	38.0	100.0	100.0	8.7
Postal service	78.9	232.2	40.5	17.8			2.9
National defense	59.2	575.9	30.4	44.2			9.7
Total	194.9	1,304.3	100.0	100.0			6.7

The figures for 1896 are as of June 30; those for 1939, as of Dec. 31, except for the postal service which is as of June 30. Postal workers are on a full-time equivalent basis. Public emergency workers are excluded.

* Denominator is zero.

CHART 8
New York State, Major Functional Categories of State Government Workers, and Population 1900 – 1940

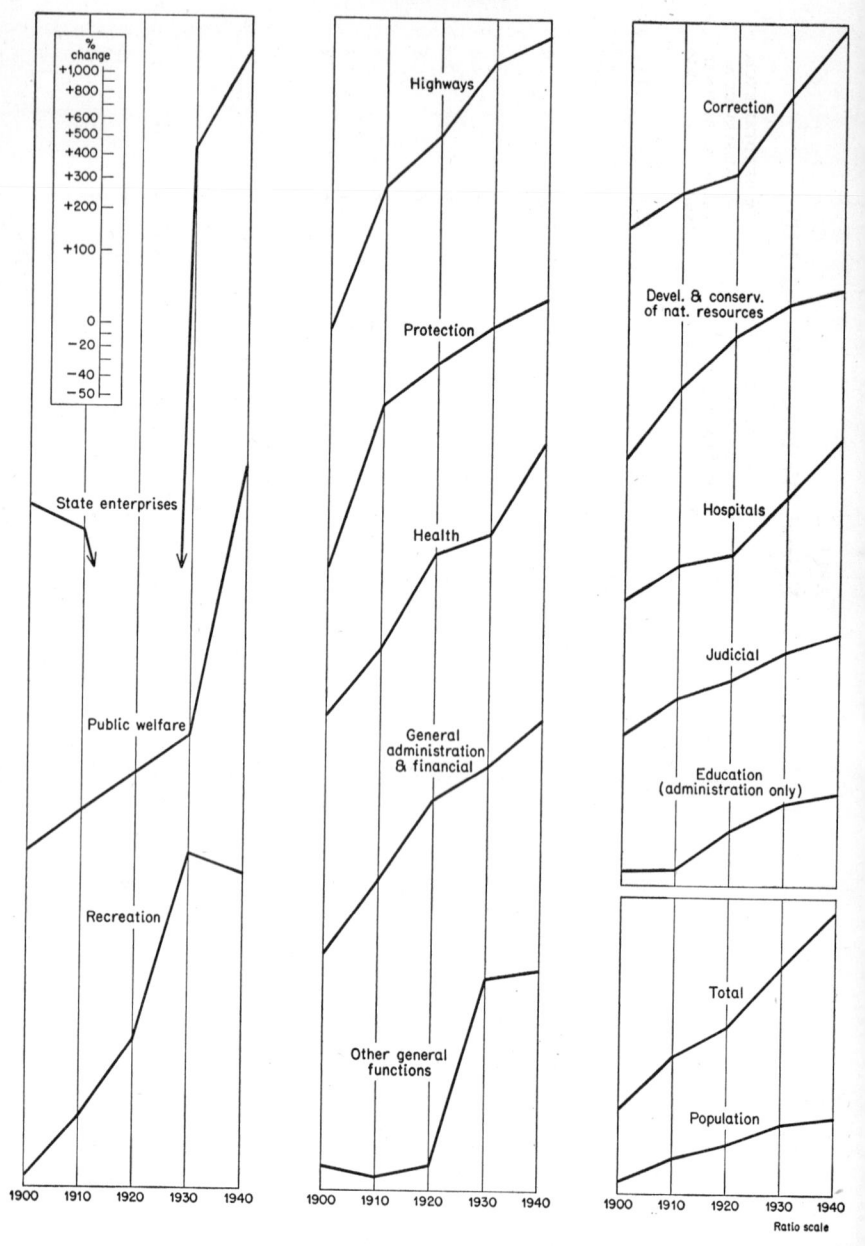

or New York State (or other states of which we have record), was the number of workers actually reduced. In no other sector of the economy would we find *every* major division expanding.

The results are almost as striking when growth in population is taken as the standard against which to set the rates of increase in individual functions. Every federal function pushed employment up more than population grew. Every New York State function pushed employment up more than the population of the state grew. As for the cities, all except three functions pushed employment up more than urban population grew.

The three municipal functions that did not grow as rapidly as urban population are the 'general control' functions, administrative, legislative, and judicial. In the federal government as well, and in part also in New York and other states, it was these functions that tended to lag.

The big percentage expansions came in activities connected with public welfare, health, conservation of resources, public works, and, at the federal level, regulation.

The functional categories used here are rather wide. Hidden within them are specific activities. To illustrate them, a few federal activities may be mentioned. Under law enforcement, for example, there is now a federal Bureau of Investigation (it had 2,400 employees in 1939), and—as a consequence of the immigration laws established in the 1920's—a greatly expanded Immigration and Naturalization Service (there were 4,000 employees in 1939 as against fewer than 300 in 1896). Public works now include construction operations of the Panama Canal and the Tennessee Valley Authority (and in 1939 also of the Federal Works Agency). The Forest, National Park, and Soil Conservation Services have swelled the number of persons engaged in conservation and development of resources. Welfare now includes the vast and various relief, social security, and other programs instituted under the New Deal, as well as the Veterans' Administration. In

TABLE 3
Functional Classification of Municipal Nonschool Payrolls and Personnel, 1903 and 1940
Cities with Populations of 25,000 or More

	PAYROLLS ($1,000,000)			PERSONNEL					
			1940 relative to 1903	Number (1,000)		1940 relative to 1903		% of Total	
	1903	1940[a]		1903	1940[a]	Direct estimate	Est. by deflation of payrolls	1903 (est.)	1940
Administrative	13.6	67.3	5.0		31.9		2.3	8.8	5.3
Legislative	1.8	5.8	3.2		3.7		1.5	1.6	.6
Judicial	5.4	17.5	3.2		6.6		1.5	2.8	1.1
Total general control	20.8	90.6	4.4		42.2		2.0	13.2	7.0
Police	36.6	215.6	5.9	34.2[b]	94.1	2.8	2.7	22.0	15.6
Fire	21.6	159.4	7.4	20.6[b]	71.3	3.5	3.4	13.3	11.8
Highways	12.8	82.0	6.4		52.4		2.9	11.3	8.7
Sanitation	14.4	92.5	6.4	19.5	61.4	3.1	2.9	13.2	10.2
Health	2.4	28.7	11.9		16.9		5.4	2.0	2.8
Hospitals	1.9	52.0	26.8		53.1		12.2	2.7	8.8
Public welfare	1.7	33.8	20.3		23.6		9.2	1.6	3.9
Water supply	9.4	73.6	7.9		42.8		3.6	7.5	7.1
Electricity	.4	23.8	52.8		12.6		24.0	.3	2.1
All other	15.4	219.1	14.2		133.1		6.5	12.9	22.1
Total	137.3	1,071.1	7.8	170.3	603.5	3.5[c]		100.0	100.0

[a] October 1940; payrolls were multiplied by 12. Part-time workers are included.
[b] Excludes callmen, volunteers, substitutes, and supernumeraries.
[c] Estimated from the figure for all cities by applying the relative increase in population. The population in cities of 25,000 or more was 22,292,000 in 1903, and 52,908,000 in 1940.

TABLE 4

Distribution of Government Workers by Main Functional Categories, 1900 and 1940

	Number (1,000)		Percentage of				1940 Relative to 1900
			Grand total		Total excl. emergency workers		
	1900	1940	1900	1940	1900	1940	
National defense	160	788	13.8	12.7	13.8	17.9	4.9
Schools	467	1,228	40.2	19.8	40.2	27.9	2.6
Public service enterprises	129	432	11.1	7.0	11.1	9.8	3.3
All other regular employees	405	1,950	34.9	31.5	34.9	44.3	4.8
Total regular employees	1,161	4,398	100.0	71.0	100.0	100.0	3.8
Public emergency workers	0	1,800	0.0	29.0			*
Grand total	1,161	6,198	100.0	100.0			5.3

This is a rough distribution of the full-time equivalent number. The national defense estimate for 1900 is based largely on the 1901 figure. The 1900 estimate for state and local public service enterprise employees is very rough, but the figure was certainly very small.

* Denominator is zero.

1896 the only 'welfare' activities of the federal government we could identify as such were the supervision of Indian affairs and operation of federal penitentiaries.

The federal agencies that appeared on the scene after 1896 employed 264,000 persons by 1939. Agencies in existence in 1896 (other than the postal and national defense services) employed only 193,000 in 1939. Excluding the post office and national defense, then, over half of federal employment in 1939 was in bureaus and divisions not organized in 1896. Corresponding or even larger proportions characterize agencies associated with such functions as conservation and development, welfare, regulation, general information and research, and public service enterprises (other than the postal system).

Measured by 1939 employment, the big additions to federal agencies came during the seven years beginning with 1933. Yet, in every decade the agencies and functions of the federal government were added to: for example, the early conservation agencies and the Panama Canal were established during 1903-12; and in every period the number of workers engaged in existing agencies and functions increased.

III Factors Affecting the Trend of Government Employment

The factors underlying the rising trend of government employment may be put into two groups: first, those affecting the relation between the number of government workers employed and the services they perform; second, those affecting the volume of government services.

Relation between Employment and Output
Influencing the ratio of employment to production are: change in hours worked by government employees; substitution of capital goods, and materials, supplies, and services purchased from the nongovernment sector, for the labor of government workers (or the reverse); and change in the efficiency of utilization of labor and other resources

in government activities. Interactions among these factors are also involved. Some factors contributed to the rise in government employment, some to its retardation. Even in this brief Paper we must at least list such factors and comment on them.

In practically all industries in the private sector of the economy—the outstanding exception may be agriculture—hours of labor put in by workers declined between 1900 and 1940. The average reduction was probably about 20 percent including agriculture, perhaps 25 or 30 percent excluding agriculture. In government, also, hours declined on the average. In some types of government work, it is true, hours have not fallen by as large a percentage as in private establishments. Such a difference in trend is suggested by the probable decline in the relative importance of part-time government work, the lengthening of the average public school year, and strong pressures towards shorter hours in private industry (especially after 1929) not as successfully matched by corresponding pressures in government. On the other hand, hours put in by policemen, hospital employees, and similar groups have probably declined more than average hours in private industry.

Any fall in the hours of government work per week tends to push government employment up. In some cases the effect of fewer hours might be partly offset by the higher productivity induced by the reduction. But this offset could hardly be complete. The maintenance of certain government services, at least, requires a fixed number of manhours per unit of service rendered. Police protection provided by foot patrol is an example. In such cases, reductions of hours would lead to exactly corresponding rises in employees per unit of service rendered.

The history of internal governmental operations suggests that capital goods and other purchases have to some extent tended to supplant labor in all or most individual functions of government. As in private industry, governments now use motor trucks, mechanical shovels, typewriters, carbon paper, and telephones on a scale not dreamed of at the opening of the century. This seems to have been accomplished by a different kind and better quality of capital assets (not reflected in measures of deflated assets) and by greater efficiency in the use of capital and other resources, rather than by more capital per worker. The figures suggest, indeed, that between 1900 and 1940 real capital per worker declined on net balance in most individual nonwar functions of government, with the major exception of education. (Data on military assets are not available.)

Heightened productivity, that is, reduction in the quantity of resources required to produce a 'unit' of government services, also would tend to keep down the rate of growth in government employment, as well as in other resources used by government. Review of some factors affecting the trend of government productivity—the use of improved technology and equipment, the spread of the merit system, the introduction of centralized purchasing, and various other advances in public administration—leaves the strong impression that the savings effected by their means have been far from negligible. Indeed, it is hard to think of any factor tending in the opposite direction except possibly the very increase in the scale of government operations. A tendency for unit costs to rise when size of establishment increases beyond some optimum level, supposed to affect private operations, might have affected government operations. On the other hand, the same reasoning suggests that an increase in scale of operations before the point of optimum size has been reached reduces costs; and some of the growth in government operations might have had this effect.

Unable to weigh all the factors affecting productivity, we cannot be sure what the net balance is. Yet, as has been suggested, governmental operations are not altogether unlike those of private enterprise, however different the objectives and means of financing may be; nor are government bureaus cut off from technological changes in the world in which we live. For the few areas of government for which some sort of measure can be attempted (for example, the postal service), there is clear evidence of substantial advance in productivity. I think it is safe to assume, therefore, that as in practically all private industry, a given volume of government production is turned out today with a smaller input of resources than at the opening of the century. The long-term trend in government's productivity has probably been upward.

Whether government productivity rose more or less rapidly than productivity in private enterprise is another matter, but one on which lack of information makes it idle to speculate. Another disclaimer may be in order. To hold that government productivity has probably advanced does not imply an opinion about its absolute level or the relation of that level to the level in private business. Whether government is more or less efficient than nongovernment enterprise also is an important question, but one not immediately relevant to the matter under discussion, and in any case not answerable with the data we have considered.

To sum up: Reduction in hours probably tended to raise employment per unit of government product. The other factors we have noted probably worked in the opposite direction. The net result has probably been a decline in employment relatively to output. This much, at least, we may conclude with confidence: if the ratio of employment to product rose, it did not rise very much. More likely, it fell. Not much, if any, of the big increase in government employment since 1900 can be attributed to the factors affecting the ratio between employment and output.

The Trend in Government Output

The major factor accounting for the increase in government employment has been the growth in government services, reflecting growth in both population and government services per capita.

Between 1900 and 1948 the population almost doubled. This is merely a rough index of the effect of population growth on government employment, however. The trend in school employees, for example, depends upon the age distribution as well as upon the size of the total population; and there may be indirect effects of population growth; for example, on the scale of operations and therefore on government's 'productivity'. Nevertheless, it seems safe to conclude that a doubling of the population would, apart from the effects of other factors, be accompanied by something like a corresponding rise in government workers. But that number rose 450 or 500 percent. While considerable, population growth alone accounts for only a part of the trend in government employment.

More important has been ampler provision of government services per capita. Services rendered in 1900 are on a larger scale today. And services are provided today that were not available at all in 1900. The simple arrays of figures in our tables, which portray the functional distribution of government workers, have something to tell us about these changes.

The contribution of national defense to government employment in the form of a standing army and navy has been indicated by Chart 4. There are interesting and distracting differences among the decades covered, but from the trend as a whole it appears that even before World War I—and certainly for the entire period—the armed forces at least kept pace with other government personnel. This means, of course, that the army and navy grew more rapidly than total population. Civilian employees participating directly in national defense increased even more rapidly than the armed forces (Chart 7). In the conditions and policies determining the magnitude of the peacetime defense effort we have, then, another factor contributing substantially to the growth in government employment.

The continued trend towards urbanization also has played a role. More and more of our people reside in incorporated places. In 1900 the urban population constituted about 48 percent of the total. By 1940 the percentage had risen to almost 65, and is higher still today. Further, a bigger fraction of the urban population now lives in the larger cities, which typically provide more municipal services and employ more municipal government workers per capita than the smaller cities. These shifts in population have thus acted to increase the number of municipal government workers per capita, as has expansion in the types of municipal service rendered by cities of all sizes.

In this connection it is interesting to observe that the distribution of employees among the various classes of state and local governments (Chart 3) reveals no pronounced trend, upward or downward, in the share of urban governments in total state and local personnel, whether including or excluding education. Increasing urbanization, with its shift of people to areas in which more government services per head are commonly rendered, though important, was not dominant in adding to state and local government workers.

The increases in employment in certain municipal functions—sanitation and streets—seem, indeed, to be very modest, barely exceeding the increase in municipal population. Does this mean that the volume of these services rendered per capita of the city population did not change appreciably or that more services were rendered more efficiently? The latter, I think, is the correct answer. And it explains also the modest rises in the number of government workers engaged in the general control function and police and fire protection. In the case of the post office, we know definitely that service per worker and per capita has expanded greatly.

Did absorption by government of functions commonly performed at the opening of the century by private enterprise play any role in expanding government employment? Employees engaged in public service enterprises rose only slightly more rapidly than population. Measured in this way and in this sense, increased 'socialization' of production does not appear to have been a significant factor. Attention may not be confined to public service enterprises (the postal service, municipal electric light systems, and the like), which are simply those so operated that their costs are largely or entirely borne by fees or charges levied on the user of their services. Government may encroach on the private sphere also by expanding the services (medical and health, for example) for which it levies no specific or significant charge on the consumer. Yet even the few facts we have observed give some basis for believing that this kind of encroachment on the private sphere has not done much to swell government employment. Encroachment through loans, subsidies, regulation, and similar means not involving direct ownership and operation is, of course, another matter.

There are, finally, 'new' government services. Not until the twentieth century did the nation really try to conserve its natural resources. Conservation of human resources also made headway. It took on new forms and old forms grew. Government employment in these functions expanded. Public health, hospitals, recreation and parks, charities, farm resettlement, public housing, unemployment compensation, 'other protection' (such as inspection of factories, foods, and drugs)—all growing more rapidly than the average for government functions—contributed considerably to the increase in government workers. Even federal workers engaged in Indian activities increased, though at a lower than average rate.

The great depression and the New Deal further stimulated the conservation of both natural and human resources. But the upward trend originated in earlier decades.

New and far-reaching regulatory activities, especially by the federal government, also appeared during the period covered. In terms of number of workers, however, these still account for only a small part of the whole job of government.

To explain why these various increases in government production occurred raises another type of question. Here it is only necessary to observe that the explanation is to be sought in several developments.

First, the rise of national income per capita made it possible to add to the government services provided final consumers and at the same time pushed up demand for these services. Despite the absence of definitive figures, it seems clear that aggregate government services rendered final consumers rose more rapidly than the rest of the nation's real product.

Second, the developments underlying the rise in national income brought with them certain costs which were met by government action. Among these are the costs of providing services essential to urban life. There are also the costs of regulating our increasingly complicated, interdependent economy and providing relief from the aberrations of its operation. The nation's progressive recognition of its responsibility created the demand for these services, and ensured satisfaction of this demand by government. Whether this sense of responsibility would have deepened as it did in an environment not characterized by a rising secular trend in income per capita or whether it is being satisfied in the most effective way by current government activity are questions into which I shall not go.

The third development may be described most simply and vividly in terms of some of the figures assembled here. In 1900 only about 160,000 persons—civilians in the nation's military establishment as well as uniformed men in the armed forces—were directly engaged in national defense. By 1925, at the middle of the period under review, the number was more than double, 350,000. Today it is 2.3 million, over six times the 1925 figure. Third, then, is the changing international scene and our reactions to it.

Note on Statistical Sources

The Census of Population data on government employment, plotted in Charts 1, 2, and 6, are derived from Bureau of the Census reports on the status of employers (1940 and 1948), on occupations and industries (1910 and 1930), or on occupations alone (1900 and 1920). The 1900-40 data are actual censuses for Census dates; the 1948 data are based on Bureau of the Census sample surveys for the week of March 7-13 published in the *Monthly Report on the Labor Force*. In preparing the 1900-30 figures Daniel Carson's estimates of the industrial distribution of the working force were used. The employment figures for years prior to 1930 are rough estimates derived from labor force figures.

The payroll data in Charts 1-5, 7, and 8, and in Tables 1-4, are derived from government reports on the number employed. The federal data are primarily from Civil Service Commission annual reports, supplemented by a special report for 1896 and unpublished data, and annual reports of the War, Navy, and Post Office Departments. The data on schools are chiefly from the Office of Education for years before 1946, and from Bureau of the Census reports on government employment for 1946-48. The state and local government nonschool data are from Bureau of the Census reports on government employment for 1940-48; the WPA-BLS study of public employment for 1929-39; Census reports on financial and other statistics of cities for 1903; employment reports from a rather small sample of cities and states for years before 1929; and the Census report on financial statistics of local government for 1902 (used to estimate the 1900 figure for 'other local, nonschool' in Chart 3). The public emergency data are from the Department of Commerce, National Income Division. There was probably some 'made-work' during depressions before that of the 1930's, but to judge from available information it was negligible.

The full-time equivalent numbers of state and local government nonschool employees are the sums of the full-time numbers plus one-third of the part-time and temporary numbers reported by the Bureau of the Census for 1940-48 (the ratio used by the Department of Commerce, National Income Division); prior to 1940, the 1940 proportion of the full-time equivalent to the total was assumed to prevail. We took the Department of Commerce proportion for schools too. For the federal government, only one adjustment was made: the number of fourth class postmasters and third and fourth class postal clerks was reduced three-quarters to yield a full-time equivalent.

Payroll data are either annual averages or as of June 30. Since the federal series covers 'off-continent' employees it may include a fairly considerable number of nonresident foreigners, especially during 1943-46.

All sources and methods for the charts and tables, and other figures mentioned in the Paper, will be described in detail in the full report.

Officers

C. REINOLD NOYES, *Chairman*
H. W. LAIDLER, *President*
HARRY SCHERMAN, *Vice-President*
GEORGE B. ROBERTS, *Treasurer*
W. J. CARSON, *Executive Director*
MARTHA ANDERSON, *Editor*

Directors at Large

DONALD R. BELCHER, *American Telephone and Telegraph Co.*
OSWALD W. KNAUTH, *New York City*
SIMON KUZNETS, *University of Pennsylvania*
H. W. LAIDLER, *Executive Director, League for Industrial Democracy*
SHEPARD MORGAN, *Finance Adviser, OMGUS, Germany*
C. REINOLD NOYES, *New York City*
GEORGE B. ROBERTS, *Vice-President, National City Bank*
BEARDSLEY RUML, *New York City*
HARRY SCHERMAN, *President, Book-of-the-Month Club*
GEORGE SOULE, *New York City*
N. I. STONE, *Consulting Economist*
J. RAYMOND WALSH, *WMCA Broadcasting Co.*
LEO WOLMAN, *Columbia University*
THEODORE O. YNTEMA, *Vice President - Finance, Ford Motor Company*

Directors by University Appointment

E. WIGHT BAKKE, *Yale*
C. C. BALDERSTON, *Pennsylvania*
ARTHUR F. BURNS, *Columbia*
G. A. ELLIOTT, *Toronto*
H. M. GROVES, *Wisconsin*
GOTTFRIED HABERLER, *Harvard*
CLARENCE HEER, *North Carolina*
R. L. KOZELKA, *Minnesota*
PAUL M. O'LEARY, *Cornell*
T. W. SCHULTZ, *Chicago*
ROBERT B. WARREN, *Institute for Advanced Study*

Directors Appointed by Other Organizations

PERCIVAL F. BRUNDAGE, *American Institute of Accountants*
ARTHUR H. COLE, *Economic History Association*
FREDERICK C. MILLS, *American Statistical Association*
STANLEY H. RUTTENBERG, *Congress of Industrial Organizations*
MURRAY SHIELDS, *American Management Association*
BORIS SHISHKIN, *American Federation of Labor*
WARREN C. WAITE, *American Farm Economic Association*
DONALD H. WALLACE, *American Economic Association*

Research Staff

ARTHUR F. BURNS, *Director of Research*
G. H. MOORE, *Associate Director of Research*

MOSES ABRAMOVITZ
HAROLD BARGER
MORRIS A. COPELAND
DANIEL CREAMER
DAVID DURAND
SOLOMON FABRICANT
MILTON FRIEDMAN
MILLARD HASTAY
W. BRADDOCK HICKMAN
F. F. HILL
THOR HULTGREN
SIMON KUZNETS
CLARENCE D. LONG
RUTH P. MACK
FREDERICK C. MILLS
RAYMOND J. SAULNIER
GEORGE J. STIGLER
LEO WOLMAN

Other National Bureau Publications on Employment and Productivity

The Output of Manufacturing Industries, 1899-1937 (1940)
Solomon Fabricant   710 pp., $4.50

Employment in Manufacturing, 1899-1939: An Analysis of its Relation to the Volume of Production (1942)
Solomon Fabricant   382 pp., 3.00

*American Agriculture, 1899-1939: A Study of Output, Employment and Productivity (1942)   462 pp., 3.00
Harold Barger and H. H. Landsberg

*The Mining Industries, 1899-1939: A Study of Output, Employment and Productivity (1944)   474 pp., 3.00
Harold Barger and S. H. Schurr

Output and Productivity in the Electric and Gas Utilities, 1899-1942 (1946)   208 pp., 3.00
J. M. Gould

Trends in Output and Employment (1947)   80 pp., 1.00
George J. Stigler

Studies in Income and Wealth, Volume Eleven   464 pp., 6.00
Part I consists of a paper by Mr. Fabricant, 'The Changing Industrial Distribution of Gainful Workers: Comments on the Decennial Statistics, 1820-1940', and one by Daniel Carson, 'Changes in the Industrial Composition of Manpower since the Civil War'.

OCCASIONAL PAPERS

*1 *Manufacturing Output, 1929-1937* (Dec. 1940)   .25
Solomon Fabricant

*4 *The Relation between Factory Employment and Output since 1899* (Dec. 1941)   .25
Solomon Fabricant

*7 *Productivity of Labor in Peace and War* (Sept. 1942)   .25
Solomon Fabricant

14 *The Labor Force in Wartime America* (March 1944)   .50
Clarence D. Long

23 *Labor Savings in American Industry, 1899-1939* (Nov. 1945)
Solomon Fabricant   .50

24 *Domestic Servants in the United States, 1900-1940* (April 1946)
George J. Stigler   .50

*Out of print.

Costs and Returns on Farm Mortgage Lending

by

Life Insurance Companies, 1945-1947

R. J. SAULNIER

FINANCIAL RESEARCH PROGRAM
NATIONAL BUREAU OF ECONOMIC RESEARCH

Costs and Returns on Farm Mortgage Lending

by

Life Insurance Companies, 1945-1947

R. J. SAULNIER

Occasional Paper 30: August 1949

FINANCIAL RESEARCH PROGRAM
NATIONAL BUREAU OF ECONOMIC RESEARCH
1819 Broadway, New York 23, N. Y.

Price: One Dollar

COPYRIGHT, 1949, BY NATIONAL BUREAU OF ECONOMIC RESEARCH, INC.
1819 BROADWAY, NEW YORK 23, N. Y.   ALL RIGHTS RESERVED
MANUFACTURED IN THE UNITED STATES OF AMERICA BY
THE JOHN B. WATKINS COMPANY, NEW YORK

Acknowledgments

The investigator's debt to those who supply primary data for his researches is more than usually heavy in the case of this work. As will be evident from the following sections, the study is based entirely on primary materials of a specialized and technical nature made available on a voluntary basis by a number of life insurance companies. Each company reported on a standard form, prepared with the advice of mortgage lending officers, and while this solved some of the problems of assembling data it could not avoid a good deal of necessary rearrangement and processing of the ordinary management records. We are particularly grateful, therefore, to the officers and staffs of those companies that responded to our requests for information.

This study is part of the Agricultural Finance Project of the Financial Research Program and will be followed by others dealing with related problems in the financing of agriculture. All of these are being prepared under generous grants of funds from the Association of Reserve City Bankers, the Life Insurance Investment Research Committee, acting for the American Life Convention and the Life Insurance Association of America, and the Rockefeller Foundation.

A good deal of the analytical work for the section in which findings are summarized, as well as a first draft of that section, were done by Mrs. Doris Warner of the Financial Research Program staff. It is a pleasure to acknowledge her contribution and that of Miss Katherine Krenning, who edited the manuscript.

R. J. SAULNIER
Director, Financial Research Program

August 1949

Table of Contents

	PAGE
I. INTRODUCTION	1
II. CONCEPTS AND METHODS IN MEASURING LENDING COSTS	5
ALTERNATIVE ACCOUNTING APPROACHES IN MEASURING LENDING COSTS	5
CONCEPTS AND ANALYTICAL METHODS	9
THE UNIT OF OUTPUT	9
THE UNIT OF COST	10
TIME-PERIOD VERSUS CROSS-SECTION STUDIES OF COST-INVESTMENT RELATIONSHIPS	10
NATURE AND CLASSIFICATION OF LENDING COSTS	12
III. FINDINGS	15
COVERAGE OF THE COST SURVEYS	15
SURVEY FINDINGS	17
GROSS INCOME	17
TOTAL COSTS	20
Components of total cost	24
NET INCOME ON LOAN INVESTMENT	28
NET INCOME ON LOAN PLUS REAL ESTATE INVESTMENT	31
NET INCOME AFTER OPERATING AND NONOPERATING INCOME AND COSTS	33
NET INCOME ON MORTGAGE LOANS AFTER ALLOWANCE FOR POTENTIAL LOSS	33
LOAN ACCOUNT TURNOVER AND NET RETURN ON INVESTMENT	34
EXPECTED YIELD	35
APPENDIX A—DESCRIPTION OF FARM MORTGAGE LENDING COST SCHEDULES FOR 1945-47	36
APPENDIX B—TABLES OF INCOME AND COST RATIOS, 1945-47	49

List of Tables

1. RELATIVE IMPORTANCE OF REPORTING COMPANIES AMONG ALL LIFE INSURANCE COMPANIES HAVING FARM MORTGAGE PORTFOLIOS, 1945-47   16
2. REPORTING COMPANIES CLASSIFIED ACCORDING TO GROSS INCOME RATIOS, 1945-47   18
3. INCOME AND COSTS IN PERCENT OF FARM MORTGAGE INVESTMENT FOR 18 INSURANCE COMPANIES, CLASSIFIED ACCORDING TO AMOUNT OF LOAN INVESTMENT, 1945-47   21
4. REPORTING COMPANIES CLASSIFIED ACCORDING TO NET INCOME RATIOS, 1945-47   31
5. REPORTING COMPANIES CLASSIFIED ACCORDING TO TURNOVER PERIODS OF FARM MORTGAGE LOAN PORTFOLIOS, 1945-47   35

List of Charts

1. GROSS INCOME IN PERCENT OF FARM MORTGAGE INVESTMENT RELATED TO AMOUNT OF LOAN INVESTMENT, 1945-47   19
2. TOTAL COST IN PERCENT OF FARM MORTGAGE INVESTMENT RELATED TO AMOUNT OF LOAN INVESTMENT, 1945-47   23
3. ORIGINATING FEES PAID TO CORRESPONDENTS IN PERCENT OF FARM MORTGAGE INVESTMENT RELATED TO AMOUNT OF LOAN INVESTMENT, 1945-47   26
4. SERVICING FEES PAID IN PERCENT OF FARM MORTGAGE INVESTMENT RELATED TO AMOUNT OF LOAN INVESTMENT, 1945-47   27
5. SERVICING FEES PAID IN PERCENT OF LOANS SERVICED RELATED TO AMOUNT OF LOANS SO SERVICED, 1945-47   29
6. HOME OFFICE EXPENSES IN PERCENT OF FARM MORTGAGE INVESTMENT RELATED TO AMOUNT OF LOAN INVESTMENT, 1946 and 1947   30
7. NET INCOME IN PERCENT OF FARM MORTGAGE INVESTMENT RELATED TO AMOUNT OF LOAN INVESTMENT, 1945-47   32

Introduction

No price, or set of prices, in our economic system has been the focus of such widespread and continuing attention as the price of borrowed money — the interest rate. It figures prominently in a wide range of discussions extending from those concerned with the direct and immediate interests of borrowers and lenders to those relating to broad economic policy and to the influence of interest rates on prices and production. Despite the vital importance of these problems, and the fact that a knowledge of what it costs a lending agency to provide funds for investment purposes is essential for analysis of any one of them, economic literature is notably deficient in the light it throws on lending costs.

The subject of the present study is lending costs in a single, highly specialized sector of the credit system — farm mortgage lending by life insurance companies. Its purposes are to explore some of the problems involved in measuring the costs incurred in the origination and servicing of loans — that is, the element in interest rates commonly referred to in economic literature as the "costs of loan administration" — to present one such method in some detail, along with certain data on lending costs for the years 1945-47, and to consider the relationship between the level of lending costs and the amount of a company's farm mortgage investment. While the data used in the analysis are drawn from a restricted segment of the market for borrowed funds, it is hoped that the conclusions to which the analysis leads will suggest relationships between lending costs and the scale of financing activities in other credit areas.

Improved knowledge of loan administration costs is increasingly important to public and private lending agencies. From the viewpoint of private investment, cost information is essential when the managements of life insurance companies must decide on the relative profitability of the several broad lines of investment open to them. Even in farm mortgage investment, information on lending costs is necessary to determine the attractiveness of particular mortgage offerings. From the standpoint of public policy, factual studies of the costs of extending long-term agricultural credit are useful in revealing certain implications inherent in government policies that determine, or influence, the interest rates chargeable to farmers. Only with reliable knowledge of the costs of loan administration can the adequacy or inadequacy of interest rate levels, in terms of the lending agency's net return at given levels, be judged intelligently.

Obviously, there would be a broader range of uses for studies of lending costs if reasonably accurate measures could be made of differences in the level of loan administration costs among various types and sizes of farm mortgage loans. How, for example, do costs vary among loans of different sizes on comparable types of farms, and among loans on farms alike except for soil quality or type of farming? If it were feasible, which it is not at present, to measure costs to this degree of refinement, lending agencies could formulate their policies to maximize more nearly their net returns, and it would be possible to foretell with greater accuracy the effects likely to flow from a public policy that applies a standard interest rate to all mortgage loans, regardless of size of loan or character of security. While the present study cannot answer all these questions, it does provide a basis for making estimates on many of them, and for pushing forward with additional studies aimed at clarifying others. It is hoped that the study will contribute, in this way, to a better understanding of the implications of certain policy decisions in both the public and private spheres of finance.

In planning this analysis of lending costs it was possible to draw on a few earlier empirical cost studies but, in general, economic literature contains little that bears directly on the subject.[1] This

---

[1] *Cost Behavior and Price Policy* (National Bureau of Economic Research, 1943), Chapter 2, provides a useful review of empirical cost studies for manufacturing and trade industries; Joel Dean's *The Relation of Cost to Output for a Leather Belt Shop* (National Bureau of Economic Research, Technical Paper No. 2, December 1941) is indispensable to any worker in the field of cost relationships, and his unpublished study, *A Statistical Examination of the Behavior of Average and Marginal Costs* (University of Chicago Ph.D. thesis, 1936), was drawn on freely in the present paper. Another interesting lending cost study, also unpublished, is W. A. Peterson's *Factors Influencing the Cost of the Small Loan Business* (University of Chicago M.A. thesis, 1934), an investigation of cost functions in the personal finance industry.

lack of relevant studies in the field of mortgage lending is not difficult to explain. During the 1920's and earlier the level of interest rates was so high that lending officers could be satisfied with rough estimates of cost. While the expenses of lending rose sharply during the early 1930's, owing to widespread loan delinquencies and foreclosures, this supplied little motivation to study lending costs since the higher expenses were not of the type that could be controlled.

A real stimulus to the study of lending costs did not come until the late thirties. By that time loan delinquencies had been largely cleared up and much of the real estate acquired through foreclosure in earlier years had been sold. Net income margins, however, were being further reduced by increased competition and by the shift from the borrower to the lender of certain costs, such as the finder's fee paid to the correspondent. Naturally, the attempts that were made to measure costs were restricted mainly to the experiences of individual companies; as a result, they were far from comparable, one with another. The principal object of the present study has been to design a basis for recording costs that will be comparable among companies and to use certain data assembled on this basis to indicate the general range of cost variation in the industry as a whole.

The general plan of this paper is first to discuss certain problems of measuring lending costs and then to present the main statistical findings. Detailed definitions of terms are provided in Appendix A, along with facsimiles of the schedules used in reporting data, and the instructions supplied to cooperating companies. Statistical tables giving data for individual companies (unidentified) are found in Appendix B.

Concepts and Methods in Measuring Lending Costs

The primary obstacle to a better understanding of the level of net returns on mortgage investments has been the use of dissimilar accounting methods in cost analyses. As a result, comparisons of individual studies, and the rough checks on accuracy which such comparisons provide, have been almost impossible. Since widely varying results can be achieved from different accounting procedures and types of analyses, it is essential, when interpreting cost figures, to have clearly in mind the nature of the analytical approach used. Differences can exist not only in the basic character of the accounting method but also in the range of costs included in the analysis and in the details of cost allocation procedures. Other difficulties arise when concepts employed in cost analyses are ambiguously, or otherwise inadequately, defined. It is important, therefore, to review briefly the principal alternative accounting approaches to a study of lending costs, and to describe the method and concepts selected for this investigation.

Alternative Accounting Approaches in Measuring Lending Costs

The chief difference among lending cost studies is generally found in the type of yield measurement used. Some studies attempt to measure the *present yield,* after costs of loan administration, on a portfolio of farm mortgages; others aim to measure the *expected yield* on "new business," that is, on an additional investment of a given amount in mortgage loans made at a given rate of interest. Studies of the first-mentioned type use what may be termed a "present portfolio yield" approach and the second an "expected yield" approach.

In measuring present portfolio yields, income and costs may be treated by the *accrual* or by the *cash* methods of accounting. The following illustration will clarify the essential differences between these two methods and show how each affects the final estimates of costs and yield. Let us assume that we are dealing with a portfolio of mortgages on which loan correspondents were paid fees, at the time the loans were closed, of 1.50 percent of the original amount of the loan in return for their activities in loan-origination, and servicing fees, disbursed at intervals over the life of the loan, for making collections on the mortgage, for periodically inspecting the property, and for performing any other agreed-upon servicing functions. The degree of dependence on correspondents or other outside agents for the acquisition and servicing of loans varies considerably from one company to another. In the farm loan business, however, a smaller proportion of new loan volume is acquired in this way than in lending on urban properties.

Handling these mortgages involves still other costs for the insurance company. A department for coordinating lending policy and for general administration of the mortgage portfolio must be maintained at the home office. Branch offices as well are operated by the great majority of companies making farm mortgage loans. If a mortgage goes into default and property is acquired, expenditures will be incurred in managing the foreclosed real estate, and either a profit or loss will be registered for the whole transaction when it is finally sold or exchanged. Each of these expenditures raises certain accounting problems, but to illustrate the differences between the cash and the accrual methods only the problem of handling originating fees paid to correspondents will be considered.

If the fees paid for loan origination are treated on an accrual basis, they are spread over the projected lives of the loans according to some assumption as to how long these loans will stay on the books.[2] The loan portfolio income of a given year is charged, there-

---

[2] Customarily mortgage lending institutions amortize the fee by annually charging against income a proportion of the fee equal to the reciprocal of the number of years the loan is expected to be an active balance. If the loan is paid off before the anticipated extinguishment date, the unamortized portion of the fee is charged against the income of the final year of the loan's life, with no attempt to recompute the income of previous years. This method is correct in the case of unamortized mortgages, but on an amortized mortgage the practice of charging the fee at a constant amount against loan income, the absolute amount of which decreases proportionately with

fore, with a proportion of the fees disbursed for that year and with portions of the still not fully amortized acquisition fees disbursed in earlier years.[3] On the other hand, if the cash principle of accounting is followed, the full amount of the fee is charged against the loan portfolio income of the year in which the fee was actually disbursed. In the same way, all other expenditures, whether for acquisition or servicing, are charged in full against the loan portfolio income of the year in which they were disbursed.[4]

The accrual and cash methods will give the same results in measuring yield after loan administration costs when the amount of loan balances outstanding, the rate at which new loans are being made, and the level of fees paid are constant. However, if the volume of new loans is increasing, whether outstandings are rising or not, discrepancies appear between the two measures of cost. As long as new loan volume rises, the accrual, or amortizing, method will give lower loan administration costs than the cash, or current charging, method. The opposite is true when the volume of new loans is falling.[5]

The other general type of yield measure — expected yield — requires a quite different accounting approach from the one just described. In this case there is the question: What will be the future yield of new business contracted today on given conditions of inter-

---

the loan balance, means that the fee bears more and more heavily on loan income as the balance falls. To distribute the fee "fairly" in such cases it is necessary to charge against income in each period an amount proportional to the unpaid balance of that period. This can be done by finding the factor F which, multiplied by the unpaid balances of the several periods $(P_1, P_2, P_3 \cdots P_r)$, will equal the total fee (C) to be charged against income. That is, we must find the value of F where $F(P_1 + P_2 + P_3 + \cdots P_r) = C$.

[3] Any other acquisition expense incurred for an individual loan, such as that portion of home office costs attributable to loan acquisition, should also be treated in this way. However, it is difficult to allocate home office or branch office costs to the separate functions of loan acquisition, loan servicing and real estate management, and companies do not attempt to spread any part of these costs, despite the logic of the case. Even if the process were not practically impossible, the costs involved are so small that the refinement would hardly be justified.

[4] Expenditures for office equipment and other capital items would be amortized, of course, in either case.

[5] It must be emphasized, as a final observation on these two methods, that consistency is essential no matter which one is followed. Income and expense, and every type of each, must be handled on the same basis. Ordinarily the treatment of interest income presents no difficulties (except for interest delinquencies), but serious problems arise in handling income from owned real estate as well as profit or loss on the whole transaction.

est rate and costs? In most respects, this problem is simpler than measuring present portfolio yields. Suppose that mortgages are made with the expectation that they will be repaid in ten years. From the gross interest received, it will be necessary merely to subtract annually a portion of the originating fee paid at the time the loan was closed and two other amounts, one representing a service fee paid periodically to the correspondent and the other an estimate of what should be charged continuously against the loan balance to cover costs of operating the home office mortgage loan department and to meet general administrative expenses.

Thus, a calculation of the expected yield on new loans acquired and serviced through correspondents can be made easily if one can (a) estimate the life of new loans with reasonable accuracy and (b) apply a reasonably accurate factor to cover home office costs. All other factors — originating cost and servicing fee — are given in the conditions of the problem. This is not the case, however, if a company acquires and services its loans without correspondents, or even if it acquires loans from correspondents but does its own servicing. In other words, the simplicity of the expected yield approach vanishes when a lending business not fully operated through correspondents or other outside agents is considered.

So much for the two principal ways of measuring lending costs. In this study the present portfolio yield approach, utilizing a "cash" or "current" accounting procedure, has been followed. It was not a difficult choice after all conditions had been examined. Calculation of the expected yield is, in a sense, a by-product of the measurement of present portfolio yield. Put more strongly, it is impossible to calculate expected yield without having measures of home office and branch office costs, and these can be developed only in the present portfolio yield type of study. Further, the expected yield calculation is feasible only when correspondents are widely used in servicing as well as in acquiring loans, and when home office and branch office costs — which present the most difficult problems in cost allocation — are at a minimum. And in the final analysis, the cash method of accounting was the only practical basis on which to ask individual companies to prepare their cost reports. The accrual method, used consistently for a large number of companies, would, in fact, have required a recalculation of income on thousands of loans.

Concepts and Analytical Methods

In addition to accounting difficulties, the measuring and analysis of lending costs involve certain other concepts and problems which it will be useful to discuss at this point.

THE UNIT OF OUTPUT

A principal object of cost studies is to determine the relationship between unit cost and the amount of business done, that is, the relationship between cost and output. Then the question arises: What should be used as the unit of output? In studies of agricultural and manufacturing costs a "physical" or "value" unit is ordinarily used, while in trade industries the choice is between a value unit (e.g., dollar volume of sales) and an "activity" unit (e.g., number of sales transactions completed).[6] In finance, the problem is more akin to trade than to agriculture or manufacturing. The lending institution's object is to keep its funds in use and, accordingly, cost studies must determine whether (a) the cost of keeping money at work varies significantly with the amount at work or with how it has been lent out (in large or small amounts; on different types of security; for different periods of time, etc.) and (b) the costs of handling an additional investment of funds, and the additional income expected therefrom, warrant making the investment.

In both cases the unit of output is an amount of money at work, or to be at work,[7] but other investigations may require a different unit, for example, an activity unit, such as the number of loans closed in a given period or the number outstanding at a given time. In a cost study in the personal loan field[8] the number of active

---

[6] See Joel Dean, "Statistical Determination of Costs, with Special Reference to Marginal Costs," *The Journal of Business of the University of Chicago*, Vol. 9, No. 4, Part 2, October 1936, pp. 25-28, for a discussion of units of measurement for output and costs; see also *Cost Behavior and Price Policy* (National Bureau of Economic Research, 1943) pp. 85-87.

[7] Accordingly, it is appropriate to use the expression "cost-investment relation" in place of the familiar term "cost-output relation."

[8] W. A. Peterson, *Factors Influencing the Cost of the Small Loan Business* (University of Chicago M.A. thesis, 1934).

accounts was used as the output variable, but this would be unworkable in mortgage studies where the average size of new loans (or of outstanding balances) varies greatly from company to company, and where costs vary greatly for different types of loans.

In the present study it has been practical to take a dollar of outstanding loan balances as the unit of output and to use the dollar amount of the mortgage portfolio as the independent variable. This is not to say that the number of loans made or outstanding, or some combination thereof, would not be a useful variable; indeed, the amount of loans made has been used occasionally in this investigation. In general, however, there is greater interest in the amount of outstanding loan balances.

THE UNIT OF COST

There is no problem in studies of the present type as to the unit of cost to be used as a dependent variable — it must be a dollar of expenditures. Nevertheless, the relationship between the number of employees and the number of accounts outstanding is of interest in other financial fields. In general, studies of this nature would be appropriate for the small loan business or, in the mortgage field, for investment activities involving nothing but insured loans on single family dwellings. In both cases mortgage handling practices are sufficiently standardized to assure that the relationship arrived at would be broadly indicative of the economy of labor-use at different levels of portfolio size.

TIME-PERIOD VERSUS CROSS-SECTION STUDIES
OF COST-INVESTMENT RELATIONSHIPS

A more important problem in planning studies of lending costs is whether to seek (a) cost-investment relationships over a number of years for one or a small number of companies or (b) cost-investment relationships for a single year for a large number of lenders having portfolios of different sizes. The former may be called the "time-period" and the latter the "cross-section" type of cost analysis.

Both analyses would be useful, but only the last-named was made in the present investigation owing to certain difficulties relating to the collection and adjustment of data. It was possible to obtain data readily for 1945 (and later for 1946 and 1947) from a large number of companies, whereas it would have been almost impossible to obtain adequate cost data for a longer period of years for any single company. But disregarding this practical matter, the technical difficulties of adjusting time-period data to eliminate all cost-influencing factors and conditions, other than the ones to be examined, are sufficient reason for avoiding the time-period type of analysis.[9]

Data adjustments are always troublesome but particularly so in this instance because mortgage financing has undergone marked institutional changes in recent years. Many companies have shifted from "correspondent" to branch office operations (particularly in farm mortgage lending), and since the late thirties the proportion of owned real estate to total loan and real estate investment has fallen abruptly. Both of these developments have greatly influenced costs, and there is no method of adjusting data to eliminate their effects. The only way to meet these problems (and the similar problem of change in type of loan) is to find a lender who has operated within a fairly stable framework over the whole period. Where such an opportunity is available it should be grasped; unfortunately the option was not open in the present investigation.[10]

Finally, if a time-period analysis is used it is necessary to disentangle the influence of loan delinquency from the joint effect of all elements affecting the cost-investment relation.[11] It is not unusual to find instances where the percentage of delinquent loans to the total amount of loans outstanding has changed since the late twenties from less than 5 percent to over 50 percent and back to less than 1 percent. This is only a forerunner of the larger problem presented

[9] See Joel Dean, *The Relation of Cost to Output for a Leather Belt Shop* (National Bureau of Economic Research, Technical Paper No. 2, December 1941) pp. 12-18, for a discussion of data adjustments of this type.

[10] It is necessary to adjust time-period data for changes in prices of labor and materials, which raises a very difficult problem in mortgage financing. Since the mid-thirties lenders have absorbed two costs — originating fees and compensation to outside agents for loan servicing — formerly borne by the mortgagor.

Not all problems of data adjustment are avoided in the cross-section approach. Companies vary, even at one point in time, in lending practices and in types of loans handled, but this difficulty can be met by selecting broadly similar cases and grouping companies for separate analyses. As will be noted, cases were grouped in the present study into "branch" and "nonbranch" companies; in some instances the separation was made arbitrarily since there is no clear dividing line between the two groups.

[11] W. A. Peterson, *op. cit.*, uses an ingenious means of correcting for changes in delinquency ratios. His data are of the cross-section type and cover a number of offices operated by a large personal finance company, which were located in different

by changes in the proportion of owned real estate to total loan and real estate investment, yet it presents somewhat more formidable difficulties since real estate management costs are separable from loan portfolio costs, whereas the costs of handling loan delinquencies are inseparable from other loan department expenses.

Loan delinquency would not influence costs if loans expired quietly into the charge-off category.[12] However, this seldom happens; in fact, a loan may end a long and troublesome life without ever having been charged off. An investigator wishing to pursue the time-period approach can do little but devise a scheme for "adjusting" his data, or look for a company without a variable delinquency ratio.

NATURE AND CLASSIFICATION OF LENDING COSTS

A few general comments on the nature of lending costs and the categories of costs that can be used effectively in analytical studies should be made at this point. First, in finance as in manufacturing there is a time lag, perhaps substantial, between the incurrence of an expense (e.g., the payment of an originating fee) and the receipt of the income resulting in whole, or in part, from this expenditure. This is significant for cost and yield analyses because it is impossible, by taking observations over a single time period (except from the very beginning of lending operations to the very end), to compare inputs of resources at given costs with outputs of income produced thereby. The only real solution to this problem is to reallocate expenditures, or receipts, so as to match inputs and outputs, but this is virtually impossible as an accounting procedure. Obviously, the seriousness of the problem increases with the maturity of loans

---

communities and experienced different delinquency conditions. Briefly, his theory is that those cost differentials among offices which cannot be explained by differences in the number of active accounts held and in the population size of the territory served are attributable to differences in delinquency ratios. This seems reasonable for the small loan business but there are many more cost-influencing factors at work in mortgage lending (at least where different types of mortgage security are taken) and they are, unfortunately, not all measurable in terms that permit analytical treatment. Peterson's lead might be followed, perhaps, in studies of cost-investment relations in savings and loan associations since these agencies provide the closest counterpart in mortgage lending to the conditions of his experiment.

12 Since charge-offs and reductions in valuation allowances and their opposites — recoveries and increases in valuation allowances — are separable accounting entries, their adjustment can be handled without special difficulty, provided the reporting is convenient.

made. It would be relatively easy to cope with if loan life averaged less than one year, but in mortgage lending loans run for a much longer time.

Second, the full costs of any given increment of loan investment are not incurred except over a substantial period of time, and cannot be precisely forecast before the first "instalment" of total expenditure is made.[13] As a result, only an approximate judgment is possible as to whether a given investment will be profitable. For example, one can estimate only very roughly the percentage of loans that will become delinquent and the extent of the losses that will be sustained on foreclosed loans. Accordingly, expected cost-investment relations based on portfolios showing little or no delinquency can be upset in a very short time.

Third, interesting and important questions are involved in selecting the categories of expenditures that can be used most effectively in studies of lending costs. Perhaps the most commonly used classification is that in which expenditures are grouped according to the identity of the goods or services purchased (e.g., labor, office supplies, heat, light, taxes, telephone, etc.). Such subclassifications are useful to management, but have only limited value from the economic viewpoint. In this investigation costs are classified according to whether they were incurred in the operation of branch offices or in the home office loan department and each of these groups is further classified into costs arising out of the functions of loan acquisition, loan servicing, and real estate management. This procedure was adopted because it provides direct answers to the main problems of the investigation; fortunately it was also the most convenient form of reporting for respondents.

There is little resemblance between this grouping of costs and those most frequently used in nonempirical studies. It is interesting to inquire, therefore, into the usefulness and adaptability for lending cost analyses of the conventional grouping of costs into those that are "fixed" in the short period and those that are "variable." The fact of primary importance in considering the usefulness of this

---

[13] The investigator should not be pressed too hard to define what is meant by the "first" expenditure. I have had the originating fee of a particular loan in mind (to take a relatively simple case) but there is no "first" expenditure short of the initial disbursement made by the company at its very beginning, if we have in mind the maintenance of a whole investment portfolio.

classification of costs is that there is no single variable in relation to which mortgage lending costs can be said to be either fixed or variable. Some costs vary with the number or dollar amount of loans outstanding; others vary with the number or dollar amount of loans made. Furthermore, some costs are fixed for substantial ranges of portfolio size and some for shorter ranges; others vary with the slightest change in portfolio size; and there are no clear lines separating one group from the next. While costs cannot be studied along these conventional lines the same questions can be explored by other methods. Costs can be aggregated and, without regard to the variability of the different elements of total cost, an "average incremental cost" can be calculated by dividing the difference between total costs at successive, fairly widely separated levels of outstandings by the amount of the difference in outstandings.[14] From the movement of a curve of average incremental cost computed on this basis, it is possible, of course, to indicate the behavior of marginal cost. As will be seen in the following section, the total unit cost of lending funds on farm mortgage security is roughly constant, at least for the range of portfolio amounts above $20 million. Since fixed costs are small relative to variable costs at present levels of lending activity, it may be inferred that average variable costs and marginal costs are also constant, or nearly so.

[14] This procedure was followed by W. A. Peterson, *op. cit.*

Findings

The primary data on which this study is based were obtained directly from life insurance companies. Schedules for reporting 1945 costs and other related information were mailed to all 369 legal reserve life insurance companies in June 1946, and in June 1947 and May 1948 somewhat simplified sets of schedules securing cost data for 1946 and 1947, respectively, were sent to all companies except those that had reported no mortgages in the returns of the previous year.[15] The coverage of the three surveys and the principal findings from analyses of these data are summarized in this section.

COVERAGE OF THE COST SURVEYS

Schedules sufficiently complete to be used in most phases of the analysis were received from 43 companies in 1945, 45 in 1946, and 31 in 1947.[16] Only a small number of companies reported on these schedules, but the fact that many of them had large farm mortgage portfolios gives the survey a wide coverage. As shown in Table 1, the 43 companies reporting fully in 1945 represented 20 percent of the number and 58 percent of the admitted assets of all legal reserve life insurance companies having farm mortgage loan portfolios, as well as 61 percent of the farm mortgage holdings of all such companies. Coverage for companies with large total assets was especially good. Eight of the 10 companies with admitted assets of $1 billion and over, and a large percentage of those with total assets of $100 million and over, replied.

[15] Copies of the 1945 and 1946 schedules and the instructions which accompanied the 1946 schedules are reproduced in Appendix A. The 1947 schedule has not been reproduced since it is identical with the 1946 schedule.

[16] More than this number of companies returned schedules, but many stated that costs could not be determined according to our instructions. Others were eliminated because their mortgage holdings were too small to warrant accurate cost determination.

TABLE 1 — RELATIVE IMPORTANCE OF REPORTING COMPANIES AMONG ALL LIFE INSURANCE COMPANIES HAVING FARM MORTGAGE PORTFOLIOS, 1945-47 [a]

Size of Company (admitted assets in millions of dollars)	Number of Reporting Companies	Number of Companies	Total Admitted Assets	Farm Mortgage Holdings [b] (1)	(2)
1945					
Less than $1	1	6%	3%	20%	20%
1-99.9	22	13	17	15	13
100-499.9	9	47	52	75	66
500-999.9	3	75	75	75	73
1,000 and over	8	80	62	78	70
Total	43	20%	58%	68%	61%
1946					
Less than $1	2	13%	11%	9%	
1-99.9	24	15	27	40	
100-499.9	8	42	46	79	
500-999.9	3	75	76	82	
1,000 and over	8	73	59	74	
Total	45	21%	56%	71%	
1947					
Less than $1	0	0%	0%	0%	
1-99.9	12	7	11	8	
100-499.9	8	38	44	68	
500-999.9	3	75	76	87	
1,000 and over	8	73	65	80	
Total	31	13%	59%	68%	

[a] From *The Spectator Insurance Year Book* (1946, 1947, and 1948) and *Best's Life Reports* (1946).

[b] The farm mortgage holdings of reporting companies taken as a percent of the farm mortgage holdings of all insurance companies are overstated in column (1) since the figures for reporting companies include real estate sales contracts, while farm mortgages for all companies are used exclusive of real estate sales contracts. When the 1945 data are corrected for this discrepancy, as in column (2), the percents are somewhat lower: 61 percent for the total of all classes instead of 68 percent, etc. Since the 1946 and 1947 data were not broken down into mortgages and real estate sales contracts, it was impossible to compute a correct percentage for these years.

In the 1946 survey the number of companies reporting and their relative importance among all insurance companies with farm mortgage portfolios was about the same as in the 1945 survey. Twenty-nine of the 45 companies responding to the 1946 survey submitted schedules the previous year, although the completeness of the reports of a particular company varied to some extent in the two years.

Among companies with assets under $100 million, the response to the 1947 survey was about 50 percent smaller in number than in the previous years. Among companies with assets of $100 million and over, however, the coverage was about the same in all three years. One company with assets of $1 billion and over dropped out in the 1947 survey but was replaced by another company in this size class. Twenty-four of the 31 companies responding to the 1947 survey participated in the other two years.

Not all of the companies referred to above as reporting in 1945, 1946, and 1947 submitted complete reports, or reports that were usable in all sections of the analysis, with the result that the number of reporting companies found in the different tables and charts of this section varies considerably. The largest representation is in the charts on gross income; the analysis of certain components of cost is next in terms of the number of reports used, followed by the analysis of total cost. As would be expected, many reports usable in other respects had to be discarded when studying the entire structure of costs, since this required a complete return.[17]

Survey Findings

GROSS INCOME

As the first step in our analysis, the gross income of each reporting company (interest income on farm mortgage loans and real estate sales contracts, prepayment premiums, and all other income except that earned on owned real estate) was expressed as a percentage of the company's loan investment.[18] These percentages, henceforth referred to as gross income ratios, are presented first in Table 2 which shows that in each of the three years 1945, 1946, and 1947 over one-half of the companies reported gross incomes between 4.00 and 4.75 percent of their loan investments.[19] Income ratios of report-

[17] Whenever it appeared that an otherwise acceptable schedule contained a reporting error, the company was requested to explain the questionable item. In this way a number of schedules for larger companies were made usable.

[18] Loan investment is the average of farm mortgage loans outstanding at the beginning and end of the year. For more precise definitions of terms used in this section, see Appendix A.

[19] The 1945 schedule called for a breakdown of income by source in order to determine whether the gross income ratios were unduly affected by receipts of income other than interest on loans. Returns showed that the 30 companies reporting a breakdown earned 89 percent of their gross income from interest on farm mortgage loans, 10 percent from interest on real estate sales contracts, and 1 percent from prepayment premiums. Furthermore, it was found in 1945 that the ratio of gross income

ing companies fell somewhat during this period. For a sample of 18 identical companies, the average gross income ratio, weighted by the size of loan investment, declined from 4.65 percent in 1945 to 4.46 percent in 1946 and to 4.26 percent in 1947. Eleven of the 18 companies reported a decline in their gross income ratio from 1945 to 1946, while 14 showed a decline from 1946 to 1947.

TABLE 2 — REPORTING COMPANIES CLASSIFIED ACCORDING TO GROSS INCOME RATIOS, 1945-47

Gross Income Ratios	Number of Companies		
	1945	1946	1947
Under 4.00%	0	0	4
4.00-4.24	5	8	4
4.25-4.49	8	7	8
4.50-4.74	7	10	8
4.75-4.99	4	3	2
5.00-5.24	5	5	1
5.25 and over	6	3	2
Total	35	36	29

Do companies with large farm mortgage loan portfolios have higher or lower gross income ratios than companies with small portfolios? Answers to this and related questions are provided by the data in Chart 1 in which the three panels refer to 35 companies in 1945, 36 companies in 1946, and 29 companies in 1947.[20] The majority of companies with small portfolios reported gross income ratios between 4.00 and 5.00 percent in 1946 while, in all but two

---

from real estate sales contracts to the average amount of such contracts outstanding was 4.66 percent compared with 4.56 percent for interest income on loans. Sales contracts produced an abnormal level of income in only a few companies and in all of these cases it was much lower than average.

[20] It will be noted that the scale has been omitted from the horizontal axis in all charts. Companies reported in each of the surveys on the assurance that the data would be presented so that individual companies could not be identified. The device of omitting the scale was adopted rather than the alternative of averaging individual company returns in order to preserve as much as possible of the primary information.

As an aid to the interpretation of the charts (other than Chart 5), each of the panels has been broken into two parts: the smaller left-hand section includes the companies with small portfolios; the larger right-hand section includes all other companies. The base is marked off in equal ranges of portfolio size and each observation has been plotted in its proper position. In this way relative positions of individual observations can be judged, although the amount of loans in any one portfolio cannot be determined. On Chart 5, the horizontal axis is divided into equal ranges representing amount of loan balances serviced by correspondents. Also, data on income, costs, and returns are given in Table 3 in the form of averages for companies grouped according to size of portfolio.

CHART 1 — GROSS INCOME IN PERCENT OF FARM MORTGAGE INVESTMENT RELATED TO AMOUNT OF LOAN INVESTMENT, 1945-47

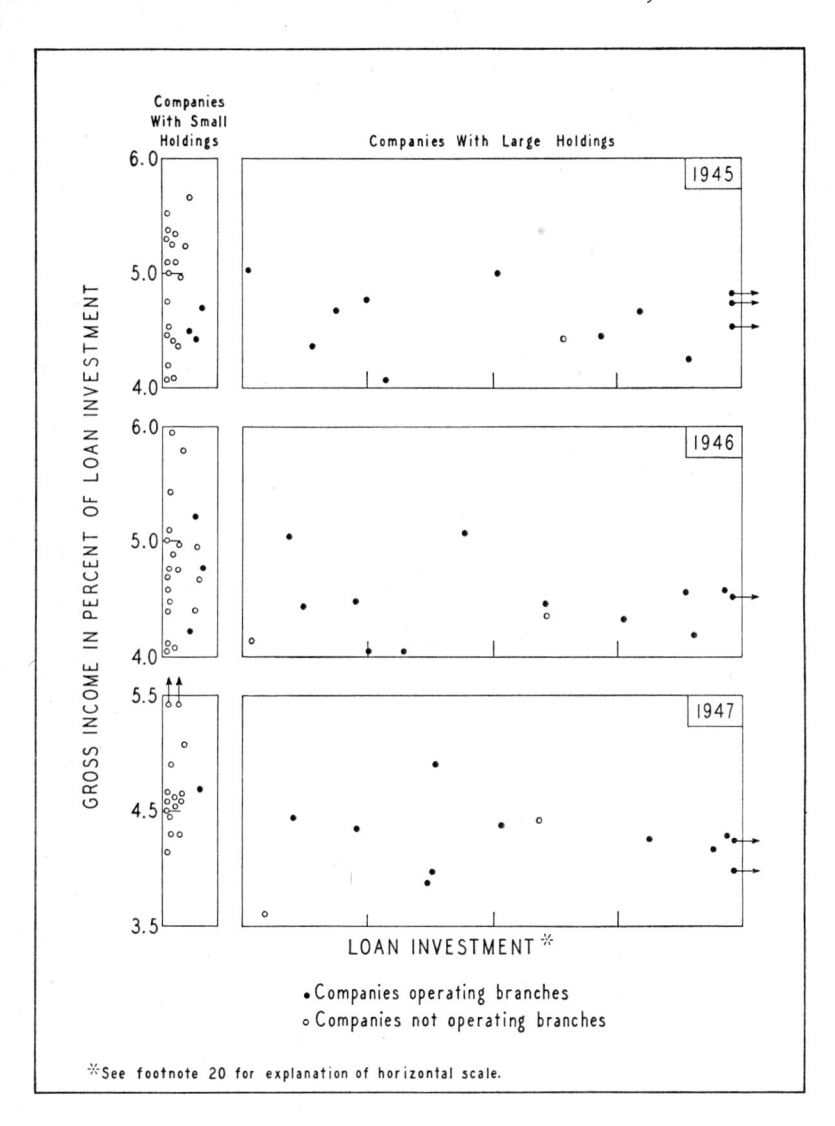

• Companies operating branches
○ Companies not operating branches

*See footnote 20 for explanation of horizontal scale.

Gross income ratios of companies with small holdings of farm mortgage loans varied more widely than gross income ratios of companies with large holdings. The former also had a somewhat higher average gross income.

of the reported cases, the ratios of companies with larger holdings were confined within the range of 4.00 to 4.60 percent. The pattern of distribution of gross income ratios in the other two years was similar, although the general level of the income ratios, as indicated in Chart 1, fell from year to year. The two outstanding characteristics of these distributions, therefore, are (1) the wider range of operating results for companies having small portfolios and (2) the tendency for the income ratios of companies with small farm loan holdings to average higher than those for companies with large farm loan holdings.

There is no conclusive evidence to explain these relationships, but the greater dispersion of gross income ratios for the small, as compared with the large, portfolio companies is probably due to the fact that there is less chance in small companies for individual interest rates to average out to a figure comparable with that of other companies and also to the possibility that their accounting practices may be less standardized than those of companies with large holdings. The tendency for the gross income ratios of small portfolio companies to average somewhat higher than those of larger lenders is probably due to lending by the former in less highly competitive areas and on farms of specialized type, possibly of relatively low quality. However, present information is insufficient to test these suppositions.

TOTAL COSTS

In order to compare costs among individual companies, and to arrive at a net income ratio, the several elements of total cost — branch office expenses, originating fees paid to correspondents, servicing fees, and home office expenses — have been aggregated and expressed as a percent of loan investment. This is referred to as the total cost ratio.[21] The elements comprising total cost are similarly expressed.

Eighteen companies reporting for the entire three-year period have been classified in Table 3 into three groups, according to the size of the company's portfolio, and average ratios have been computed for each group. The total cost ratios present a conflicting picture as regards the relationship between company size and the level of operating costs. Companies with small holdings had a higher

[21] More correctly, we deal with ratios of total *operating* costs. Losses, credits to reserves, and other *nonoperating* expenses are excluded.

level of total costs in 1946 than did large companies and a lower level in 1947. The pattern in 1945 was still different, with the middle-sized group reporting the highest total cost ratios. Considerations having to do with company organization must be introduced to explain differences in the level of the various elements of total costs among the various-sized groups of companies. Since small companies generally do not operate branches, while large companies depend heavily on them, the branch office costs of the latter are rela-

TABLE 3 — INCOME AND COSTS IN PERCENT OF FARM MORTGAGE INVESTMENT FOR 18 INSURANCE COMPANIES, CLASSIFIED ACCORDING TO AMOUNT OF LOAN INVESTMENT, 1945-47 [a]

Income and Cost Items (in percent of loan investment)	Year	Companies with Portfolios of:		
		Under $5 Million [b]	$5 to $20 Million [c]	$20 Million and Over [c]
Gross income	1947	5.05%	4.10%	4.28%
	1946	5.24	4.24	4.49
	1945	5.11	4.48	4.67
Total costs	1947	.93	1.14	1.51
	1946	1.27	1.22	1.17
	1945	.93	1.12	.88
Originating fees paid	1947	.23	.20	.35
	1946	.24	.22	.21
	1945	.16	.16	.11
Servicing fees paid	1947	.14	.12	.03
	1946	.11	.12	.03
	1945	.10	.11	.04
Branch office expenses	1947	.00	.53	.88
	1946	.00	.50	.71
	1945	.00	.47	.51
Home office expenses	1947	.56	.29	.25
	1946	.92	.38	.22
	1945	.67	.38	.22
Net income	1947	4.12	2.96	2.77
	1946	3.97	3.02	3.32
	1945	4.18	3.36	3.79
Number of reporting companies		7	5	6

[a] Averages of individual company ratios weighted by portfolio size. Ratios of individual companies are found in Appendix B; for example, the seven companies with portfolios under $5 million in 1945 are companies A through G in Appendix Table B1.

[b] Includes only companies not operating branch offices. Only three companies with portfolios under $5 million reported that they operated branch offices.

[c] Includes only companies operating branch offices. The one branch office company with a portfolio under $5 million that responded in all three years has been included in the $5 to $20 million class, while the one large company not having a branch office system, but reporting in all three years, has been excluded from this table.

tively high. On the other hand, small companies depend more heavily on home office operations, giving them a higher cost ratio in this respect.

To show the range of intercompany differences, total cost ratios are presented in Chart 2 as a scatter diagram. It will be observed, first, that costs vary less widely among companies with large portfolios than among those with small holdings. Total cost ratios of large portfolio companies tended to concentrate within fairly narrow limits in 1945 and 1946, ranging in general between 0.70 and 1.15 percent of their respective loan investments in 1945, and between 0.95 and 1.20 percent in 1946. The cost ratios of large portfolio companies were considerably less concentrated in 1947, falling between 0.95 and 1.65 percent of loan investment.

Companies with small portfolios reported both the highest and the lowest total cost ratios. This suggests that there is greater similarity among large portfolio companies than among those with small holdings in respect to organization, type of farming area served, and type and average size of loans made. In addition, it might be expected that special conditions resulting in relatively low or relatively high costs on a few loans would considerably influence the cost ratios of companies with small portfolios, whereas in companies with large or very large portfolios the chances are greater that costs would average out to a ratio close to the average for the whole group.

Finally, the upward movement of lending costs from 1945 to 1947 is mainly evident in the ratios of those companies with very large portfolios of farm mortgages. As indicated in Table 3, increased branch office expenses and originating fees, attributable to the increased volume of new loans made in 1946 and 1947, were largely responsible for this increase.[22]

Two additional factors were examined in an attempt to explain intercompany differences in total cost ratios: the average size of a company's individual loan balances and its activity in extending new credits (measured by the ratio of loans closed in 1946, exclu-

[22] While it would be interesting to utilize these data to answer the question whether companies operating on a branch system have a higher or lower ratio of total costs to their loan investment than nonbranch companies with the same loan investment, comparison is impossible because all the reporting companies with large holdings of farm mortgage loans are in the branch company class and there are only a few branch companies among those with small portfolios.

CHART 2 — Total Cost in Percent of Farm Mortgage Investment Related to Amount of Loan Investment, 1945-47

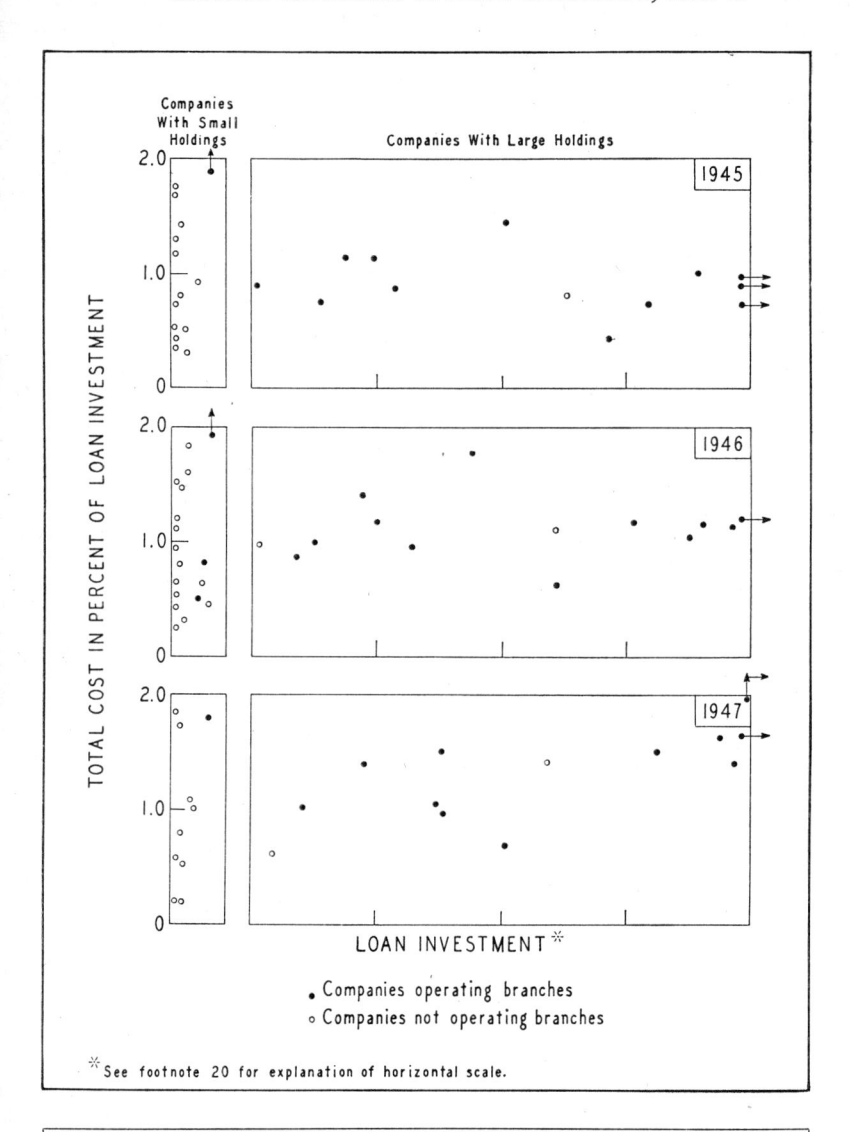

*See footnote 20 for explanation of horizontal scale.

- Companies operating branches
- Companies not operating branches

Companies with small holdings had more widely dispersed total cost ratios than companies with large holdings. The increase in total cost ratios from 1945 to 1947 was most pronounced among the companies with the largest portfolios.

sive of loans refinanced, to the amount of loan balances outstanding at the beginning of the year).[23] No systematic relationship was found between the total cost ratio and the average size of individual loan balances. Doubtless, this is because small balances are mainly held by small portfolio companies, and these companies are almost equally divided between those with high, and those with low, total cost ratios.

While a definite relationship would be expected between the level of a company's lending activity and its lending costs, this is not apparent in the evidence for companies with portfolios of $5 million and over. There are only a few such reporting companies, in any case, and they do not differ greatly with respect to lending activity; consequently, no significant cost differentials were apparent in the experimental analysis. Among companies with portfolios of less than $5 million there was some evidence that high levels of lending activity were associated, in general, with high cost ratios, but even here there were a number of striking exceptions to this generalization.

Components of total cost

That companies are differently organized for the conduct of mortgage lending, and follow different practices in compensating their correspondents and other outside agents, such as brokers, means that intercompany differences are far greater with respect to the ratios of these cost components to the investment base than for the ratios of total cost to loan investment. Nonetheless, certain aspects of the cost structure of farm mortgage lenders are clarified by this breakdown of expenses. In particular, information is provided on the level of home office loan department costs relative to loan investment and on the relation of this cost factor to the size of a company's portfolio.

A. BRANCH OFFICE EXPENSES

Naturally, branch office cost ratios vary widely from company to company, since not all companies handle the same proportion of their business through a branch system. Ratios of branch office ex-

[23] The analysis was not made for 1947 owing to the smaller number of reports available in that year. Charts are not included for the analysis of cost relationships with average loan balance and with lending activity.

penses to average loan investment tended to cluster fairly closely for the few companies with the very largest portfolios; ratios for companies outside this group are very widely dispersed. The five companies reporting the largest portfolios in 1945 had ratios of branch office expense to total loan investment that ranged between 0.40 and 0.55 percent, and the five largest concerns reporting in 1946 had ratios that fell between 0.50 and 0.75 percent. The same concentration of ratios occurred in 1947, although the general level of branch office expense ratios in that year was over 0.70 percent.

B. ORIGINATING FEES, COMMISSIONS, AND PREMIUMS

Fees and commissions paid to correspondents and other outside agents during the year may be expressed as a percentage of loan investment, as in Chart 3, or as a percentage of the amount of loans acquired during the year through correspondents. Chart 3 shows that for the majority of companies originating fees were less than 0.15 percent of loan investment in 1945 and over 0.25 percent in 1947. The marked rise in this category of costs from 1945 to 1947 was to a large extent due to the increased volume of new loans acquired and in part to an increase in the rate of commission paid to correspondents for originating loans. The ratio of fees paid to the volume of loans acquired through correspondents ranged between 1.30 and 1.60 percent for half of the companies reporting in 1946 but the number of companies reporting this item in 1945 and 1947 was too small to permit comparison of this range with commission rates paid in these years.

As would be expected, the ratios of originating fees to loan investment for small portfolio companies vary over a much wider range than do the ratios for companies with large holdings. Differences in the proportions of new loans which companies acquire through outside agents, branches, and home office staffs are so great that intercompany comparisons of these ratios are of little value.

C. SERVICING FEES

Measures similar to those discussed in the previous section can also be used to show the level of servicing fees. Chart 4 reveals that these fees amounted in the three years 1945-47 to less than 0.10 percent of loan investment for the majority of companies. The highest ratios were reported by the small portfolio companies, probably because

CHART 3 — ORIGINATING FEES PAID TO CORRESPONDENTS IN PERCENT OF FARM MORTGAGE INVESTMENT RELATED TO AMOUNT OF LOAN INVESTMENT, 1945-47

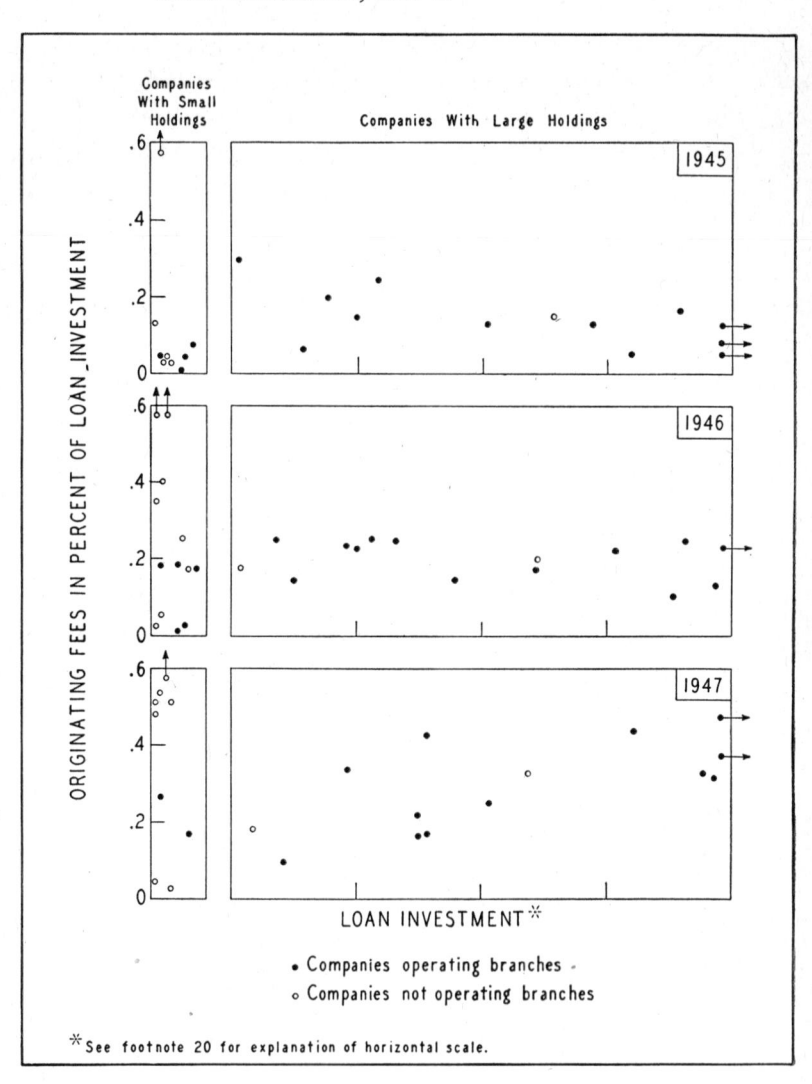

• Companies operating branches
○ Companies not operating branches

*See footnote 20 for explanation of horizontal scale.

For most companies, originating fees paid were under 0.15 percent of loan investment in 1945, between 0.15 and 0.25 percent in 1946, and above 0.25 percent in 1947. The increase in originating fees from 1945 to 1947 doubtless reflects both the growth in loan activity and the increase in commission rates.

CHART 4 — SERVICING FEES PAID IN PERCENT OF FARM MORTGAGE INVESTMENT RELATED TO AMOUNT OF LOAN INVESTMENT, 1945-47

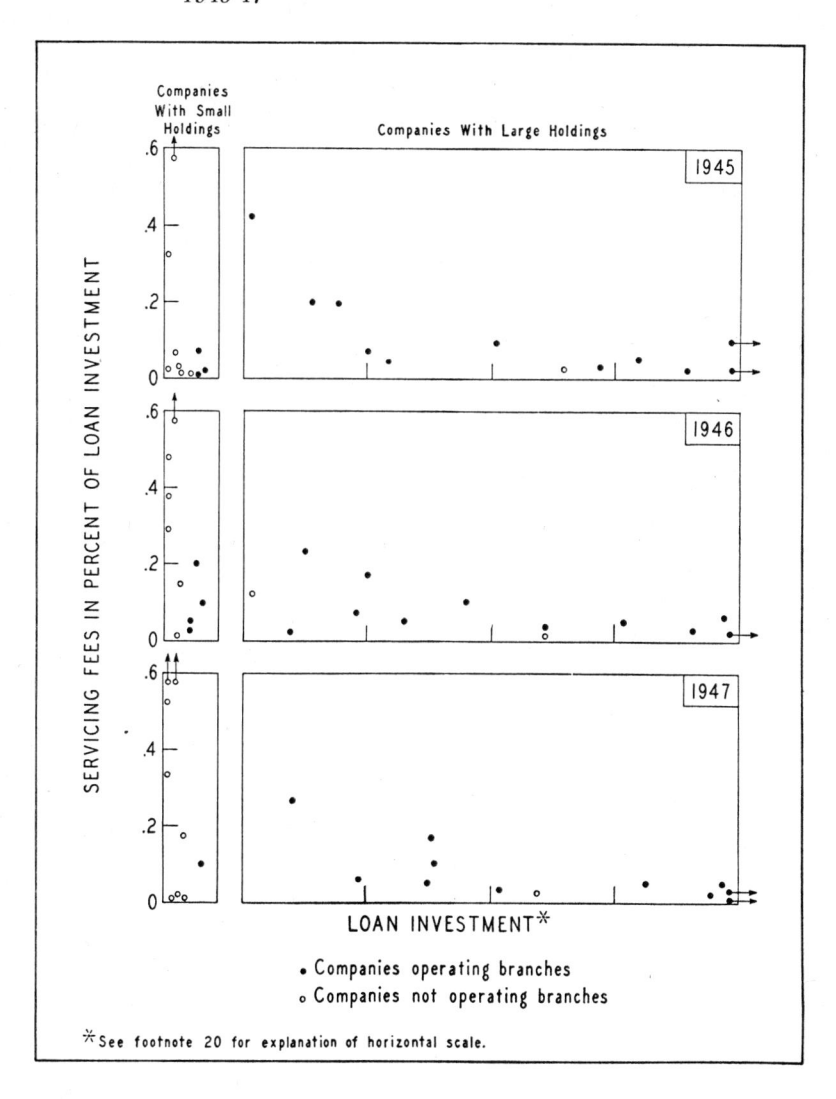

- Companies operating branches
- Companies not operating branches

*See footnote 20 for explanation of horizontal scale.

> Servicing fees paid in 1945-47 were less than 0.10 percent of loan investment for most companies. Companies with the largest portfolios paid out the smallest amounts relative to their loan investment, reflecting their greater independence of outside loan servicing agencies.

they frequently make the most extensive use of outside agents to service loans.

Ratios of greater significance are given in Chart 5 which shows, for individual companies, the ratios of servicing fees paid during the year to the amount of the balances so serviced, arranged according to the amount of the loan balances being serviced. The chart indicates, first, that the majority of companies were paying fees for loan servicing between 0.20 and 0.60 percent of the amount of the loan balances being serviced and, second, that the cost ratios did not vary with the amount of loan balances being serviced.

One would not expect servicing fees to vary with the total amount of the loan balances being serviced for a given company since this total is an aggregate of amounts serviced by a number of correspondents. Doubtless there is a tendency for fees to be lower where the amount of loans serviced by a single correspondent is large and where the average size of the balances is large, but available data are not adequate to determine the character of these relationships.

D. HOME OFFICE EXPENSES

The only meaningful measure of this final cost component is the percent of home office expenses to loan investment. For the 11 large portfolio companies reporting for the whole 1945-47 period, the weighted average home office expense ratio was 0.25 percent in each year. For half of these large portfolio companies the cost of operating a home office farm mortgage loan department ranged, in 1946, between 0.20 and 0.30 percent of loan investment, while in 1947, as shown in Chart 6, the scatter was greater than in the previous year. Conforming with the results presented in Table 3, Chart 6 indicates that home office expenses, for companies operating branch office systems, average somewhat lower for companies with very large portfolios than for those with small holdings.

NET INCOME ON LOAN INVESTMENT

The ratios of net income after costs to loan investment for individual companies are shown in Table 4; weighted averages for all companies included in the table for 1945, 1946, and 1947 are 3.71, 3.34, and 2.68 percent, respectively. It will be noted that net income ratios were concentrated between 3.50 and 3.99 percent of loan

CHART 5 — SERVICING FEES PAID IN PERCENT OF LOANS SERVICED RELATED TO AMOUNT OF LOANS SO SERVICED, 1945-47

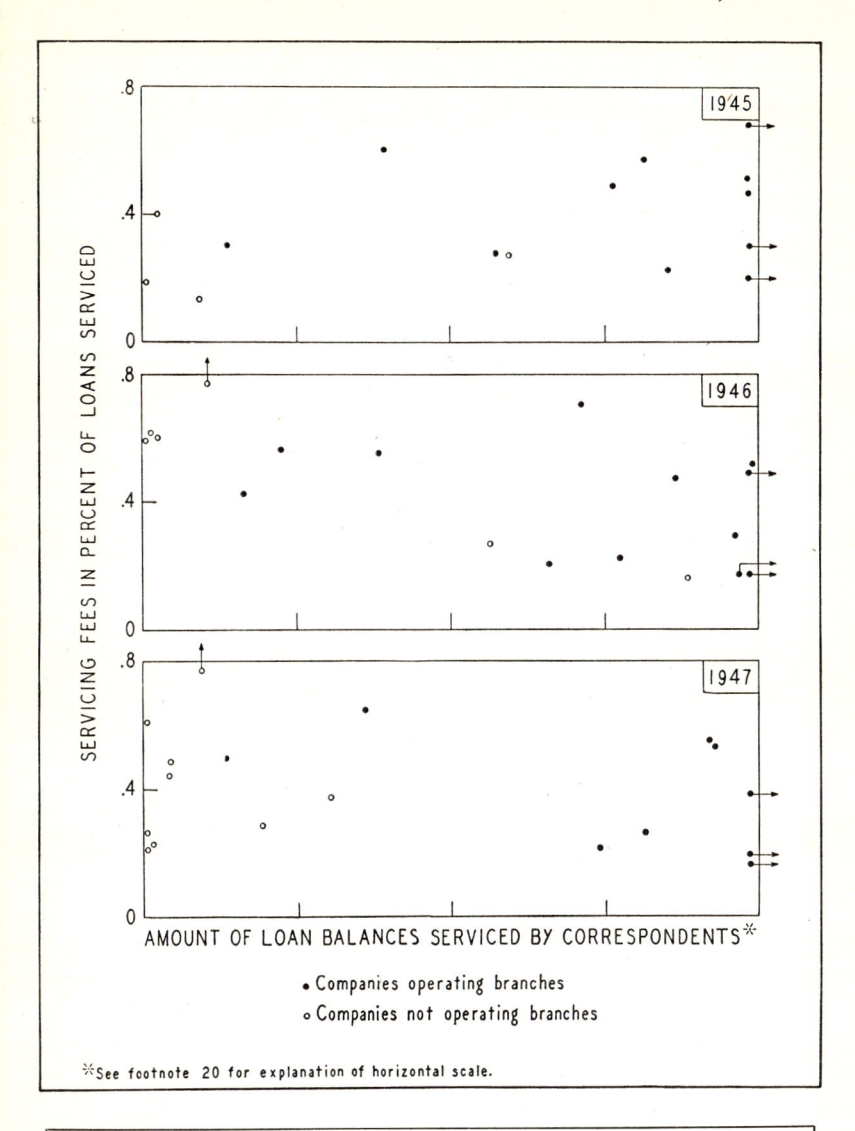

- Companies operating branches
- Companies not operating branches

*See footnote 20 for explanation of horizontal scale.

When expressed as a percent of the amount of loan balances serviced by outside agents, servicing fees ranged from 0.20 to 0.60 percent for most companies in 1945-47.

CHART 6 — HOME OFFICE EXPENSES IN PERCENT OF FARM MORTGAGE INVESTMENT RELATED TO AMOUNT OF LOAN INVESTMENT, 1946 AND 1947

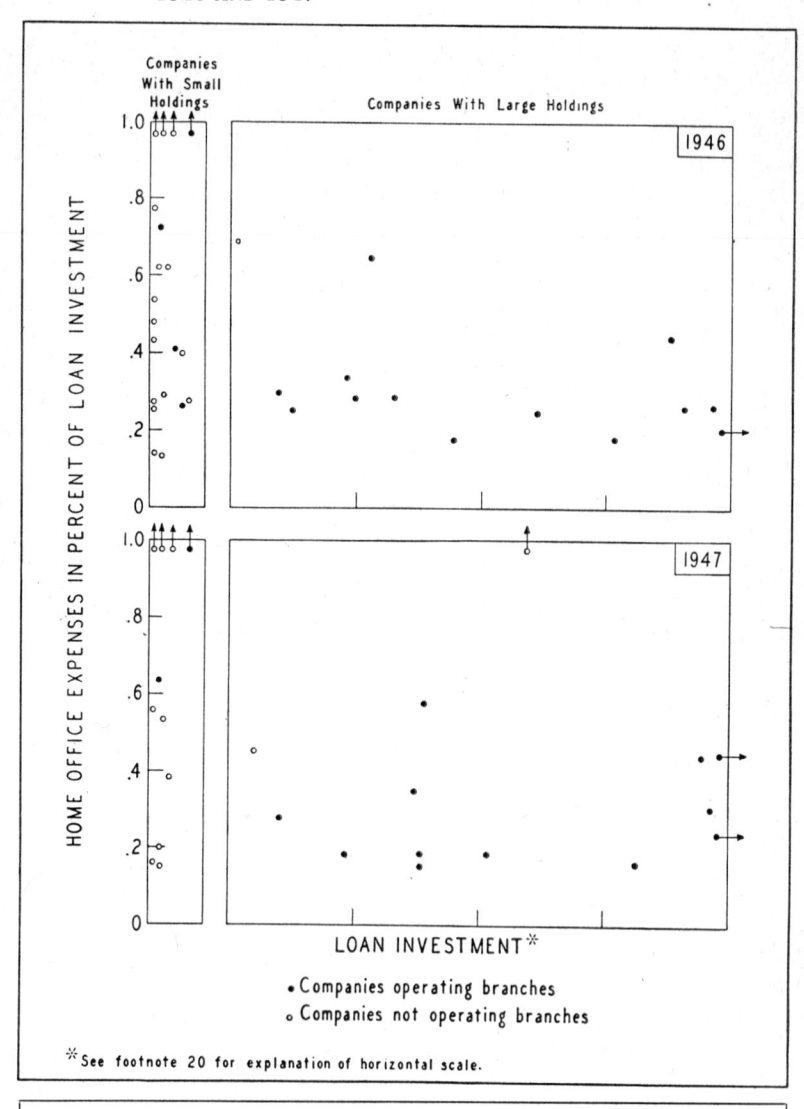

* See footnote 20 for explanation of horizontal scale.

Home office expenses varied widely for companies with small portfolios. For most large portfolio companies in 1946 these expenses were from 0.20 to 0.30 percent of loan investment.

investment in 1945, between 3.00 and 3.49 percent in 1946, and between 2.50 and 2.99 percent in 1947.

TABLE 4 — REPORTING COMPANIES CLASSIFIED ACCORDING TO NET INCOME RATIOS, 1945-47

Net Income Ratios	Number of Companies		
	1945	1946	1947
Under 2.50%	2	1	2
2.50-2.99	0	3	12
3.00-3.49	3	12	2
3.50-3.99	13	9	3
4.00-4.49	7	5	2
4.50 and over	3	2	3
Total	28	32	24

We may now turn to the question: How is net income after costs related to the size of the companies' portfolios of farm mortgages? It is clear in Chart 7 that in all three years the greatest variability in net income ratios was among small portfolio companies. As with our measures of gross income and all elements of operating cost, the large portfolio companies conformed closest to a standard pattern of performance. This chart also makes it plain that the level of net income ratios for companies with large holdings of farm mortgages did not vary with the size of the portfolio held. Further, it is apparent that the downward movement of net income ratios from 1945 to 1947 was more characteristic of companies with large portfolios than of those with small holdings.

NET INCOME ON LOAN PLUS REAL ESTATE INVESTMENT

The foregoing discussion has dealt only with costs incurred, and income earned, on portfolios of loans and real estate sales contracts, but to describe adequately farm mortgage investment experience it is essential to consider the income earned, and the expense incurred, on owned real estate. The latter is clearly only a transformation of the mortgage loan account, except where the real estate was acquired for investment. The data for computing this over-all ratio were provided for in the 1945 schedule by separate reports of income earned on the real estate account and costs incurred — either at branches or at the home office — in the management of owned real

CHART 7 — NET INCOME IN PERCENT OF FARM MORTGAGE INVESTMENT RELATED TO AMOUNT OF LOAN INVESTMENT, 1945-47

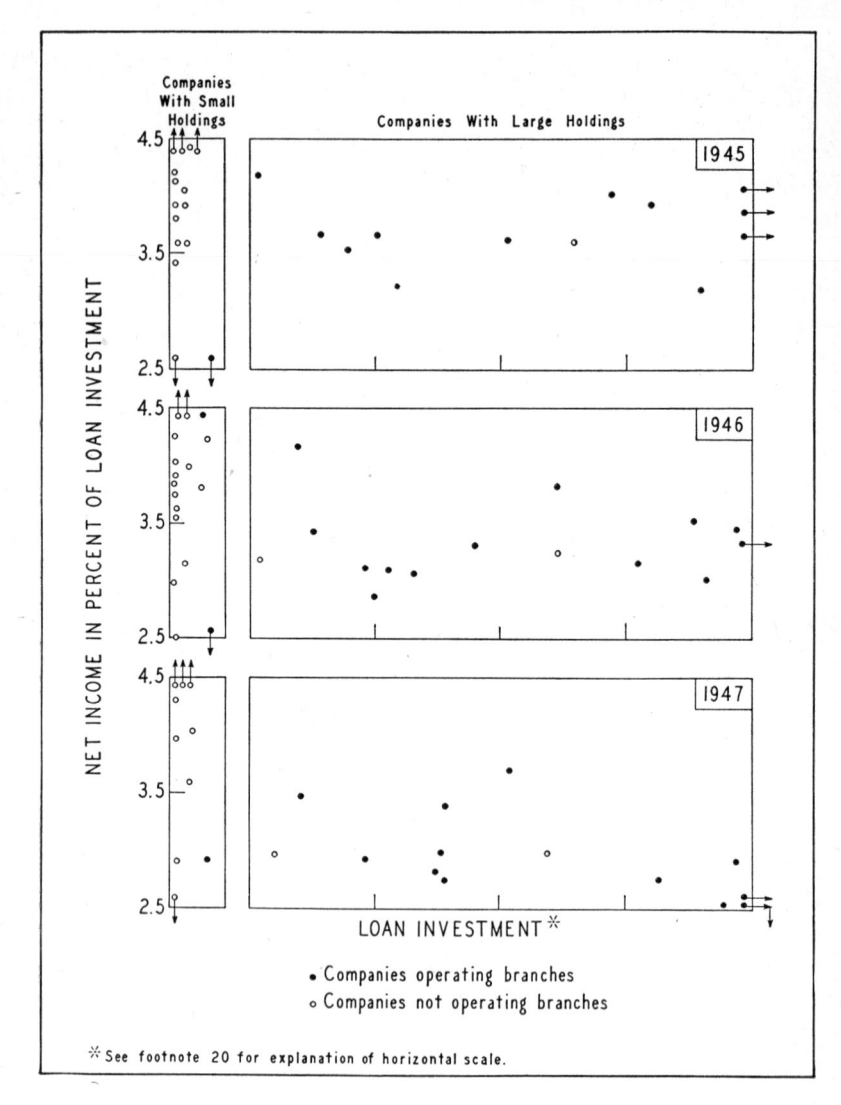

Net operating income ratios, like gross income ratios, were generally higher, as well as more dispersed, for companies with small holdings than for those with large holdings.

estate.[24] Such data were not asked for, however, in the 1946 and 1947 surveys mainly to simplify reporting.

Ratios of net income after costs on the combined mortgage, real estate sales contract, and owned real estate accounts are given in Appendix Tables B1 and B2 for the companies that reported the necessary data. These ratios vary much more widely from company to company than do the ratios of net income on the loan account. In general, the over-all ratios are higher in 1945 than the ratios of net income on the loan account taken by itself, but of course this would not be true if the data referred to a year in which real estate properties were in surplus supply.

NET INCOME AFTER OPERATING AND NONOPERATING
INCOME AND COSTS

A final calculation of the portfolio yield on a mortgage loan investment requires that items of nonoperating income and expense, arising mainly out of profits or losses on the sale of owned farm real estate, be taken into account. Findings on this measure of investment experience are also given in Appendix Tables B1 and B2. The resulting ratios vary widely from company to company and, due to the extremely favorable real estate market conditions of 1945, they are, in the main, considerably higher than the ratios of net income which take account only of operating income and cost.

NET INCOME ON MORTGAGE LOANS AFTER ALLOWANCE
FOR POTENTIAL LOSS

No allowance for potential loss on the mortgage loan account has been incorporated in the foregoing analysis, but, clearly, provision must be made for this cost element at some point in the calculation of net yields. Mortgage loan losses were negligible in 1945-47, but they have been high in some past years and may be so again. It was not clear what allowance should be made for potential loss and, accordingly, reporting companies were asked in the 1945 schedule to estimate the "risk factor" which they believed inherent in their portfolios of farm mortgage loans. Estimates varied so widely, however, that they provided no basis on which to adjust the net income ratio. In the absence of a reliable factual basis for correcting net income

---

[24] The item reported on our schedule as income on owned farm real estate is, of course, farm income net of farm operating costs.

it is perhaps admissible to use a loss or risk factor of 0.25 percent, the rate at which home mortgages are insured by the Federal Housing Administration. When the net income ratios of large portfolio companies, among whose holdings the risk element is likely to vary only moderately, are adjusted by 0.25 percent in 1946, the net income for the largest concentration of companies shown in Chart 7 would range from 2.75 to 3.24 percent. The data for 1947 indicate that the majority of reporting companies had net incomes after costs, and after an allowance for potential loss of 0.25 percent, ranging from 2.25 to 3.24 percent, with the largest lenders at the lower limit of this range of net returns. It should be indicated, however, that the heavy volume of acquisition costs incurred in these years, being fully charged in this analysis to current operating income, produces a net income, after costs and allowance for potential loss, which is lower than that which would result if the costs were amortized over the expected life of the loan balances. However, this correction would not greatly alter the results, owing, as will be seen in the following section, to the high rate at which loans were being repaid in these years.

LOAN ACCOUNT TURNOVER AND NET RETURN ON INVESTMENT

The findings of this study indicate a return on farm mortgage loans which is low relative to what might be expected from a type of investment which has in the past experienced much delinquency and loss. However, in the years 1945-47 the low net income ratios were due in large part, as indicated above, to the rapid rate of loan repayment, a condition subject to change as farm economic conditions alter. Accordingly, what the surveys indicate about the period of turnover on farm mortgage loan accounts is of interest.

Periods of turnover were calculated for individual reporting companies by dividing loan repayments during the year into the amount of their average loan investment for the year. This gives the number of years that it would take, at the rate loans were being repaid in the years in question, for the whole portfolio to be retired. Turnover periods are given in Table 5. Thirty-three out of 43 companies in 1946 and 24 out of 31 companies in 1947 reported repayments at a rate that would have retired their entire portfolios in two to five years.

TABLE 5 — Reporting Companies Classified According to Turnover Periods of Farm Mortgage Loan Portfolios, 1945-47

Turnover Periods (years)	Number of Companies 1945	1946	1947
Under 2	1	2	0
2 to 3	4	7	5
3 to 4	10	14	7
4 to 5	11	12	12
5 to 6	8	2	2
6 and over	6	6	5
Total	40	43	31

EXPECTED YIELD

Having measured the components of cost and the turnover period of loan portfolios, it is now possible to estimate the expected yield on mortgage loan investments. It will simplify the making of this estimate to assume that loans are made on a nonamortized basis and are acquired and serviced by outside correspondents. Specifically, it may be assumed that (a) the mortgages are acquired at the rate current in 1945-47 — 4.00 percent, (b) correspondents are paid an originating fee of 1.50 percent of the original amount of the loan, (c) the company pays correspondents an annual service fee of 0.25 percent of the amount of the loan balance, (d) home office loan department expenses are 0.25 percent, and (e) the loans are expected to remain on the books for five years. The interest rate and the correspondent's fee and servicing charge are unlikely to change over the life of the loan, although the cost of operating the home office loan department may change and the actual life of a loan may not be according to original expectations. However, if it is expected that the conditions stated above will be maintained, the "expected yield" on the company's investment in loans of this type will be 3.20 percent before any allowance for the risk factor.[25] If we were to take 0.25 percent as an allowance for potential loss we would have an expected yield of 2.95 percent.

[25] Expected yield equals the contract interest rate less the originating fee divided by the number of years the balance is expected to continue, less the servicing fee, and less the home office expense ratio. Thus, 3.20 percent = 4.00 percent − (1.50 percent ÷ 5) − 0.25 percent − 0.25 percent.

Appendix A

DESCRIPTION OF FARM MORTGAGE LENDING COST SCHEDULES FOR 1945-47

In order fully to understand the meaning of the findings of a study of this type it is essential to have clearly in mind the definitions of the categories of income and cost which it employs. It is hoped that this Appendix will satisfy that need. The several items of information called for on the schedules on which cooperating companies reported their mortgage lending costs are defined in all the detail deemed necessary, and these explanations are followed by facsimiles of the schedules used in 1945 and 1946 and the instructions circulated to companies in connection with the 1946 schedule. The 1947 schedule has not been reproduced since it is identical with that for 1946. While the Appendix provides more detail than is necessary for the general reader, it is hoped that it will be useful to investigators who may attempt further studies of mortgage lending costs and, furthermore, that it will supply useful procedural suggestions for those who may wish in the future to pursue similar studies in other credit areas.

Definition of Schedule Items

Survey schedules were divided into two sections. Part I called for certain general data, such as loan balances outstanding, volume of loans made, gross income, etc. and Part II called for the reporting company's estimates of the primary elements of its operating costs.

Specifically, Part I of the 1946 and 1947 schedules requested the *number and amount of mortgage loan and real estate sales contract balances outstanding at the beginning and end of the year* (Item 1) and *the amount of mortgage loans made during the year* (Item 2). The latter item was to be classified into new loans (including additional amounts advanced on outstanding balances) and all other loans (i.e., loans renewed, extended, or otherwise rewritten). Data on balances outstanding, when averaged, gave a figure of loan investment to which both income and costs were related to produce operating ratios. Loan investment was also used as a measure of portfolio size in the analyses of the cost-investment relationship. New loans were separated from all other loans because the costs of making the former were thought to be greater than for the latter and because a measure of new loan volume was essential in the computation of acquisition cost ratios and loan turnover periods.

In the 1945 schedule, companies were asked to report separately on their outstanding balances of mortgage loans and real estate sales contracts and on the income earned from each, but not on the amount of real estate sales contract balances created during the year.[1] However, this information proved to be of very limited value as well as difficult to give; accordingly, these breakdowns were not asked for in the 1946 and 1947 schedules.

Certain problems involved in the payment of servicing fees to correspondents should be noted in connection with Item 3 of Part I, *gross income from mortgage loans and real estate sales contracts*.[2] Some companies allow correspondents to retain part of the interest income as compensation for making collections on mortgages, for occasionally inspecting the property, and for otherwise servicing the mortgage; others receive the full income and make a separate payment of servicing fees to the correspondent. All companies were asked to report interest income *gross* of such servicing fees and to report elsewhere in the schedule the amounts retained by outside agents as servicing fees. However, in some instances this proved to be difficult. Where income could not be reported on a gross basis, companies were asked to indicate by footnote that they were reporting income net of servicing fees retained by outside agents. While all reports were usable in the analysis of net income after total costs,

---

[1] The volume of real estate sales contracts originated during the year may be estimated by adding the amount of real estate sold in that period and held under sales contract at the beginning of the year to the difference between the book value of real estate under sales contract at the beginning and at the end of the year. This method fails to include the amount of real estate sales contracts entered into after the beginning of the year and deeded out before the year's end, but we are assured by experienced loan officers that this amount is not large.

[2] Income was reported on a cash, or current, basis, that is, so as to include all interest and other income received during the year on loans and sales contracts.

reports from only those companies reporting income on a *gross* basis could be used in the analysis of gross income ratios.

To measure the importance of the several main types of income, companies were requested on the 1945 schedule to divide total gross income into (a) interest income on loans, (b) interest income on real estate sales contracts, (c) prepayment premium income,[3] and (d) other income. Not all companies could report in such detail but those that did showed insignificant or no amounts under (c) and (d). Therefore, separate information on these items was not requested in the 1946 and 1947 schedules, and since these schedules abandoned the distinction between loans and real estate sales contracts, the end result was that no breakdown of gross income was requested.[4]

Finally, among the general items in Part I of the schedule are the *amount of farm mortgage loans acquired during the year through correspondents or other outside agents* (Item 4) and *the amount of loan balances outstanding at the end of the year which were serviced for the company by some outside agent* (Item 5). These figures were requested in order to calculate ratios of the amount of originating fees paid to correspondents and other outside agents to the amount of loans originated by these agents and ratios of servicing fees paid to the amount of loans serviced.

In Part II of the schedule, which includes all cost items, companies were asked to report the amount of their *branch office farm loan costs* (Item 1). They were instructed to include under branch office costs all those expenses properly attributable to the conduct of farm mortgage lending activities, such as salaries, rent, light, telephone, travel, and miscellaneous office expenditures. In the 1945 schedule this total of branch office costs was broken down into its three compo-

---

[3] Some, but by no means all, loan agreements provide that if the mortgagor prepays the loan within a specified period he must pay a specified premium. The purpose is to protect the lender from refinancing, or unexpectedly early repayment out of income, which would make the income from the loan insufficient to cover the initial costs of putting it on the books.

[4] All income from owned real estate, such as lease, crop, and mineral income, was reported separately in the 1945 schedule and excluded from the 1946 and 1947 schedules. Some of the problems in studies of this kind are illustrated by crop income which is received *after* the farm is sold and mineral income which continues to be received long after the property has disappeared as an asset of the reporting company. However, the figures suggest that the present analysis was affected little, if any, by circumstances of this sort.

nents: the costs of loan acquisition, loan servicing, and real estate management. In 1946 and 1947 the first two were combined and the third was dropped from the schedule.

To get a loan portfolio yield figure, branch office costs attributable to the acquisition and handling of loans and real estate sales contracts, along with certain other lending costs, must be separated from branch office costs incurred in the management of owned real estate. A separate listing of loan acquisition and loan servicing costs is essential to a functional analysis of costs, but the distinction was exceedingly difficult to make. Some companies reported the breakdown fairly accurately but there were not enough such reports to warrant continuation of this breakdown on the 1946 and 1947 schedules. The fact that owned farm real estate had practically disappeared from insurance company holdings in 1945-47 meant that the problem of separating real estate management costs from costs of loan acquisition and servicing was at a minimum.[5]

Item 2 in Part II is *the amount paid out during the year to correspondents or other outside agents at the time of acquiring farm mortgages.* This refers to all lump-sum payments made to outside agents when loans are made, including originating fees to correspondents, fees or commissions to loan brokers, and premiums for the purchase of mortgages. Unfortunately, these payments are not made purely for loan acquisition. In some instances they are intended also to compensate the outside agent for servicing loan balances. Some companies make a relatively large payment to the correspondent when the loan is made and a smaller continuing payment for servicing of the loan balance; other companies do the opposite. As a practical matter, therefore, it is impossible to get a breakdown of costs for a group of companies that follows purely functional lines. This was not fully understood when the 1945 schedule was prepared, but the relevant points were rectified on the 1946 and 1947 forms.

Item 3, *servicing fees and other compensation paid to correspond-*

[5] If costs of real estate management are merged with loan administration costs at the branches, they must be combined at the home office level and income from real estate must be merged with income from loans. This, however, is an unsatisfactory procedure. Real estate income and expenses for 1945 were studied separately, and it was shown that merging the operating income and expense for loans and real estate would distort the analysis to the point where it would fail to reveal operating results on either loans or real estate.

ents and other outside agents on a continuing basis,[6] refers to all payments actually dispersed to outside agents subsequent to the loan's origination. As stated above, such payments are mainly for a loan servicing function, but they are sufficiently mixed with deferred acquisition fees to preclude their use as an accurate measure of compensation for the servicing function alone.

Finally, companies were requested to report the *expenses of operating their home office farm mortgage loan department and their general home office administrative expenses* (Item 4). On the 1945 schedule the home office loan department costs were divided into (a) direct departmental expenditures attributable to loan acquisition, (b) direct departmental costs of loan servicing, (c) departmental expenses incurred in managing owned real estate, and (d) expenses incurred by other departments of the company in providing legal, audit, and other services.[7] Some company overhead costs, such as light, heat, etc., were taken into account in calculating home office mortgage loan department costs (Item 4a). But in defining *general home office administrative expenses,* there were the alternatives of attempting to allocate all overhead costs which might be attributed in some part to the mortgage loan department or of ignoring all overhead costs except those which could be directly attributed to farm mortgage lending activities, such as the expenses of the company's finance, investment, or loan committee. It was impractical to adopt the first alternative and consequently our final figures are a slight underestimate of total costs.

The objective of the 1945 schedule was a breakdown of costs that would divide total costs into three functional classes: costs of loan acquisition, costs of loan servicing, and costs of real estate management. Actually, it was impossible to break costs down in this way and the plan was abandoned in the 1946 and 1947 schedules in favor of classifying costs into (a) branch office expenses, (b) home office expenses, (c) originating fees, and (d) servicing fees paid to outside agents.

[6] An additional item, *commissions paid to brokers and others for the sale of farm real estate,* was included in the 1945 schedule but dropped in 1946 and 1947 when the survey was restricted to "loan administration" costs.

[7] In some cases the extra-departmental expenses were fairly substantial; in others they were negligible. Distribution depended on company organization. Some firms had nearly self-sufficient mortgage loan departments and others had departments largely dependent on the general service divisions of the company.

As the survey results show, total costs can be measured with reasonable accuracy and movements in the various elements of total costs for particular companies can be compared from one year to another. However, the organization and practices of individual companies are so different that intercompany comparisons of particular items of cost are precluded. One exception is in the analysis of home office expenses, where the findings suggest that intercompany comparisons are valid. This is fortunate indeed, since the home office expense ratio is the single figure essential to the calculation of an expected yield which must be determined by cost accounting methods.

National Bureau of Economic Research
Financial Research Program   Company Code No. . . . .

SCHEDULE FOR COST DATA ON FARM MORTGAGE FINANCING BY LIFE INSURANCE COMPANIES, 1945

PART I — GENERAL DATA
(Report amounts in dollars only; omit cents.)

	Farm Mortgage Loans	
	Number	Amount

1. Mortgage loan balances outstanding
    December 31, 1944 . . . . | | $
    December 31, 1945 . . . . |

2. Book value of real estate sales contracts outstanding
    December 31, 1944 . . . .
    December 31, 1945 . . . .

3. Mortgage loans made during 1945 — total . . . . . .
    a. New loans made, including increases in outstanding balances . . . .
    b. All other loans made, i. e., refinancing, renewals, and extensions . . . .

4. Real estate owned
    December 31, 1944 . . . .
    December 31, 1945 . . . .

5. Real estate acquired during 1945 . . . .

6. Real estate sold during 1945 — total . . . .
    a. Under sales contract on December 31, 1944 . . .
    b. Not under sales contract on December 31, 1944 . .

7. Gross income from mortgage loans and real estate sales contracts during 1945 — total . . . . x x x
    a. Interest income on loans* . . . . x x x
    b. Prepayment penalties . . . . x x x
    c. Interest on real estate sales contracts . . . . . x x x
    d. Other income . . . . x x x

8. Net profit or loss on sale of real estate during 1945 . . . x x x

9. Net income on real estate owned during 1945 . . . . . x x x

10. Net change by adjustment during 1945:
    a. Increase or decrease in book value of farm real estate, including acquisition costs and advances charged off and changes by adjustment in book value . . . . x x x
    b. Increase or decrease in book value of farm mortgage loans, excluding write-downs of book value made in connection with the amortization of premiums paid on the acquisition of loans . . . x x x

* Interest income on mortgage loans is reported $\genfrac{}{}{0pt}{}{\text{net} \ldots}{\text{gross} \ldots}$ of participation in interest by correspondents or others. (Check one.)

FARM COST SCHEDULE, 1945 (continued)

PART II — Cost Data, Covering the Year 1945
(Report amounts in dollars only; omit cents.)

	Farm Mortgage Loans

1. Expenses of operating branch offices — total . . . . $
   a. Farm loan acquisition and servicing costs — total . .
      (1) Loan acquisition costs . . . .
      (2) Servicing costs . . . .
   b. Branch office farm real estate administrative costs . .
2. Commissions and premiums paid to correspondents and others at time of acquisition of farm mortgages — total . . .
3. Commissions paid to brokers and others in connection with the sale of farm real estate — total . . . .
4. Participations in interest and other fees paid to correspondents and others on a continuing basis — total . . .
5. Expenses of operating home office farm mortgage loan department and general administrative expenses — total . . .
   a. Home office farm mortgage department costs — total .
      (1) Loan acquisition and servicing costs — total . .
         (i) Loan acquisition costs . . . .
         (ii) Loan servicing costs . . . .
      (2) Farm real estate management costs . . . . .
      (3) Expenses of legal, audit, and other services supplied by another division of company . . . .
   b. General home office administrative expenses . . . .

PART III — General Questions
(Report amounts in dollars only; omit cents.)

1. Total admitted assets of company, as of December 31, 1945 . $
2. a. *All* real estate sales contracts outstanding at end of 1945:
      Book value . . . .
      Amount actually due company . . . .
   b. Real estate sales contracts outstanding *on which interest income was not yet being earned* at end of 1945:
      Book value . . . .
      Amount actually due company . . . .
3. State, or estimate as nearly as possible:
   a. Amount of farm mortgages closed during 1945 which were acquired through:
      (1) Correspondents or other outside agents . . . .
      (2) Branch office operations . . . .
      (3) Home office operations . . . .
   b. Amount of farm mortgage loan balances outstanding at end of 1945 which were serviced during the year through:
      (1) Correspondents or other outside agents . . . .
      (2) Branch office operations . . . .
      (3) Home office operations . . . .

(Continued on next page)

Farm Cost Schedule 1945 (concluded)

PART III — GENERAL QUESTIONS

4. Number of branches: (a) originating farm loans in 1945 . . . _____

                          (b) servicing farm mortgage loans in 1945 _____

5. Number of correspondents or other outside agents:
   (a) from whom farm mortgage loans were acquired in 1945 . _____

   (b) who serviced farm mortgage loans in 1945 . . . . . _____

6. How many years do you estimate that farm loans made during 1945 will remain among the company's assets, on present and probable future conditions? . . . . _____ years

7. If you follow the practice of amortizing premiums and commissions paid for the acquisition of loans over a period of years, what expected period are you now using on farm loans? . . . . _____ years

8. Have you arrived at a figure representing the risk factor? If so, indicate the percent of the principal per annum which you think fairly represents the risk inherent in farm mortgage loans . . . _____%

National Bureau of Economic Research
Financial Research Program

Company Code No. . . . .

SCHEDULE FOR COST DATA ON FARM MORTGAGE LENDING BY LIFE INSURANCE COMPANIES, 1946

PART I — GENERAL DATA
(Report amounts in dollars only, omit cents)

	Farm Mortgage Loans	
	Number	Amount (in dollars)
1. Mortgage loan and real estate sales contract balances outstanding		$
December 31, 1945		
December 31, 1946		
2. Mortgage loans made during 1946 — total	x x x	
a. New loans made, including increases in outstanding balances	x x x	
b. All other loans made, i.e., refinancing, renewals, and extensions	x x x	
3. Gross income from mortgage loans and real estate sales contracts during 1946 — total*	x x x	
4. Farm mortgage loans closed during 1946 which were acquired through correspondents or other outside agents .	x x x	
5. Farm mortgage loan balances outstanding at end of 1946 which were serviced through correspondents or other outside agents	x x x	
6. Total admitted assets as of December 31, 1946	$	

* Interest income on loans is reported $\frac{\text{net} \ldots}{\text{gross} \ldots}$ of servicing fees paid to correspondents or others. (Check one.)

PART II — COST DATA, COVERING THE YEAR 1946
(Report amounts in dollars only, omit cents)

	Farm Mortgage Loan Costs (in dollars)
1. Branch office farm loan acquisition and servicing costs . . .	$
2. Originating fees and premiums paid to correspondents and others at time of acquisition of farm mortgages	
3. Service fees and other compensation paid to correspondents and others on a continuing basis	
4. Expenses of operating home office farm mortgage loan department and general administrative expenses — total . .	
a. Home office farm mortgage department costs — total .	
(1) Loan acquisition and servicing costs	
(2) Expenses of legal, audit, and other services supplied by another division of company	
b. General home office administrative expenses	

NOTES AND DEFINITIONS TO BE FOLLOWED IN REPORTING FARM MORTGAGE LENDING COSTS OF LIFE INSURANCE COMPANIES, AND CHECK LIST OF MORTGAGE LENDING COSTS — 1946

Part I — General Data

Item 1

This combined figure can be taken from the Annual Statement. The amount of outstanding loan balances included in Item 1 is the book value, at year end, of owned mortgages reported as "farm mortgages" in item 23 of Schedule B — Part 1 — Section 2 of the Annual Statement; the number of farm mortgages owned can be taken from Schedule B — Part 1 — Section 2 of the Annual Statement. The number and amount of farm real estate sales contract balances outstanding are the number of items and the book value of farm properties held under sales contract as these are reported in items c,7 and d,7 of Schedule A — Part 1 of the Annual Statement.

Item 2a

The amount of new farm mortgage loans made during the year, and increases in outstanding balances under these loans, can be determined by adding items 2 to 7, inclusive, of Schedule B — Part 1 — Section 1 of the Annual Statement, for "farm mortgages." These are (i) loans in cash, or granted on disposal of real estate, (ii) amount of mortgages purchased, (iii) additional cash loaned on refunded mortgages, (iv) interest covered by increase in, or refunding of, mortgages, (v) taxes covered by increase in, or refunding of, mortgages, (vi) other items covered by increase in, or refunding of, mortgages.

Where refunding or extension of a mortgage involved the advance of additional cash, the amount of additional cash advanced should, as indicated in the preceding paragraph, be included in Item 2a. However, the amount of such a transaction which consists merely of the refunding of an existing balance should be included under Item 2b, below.

Item 2b

Include under this heading (i) all refundings, renewals, and extensions involving no advance of additional cash, and (ii) that portion of refunded loans involving an advance of additional cash which consists merely of the refunding of existing loan balances.

Item 3

Income should be reported on a *current* basis, including only actual collections and excluding accruals. Income received in the form of prepayment premiums should be included, along with interest income; mineral income and crop income should be excluded since this arises from the owned real estate account rather than the loan account. Wherever possible income should be given before deduction of any servicing fees or other compensation paid to correspondents and others on a continuing basis. Amounts actually retained by, or paid to, correspondents during the year under a loan servicing agreement should be interpreted as a cost and included among the cost data in Part II of this schedule. *It should be indicated in the footnote to Item 3 whether income reported is gross or net of servicing fees paid to correspondents or others.*

Interest income on real estate sales contracts should be reported *net* of any amounts expended for taxes, repairs, and other expenses, if there are such. Income, *other than interest income,* on sales contracts should be excluded as should down payments and other payments on principal under sales contracts.

Item 4

Report the amount of all farm mortgages closed during 1946 which were acquired through correspondents or other outside agents.

Item 5

Report the amount of all farm mortgage loan balances outstanding as of the end of 1946 which were serviced through correspondents or other outside agents.

Item 6

Give total admitted assets as reported in Part 1 of the Annual Statement.

Part II — Cost Data

Item 1

This item refers to those expenses of operating branch offices that are properly attributable to the conduct of farm mortgage lending activities. Branch office costs should include only those amounts *actually disbursed* during the year, such as salaries of branch office personnel, rent, light, telephone, travel, and miscellaneous office expenditures, whether paid from the home office or in the field. (See appended check list of mortgage lending costs.) Any expenses incurred in supervising farm loan branch office operations from the home office should be considered a home office expense. *Exclude all expenses incurred by branch offices in connection with the operation and management of owned real estate.*

Item 2

Originating fees paid to correspondents and others at the time of acquisition of loans, including premiums paid in connection with the purchase of mortgage loans, should be reported on a *current* basis. Include under this heading all disbursements actually made during the current year, whether from branch offices or home office, regardless of the fact that it might be the company's policy to amortize these over a period of years. Likewise, the report should exclude all charges against income during the current year arising out of the amortization of commissions or premiums actually disbursed in earlier years. As in Item 1, above, include only those expenses for which disbursements have actually been made, excluding amounts for which commitments have been made but which have not yet been disbursed.

Item 3

Fees for servicing loan balances and other compensation paid to correspondents and others on a continuing basis should be reported here, as distinct from lump-sum payments paid at the time a loan is acquired, which are reported in Item 2 above. In connection with the compilation of data on servicing fees see the note referring to Item 3 of Part I, above.

Item 4a

All operating expenses incurred *directly* by the farm mortgage loan department in acquiring and servicing mortgage loan balances should be included under heading

47

(1). These costs would include charges for salaries, space, light, heat, maintenance, travel, office supplies, etc. (See appended check list of mortgage lending costs.) If officers or other personnel of the farm mortgage loan department spend part of their time on activities *outside* of this department (e.g., on city mortgages or on the bond account) their salaries should be prorated according to an estimate of how their time is divided. All expenses incurred by the farm loan department in connection with the operation and management of owned real estate should be *excluded* here.

If legal, auditing, and other services are supplied to the farm mortgage loan department by *other* departments of the company, the expenses of operating such departments should be prorated and included under subhead (2).

Item 4b

General home office administrative expenses should include *only* fees paid in connection with the Investment, Finance, or Mortgage Loan Committee and other expenses of this Committee. Where the Committee involved has responsibility for investments other than farm mortgage loans, its expenses should be prorated according to the proportion of farm mortgages and farm real estate owned to the total investment for which the Committee was responsibible at the end of 1946.

Check List of Mortgage Lending Costs

In preparing data for the schedule of mortgage lending costs it may be helpful for companies to refer to the following check list of types of operating costs, which is meant to illustrate the various kinds of costs that might be included in the expenses of operating branch offices and the home office farm loan department. The list is given only for reference and to obviate the possibility of significant items of cost being overlooked in the compilation of cost reports; *it is not expected that costs will be broken down according to these categories.*

Check list of costs
1. Salaries
2. Rent, heat, and light
3. Telephone and telegraph
4. Postage and express
5. Supplies, including printing
6. Rental and servicing of office equipment
7. Repairs: furniture and fixtures
8. Depreciation: furniture, equipment, and fixtures
9. Advertising
10. Credit reports
11. Revenue stamps
12. Checking taxes
13. Recording and/or filing fees
14. Title examinations
15. Employee bonds and insurance
16. Dues and subscriptions
17. Travel
18. Car expense
19. Entertaining, suppers, etc.
20. Donations and charity
21. Lunch room, infirmary, and other employee welfare expenses
22. Other expenses, not elsewhere classified

Appendix B
TABLES OF INCOME AND COST RATIOS, 1945-47

Appendix B presents income and cost ratios for 27 companies in 1945, 31 companies in 1946 and 23 companies in 1947, classified according to size of portfolio. The companies in these tables are identified so that changes from 1945 to 1947 in ratios for a given company may be compared. That is, Company A in Table B1 is the same as Company A in Tables B3 and B5.

Ratios are given for each of the individual companies included in the weighted average income and cost ratios shown in Table 3; companies not included in Table 3 are identified by footnote.

Companies are classified according to their average portfolio size for the first year in which they reported. With two exceptions, companies remained in the same size class in all the years in which they reported; two branch office companies with average portfolios between $5 and $20 million in 1945 and 1946 reported portfolios slightly over $20 million in 1947. These two companies have been left in the smaller portfolio-size class.

TABLE B1 – GROSS INCOME, COSTS, AND NET INCOME IN PERCENT OF FARM MORTGAGE LOAN AND REAL ESTATE SALES CONTRACT INVESTMENT, 1945

(Companies not operating branches)

Company	Gross Income	In Percent of Farm Mortgage Loan Investment [a]					Net Income in Percent of Mortgage Loan Investment and Real Estate Owned [e]	
		Costs				Net Income [d]	Before Non-operating Adjustments	After Non-operating Adjustments
		Total Cost	Originating Fees [b]	Servicing Fees [b]	Home Office Expenses [c]			
Portfolios Under $5 Million								
A	4.94%	.53% [f]	.00%	.03%	.50% [f]	4.41%	6.72%	13.73%
B	5.35	1.43	.98	.06	.39	3.92	g	g
C	5.62	.92	.00	.01	.91	4.70	4.80	10.90
D	4.38	.80	.00	.67	.13	3.58	2.74	2.12
E	5.34	1.17	.13	.02	1.02	4.17	h	h
F	4.09	1.76	.00	.00	1.76	2.33	h	h
G	4.51	.72	.00	.00	.72	3.79	h	h
H [i]	5.50	1.29	.00	.00	1.29	4.21	3.60	4.51
I [i]	4.46	.54	.00	.32	.22	3.92	5.46	9.23
J [i]	5.32	.40 [f]	.00	.00	.40 [f]	4.92	4.85	5.11
K [i]	5.08	.36 [f]	.00	.00	.36 [f]	4.72	3.36	23.02
L [i]	5.10	1.69 [f]	.00	.00	1.69 [f]	3.41	4.23	4.07
M [i]	4.36	.31 [f]	.04	.02	.25 [f]	4.05	4.37	2.76
Portfolios of $20 Million and Over								
W [1]	4.40%	.81%	.15%	.02%	.64%	3.59%	g	g

[a] Investment includes real estate sales contracts.
[b] Represents fees and commissions paid to correspondents and to other outside agents.
[c] Excludes real estate management costs, except as indicated.
[d] Excludes income on owned real estate.
[e] Includes net income on mortgage loans, real estate sales contracts, and owned real estate.
[f] Includes real estate management costs.
[g] Not available.
[h] No real estate owned.
[i] Not included in the weighted averages shown in Table 3.

TABLE B2 — GROSS INCOME, COSTS, AND NET INCOME IN PERCENT OF FARM MORTGAGE LOAN AND REAL ESTATE SALES CONTRACT INVESTMENT, 1945
(Companies operating branches)

		In Percent of Farm Mortgage Loan Investment [a]							Net Income in Percent of Mortgage Loan Investment and Real Estate Owned [e]	
				Costs						
Company	Gross Income	Total Cost	Originating Fees [b]	Servicing Fees [b]	Branch Office Expenses [c]	Home Office Expenses [c]	Net Income [d]		Before Non-operating Adjustments	After Non-operating Adjustments

X | 4.69% | 3.31% | .07% | .02% | .62% | 2.60% | 1.38% | | 1.35% | 2.09%

Portfolios Under $5 Million

Z | 4.74% | 1.14% | .14% | .07% | .69% | .24% | 3.60% | | 4.91% | 5.82%
AA | 4.34 | .74 | .06 | .20 | .30 | .18 | 3.60 | | 3.56 | 5.94
AB | 4.65 | 1.14 | .19 | .19 | .46 | .30 | 3.51 | | f | f
AC | 4.06 | .86 | .24 | .05 | .35 | .22 | 3.20 | | 4.37 | 5.52
AD [g] | 5.04 | .89 | .29 | .42 | .09 | .09 | 4.15 | | 4.15 | 4.17

Portfolios of $5 to $20 Million

Portfolios of $20 Million and Over

AF | 4.99% | 1.39% | .13% | .09% | .99% | .18% | 3.60% | | 3.83% | 5.21%
AG | 4.76 | .71 | .05 | .10 | .40 | .16 | 4.05 | | 4.06 | 4.46
AH | 4.77 | .94 | .13 | .02 | .54 | .25 | 3.83 | | 3.90 | 5.53
AI | 4.64 | .74 | .05 | .05 | .51 | .13 | 3.90 | | 4.55 | 5.84
AJ | 4.23 | 1.06 h | .16 | .02 | .53 | .35 h | 3.17 | | 3.95 | 5.79
AK | 4.43 | .42 | .12 | .03 | .10 | .17 | 4.01 | | 4.05 | 4.12
AL [g] | 4.53 | .89 h | .08 | .00 | .42 h | .39 | 3.64 | | 4.20 | 5.00

[a] Investment includes real estate sales contracts.
[b] Represents fees and commissions paid to correspondents and to other outside agents.
[c] Excludes real estate management costs, except as indicated.
[d] Excludes income on owned real estate.
[e] Includes net income on mortgage loans, real estate sales contracts, and owned real estate.
[f] Not available.
[g] Not included in the weighted averages shown in Table 3.
[h] Includes real estate management costs.

TABLE B3 — Gross Income, Costs, and Net Income in Percent of Farm Mortgage Loan and Real Estate Sales Contract Investment, and Other Related Ratios, 1946
(Companies not operating branches)

Company	Gross Income	In Percent of Farm Mortgage Loan Investment [a]					Originating Fees Paid in Percent of Loans Acquired from Correspondents	Servicing Fees Paid in Percent of Loans Serviced by Correspondents
		Costs				Net Income [d]		
		Total Cost	Originating Fees [b]	Servicing Fees [b]	Home Office Expenses [c]			

Portfolios Under $5 Million

A	4.99%	.30%	.00%	.01%	.29%	4.69%	.00%	.59%
B	4.73	1.59	.84	.13	.62	3.14	1.84	e
C	5.79	1.83	.00	.00	1.83	3.96	.00	.00
D	5.92	.78	.00	.65	.13	5.14	.00	1.05
E	4.68	.43	.00	.00	.43	4.25	.00	.00
F	4.02	1.52	.00	.00	1.52	2.50	.00	.00
G	5.09	1.47	.40	.00	1.07	3.62	1.00	.00
H [f]	5.00	.96	.00	.48	.48	4.04	.00	e
I [f]	4.56	.65	.00	.38	.27	3.91	.00	.61
N [f]	4.38	.53	.00	.00	.53	3.85	.00	.00
O [f]	4.01	.25	.00	.00	.25	3.76	.00	.00
P [f]	4.72	1.19	.76	.29	.14	3.53	1.48	.60
Q [f]	4.08	1.11	.35	.00	.76	2.97	1.05	.00
R [f]	4.66	.44	.17	.00	.27	4.22	1.84	.00
S [f]	4.44	.65	.25	.00	.40	3.79	1.53	.00

Portfolios of $5 to $20 Million

| U [f] | 4.14% | .98% | .17% | .12% | .69% | 3.16% | .55% | .16% |

Portfolios of $20 Million and Over

| W [f] | 4.36% | 1.11% | .20% | .02% | .89% | 3.25% | 1.50% | .27% |

[a] Investment includes real estate sales contracts.
[b] Represents fees and commissions paid to correspondents and
[c] Excludes real estate management costs.
[d] Excludes income on owned real estate.

TABLE 21

CONTRACT INVESTMENT, AND OTHER RELATED RATIOS, 1946

GROSS INCOME, COSTS, AND NET INCOME IN PERCENT OF FARM MORTGAGE LOAN AND REAL ESTATE SALES

(Companies operating branches)

Company	Gross Income	Costs — Total Cost	Originating Fees [b]	Servicing Fees [b]	Branch Office Expenses [c]	Home Office Expenses [c]	Net Income [d]	Originating Fees Paid in Percent of Loans Acquired from Correspondents	Servicing Fees Paid in Percent of Loans Serviced by Correspondents
Portfolios Under $5 Million									
X	4.73%	2.63%	.17%	.10%	.49%	1.87%	2.10%	e	.42%
Y [f]	5.22	.80	.02	.20	.32	.26	4.42	e	.56
Portfolios of $5 to $20 Million									
Z	4.50%	1.40%	.23%	.07%	.77%	.33%	3.10%	1.48%	.55%
AA	4.42	1.00	.14	.23	.38	.25	3.42	1.30	.49
AB	4.03	1.17	.22	.17	.50	.28	2.86	.52	.17
AC	4.01	.95	.25	.05	.37	.28	3.06	e	.17
AE [f]	5.03	.87	.25	.02	.30	.30	4.16	1.34	e
Portfolios of $20 Million and Over									
AF	5.09%	1.77%	.14%	.10%	1.37%	.17%	3.32%	.55%	.52%
AG	4.56	1.12	.13	.06	.67	.26	3.44	1.51	e
AH	4.52	1.19	.23	.02	.73	.21	3.33	e	.71
AI	4.31	1.17	.22	.05	.73	.18	3.14	1.16	.47
AJ	4.18	1.15	.24	.02	.64	.26	3.03	1.58	.21
AK	4.44	.63	.17	.03	.19	.24	3.81	1.40	.22
AL [f]	4.55	1.04 [g]	.10	.00	.50 [g]	.44	3.51	e	.00

[a] Investment includes real estate sales contracts.
[b] Represents fees and commissions paid to correspondents and to other outside agents.
[c] Excludes real estate management costs, except as indicated.
[d] Excludes income on owned real estate.
[e] Not available.
[f] Not included in the weighted averages shown in Table 3.
[g] Includes real estate management costs.

TABLE B5 – GROSS INCOME, COSTS, AND NET INCOME IN PERCENT OF FARM MORTGAGE LOAN AND REAL ESTATE SALES CONTRACT INVESTMENT, AND OTHER RELATED RATIOS, 1947
(Companies not operating branches)

Company	Gross Income	Total Cost	Costs: Originating Fees [b]	Costs: Servicing Fees [b]	Costs: Home Office Expenses [c]	Net Income [d]	Originating Fees Paid in Percent of Loans Acquired from Correspondents	Servicing Fees Paid in Percent of Loans Serviced by Correspondents
			In Percent of Farm Mortgage Loan Investment [a]					
			Portfolios Under $5 Million					
A	4.88%	.21%	.00%	.01%	.20%	4.67%	.00%	.61%
B	4.63	1.06	.51	.17	.38	3.57	1.54	.28
C	5.81	.53	.00	.00	.53	5.28	.00	.00
D	5.97	.79	.00	.64	.15	5.18	.00	1.07
E	4.54	.56	.00	.00	.56	3.98	.00	.00
F	4.14	1.84	.00	.00	1.84	2.30	.00	.00
G	4.61	1.72	.53	[e]	1.19	2.89	1.00	.21
J [f]	4.48	.20	.04	.00	.16	4.28	1.50	.00
T [f]	5.05	1.04	.02	[e]	1.02	4.01	.88	.22
			Portfolios of $5 to $20 Million					
V [f]	3.58%	.62%	.17%	.00%	.45%	2.96%	[g]	.00%
			Portfolios of $20 Million and Over					
W [f]	4.37%	1.39%	.32%	.02%	1.05%	2.98%	[g]	.37%

[a] Investment includes real estate sales contracts.
[b] Represents fees and commissions paid to correspondents and to other outside agents.
[c] Excludes real estate management costs.
[d] Excludes income on owned real estate.
[e] Less than .005 percent.
[f] Not included in the weighted averages shown in Table 3.
[g] Not available.

TABLE B6 – Gross Income, Costs, and Net Income in Percent of Farm Mortgage Loan and Real Estate Sales Contract Investment, and Other Related Ratios, 1947
(Companies operating branches)

Company	Gross Income	In Percent of Farm Mortgage Loan Investment [a]						Originating Fees Paid in Percent of Loans Acquired from Correspondents	Servicing Fees Paid in Percent of Loans Serviced by Correspondents
		Costs					Net Income [d]		
		Total Cost	Originating Fees [b]	Servicing Fees [b]	Branch Office Expenses [c]	Home Office Expenses [c]			
Portfolios Under $5 Million
X	4.68%	1.78%	.16%	.10%	.50%	1.02%	2.90%	e	.49%
Portfolios of $5 to $20 Million
Z	4.33%	1.40%	.33%	.06%	.83%	.18%	2.93%	1.12%	.54%
AA	4.47	1.02	.09	.26	.40	.27	3.45	1.07	.55
AB	3.93	.97	.16	.16	.47	.18	2.96	.37	.19
AC	3.85	1.05	.21	.05	.44	.35	2.80	e	.17
Portfolios of $20 Million and Over
AF	4.88%	1.49%	.16%	.10%	1.08%	.15%	3.39%	e	53%
AG	4.29	1.40	.31	.05	.74	.30	2.89	e	e
AH	4.24	1.65	.38	.02	1.01	.24	2.59	e	e
AI	4.24	1.51	.42	.05	.88	.16	2.73	1.38	.38
AJ	4.14	1.62	.32	.02	.85	.43	2.52	1.36	.26
AK	4.35	.67	.24	.03	.22	.18	3.68	1.11	.21
AM [f]	3.99	2.33	.47	.01	1.40	.45	1.66	e	e

[a] Investment includes real estate sales contracts.
[b] Represents fees and commissions paid to correspondents and to other outside agents.
[c] Excludes real estate management costs.
[d] Excludes income on owned real estate.
[e] Not available.
[f] Not included in the weighted averages shown in Table 3.

National Bureau of Economic Research

Officers
C. REINOLD NOYES, *Chairman*
H. W. LAIDLER, *President*
HARRY SCHERMAN, *Vice-President*
GEORGE B. ROBERTS, *Treasurer*
W. J. CARSON, *Executive Director*
MARTHA ANDERSON, *Editor*

Directors at Large
DONALD R. BELCHER, *American Telephone and Telegraph Company*
OSWALD W. KNAUTH, *New York City*
SIMON KUZNETS, *University of Pennsylvania*
H. W. LAIDLER, *Executive Director, League for Industrial Democracy*
SHEPARD MORGAN, *Vice-President, Chase National Bank*
C. REINOLD NOYES, *New York City*
GEORGE B. ROBERTS, *Vice-President, National City Bank*
BEARDSLEY RUML, *Chairman, Board of Directors, R. H. Macy & Company*
HARRY SCHERMAN, *President, Book-of-the-Month Club*
GEORGE SOULE, *New York City*
N. I. STONE, *Consulting Economist*
J. RAYMOND WALSH, *WMCA Broadcasting Company*
LEO WOLMAN, *Columbia University*
T. O. YNTEMA, *Vice-President — Finance, Ford Motor Company*

Directors by University Appointment
E. WIGHT BAKKE, *Yale*
C. C. BALDERSTON, *Pennsylvania*
ARTHUR F. BURNS, *Columbia*
G. A. ELLIOTT, *Toronto*
H. M. GROVES, *Wisconsin*
GOTTFRIED HABERLER, *Harvard*
CLARENCE HEER, *North Carolina*
R. L. KOZELKA, *Minnesota*
PAUL M. O'LEARY, *Cornell*
THEODORE W. SCHULTZ, *Chicago*
R. B. WARREN, *Institute for Advanced Study*

Directors Appointed by Other Organizations
PERCIVAL E. BRUNDAGE, *American Institute of Accountants*
ARTHUR H. COLE, *Economic History Association*
FREDERICK C. MILLS, *American Statistical Association*
STANLEY H. RUTTENBERG, *Congress of Industrial Organizations*
MURRAY SHIELDS, *American Management Association*
BORIS SHISHKIN, *American Federation of Labor*
WARREN C. WAITE, *American Farm Economic Association*
DONALD H. WALLACE, *American Economic Association*

Research Staff
ARTHUR F. BURNS, *Director of Research*
G. H. MOORE, *Associate Director of Research*

MOSES ABRAMOVITZ
HAROLD BARGER
MORRIS A. COPELAND
DANIEL CREAMER
DAVID DURAND
SOLOMON FABRICANT
MILTON FRIEDMAN
MILLARD HASTAY
W. BRADDOCK HICKMAN

F. F. HILL
THOR HULTGREN
SIMON KUZNETS
CLARENCE D. LONG
RUTH P. MACK
FREDERICK C. MILLS
RAYMOND J. SAULNIER
GEORGE J. STIGLER
LEO WOLMAN

Relation of the Directors to the Work of the National Bureau of Economic Research

1. The object of the National Bureau of Economic Research is to ascertain and to present to the public important economic facts and their interpretation in a scientific and impartial manner. The Board of Directors is charged with the responsibility of ensuring that the work of the Bureau is carried on in strict conformity with this object.

2. To this end the Board of Directors shall appoint one or more Directors of Research.

3. The Director or Directors of Research shall submit to the members of the Board, or to its Executive Committee, for their formal adoption, all specific proposals concerning researches to be instituted.

4. No report shall be published until the Director or Directors of Research shall have submitted to the Board a summary drawing attention to the character of the data and their utilization in the report, the nature and treatment of the problems involved, the main conclusions and such other information as in their opinion would serve to determine the suitability of the report for publication in accordance with the principles of the Bureau.

5. A copy of any manuscript proposed for publication shall also be submitted to each member of the Board. For each manuscript to be so submitted a special committee shall be appointed by the President, or at his designation by the Executive Director, consisting of three Directors selected as nearly as may be one from each general division of the Board. The names of the special manuscript committee shall be stated to each Director when the summary and report described in paragraph (4) are sent to him. It shall be the duty of each member of the committee to read the manuscript. If each member of the special committee signifies his approval within thirty days, the manuscript may be published. If each member of the special committee has not signified his approval within thirty days of the transmittal of the report and manuscript, the Director of Research shall then notify each member of the Board, requesting approval or disapproval of publication, and thirty additional days shall be granted for this purpose. The manuscript shall then not be published unless at least a majority of the entire Board and a two-thirds majority of those members of the Board who shall have voted on the proposal within the time fixed for the receipt of votes on the publication proposed shall have approved.

6. No manuscript may be published, though approved by each member of the special committee, until forty-five days have elapsed from the transmittal of the summary and report. The interval is allowed for the receipt of any memorandum of dissent or reservation, together with a brief statement of his reasons, that any member may wish to express; and such memorandum of dissent or reservation shall be published with the manuscript if he so desires. Publication does not, however, imply that each member of the Board has read the manuscript, or that either members of the Board in general, or of the special committee, have passed upon its validity in every detail.

7. A copy of this resolution shall, unless otherwise determined by the Board, be printed in each copy of every National Bureau book.

(*Resolution adopted October* 25, 1926, *and revised February* 6, 1933, *and February* 24, 1941)

Financial Research Program: Committee

In the planning and conduct of all research under the Financial Research Program the National Bureau benefits from the advice and guidance of its Committee on Research in Finance. The functions of this committee are to review and supervise the specific research activities of the Program staff.

RALPH A. YOUNG, Chairman pro tempore — *Associate Director, Division of Research and Statistics, Board of Governors of the Federal Reserve System*

RAYMOND J. SAULNIER, Secretary — *Barnard College, Columbia University; Director, Financial Research Program, National Bureau of Economic Research*

BENJAMIN HAGGOTT BECKHART — *Columbia University; Director of Research, The Chase National Bank*

ARTHUR F. BURNS — *Columbia University; Director of Research, National Bureau of Economic Research*

WILLIAM J. CARSON — *University of Pennsylvania; Executive Director, National Bureau of Economic Research*

GEORGE W. COLEMAN — *Economist, Mississippi Valley Trust Company*

ERNEST M. FISHER — *Columbia University*

E. A. GOLDENWEISER — *Institute for Advanced Study*

F. CYRIL JAMES — *Principal and Vice-Chancellor, McGill University*

WALTER LICHTENSTEIN — *Chicago, Illinois*

WALTER L. MITCHELL, JR. — *Managing Director, Controllers Institute of America*

SHEPARD MORGAN — *Vice-President, The Chase National Bank*

WILLIAM I. MYERS — *Dean, College of Agriculture, Cornell University*

JACK H. RIDDLE — *Vice-President, Bankers Trust Company*

GEORGE BASSETT ROBERTS — *Vice-President, The National City Bank; Treasurer, National Bureau of Economic Research*

HAROLD V. ROELSE — *Vice-President, Federal Reserve Bank of New York*

CASIMIR A. SIENKIEWICZ — *President, Central-Penn National Bank of Philadelphia*

WOODLIEF THOMAS — *Director, Division of Research and Statistics, Board of Governors of the Federal Reserve System*

DONALD S. THOMPSON — *Vice-President, Federal Reserve Bank of Cleveland*

ROBERT B. WARREN — *Institute for Advanced Study*

JOHN H. WILLIAMS — *Graduate School of Public Administration, Harvard University; Economic Advisor, Federal Reserve Bank of New York*

JOHN H. WILLS — *Second Vice-President, Northern Trust Company*

LEO WOLMAN — *Columbia University; Research Staff, National Bureau of Economic Research*

DONALD B. WOODWARD — *Second Vice-President, Mutual Life Insurance Company of New York*

Occasional Papers in Print

1. MANUFACTURING OUTPUT, 1929-1937 (December 1940)
   Solomon Fabricant 25
3. FINISHED COMMODITIES SINCE 1879, OUTPUT AND ITS COMPOSITION (August 1941)
   William H. Shaw 25
5. RAILWAY FREIGHT TRAFFIC IN PROSPERITY AND DEPRESSION (February 1942)
   Thor Hultgren 25
10. THE EFFECT OF WAR ON BUSINESS FINANCING: Manufacturing and Trade, World War I (November 1943)
    R. A. Young and C. H. Schmidt 50
11. THE EFFECT OF WAR ON CURRENCY AND DEPOSITS (September 1943)
    Charles R. Whittlesey 35
12. PRICES IN A WAR ECONOMY: Some Aspects of the Present Price Structure of the United States (October 1943)
    Frederick C. Mills 50
13. RAILROAD TRAVEL AND THE STATE OF BUSINESS (December 1943)
    Thor Hultgren 35
14. THE LABOR FORCE IN WARTIME AMERICA (March 1944)
    Clarence D. Long 50
15. RAILWAY TRAFFIC EXPANSION AND USE OF RESOURCES IN WORLD WAR II (February 1944)
    Thor Hultgren 35
16. BRITISH AND AMERICAN PLANS FOR INTERNATIONAL CURRENCY STABILIZATION (January 1944)
    J. H. Riddle 35
17. NATIONAL PRODUCT, WAR AND PREWAR (February 1944)
    Simon Kuznets 50
18. PRODUCTION OF INDUSTRIAL MATERIALS IN WORLD WARS I AND II (March 1944)
    Geoffrey H. Moore 50
19. CANADA'S FINANCIAL SYSTEM IN WAR (April 1944)
    Benjamin H. Higgins 50
20. NAZI WAR FINANCE AND BANKING (April 1944)
    Otto Nathan 50
22. BANK LIQUIDITY AND THE WAR (May 1945)
    Charles R. Whittlesey 50
23. LABOR SAVINGS IN AMERICAN INDUSTRY, 1899-1939 (November 1945)
    Solomon Fabricant 50

24. Domestic Servants in the United States, 1900-1940 (April 1946)
   George J. Stigler 50
25. Recent Developments in Dominion-Provincial Fiscal Relations in Canada (March 1948)
   J. A. Maxwell 50
26. The Role of Inventories in Business Cycles (May 1948)
   Moses Abramovitz 50
27. The Structure of Postwar Prices (July 1948)
   Frederick C. Mills 75
28. Lombard Street in War and Reconstruction (July 1949)
   Benjamin H. Higgins 1.00
29. The Rising Trend of Government Employment (July 1949)
   Solomon Fabricant 50

Technical Papers in Print

3. Basic Yields of Corporate Bonds, 1900-1942 (June 1942)
   David Durand 50
4. Currency Held by the Public, the Banks, and the Treasury, Monthly December 1917 to December 1944 (January 1947)
   Anna J. Schwartz and E. Oliver 75
5. Concerning a New Federal Financial Statement (December 1947)
   Morris A. Copeland 1.00
6. Basic Yields of Bonds, 1926-1947: Their Measurement and Pattern (December 1947)
   David Durand and Willis J. Winn 75